Evguenia Davidova is Associate Professor of International Studies at Portland State University, Oregon. She has published extensively on the nineteenth-century socio-economic history of the Ottoman Balkans. Davidova is the author of *Balkan Transitions to Modernity and Nation-States: Through the Eyes of Three Generations of Merchants (1780s–1890s)* (2013).

"This collection of articles on wealth and poverty in the late Ottoman and early post-Ottoman Balkans offers a refreshingly multifaceted and often intriguing panorama of Balkan society in a crucial era of transition. Covering most of the Balkan countries, the volume pays attention not only to economic and social factors, but also to institutional and cultural aspects of wealth and poverty, dealing with often unexplored but highly relevant case studies. Written by a group of renowned historians of the Balkans, the book represents a thought-provoking addition to mainstream Balkan historiography on the topic."

Raymond Detrez, University of Ghent

"This volume is a truly original intervention into both Balkan and Ottoman history. Dispensing with the tired old frame of nationalism, it repeatedly crosses local, regional, national and imperial boundaries to bring us a set of deeply researched articles on wealth and poverty from Athens to Istanbul, and many places in between, during the long and dramatic nineteenth century. The perspectives are fresh and the attention to locales which are usually ignored in grand narratives is very welcome."

Molly Greene, Princeton University

WEALTH IN THE OTTOMAN AND POST-OTTOMAN BALKANS

A Socio-Economic History

Edited by
EVGUENIA DAVIDOVA

I.B. TAURIS
LONDON · NEW YORK

Published in 2016 by
I.B.Tauris & Co. Ltd
London • New York
www.ibtauris.com

Library of Ottoman Studies 52

ISBN: 978 1 78453 439 4
eISBN: 978 0 85773 949 0

A full CIP record for this book is available from the British Library
A full CIP record is available from the Library of Congress

Library of Congress Catalog Card Number: available

Typeset in Garamond Three by OKS Prepress Services, Chennai, India
Printed and bound by CPI Group (UK) Ltd, Croydon, CR0 4YY

MIX
Paper from responsible sources
FSC® C013604

CONTENTS

LIST OF ABBREVIATIONS

a.e.	*arkhivna edinitsa* (archival unit)
AA	*Antolikos Astēr/Astir*
AG	*Arhiva Genealogică*
AIU	Alliance Israélite Universelle
AKA	Alexandros Karatheodores Archive, Institute for Hellenic Studies, Athens
BAR	Biblioteca Academiei Române
BIA-NBKM	Bŭlgarski istoricheski arkhiv, Narodna Biblioteka "Sv. Kiril i Metodii"
BNF	Bibliothèque Nationale de France
BOA	Başbakanlık Osmanlı Arşivi
	C.AS. — Cevdet Askeriye
	C.IKTS. — Cevdet Iktisat
	C.MTZ — Cevdet Eyalet-i Mümtaze
	HAT — Hatt-ı Hümayun
	ML.VRD.TMT.d — Maliye Nezareti Varidat Muhasebesi Temettuat defterleri
BS	*Balkan Studies*
DARM	Drzhaven Arhiv na Republika Makedonija, Skopje
dr.	drachma
EB	*Etudes Balkaniques*
FO	Foreign Office
g.	*grosia, grosha, guruş*

GAK	General State Archives of Greece	
	Efeteio	Civil Law Decisions of the Court of Appeals of Athens
	Leonidio	Leonidio Notarial Archive
	Mykonos	Mykonos Notarial Archive
h.	*hacı, hadzhi*	
HMG	*Hanımlara Mahsus Gazete*	
I.A.Y.E.	Historical Archive of the Greek Ministry of Foreign Affairs	
IČ	*Istorijski časopis*	
IEEE	Historical and Ethnological Society of Greece	
	Mykonos	Mykonos Notarial Archive
	Naxos	Naxos Notarial Archive
IJMES	*International Journal of Middle East Studies*	
IL	*Indreptarea legii*	
IP	*Istoricheski pregled*	
JEH	*Journal of Economic History*	
JESHO	*Journal of the Economic and Social History of the Orient*	
JFH	*Journal of Family History*	
JMGS	*Journal of Modern Greek Studies*	
k.	*kuruş*	
LC	*Logiuirea Caragea*	
MES	*Middle Eastern Studies*	
MH	*The Missionary Herald*	
NPT	*New Perspectives on Turkey*	
OM	*Oriente Moderno*	
ON	*Opštinske novine*	
p.	*para*	
RGADA	Rossiskii Gosudarstvennyi Arkhiv Drevnykh Aktov	
RGVIA	Rossiskii Gosudarstvennyi Voenno-Istoricheskii Arkhiv	
RIM	Regionalen istoricheski muzeĭ, Gabrovo	
SBAN	*Sbornik na Bŭlgarskata Akademia na Naukite*	
SN	*Srpske novine*	

GLOSSARY

ahtar – apothecary
akçe – small silver coin
antikatastatika – replacement documents
ayan – local notable
ban – governor
berat – patent
boyar – member of aristocracy
cizye – poll tax paid by non-Muslim male adults
çiftlik, *chiflik* – farm, estate
çorbacı, chorbadzhi – village representative, notable
dervendzhi – guardian of a pass
dolapcı – silk producer
donatio propter nuptias (progamiaia dorea) – betrothal gift
dram – 3.10 grams
dükkân – shop
dzhelep, *dzhelepkeshan* – trader in animals; trader/producer of animal products
ephor – overseer
esnaf – guild
ferman, firman – imperial decree
gerontism – system of elders (gerontes), a permanent Holy Synod of metropolitans of the bishoprics near Constantinople
grosia, groša, grosha, guruş, see *kuruş*
hacı, *hadji*, *hadzhi* – pilgrim who visited the Holy Lands
hekim – doctor

kadı – judge
kamini, cămin – ancestral eponymous land
kaymakam – governor of a *kaza*
kaza – administrative district
kirdzhalis, *karjalee* – brigands
kocabaşlar – village headmen
kuruş – silver coin, equaled 40 para or 120 *akçe*
logothete – secretary of a dignitary
meclis – council
millet – officially recognized non-Muslim religious community
muhtar – village elder
mutesarrıf – governor of sancak
okka – around 1.28 kg
paharnic – high dignitary
para – silver coin, one fortieth of a *kuruş*
Phanariots – Orthodox laic elite with strong ties to the Patriarchate and the Ottoman administration
postelnic – chamberlain
reaya – tax-paying Ottoman subjects
sapundzhi – soap maker
spitseria – pharmacy
stolnic – high dignitary
temettuat defter – tax register
vali – governor of *vilayet*
vilayet – province
vornic – high judge
voyvoda – governor
waqf – pious endowment

LIST OF CONTRIBUTORS

Nikolay Aretov is a professor (Dr. habil., 2006) at the Institute for Literature, Bulgarian Academy of Sciences, Editor-in-chief of *Literaturna misal journal*, and lecturer at Sofia University. He has published several books in Bulgarian, among them *The Bulgarian Murder: Plots with Crimes in Bulgarian Literature* (1994, 2007); *The Bulgarian National Revival and Europe* (1995; 2001); and *National Mythology and National Literature* (2006). He has edited several collections on Bulgarian and Balkan culture. Aretov is also a coordinator of interdisciplinary projects on collective identities and their representations in culture; and President of the Bulgarian Academic Circle of Comparative Literature. His research interests include: Bulgarian literature (eighteenth–twentieth century), comparative literature, cultural studies, nationalism and national mythology, and crime literature.

Evguenia Davidova is Associate Professor of International Studies at Portland State University, Oregon. She completed her PhD in history at the Bulgarian Academy of Sciences (1998) and held a post-doctorate at Oxford University (1999–2000). Her research interests focus on the Ottoman and post-Ottoman Balkans: commerce, modernization, nationalism, and medical practices (nineteenth–twentieth century). She has published several articles in various journals, including *Turcica*, *Balkanologie*, and *New Perspectives on Turkey*. Davidova is the author of *Balkan Transitions to Modernity and Nation-States: Through the Eyes of Three Generations of Merchants (1780s–1890s)* (2013).

Evdoxios Doxiadis completed his PhD at the University of California, Berkeley (2007). He was the Ted and Elaine Athanassiades post-doctoral fellow at Princeton University (2007–8), and has since worked at the International Center for Hellenic and Mediterranean Studies in Athens and at San Francisco State University before moving to Simon Fraser University. His research is on Greek, Balkan and Mediterranean history with a focus in the eighteenth and nineteenth centuries and a particular interest in gender, law, state formation, and minorities. He has published one book, *The Shackles of Modernity: Women, Property, and the Transition from the Ottoman Empire to the Greek State, 1750–1850* (2011), and several articles in various journals, including *Past and Present*, *Journal of Modern Greek Studies*, and *Journal of Byzantine and Modern Greek Studies*.

Gergana Georgieva is Associate Professor at the Faculty of History, University of Veliko Turnovo. She has a PhD in history from the Institute of Balkan Studies, Bulgarian Academy of Sciences (2006) and several doctoral and post-doctoral fellowships at the Center for Advanced Studies, Berlin; New Europe College, Bucharest; and the American Research Institute in Turkey. Her research focuses on the Ottoman Balkans: eighteenth- to nineteenth-century urban history; imperial governing; provincial administration systems; heterodox Muslim communities and Muslim mystical orders. Her recent publications include a contribution to *Encyclopedia of Islam*, 3rd edn (2015), and the book *Arbanasi in the Fifteenth–Nineteenth Centuries: A Socio-Economic Profile* (in Bulgarian).

Eyal Ginio is the former Chair of the Department of Islam and Middle Eastern Studies, the Hebrew University of Jerusalem (2009–12). He is also a coordinator of the Forum of Turkish Studies at the Institute of Asian and African Studies, the Hebrew University. He completed his PhD at the Hebrew University in Middle East Studies (1999) and held a post-doctorate at Oxford University (1999–2000). His research and publications in English, French, Hebrew, and Turkish focused on the social history of the Ottoman Empire with an emphasis on eighteenth-century Salonica and its region.

Andreea-Roxana Iancu is an independent scholar who lives in France. She was a research fellow at the "Nicolae Iorga" Institute of History in Bucharest (2000–13). She holds a PhD in history from the École des

Hautes Études en Sciences Sociales. Her research interests include social history and juridical anthropology of property, inheritance, and legal plural systems in Walachia and Moldavia (eighteenth–nineteenth century). Iancu has published several articles in Romanian and French journals.

Dalibor Jovanovski is Associate Professor of Modern Balkan History at the Faculty of Philosophy and Institute for History in Skopje. His main academic interest is the history of the Balkan states, especially their political, economic and social developments. Aside from his books *Greek Balkan Policy and Macedonia 1830–1881* and *Balkans 1826–1913* (both in Macedonian), he has published numerous articles. He is a member of the editorial board of *Macedonian Historical Review*.

Efi Kanner is Lecturer of Turkish Culture and Society in the Department of Turkish and Modern Asian Studies at the University of Athens. She holds a DEA from the École des Hautes Études en Sciences Sociales and a PhD from the University of Athens. She has researched various aspects of embourgeoisement among Orthodox and Muslim populations in the late Ottoman period and early Turkish Republic, i.e. national identities, politics towards poverty, concepts of childhood, privacy. Her more recent interests relate to micro-history as a field of investigation of the construction of bourgeois subjectivities, trans-cultural encounters and the formation of gender patterns in various ethno-religious environments. She has authored two books in Greek: *Gender-based Social Demands from the Ottoman Empire to Greece and Turkey: The World of a Greek-Orthodox Female Teacher* (2012); and *Poverty and Philanthropy in the Istanbul Orthodox Communities (1753–1912)* (2004).

Eleonora Naxidou is Assistant Professor of Modern History of Southeastern Europe at the Department of History and Ethnology at Democritus University of Thrace, Komotini. Her research area is the Balkans and her publications focus on nationalism, national identity, church and national ideology, and ethnic minorities. She is currently working on a book about the Bulgarian national movement during the nineteenth century. Among her more recent publications are: "Nationalism versus multiculturalism: the minority issue in twenty-first-century Bulgaria", *Nationalities Papers* 40 (2012), and "Traditional Aspects of Modernity in the Nineteenth-Century Balkans: The Ecclesiastical

Dimensions of the Bulgarian National Movement", in *Power and Influence in South-Eastern Europe: 16th–19th Century* (2013).

Evelina Razhdavichka-Kiessling is a research associate at the Institute of Balkan Studies, Sofia. She devotes her scholarly work to nineteenth-century Balkan socio-economic and cultural history. She has been a scholarship holder at the Eötvös Loránd University, Europa Institut Budapest, Institute for Advanced Study Berlin, Bielefeld Graduate School in History and Sociology, and Leibniz Institute of European History, Mainz. She is the author of numerous articles and chapters in specialized journals and books.

Andrew Robarts is Assistant Professor of History at the Rhode Island School of Design (RISD). He is a published scholar on labor migration, Ottoman Bulgaria, Ottoman–Russian relations, and the Black Sea region. Between his MA in international relations and PhD in history (both from Georgetown University), Robarts worked for seven years in the field of humanitarian and refugee relief with the International Rescue Committee and the UN High Commissioner for Refugees. His research languages include Bulgarian, Ottoman Turkish, and Russian.

Momir Samardžić is Associate Professor at the Faculty of Philosophy, University of Novi Sad. He received his PhD in history from the University of Novi Sad. He is the author of *Roads to Europe: Serbian Politics and the Railway Issue, 1878–1881* (2010). Until recently, his main field of research has been international relations in the nineteenth century and the Eastern Question within the context of the Serbian foreign policy and inter-Balkan relations of the newly emerging nation-states. Recently, he has focused more on foreign influences in Balkan politics and society and their impact on the economy and the development of infrastructure.

Dimitris Stamatopoulos is Associate Professor of Balkan and Late Ottoman History in the Department of Balkan, Slavic and Oriental Studies at the University of Macedonia, Thessaloniki. He has received many fellowships and was a member of the School of Historical Studies in the Institute for Advanced Study at Princeton (2010–11). He is the author of many articles concerning the history of the Christian populations in the Ottoman Balkans and two books in Greek – *Reform and Secularization: Towards a Reconstruction of the History of the Ecumenical*

Patriarchate in the Nineteenth Century (2003); and *The Byzantium after the Nation: the Problem of Continuity in the Balkan Historiographies* (2009) – and has co-edited (in Greek) *Orientalism at the Limits: From the Ottoman Balkans to the Contemporary Middle East* (2008).

INTRODUCTION

Evguenia Davidova

> The victims [of fever and ague] are principally from the poorer classes, whose scanty, unwholesome food, and habits of intemperance, render them perpetually liable to the attacks of the malady, but yet, amongst the highest society, the sallow cheek and bloodless lip are a constant proof that even the most careful diet and regular living will not ensure safety ...[1]

This commentary on social disparities in Salonika belongs to the seasoned British traveler Mary Walker, who visited the city in 1860. Whereas diseases and lifestyle affected health and status, as she aptly noted, socio-economic causes and factors, which she casually omitted, impacted chances for economic survival, social mobility, and political and cultural aspirations. This volume seeks to flesh out the complex socio-economic, cultural, political, and institutional framework within which wealth was accumulated and poverty was maintained in the Ottoman and post-Ottoman Balkans.

Who was wealthy and how in its assorted incarnations was fortune represented? What were the distinctions between the deserving and undeserving poor? How were concepts of prosperity and progress and poverty and failure socially produced in various contexts? This collection examines the intersection between diverse practices and discourses entailing social and civic inclusion/exclusion through the lenses of ethnic, religious, class, and gender-sensitive approaches. The markers of wealth accumulation and corresponding pauperization, and the ways they were experienced elucidate the relationships among state, economy, society, modernity, and national identity against the backdrop of Balkan, Ottoman, and European developments. The contributors add neglected dimensions to a major historiographical theme of socio-economic transformations and, more specifically, the disaggregating and remixing of emerging middle classes, the daily negotiations between old and new elites, the secularization and commodification of social standing and values, and the debates about the Ottoman Empire and its heritage in the Balkans.

Employing different social categories as a tool for historical analysis, this inquiry into social, economic, cultural, and political interactions is informed by the following guiding questions: How did state, society, market, religious, and various other institutions influence each other's concepts of wealth/poverty and success/failure? In what ways did diverse social actors employ such key categories for maintaining social cohesion? How was social status negotiated between traditional values and modern sensibility? What were the ethnic and gender configurations? How did discourses of modernization conceptualize wealth as a social category of progress? What were the exchanges, differences, and similarities between East and West? Such examination of historical experiences is implicitly based on Henry Lefebvre's conceptualization of socially produced relations: "*(Social) space is a (social) product*" (emphasis in original).[2] Therefore, the social practices, discourses, and actors under investigation are located within contested physical and symbolic social space wherein relations of power (re)production are historically bound. Thus, the collection examines multiple levels of social transformations: rural/urban, illiterate/literate, pre-industrial/industrial, empire/nation-states, subjects/citizens, pre-modern/modern. But these binary oppositions are not and should not be seen as mutually exclusive.

The volume is grounded in original empirical research and comprises both a qualitative and quantitative analysis, including some in-depth case studies. Methodological approaches vary from microhistory to multiscopique to alltagsgeschichte to histoire croisée; it is the latter with its emphasis on "multiplicity of possible viewpoints and the divergences resulting from languages, terminologies, categorizations and conceptualizations, traditions, and disciplinary usages" that allows for a richer contextualization of the shared Balkan past.[3] Primary sources in various languages frame the comparative analysis, which reconstructs social hierarchies rooted in real or symbolic ownership of scarce (and cherished) resources. This collection is intended as a multi-dimensional interpretation of social order and re-ordering. The contributing 13 scholars also address major discourses in various national historiographies with regard to social transformations, nationalism, modernity, and the Ottoman legacy.

The chronological period spans from the late eighteenth to early twentieth century and comprises broader processes of the economic incorporation of the Ottoman Empire, the Tanzimat institutional reforms, the outburst of successful (and not so) nationalist movements, the escalation of the Eastern Question, and the emergence of nation-states. Nationalism and market expansion brought up into existence unprecedented levels of competitiveness, mobility, hierarchies of power, and burgeoning inequalities. These social reconfigurations were taking on new social meanings and attendant diverse forms of expression that transgressed ethnic, religious, and gender boundaries. Concurrently, the secularization of social status, nationalization of discourses, and commodification of values both reflected and constituted modernity. The latter is conceived in plural as continually evolving "multiple modernities",[4] where borrowing from the West was resourcefully embraced within a rich and fluid social tapestry, and often conceived as a weapon against dependence on the West.

The volume explores both discourses about wealth (and success) in the broadest sense and the practices of its accumulation, material manifestations, and representations. The book also examines the antipode – poverty (and failure) – society's revised ideas about poverty as fate, social evil, philanthropy, welfare, and the language of social exclusion. It also interprets these fundamental social identities as abstract categories (ethnic/national) and as material embodiments (property, fortune, consumption, status, occupation and/or the lack thereof). What makes the topic intrinsically interesting is its focus on social values (as tacitly understood) that were redefined and then normalized under new conditions: incorporation into a world economy, the system of nation-states, secular worldviews, and modern sensibilities.

Some caveats are in order. First, the geographic scope reflects the contributors' research interests and expertise and does not include all parts of the Balkans. Second, due to space limitations, some themes are only broached without elaboration. Third, as the authors come from various national historical schools, the terminology and transliteration of some terms vary and are left in their original form.

The contributions are organized in four sections with the intention to emphasize the common themes and intercrossings that emerge. Part One, "Wealth, Property, and Social Status", focuses on the intersection of social standing and its measurability within expanding commercialization and state centralization. The fundamental category of property, ownership, and patterns of investment are examined from different angles. In Chapter 1, Evdoxios Doxiadis suggests that the legal status of women in the early independent Greece demonstrated continuity from the late Ottoman period with regards to property rights. It was the very establishment of the modern state and the concomitant social transformations in Greece that gradually hindered the control women exercised over their property (and status) in practice. Evelina Razhdavichka-Kiessling, in Chapter 2, examines the history of a prosperous multigenerational business. The Khadzhitoshev family serves as an example of strategies for accumulation of economic, social, and cultural capital and its inter-generational transmission and transformation. Andreea-Roxana Iancu, in Chapter 3, discusses the *boyars'* inheritance practices within the context of state bureaucratization and synthesis of plural law system in Wallachia. As a result, a new relationship between the individual as legal subject and land property was established, which created new possibilities to legitimate aristocratic genealogies.

Section Two, "Institutional and Social Practices", explores forms of state regulation and their impact on various institutional contexts within new market practices. In Chapter 4, Andrew Robarts focuses on the revitalization of social and economic exchanges in pre-Tanzimat Ottoman Bulgaria. The Russo–Ottoman War of 1828–9 acted as catalyst for both material destruction and demographic and economic recovery, facilitated by judicious local administration and cooperation of non-Muslim elites. Dimitris Stamatopoulos, in Chapter 5, explores the Patriarchate's financial and institutional restructuring that was linked to increased secular interventions that ultimately undermined its ecumenical legitimacy, financial viability, and political autonomy. In another context, Evguenia Davidova, in Chapter 6, suggests that commodification of medical services and social stratification were mutually constitutive. Doctors, as part of the new professionally educated elites, were not only dependent on the expanding modern state but were also involved in economic entrepreneurship and innovative marketing practices, which engendered a host of new modern sensibilities. In pursuit of social cohesion and dominance, as Efi Kanner demonstrates in Chapter 7, secular elites, among other means, exercised control over poverty through philanthropy. This was true not only in the case of both non-Muslims and Muslims who adopted middle-class liberal values but also the Ottoman government that embraced philanthropy as a means of political integration and legitimization. Furthermore, philanthropy had strong gender dimensions with both negative and positive ramifications.

Part Three, "Transnational Networks and Exchanges", shifts the geographic scope to the broader and shrinking map of the Ottoman Empire and its neighbors. In Chapter 8, Gergana Georgieva traces the expanding commercial and social interethnic networks from their starting point – the prosperous village of Arbanasi – in various directions: Istanbul, Wallachia, Moldavia, and Transylvania. By contrast, as Dalibor Jovanovski in Chapter 9 shows, the Balkan Wars brought about impoverishment to Bitola, a prosperous center of an Ottoman *vilayet*. The city's inclusion in the nation-state system and subsequent geographic marginalization as a result of the new border regime led to economic and cultural decline as well as the loss of Ottoman cosmopolitanism. Eyal Ginio in Chapter 10 situates another Ottoman city, also affected by the Balkan Wars, within a broader Mediterranean context. He examines Kavala's transformation from a *lieu de naissance* of Mehmed Ali into a *lieu de mémoire* of Egypt's khedivial dynasty through a re-articulation of the notion "deserving poor" in the context of philanthropy during wartime.

The last Section, Four, "Discourses of Social and National Values", comprises three chapters. The process of growing economic incorporation, urbanization, nationalism, and the attendant social re-stratifications brought with it contested national, social, ideological, and moral dimensions. Those dynamic changes were expressed in a variety of discursive contexts. In Chapter 11, Eleonora Naxidou explores how the use of binary metaphors of wealth/poverty was employed among the nineteenth-century Bulgarian political elites within and without the Ottoman Empire. The assertion of national self-determination intertwined with ideas of classical liberalism, in pursuing both political and ecclesiastical independence, emerged as one of the major discourses in the 1860s and 1870s. Momir Samardžić, in Chapter 12, interprets another discursive theme – the concept of "people's welfare" – also shaped by a combination of nationalism and liberalism. In pre-independence Serbia, although some of the debates took on an economic meaning, the elites were seeking political solutions rather than a comprehensive economic modernization. Nikolay Aretov, in Chapter 13, analyzes how the idealization of poverty occupied crucial position in Bulgarian literature, while the amassing of wealth was often demonized. Such critical interpretations derived not only from Christian (and later socialist) contexts, but also reflected deeper social disparities and modern sensibilities.

In appreciation of this truly collaborative work, I wish to extend my thanks to all contributors for generously sharing with me their vast knowledge, keen wit, and warm collegiality. It goes without saying that all shortcomings in the organization and editing of this text rest with me.

PART I

WEALTH, PROPERTY, AND SOCIAL STATUS

CHAPTER 1

WOMEN, WEALTH, AND THE STATE IN GREECE (1750–1860)

Evdoxios Doxiadis

> Woman, as a spouse, is not master of her property, does not have the right to spend a single penny from it. For her entire life she is considered by the Law as an underage and incapable person. As a mother, she does not have any legal right over the upbringing and the future of her offspring. As a citizen, she cannot be a guardian of orphans and cannot present herself as a witness in any legal act.[1]

When the *Journal of the Ladies* (*Efimeris ton Kyrion*), published the above passage in 1895 it fit perfectly within the context of early feminist writings throughout Europe, being reminiscent of the writings of Caroline Norton 40 years earlier.[2] The image of nineteenth-century Greek women lacking civil and property rights sits well within the European context and later developments in Greece that scholars have not seriously examined the legal and material conditions of women in the nineteenth century beyond the writings of early feminists. Admittedly, sources with respect to women's employment are scarce, but there is an abundance of other sources regarding wealth from dowry contracts to wills and donations, sales documents, and court cases involving women that can be used to construct a picture of the relationship between women and wealth. What emerges is a more complex picture that seems to indicate that for most of the nineteenth century women enjoyed most of the rights whose absence is bemoaned above. They were regularly guardians of their children, they engaged in all sorts of legal and business transactions, and frequently took legal action to protect their interests.

At the same time the changes taking place in Greece appear to have undermined the economic wellbeing of women even as their rights appear unchanged from the Ottoman period through the reign of King Otto (Othon), the first King of Modern Greece. My intention is to show the legal development of women's property rights, and the material condition of women through the period from the final decades of the Ottoman period (1750–1821), the Greek War of Independence (1821–32), and the reign of King Otto (1832–63). I argue that the Greek state presents a complex picture, maintaining the fundamentals of the legal framework inherited from the Ottoman period that allowed women to enjoy greater property rights yet also adopting "modern" legal structures, regulations, and policies that were not initially intended to undermine women's property rights but gradually did so.

Women's Wealth in Ottoman Times

It is difficult to provide a comprehensive picture of the relationship between women and property for the Ottoman period in Greece. Every region, island, or village had its own customs that varied so dramatically as to make general statements meaningless. Customs ranged from the extreme of the island of Karpathos where first-born daughters received nearly the entire wealth of their mothers to inner Mani where daughters were excluded from all real property to areas where brideprice rather than dowry was the norm.[3] Some regions clearly favored matrilocal/uxorilocal marriage, while others practiced patrilocality, occasionally both types existing side-by-side.[4]

Marriage in Greece was an imperative, even as late as 1880 when 97 percent of women of marriageable age were indeed married, compared to 88 percent in Italy and 80 percent in Portugal, themselves societies where marriage was highly valued. Most Greek women married young, between the ages of 15 to 21.[5] That was when women received the bulk of their wealth as a dowry. Traditions stemming from Byzantine law considered the dowry inviolate and inalienable and husbands stood as surety over it with their own wealth. Any attempt to alienate it, as for instance in order to augment the dowries of offspring, required the consent of the wife. Women, however, did not manage their wealth nor did they profit from any income generated. Those were under the control of the husband who managed the dowry and enjoyed its fruits. Even the proceeds of the labor of a married woman belonged to her husband who "sustains the burdens of matrimony", as the *corpus juris civilis* put it.[6] In general, only at the marriage's dissolution, through divorce or death, did a wife assume full control of her wealth.

Women could receive additional wealth through inheritances, donations, gifts, etc. Such properties were under a different legal status than the dowry and were not considered inalienable even though the husband, who managed them as well, was supposed to compensate his wife for any loss. In regions like Athens women were also promised a *progamiaia dorea* (marriage donation – *donatio propter nuptias*) by their husbands that he, or his heirs, were supposed to give to the wife if the marriage was subsequently dissolved. The legal status of such payments was not very clear but their inclusion in the dowry contracts ensured that it could be pursued in a court.

Although some scholars have tried to argue for the existence of a common conjugal fund in the Ottoman period,[7] this does not seem to have been the case. The properties of men and women were kept separate, even if managed by the same individual, and there is no evidence of amalgamation even after decades of marriage.[8] Numerous bills of sale in the notarial archives show that husbands regularly compensated their wives for the sale of their properties, usually by replacing them with their own properties of comparable value either in the bills of sale or in separate documents called *antikatastatika* (replacements).[9] Alternatively, women could confirm the actions of their husbands at a later date, like Aneta Mexiou who drafted a notarial document in which she stated that her husband sold a field according to her own wishes.[10] Prohibitions regarding donations between spouses further strengthened the principle of separation of properties, prohibitions that can be traced to the introduction of the *donatio propter nuptias*.[11]

Women owned a great variety of properties ranging from houses to agricultural land, to moveable goods and animals. As others have also indicated, it is very difficult to compare the wealth of women to that of men in Ottoman Greece because dowries were simply descriptive.[12] Since the value of a field or a house can vary dramatically a comparison of properties is not meaningful. Nevertheless, it is clear that women in certain regions received wealth comparable to that of men. My research indicates that nearly all women received some sort of real property in their dowry contracts either structures (67 percent of women in Naxos, 98 percent in Mykonos, and 36 percent in Athens), or fields, vineyards, orchards (95 percent in Naxos, 96 percent in Mykonos, and 91 percent in Athens).[13] Cash was scarce in areas like agricultural Naxos, though common in others like Athens,[14] yet never the dominant component.

Women received additional wealth through inheritances and donations from third parties. Relatives without offspring regularly bequeathed or donated properties to women in return for support in their old age.[15] Husbands frequently bestowed additional property to their wives (35 percent of male wills in Mykonos, 33 percent in Naxos) often under the condition that they would "stand by his honor" and not remarry.[16] Wives also remembered their husbands in their wills (20 percent in Mykonos, 18 percent in Naxos) and women composed 56 percent of total wills in Mykonos and 47 percent in Naxos.[17]

Though the expectation was for women to receive their possessions through inheritance and dowries, some families were unable to provide daughters with the necessary wealth. As in contemporary Europe, such young women had to seek employment in order to accumulate additional wealth. Servants in Europe were common and were paid by receiving food, clothes, lodging and a small stipend, which could be saved for marriage.[18] We have numerous examples of women who sought to enter wealthier households as domestic servants in return for maintenance and the promise of a dowry. For example, the priest Panagiotis Mariotis gave his niece Panagiota to Peraki Kampini to work for 10 g. per year plus maintenance, though for the first five years she was to receive only support due to her youth and inexperience. This arrangement would allow the apparently orphaned girl to gain experience and marketable skills, plus a small sum that could eventually enable her to marry with a modest dowry.[19] Other women sought employment in urban centers such as Constantinople or Smyrna (Izmir) often, though not always, returning to their place of birth to marry once they had amassed an adequate dowry.[20]

Some women even after their marriage continued to work for pay either in the service of wealthier individuals or by producing goods for sale. The range of women's professions is not entirely known and was probably, as Merry Weisner has seen in Western Europe,[21] of fairly low status although we know of female doctors in Athens.[22] The Ottoman period provides many examples of Christian, Jewish, and Muslim women, engaged in the wider economy from manual laborers to merchant women, peddlers, shop owners, moneylenders, and artisans.[23] Women participated and even formed their own guilds, as a surviving document from Trikala (1738) indicates. According to this document, six women of the guild of the soap-makers made a deposition that no men belonged to the guild since "ancient" times, nor were men allowed to practice the craft.[24]

No such evidence exists for the regions I examined, but women clearly participated in the local economies, as demonstrated by the court case of old Anousa Touhampa who rented a coffeehouse to another woman in return for maintenance (*zootrofi*) and 10 g. per month.[25] Another woman wanted to evict a tenant in order to open a store.[26] Other women produced goods for the market though husbands often expropriated such income. This is the implication of the court case filed by Nikolas and Geronimos Kornaros against their father in which they demanded the dowry of their deceased mother and the profits from their mother's commercial weaving for over 40 years.[27] Finally, wealthier women undertook all sorts of investments including tax farming.[28]

Enforcement of Property Rights

In Byzantium women were involved in 35–71 percent of surviving legal cases, most dealing with dowries and property.[29] In the Ottoman Empire the question becomes more complex due to the existence of multiple avenues through which women could pursue legal redress starting from the Islamic *kadi* courts to the ecclesiastical courts of the Orthodox Church, to the communal courts of many communities. Women vigorously defended their property rights in all these courts, seeking advantageous divorces, or pursuing cases ranging from murder to fraud, and even rape.[30] This is not different from the rest of early modern Europe when multiple sources of law existed until their consolidation in the nineteenth century.[31] European women, like their Greek counterparts, had no problem navigating these complex systems and widows especially showed firm knowledge of property law.[32] Such knowledge was expected in Naxos where the two opponents of the widow Elenaki expressed their "amazement" that "such a woman of her age and knowledge of the local customs" would lodge a protest against them.[33]

Perhaps the most extraordinary cases involve women who assumed, or tried to assume, direct control of property while still married. Women whose husbands proved incapable of proper management went to court in order to safeguard their dowry without seeking to dissolve the marriage. Though rare, such cases were anticipated in Byzantine legislation and persisted to Ottoman times.[34] One often notices the involvement of kin signifying continuing contact and interest by her natal family, as the case of Georgios Mponis who worried that his son-in-law was selling off his wife's dowry and undertaking debts that he may have had to cover.[35] Though this seems odd in the Greek setting, scholars have argued that in some parts of the Mediterranean a father's *patria potestas* did not end with the marriage of the daughter and thus he could be liable for her debts.[36]

Women even assumed management of their husbands' affairs when the latter was absent or incapacitated, and often became embroiled in legal disputes with their husbands' creditors. An example was Eleno who managed to drag a case regarding her late husband's debts for a decade.[37] Similarly adept was Marino who insisted that she was not simply a trustee (*epitropiki*) but a procurator (*kouratoros*) appointed by her husband to collect his debts in Mykonos in his absence, and even managed to get the General Consul of Russia in Smyrna involved.[38]

Other women confronted their husbands, usually in cases involving divorce. Divorce in Ottoman times was easy in part because women could seek out divorce in Ottoman *kadi* courts, which were more obliging than ecclesiastical courts and more favorable to women in terms of support or custody of children.[39] In response, the Orthodox Church relaxed its grounds for divorce so that by the end of the Ottoman period Greek men and women could even procure consensual divorces. Though the divorce itself was always a matter for the bishop to decide, the property ramifications often involved local communal courts. For example, Mpazia and A. Kourvisanou who decided that they "could not live together" demanded a divorce on "their own free will", upon which the notables made a notarial document for divorce and separation of property and then sent the case to the "archpriest for a ruling".[40] In another case Zortzis Zakinthinos lodged a document explaining that his former wife Maria had abandoned their home in Mykonos and went to the island of Naxos where she became "the whore of the Naxian". He was granted a divorce by the archpriest but he wanted a decision by the notables regarding his two children whom Maria had taken with her, demanding custody or to cease supporting them. As an afterthought, Zortzis added that his wife had taken all her belongings when she left him.[41] These cases demonstrate the involvement of the notables in property and financial matters when a marriage fell apart. Furthermore, assuming that Zortzis' account was accurate, his was a case where an adulterous wife was able to abandon her husband with her property intact, retain custody of her children, and even achieve their support from her ex-husband, all against Byzantine stipulations.[42] This inversion of the legal norm was not rare. In a reconciliation document a couple agreed that the wife would not be able to kick her husband out of their house while he was alive and would allow him to manage her property, the rights a husband enjoyed by law.[43] Such cases indicate that above all the ability of a woman to use and manipulate the legal system was reinforced by the use of the *kadi* courts where women frequently pursued cases of divorce when they were frustrated by the ecclesiastical courts.

Women habitually managed the properties of their underage children although, again, local customs varied significantly. In some areas of maritime Greece, widows were often the sole guardians of their children while in other areas a family council assisted or even assumed that responsibility entirely.[44] On occasion, widows seem to have a leading role in family affairs even after their sons had come of age.[45] Some women were even able to participate in community deliberations and petitions, as seen in a 1794 petition from the Commons (*Koino*) of Naxos regarding the tithe system that included the signatures of two women.[46]

A Time of Rapid Changes

The Greek War of Independence saw massive social, political, cultural, and economic transformations in the provinces that revolted against Ottoman authority. While some regions escaped unscathed, most were devastated. Greece experienced massive loss of life and dislocation of population, internal as well as refugees from areas that had participated in the revolt but remained under Ottoman control. The demographic decline was indicative of the destruction. From 1821 to 1830 the population of what became the Greek state declined from 938,765 to 538,847.[47] The structures of the Ottoman state were destroyed, alongside the Muslim and Jewish populations that were massacred or forced to flee.

The decades following the establishment of the new state saw the rapid transformation of the economy including the development of a cash economy despite the early struggles of the drachma, the new currency.[48] This development was spurred by the move of the population towards new urban centers that saw Athens grow from 10,000 inhabitants in 1833 when it was declared a capital,[49] to 30,590 in 1853 and 65,499 by 1879; Patras from 15,854 in 1853 to 25,494 in 1879; Piraeus from 5,434 to 21,618 over the same period.[50] A second element that led to the establishment of a monetized economy was the emergence and expansion of salaried employment in Greece. By 1861, although the country was still predominantly rural with 147,507 agriculturalists; 38,953 shepherds; and 16,122 land holders, Greece also numbered 32,801 workers; 19,592 artisans; 12,652 male servants; 9,452 shop-keepers; 793 merchants; 5,102 clergymen; 1,346 artists; 19,303 commercial sailors; 394 lawyers; 398 medical men; 161 apothecaries, plus 9,928 government employees including public and municipal functionaries, professors and teachers. However, the only female employees mentioned were 832 midwives; 7,724 women servants, and 9,035 female students (as opposed to 42,680 male students).[51]

The economic transformation of Greece certainly affected the wealth of women, as did the loss of life that left thousands as widows. In the long run, however, the construction of the new state, which was based on the principle of complete centralization, as even contemporaries recognized,[52] was of greater importance in transforming Greece, its economy, society, and culture.

Legal and Institutional Transformations

The pre- and post-revolutionary periods could not be more different with respect to legal structures. From the diverse, multi-cultural, localized environment of Ottoman Greece, a new hierarchical, centralized system was imposed within a remarkably short period of time. Although preference for such a system was clearly expressed from the first year of the Greek revolt, the war delayed its implementation until the arrival of first governor of Greece, Ioannis Kapodistrias, and was finalized only after the establishment of the Bavarian Regency. The latter, under the direction of Georg von Maurer, a noted Bavarian legalist and a member of the triumvirate that formed the Regency, quickly set about establishing the necessary structure of a European-style legal system by promulgating new legal codes, regarded as excellent even by the critics of the Regency.[53] Justices of the Peace were assigned to every significant community, and in 1834 a decree created courts of first instance in every provincial capital, two courts of appeal, a supreme court (*Areios Pagos*) in Athens, and three commercial courts.[54] With equal rapidity a new commercial code was compiled, based upon the French Commercial Code, alongside a new penal code and new codes of civil and criminal procedure for the courts. When the new state moved to create a civil code, however, the process ground to an abrupt halt.

Unlike the other aspects of the legal system where there was a fairly broad agreement, the question of the civil code was one of intense debate and friction. Some favored the wholesale adoption of the Napoleonic Code of 1804 as a paradigm of modernity.[55] Although alien to Greek realities, the *code civil* was spreading throughout Europe and Latin America[56] and by adopting it Greece could claim to be embracing European modernity, as explicitly stated by the Proclamation of the 3rd National Assembly (1827).[57] Others wanted Greece to return to what they perceived to be her real roots. Though a few advocated the adoption of the codes used by the Church, such as the fourteenth-century *nomocanon* of Armenopoulos, known as the *exavivlos*,[58] scholars in the first decades of the new state, notably Pavlos Kalligas who dominated legal debates and influenced generations of legal scholars, preferred to go further back to the *basilika* (ninth century) or even the *corpus juris civilis* by Justinian (sixth century), as more indicative of the Greek legal spirit.[59]

There was, finally, a third group, one that had the support of Maurer himself, who believed that the existing customary laws of Greece represented the true legal spirit of the Greeks, "a true national civil law", as his associate Gustav Karl Geib stated.[60] Maurer wanted to develop a civil code based upon existing customary practices. Kapodistrias had already established the principle of equity between custom and law; Greek courts were instructed to consider customary practices as applicable. In the absence of custom, courts were to refer to Byzantine law.[61] This debate was not resolved in the nineteenth century; Greece only established a comprehensive Civil Code in 1946. These legal debates, however, did not involve mere legalistic matters, but determined to a significant degree the relationship between women, state, and wealth in the nineteenth century.

The first half of the nineteenth century was not a good period for women in Europe with respect to their legal rights. In several of the paradigmatic European states like England and France, women's wealth, and in particular married women's wealth, came under attack and in many cases was subsumed within the property of their husbands. One only has to mention the Napoleonic Code in France, which re-established patriarchy after the brief period of reform under the early revolutionary governments, even though some have argued that the actual legal situation of women was not quite as bad as the law implied.[62] Or, consider Coverture in England that robbed women of their legal personality as well as their movable property, made prior wills invalid by marriage,[63] as seen in the Dower Act of 1833.[64] To assault women's property rights jurists used the legal principles of contract to legitimize the husband's power over his wife, and considered the exchange of the dower for jointure as a bargain beneficial to women and society.[65] Only in the latter half of the century, after intensive campaigning, did married women begin to re-establish some control over their wealth through various property acts.[66]

In that environment, if Greece had, like many other European states, introduced the Napoleonic Code it would have experienced a dramatic and radical transformation of women's property rights.[67] A common conjugal fund would have replaced the legally separate properties of husband and wife, divorce would have been severely restricted, and the ability of women to act independently in defence of their rights and properties would have been curtailed. A similar, though probably far less dramatic result could be expected if the *basilika* or the *corpus juris civilis* had been adopted, especially under the influence of Western ideas regarding the common conjugal fund. The division between a public and a private space, according to gender lines, and the need for patriarchal control and supremacy was shared by most foreign-educated Greek jurists. Indeed, one may argue that this was exactly the outcome in the early twentieth century when the laws on divorce were tightened and the moveable properties of husband and wife were amalgamated in a common fund.[68]

The acceptance of customary law by the Greek state allowed women to continue to exercise some agency with respect to their wealth through most of the nineteenth century. Wives could demand that their husbands' properties be placed as surety to their dowries, a demand the husbands were legally obliged to accept.[69] Greek courts clearly accepted the viewpoint of customary law, which saw the dowry and even the *donatio propter nuptias* as belonging to the wife, even though in Byzantine legislation the betrothal gift went to the heirs of the husband in case of his death and not to the wife.[70] As in the premodern period, women were recognized as the natural custodians of their offspring as long as they did not remarry,[71] and women, like men, could adopt a clear indication of their own separate legal identity.[72] Although the prohibition of donations between spouses was reiterated,[73] widows that did not have a dowry could inherit up to one-quarter of the wealth of their husbands.[74]

Yet that is not the image that emerges from the contemporary accounts of foreigners in Greece before or after the establishment of the modern Greek state. Few, like the generally perceptive Edmond About were able to nuance the circumstances and see Greek women in a more favorable light.[75] Repeatedly travelers, ambassadors, and even foreign functionaries under the Regency, commented on the isolation and backwardness or the "semi-oriental" nature of Greek women.[76] Their accounts have flavored ideas regarding Greek women ever since, and have created an image, which if not entirely inaccurate, is certainly incomplete. Greek women in the nineteenth century may not have achieved the sociability of European bourgeois women but in terms of legal rights, they far outstripped them.

Women and Wealth: Continuity and Change

As in the Ottoman period, the dowry was the most significant component of women's wealth, and was managed by their husbands. Although, at first, the composition of dowries was similar, differences soon appeared due to the economic, legal, and bureaucratic transformations that Greece was experiencing. I will focus on the effects of two developments: the increasing monetization of the dowry and the interaction of women and the courts in their attempts to defend their properties and wealth.

Widows continued to be active in the economy and they frequently appear in court cases as a result of their business activities,[77] including the widow Kalliopi who continued to exercise the tax collection rights for the province of Navplio in 1832 that her late husband had.[78] Such prosperous and influential widows had a say in public affairs as evidenced in the dispute of the village of Plessa with the Greek state over communal lands. Eighty individuals representing their community signed the document to initiate the court case, including six widows who participated as heads of their households on an equal basis with the other heads of households.[79]

Similarly, women continued to actively pursue their rights in the courts, just as they had done in Ottoman times. From 27 January 1860 to 9 October 1860 the Court of Appeals of Athens heard 652 civil cases and petitions, 275 (42 percent) of those involving women, most involving their dowries and other properties, or actions on behalf of their underage offspring. The widow Anthi, for example, sued the brothers of her late husband for expelling her from his house, keeping her dowry, and withholding 1,000 dr. her husband had bequeathed her in his will. She also demanded material support and the interest for the proceeds of her property. She was able to win her case, though did not receive all the support she claimed.[80] The changing economic environment often complicated the position of widows. Kouzi, a widow, had to confront the new Hellenic Bank over a mortgage her late husband had taken on a house that he assigned to her as compensation for his use of her dowered properties.[81] This case was indicative of the way husbands, as managers of the wealth of their spouses, could compromise the position of their spouses although the courts, as in this occasion, often defended the property rights of widows.

As in the Ottoman period, some women were quite willing to confront their husbands by seeking divorces and separation of properties, or requesting the support husbands were legally obliged to provide.[82] Some of these cases reveal the dangers women faced in marriage, like Aspasia Triantafyllou who demanded a divorce after being repeatedly attacked by her husband. On one occasion, he injured her with a sword and on another he caused a miscarriage.[83] Even more interesting, however, are cases that indicate a continuing link between married women and their natal families. On at least three occasions in 1860 fathers intervened to defend the dowries of their married daughters that may have been in danger from their husbands. In two of the cases the daughters were still underage, but it is interesting that even after their marriage fathers continued to consider themselves their guardians, even though the courts in one of the cases were unsure about the rights of the father to represent his married daughter.[84] In the second case the father was alarmed by the financial difficulties of his son-in-law and wanted to become the administrator of his daughter's dowry until her maturity, to which the court consented.[85]

The transformation of the dowry from real property to a predominantly monetary one has often been seen as a sign of effective disinheritance of the daughter by the implication that real property was too valuable to be alienated to daughters.[86] In Greece that was not the case but, as seen elsewhere, the merging of the wife's cash dowry with the husband's estate was a real threat.[87] Scholars have advanced various possible explanations for this phenomenon.[88] One of the most convincing has tied the monetization of the dowry to the urbanization of Greece, and especially the growth of certain centers like Athens, Ermoupolis, Patras, or Piraeus. Although a dowry composed primarily of land made perfect sense in agricultural communities since it allowed the new household to begin its existence with the necessary economic foundation, such a dowry had significantly less value if the couple relocated to one of the new expanding urban centers. The need to disinvest from land that was impossible to cultivate was evident even in patrilocal or neolocal marriages that took the bride to a different village. Such marriages were followed by a flurry of sales and replacements in order to maintain the value of the dowry. From October 1835 to November 1850, for example, in the small provincial town of Leonidio the notarial records contain 96 exchanges of properties, as the one between Konstantinos Pougias alongside his wife Thomais Karamanou who gave a dowered vineyard to Dimitrios Kordogouras in return for 22 goats and sheep; in the same document the husband insured the dowry with 7 dr. per sheep and 5 dr. per goat.[89] If the couple was to settle in a town, however, a monetary dowry was more practical and useful.

This process of monetization was visible in both urban as well as rural areas, as other researchers have found. Eleftherios Alexakis, for example, has determined that the monetary component of dowries among the Arvanites of south-eastern Attica saw a significant increase from 17 percent in the second half of the nineteenth century to 35 percent in the first half of the twentieth.[90] Dimitris Psychogios has also noted the enlargement of the monetary component of dowries in the latter half of the nineteenth century,[91] as have others.[92]

A second factor that drove towards monetization of the dowry was the legal requirement from 1836 onward demanding a detailed valuation of each component and the whole of all notarized dowries.[93] The government insisted upon this in order to calculate the newly imposed stamp duty, and the law was coupled by a provision that only notarized dowries were defensible in court. Although most dowries continued to be composed of a variety of elements including moveable and real properties,[94] by expressing each item in a monetary form the law begun to alter the way people perceived dowries. The dowry certainly assumed an increasingly negative connotation as the century progressed from a vehicle for the protection of the wife to one for the enrichment of the husband. Already by the latter half of the nineteenth century we encounter frequent denunciations of the dowry by early feminists,[95] and even by foreign travelers who lamented the greed and avarice of men, especially in cities, who demanded ever-larger dowries. Dowry-hunting (*proikothiria*), they said, was a scourge in Athens, destroying the principles of good marriage unions and impoverishing families.[96]

Soon husbands would replace real properties of their wives' dowry with the equivalent value rather than with other real property undermining the long-term value of the dowry since in the absence of adjustment towards inflation a monetary dowry rapidly lost its value over time, especially in the conditions of nineteenth-century Greece with loose monetary policies.[97] In addition to inflation, monetary dowries were easier for husbands to alienate, hide, or spend, further eroding their wives' wealth. Women tried to insure their dowries either through the traditional manner of *antikatastatika*, or through notarized documents that placed real properties of the husband as surety.[98] From June 1839 to August 1850, in Leonidio, couples drafted 56 *antikatastatika*, some indicating significant prior expropriation of a wife's dowry, as was the case with Stamatou whose husband Konstas had managed to alienate a dowry worth 9,000 drachmas![99] It should be noted that in the first decades of the nineteenth century there was little evidence of permanent erosion in the records but the frequent complaints and protests seen in the latter half of the century and in the twentieth century indicate the danger of the monetization of dowries.

Modern anthropologists commented that in the twentieth century even in rural Greece the alienation of the movable dower required only informal consent of the wife unlike real estate that required a notarized contract, rendering the latter more secure.[100]

The law mandating the drafting of dowries in a notary may have had an even more sinister, though hidden, consequence. As the notarized dowries concluded in the town of Leonidio seem to indicate, it was predominantly the wealthier segments of the population that were willing to undertake the added expense of a notarized dowry.[101] Poorer families may have eschewed the cost leaving these women without the benefit of legal recourse in case of a husband's despoliation of the dowry. Thus, the law may have also inadvertently reduced the capacity of most women to defend their property rights.

Even for wealthier women, however, the new legal structures may have reduced their ability to defend their property rights in another interesting manner. In the first decades of the new state there was a veritable explosion of the number of letters of attorney in which women assign men, usually lawyers or family members, to defend their rights in court cases as compared with the Ottoman period. Such letters were not new, but they used to be rare, drafted only in extraordinary circumstances. In the post-independence Leonidio, however, such documents were among the most common documents drafted by women. As I have argued elsewhere, this proliferation of letters of attorney was indicative of the *de facto* exclusion of women from the judicial process.[102] This exclusion was the result of the nature of the new courts which lengthened the time of court cases, primarily through the appeals process, and at the same time were less accessible, affordable, and familiar, with intricate language and proceedings, necessitating the use of lawyers, and travel to the seats of the new courts.

Women's Education and Professional Occupations

This physical detachment was further reinforced by the educational developments in modern Greece, which also directly impacted the ability of women to defend their rights and their economic standing. A few years after the founding of modern Greece both men and women, in the overwhelming majority, were illiterate, 91 percent of men and essentially all women. Fifty years later the illiteracy rate for men had dropped to 69 percent but for women the rate still hovered around 90 percent.[103] This was despite the fact that in 1834 the Greek state had mandated the primary education of boys and girls up to the age of 12 and established fines for every lost hour.[104] Greece fits the pattern that Wiesner identified regarding the literacy gulf between men and women, which was more pronounced in the middle of the social scale. However, Greece at the time of independence lacked a middle class and thus the overall gulf was not significant.[105] The manufacture of the middle class in the following decades, and the openness of the class to new members, created an ever-widening gulf in literacy.

As Eleni Varika noted, the reason for this discrepancy lies within the different functions education played for men and for women.[106] At one level education was seen as a crucial element for the development of good citizens. This was identified by the earliest proponents of the establishment of a new "Greek" state, like Rigas Velestinlis who included in his Bill of Human Rights of 1797 a clause (Article 22) on mandatory primary education for boys and girls.[107] For men, however, education was also a significant tool for upward mobility.[108] The absence, and urgent need, for all sorts of professionals, lawyers, doctors, architects, engineers, pharmacists, topographers, chemists, and particularly bureaucrats, made education highly sought after since it guaranteed a career, especially in the early absence of class prejudices. Greek bureaucracy was open to everyone capable of claiming a position and the state was thus one of the very few areas in those early decades that allowed social climbing.[109]

For women, however, professional avenues were barred with the exception of midwifery and teaching. Thus, although the law mandated their education till the age of 12, this was seen as a luxury by the peasant households who would much rather use the labor of their daughters in their fields or homes. This attitude was reinforced by the warnings about "excessive" schooling for girls voiced by learned men, and the state itself reinforced this mentality by not establishing secondary schools for girls till 1917.[110] Even in the few private schools for girls catering to the slowly emerging bourgeoisie the curricula focused on "feminine arts" like sewing and embroidery as well as in the teaching of domestic economy (*oikiaki economia*) generally accepted as a useful subject for women.[111] Greek educators invariably used European examples to legitimate their views,[112] which in essence meant what has been referred to as "decorative education" especially after the 1850s.[113] The situation was further exacerbated with the ban of mixed schools in 1852,[114] since the state gave primacy to the founding of schools for boys.

The exceptions to this were the professions of teacher and midwife, which alongside servants and students formed the most significant female occupations in the nineteenth century outside agriculture.[115] The fledgling state immediately concerned itself with the question of midwives, accepting out of necessity the need to maintain the profession open to women but at the same time regularizing it and placing it under the control and authority of a newly instituted Medical Council. This was done with law 166D of 7 December 1834.[116] Within three years further laws imposed more professional limitations and brought midwifery under close state supervision. They also gave state agencies the ability to select future midwives from among the young, morally upstart, and preferably literate young women of the various provinces, a duty assigned to the municipal authorities, while the Medical Council, with its male doctors, undertook to supervise the future conduct of midwives. [117]

The profession of teacher was also of particular importance to the state, not only because of the dire lack of teachers throughout the country, but also because the profession assumed a prominent role in the nationalist imaginary of Greece. A school for male and female teachers was established as early as 1834,[118] and within 30 years Greece had 1,041 male and 165 female teachers serving 989 primary schools for boys and 138 for girls with 66,714 and 12,400 pupils, respectively.[119] With the emergence of the irredentist *Megali Idea* and the subsequent competition among the fledgling Balkan states particularly over the territory of Macedonia, idealistic teachers, many of them young women, became the missionaries of Greek nationalism in the remaining Ottoman Balkan territories. These men and women had to face the enmity of the rival Bulgarian, Serbian, Albanian, and Vlach nationalist organizations and often lost their lives in the process.[120] Besides the moral and ideological satisfactions of the profession, being a teacher also allowed a woman to live modestly but independently, their salary comparable to that of male bank clerks.[121] Not surprisingly, many of the first feminists in Greece were schoolteachers.[122]

Quite naturally, poorer women continued to work in the economy, though, perhaps not as easily as before. Certainly, Greece in the latter half of the nineteenth century continued to have a significant number of people engaged as servants, and many of those were women.[123] Some served under similar terms as during the Ottoman period, as can be seen from the few surviving contracts. In 1848, for example, the shepherd Dimitrios Iliopoulos came to an understanding with the widow Metaxou Trochani, to give the latter his tenth daughter Evgeni for five years to "serve and work" with a salary of 40 dr. a year, excepting the first year during which she would work without pay "due to her young age and her ignorance regarding her service". Metaxou undertook to feed "as customary" the young servant, without extracting such costs from her salary. Moreover, whatever "handicrafts" Evgeni produced in her spare time would be her own and she was to take them alongside her salary at the conclusion of her service.[124] Other servant contracts could be for longer duration like Aikaterini's who entered service for 11 years, and who was promised a very specific dowry including 12 shirts, eight dresses, and a number of other clothes in addition to 300 dr. in cash for a total value of 460 dr.[125] When servants did not receive what they considered to be their due they did not hesitate to seek redress against their former employers in court all the way to the Court of Appeals.[126]

On the other hand, many servants were simply salaried employees, especially in the new urban centers where the new middle-class households were a new pole for poor women seeking employment.[127] In Athens the salary of a woman servant in a wealthy household in the 1840s was 15–18 dr. a month, as compared to a male servant's 24–25 dr. The duties of a female servant were restricted to the home, male servants being dispatched to the market to shop and for all other activities outside the home.[128] For that reasons male servants were quite numerous and only in the latter half of the nineteenth century and the first quarter of the twentieth did service become increasingly feminized.[129]

Scholars have argued that the emergence of the new market economy, the introduction of salaried work and work hour, and the removal of the workplace from the home, coupled with urbanization, led to a devaluation of the place of women in the family and society, and that in Greece, unlike much of Europe, lower class women were excluded from public space alongside their middle-class counterparts.[130] Certainly, we have little data on women workers in the nineteenth century and much of the information regarding the terrible working conditions comes from novels promoted by early feminists.[131] We can hardly even talk of a working class before the 1860s or 1870s when some industrial development begun to emerge,[132] and even in the twentieth century women's participation in the labor force was stunted compared to most European states.[133] This could be one of the causes for the anemic feminist movement in Greece since demand for work was a key concern for the development of women's activism in nineteenth-century Europe.[134] Indeed, this was a focal point for the few Greek feminists at the turn of the century who suggested paid employment as an alternative to the dowry to rescue marriages from the "profitable business" they had become.[135]

The progressive character of the Greek state should be nevertheless emphasized. Mandatory elementary education for girls was only established in 1882 in France and 1880 in Germany, half a century after such clauses were inserted in the Greek revolutionary and post-revolutionary legislation.[136] Ironically, in the second half of the nineteenth century, Greek women and their roles came under increasing attacks by those who promoted reason and science as well as by those who bemoaned what they saw as the negative aspects of Westernization.[137]

A similar progressiveness was visible in other areas. Although the conclusion of the War of Independence found Greece bankrupt, its economy devastated, overrun with refugees, and with countless war widows and orphans, the state was ready to accept social responsibilities that few other states of the time considered. The willingness of the state to address the issue of widows and orphans was remarkable under the circumstances, especially as it did not show the same urgency in dealing with the problem of the unemployed, and much more dangerous, armed veterans of the war who would plague the fragile state with insurrections and banditry for decades. The only asset in the hands of the Greek government that it could utilize was the land it had expropriated from the Ottoman state and Muslim landowners, and later from monasteries. The state recognized widows as head of households, making them eligible to receive land under the schemes of land redistribution the state would attempt.[138] As early as 1823 with the 2nd National Assembly at Astros, the Greek state undertook the obligation to provide pensions to war widows and orphans, a responsibility reiterated in article 147 of the constitution drafted by the 3rd National Assembly of 1827 in Troezina.[139] Nor was this concern towards widows limited to the revolutionary period. In 1853, a quarter of a century after the establishment of the Greek state, the government passed law 880N SK' that created a fund to support widows and orphans for the duration of the former's lives or until they married, despite the woeful condition of the state's finances.[140]

Conclusions

Most negative effects on women's wealth in nineteenth-century Greece were unplanned or legislated but the result of the mere establishment of a modern state in Greece. This was the case with the creation of a modern judicial and educational system, both of which severely disadvantaged women *vis-à-vis* men. In the areas where the state consciously addressed issues that affected women, such as the civil legislation of the state, pensions and land distribution, or divorce, its attitude was one of inclusion, either accepting the *status quo* or taking into consideration the wellbeing of women. Similarly, the courts well into the second half of the century did not obviously discriminate against women in their rulings. Even servants could seek redress in the courts against their employers and receive the proper compensation for past services.[141] This pragmatism stands in marked contrast with the exhortations of the emerging Greek intelligentsia, which, adopting the contemporary European paradigms, insisted upon the removal of women from the public sphere. Although women's work was positively commented upon by foreigners at first,[142] later in the nineteenth century and up to the 1940s women's idleness was an explicit objective, even in the lower classes where such ideals were impractical, and thus women's employment remained unregistered, often piece work done in the home.[143] That such a persistent campaign would in the end influence state policies and legislation is not surprising. What is surprising was how long it took. It was at the turn of the century, and during the early decades of the twentieth century, that women's rights were compromised.

In 1922, a new law abolished consensual divorces and the state introduced the common conjugal fund. Greek courts curtailed the rights of illegitimate children, which became the sole responsibility of the mother, ostensibly in order to protect women and in openly acknowledged emulation of contemporary European legislation.[144] Three years earlier the Greek state introduced the taxation of dowries, probably due to fiscal needs.[145] By 1946, the new Civil Code enshrined this degraded position of women in the economic household. The code defined the dowry in article 1406 as "the property that the wife or somebody else on her behalf gives to the husband in order to alleviate the burdens of marriage", and added in article 1412 that the husband assumed ownership of the movable dowry and the right to manage and profit from the real estate.[146] In total, 22 articles of the new Civil Code dealt with the dowry while the code also restricted the ability of married women to pursue independent economic actions without their husbands' written consent.[147] This state of affairs would continue until the reform of the Greek family law by the first Socialist Greek government in 1983 that abolished the legal requirement for a dowry and eliminated the concept of "head of household".[148]

Why Greece regressed in this area at a time when the feminist movement in Europe and North America was gaining strength is a matter for further research. What we can conclude is that at the founding of Greece women enjoyed solid legal property rights to their wealth, and that they were willing to defend their rights in court, practices inherited from the Ottoman period. In comparison to much of Europe, they were in a favorable legal position, though not with respect to the emerging economic transformations that were favoring non-static wealth. Women were excluded from the most dynamic aspects of the economy such as the professions, the state bureaucracy, and possibly the patronage networks that would play such a significant role in Greek politics and economic development. In circumstances of rapid urbanization, rising inflation, constant budgetary crises and financial instability, their traditional legal rights may have been incapable of protecting women's wealth, though the precise manner of this development, if it indeed occurred in the nineteenth century, still needs to be uncovered.

CHAPTER 2

PEOPLE OF WEALTH AND INFLUENCE: THE CASE OF THE KHADZHITOSHEV FAMILY (1770s–1870s)

Evelina Razhdavichka-Kiessling

It is well known that accumulation, consolidation, and intergenerational transmission of wealth, accompanied by upward social mobility, cannot occur without the concomitant existence of several political, economic, and social factors. In the case of the Ottoman Balkans during the period under investigation, incorporation into the European economy contributed to the rapid expansion of cash crops and high regional product specialization, and also had as a side effect the intensification of interregional trade. One of the most essential results of these economic changes was the transformation of the Ottoman society. Both the changed economic situation and the emerging new social order left a vacuum into which non-Muslims, and in particular some Bulgarians, stepped. Moreover, the reforms promulgated with the Gülhane Rescript (1839) and *Hatt-i Hümayun* (1856) created further opportunities for strengthening their economic and social positions as well as chances to enter the Ottoman bureaucracy.[1]

Since the second half of the eighteenth century, many Bulgarian merchants became active players in the interregional and international commercial scene.[2] As some recent studies on the development of the

Bulgarian merchant stratum have shown, the emerging commercial bourgeoisie used all the given opportunities to accumulate capital.[3] Engaging simultaneously in trade, lending money at interest, tax farming, and organizing production, they came to form the most energetic and enterprising social element whose influence and control over public life increased together with its riches.

Most of these merchants ran their business as a family affair in which kinship ties were very important for establishing and maintaining commercial webs.[4] Such family enterprises were relatively stable and made possible not only accumulation of wealth but also its consolidation and transfer to future generations. However, to keep and pass riches on to descendants was a challenging task. This was especially true of the Khadzhitoshev family from Vratsa (Ivraca) whose history illustrates the role of commerce in capital formation on a local level; the fields in which it was invested; the applied strategies of its transmission to the future generations; and finally, the ways in which the fortune was manifested. Through examining the Bulgarian Khadzhitoshev family as a case study of flexible economic behavior and social and bureaucratic integration, this chapter will analyze and contextualize the emergence and strengthening of a rich and powerful merchant stratum on a local level within the changing Ottoman context.

The sources for this study are derived from the remarkably rich archive kept by the Khadzhitoshev family. This archive consists of approximately a thousand units, including *firmans*, official and private correspondence, wills, commercial contracts, accounting books, bills of exchange, created from 1750s till 1930s.[5] These documents were kept dispersed in different archives, museums, and institutions until 1984 when a team of researchers organized, translated, and published those diverse materials in two volumes in 1984 and 2002, respectively.[6] What makes these documents valuable for the present investigation is the rich information about the business, public, and private life of three generations.[7] Engaged in various commercial and public activities, primarily in their hometown of Vratsa and the adjacent regions, the family members became part of various commercial and private networks. To keep their business running under the conditions of undeveloped communication, they could rely only on regular correspondence and carefully conducted documentation. Indeed, these letters and documents disclose information about the everyday life of the merchants, and about their interpersonal relations, markets and goods, partners and clients. And all this is intertwined in a tight network of bilateral contacts on different levels, of different character, and with different duration. A close reading of these sources reveals the multiple ways in which the fortune of the Khadzhitoshev family was amassed, invested, manifested, and transferred through the generations.

Tosho Tsenov: the Initial Accumulation of Wealth and Power, 1775–1803

The founder of the Khadzhitoshev family enterprise was *hacı* Tosho Tsenov Vasilev (1745–1831) from Vratsa (see the genealogical tree).[8] In 1755, while still a child, he inherited capital in ready money from his paternal grandmother at the value of 3,070 k., which was to be kept by his guardian – his uncle Ioncho Vasilev – as well as 280 *dram* silver, one silver waist-belt, 25 beehives, two brandy distilleries, and three cauldrons. This document[9] shows that before and around the mid-eighteenth century the family was already involved in production and commercial activities, which made possible the accumulation of a fortune consisting of cash, precious metal, and chattels.

The above-cited will is also interesting from another point of view. Among the seven witnesses who signed it, there was a certain h. Vasil. The fact that at that time he was already called "*hacı*" is an important indicator for the existence of wealthy people in the town who could afford the expensive and long travel to the Holy Lands. Similarly to the grandparents of Tsenov, they could amass fortune probably by engaging in both production and commerce. Furthermore, their riches were enough not only to cover the travel expenses to Jerusalem and back, but also to secure the family's living expenses during the time when men could not exercise their business. Those two examples demonstrate an early stage of two interrelated and interdependent processes: the accumulation of fortune by the Bulgarians in Vratsa, and the formation of a new social group – the local bourgeoisie – who would later express national aspirations. The case of the Khadzhitoshev family illustrates in detail the separate steps in these processes.

As the preserved documents show, Tsenov tried not only to keep, but also to augment, the inherited family capital. It is not clear when exactly he started his commercial career, but as early as 1775 he became a business partner with his uncle. This family enterprise existed during the period 1775–88. When the partners split in 1789, the profit for the last 14 years was 54,212 k.[10] In 1775, their net annual profit was only 1,633 k., but a year later it was nearly doubled. During the next years the net returns fluctuated between 2,758 k. and 6,636 k. (See Table 1.) As their accounts show, the partners engaged simultaneously in trade in animal products (silk, wool, hides, beeswax), food (wine, honey, salt), livestock (sheep, buffaloes, and horses), and in small-scale money-lending. Additionally, they owned two *dükkâns*: a tailor shop and a grocery (the total gain from both of them was 6,750 k.). The silk trade produced the biggest profit: 22,365 k. (41.28 percent of the total profit). The partners carried out extensive trade with both premium and low-quality silks, which were bought from the so-called "*dolapcıs*" (silk producers) working in the town or the adjacent villages. The total profit from the former was 18,709 k., while the profit from the latter was very small – 3,656 k. This is not surprising since the tradition of cultivation and production of silk in Vratsa and its vicinity was quite strong.[11] Namely, the silk production in the region became one of the first "capitalist manufactures" but also became dependent on the merchants engaged in this type of trade and the organization of the process. It is worth noting that in 1786 Ioncho Vasilev intended to buy silk reeling devices (*dolaps*) from h. Andrei and Stancho Iovev from Gabrovo. Probably Tsenov and his uncle hired professional workers who used these devices to wind and spin silk. There is no other evidence to confirm that the partners became entrepreneurs in a putting-out system of silk production. However, in the same year their profit from deals in premium quality silk reached its highest value – 4,750 k.[12]

The second lucrative business of the two partners was the trade in livestock and they earned 10,034 k. They were not only buying and selling cattle and sheep but also raising livestock for sale.[13] Moreover, in this business their partners were local Christians[14] as well as Muslims. For example, in 1777 together with some "Turks" they earned 634 k. from a sale of sheep. Two years later Tsenov noted that from a deal with cattle their share of the profit (*kâr*) was 350 k.[15] The transaction was arranged by a certain "Bayraktar".[16]

The two partners also engaged as middlemen (*kalauzes*) in commercial dealings with wool. Their gain from this activity was 4,940 k.[17] As the correspondence with the brothers Anastas and Georgi Drokhna, their business partners and relatives, shows the two partners collected and bought wool on behalf of Drokhna from some remote villages located in the southern skirts of the Balkan Mountains.[18] In order to fulfill their orders and to secure the deal, the two Vratsa merchants got cash as a prepayment. Unfortunately, there is no information about the commission that the intermediaries would get in the case of a successful transaction.[19]

As merchants who worked on their own account or as commission agents, Tsenov and his uncle traded also in hides and dye, wine, wax, honey, salt, and maize. Another field in which they invested the earned capital was moneylending.[20] The sources do not reveal the rate of interest but they explicitly point out that the two business partners had lent money to the adjacent villages, probably to enable their inhabitants to meet their tax obligations to the treasury. There is only one case when the two merchants made a loan to a certain Emin ağa.[21] In 1789 when their partnership ended, Tsenov and his uncle were owed 11,366 k. by more than 20 villages for goods or sums lent at interest.[22] Besides this capital they had commodities in their two shops, not counting their goods in transit, and sums invested in livestock and cereals.[23] These accounts illustrate the strategies for capital accumulation used by the partners in order to amass their fortune. Keeping the old rule that profits come from money that changes hands often, Tsenov and Vasilev held relatively little cash and preferred to invest their capital in trade for goods in high demand on the market (silk, wool, and livestock) and through moneylending.

The family business operations were carried out through a network primarily based on kinship but also open to Christian and Muslim partners and agents in Vratsa and the adjacent area.[24] Tsenov was keeping and using some of these contacts after he ended the partnership with his uncle. As a contract signed in March 1792 witnesses, he continued to work with members of the Drokhna family. Tsenov, in partnership with Kostadin Drokhna,[25] got from Georgi Drokhna and Alexi Georgiu an advance payment of 1,000 k. to deliver premium-quality silk at market price. For their services the two partners would get a commission (*kalauzluk*) of 30 p. per *okka*. At the same time, Tsenov established new business connections and partnerships. For example, he worked as an agent for the company Angelis Kokosis & Partners from Plovdiv (Philippoupolis), buying silk for them. Satisfied with his work,

Table 1 Profit (in *kuruş*), earned by Tosho Tsenov and Ioncho Vasilev from trade in different goods and moneylending, 1775–88

Year	Silk[1]	Livestock	Wool	Tailor shop	Grocery	Usury	Other goods	Yearly profit
1775	278.20	-	634.15	245.00	115.00	-	361.50	**1,633.85**
1776	424.15	991.20	547.00	184.00	225.00	227.00	546.60	**3,144.95**
1777	707.45	1,196.00	345.20	121.00	-	75.20	313.15	**2,758.00**
1778	2,789.00	1,359.20	426.00	208.00	682.00[3]	258.00	483.00	**6,205.20**
1779	2,032.50	869.00	325.00	157.00	-	287.20	383.20	**4,053.90**
1780	1,540.00	1,120.20	295.00	85.00	750.00[4]	255.00	460.00	**4,505.20**
1781	1,889.20	614.30	346.00	230.00	-	505.00	540.70	**4,125.20**
1782	393.20	958.20	567.00	-	750.00	282.30	293.25	**3,243.95**
1783	1,914.20	642.25	276.00	189.15	-	323.30	506.55	**3,851.45**
1784	1,128.00	511.00	197.20	210.00	-	348.00	443.00	**2,837.20**
1785	1,312.00	469.00	-	150.00	535.00	672.00	332.00	**3,470.00**

1786	5,106.00	380.00	110.00	120.00	450.00	280.00	190.00	6,636.00
1787	1,502.00	463.00	547.00	245.00	359.00	450.00	386.00	3,952.00
1788	1,350.00	461.00	325.00	740.00[2]		625.00	263.00	3,764.00
Total sum	**22,365.90**	**10,034.35**	**4,940.55**	**6,750.15**		**4,588.00**	**5,501.95**	**54,180.90**
Percentage of the total	**41.28%**	**18.52%**	**9.12 %**	**12.46%**		**8.47%**	**10.15%**	**100%**

[1] Premium and low quality silk together.

[2] Together with the profit from the grocery for the same year.

[3] Sum for 1777 and 1778.

[4] Sum for 1779 and 1780.

The table is based on data extrapolated from the profit accounts kept by Tsenov. The yearly profit is the sum of the separate profits recorded for every year. They differ slightly from those of Tsenov because he made several mistakes.

Source: Vŭzvŭzova-Karateodorova 1984: 367–72.

in 1800 Kokosis asked him again to collect silk on their behalf; however, he asked that the collaboration be limited to the two of them in order to secure their profit due to the low demand for silk that year.[26]

In 1801, again as a commission agent, Tsenov bought wool on behalf of another company: Michal Kurte & Michal Goga from Craiova. A document, signed on 26 May 1801, shows that the applied scheme of work organization was the same as the above-described: Tsenov got an advanced payment of 5,000 k. to buy and deliver wool at market price but not higher than 18–20 *kuruş* per *okka*. For his work he would get a commission of one para per *okka*. Compared to the gain he got some years before on the deal for silk, this one was relatively small.[27] The merchants from Craiova, though, sent 80 sacks and 16 rolls of packthread to Vratsa, as well as two people to help with the packaging of the wool. Their agent Gecho, who was in charge of organizing the transportation of the first 30–40 ready sacks to Craiova, also came with them to Vratsa.[28] As the correspondence reveals, the ordered quantity was 40,000 *okka*: 30,000 to be delivered by Tsenov and 10,000 by a certain h. Osman ağa.[29] Despite some difficulties caused by his competitor Tosun ağa, by the end of June Tsenov had bought more than 20,000 *okka* of wool. Meanwhile, he got additional money from his partners in Craiova, needed for buying the remaining 10,000 *okka* of wool and the necessary sacks for its packaging.[30] Although the final gain for this deal remains unknown, one can surmise that Tsenov realized a net profit between 500 and 750 k. Moreover, it seems that he fulfilled the expectations of his Wallachian partners who continued to work with him during the following years.[31]

By having limited his commercial activities primarily to intermediate trade in silk, wool, and livestock, all in demand on the markets at that time, Tsenov secured relatively small but steady profits. He invested part of them in moneylending, becoming a creditor mainly to peasants, but also to artisans and some Muslims.[32] Besides these income sources his shops brought additional secure earnings. Through his extensive network, which included not only family members and relatives but also both Christian and Muslim agents and partners, Tsenov paved the way for his successful business. His commercial activities, though, required high mobility in order to meet with his partners and clients or to collect and buy needed goods. His travels took him through a broad regional area, which included Gabrovo, Koprivshtitsa, Zlatitsa,

Vidin, Oryahovo, and Craiova.[33] Taking into account these facts, one can depict Tsenov as a typical member of the first generation of the emerging Bulgarian merchant stratum, that of the "fathers", who accumulated their capital by engaging in multiple economic activities, and by relying on inter-ethnic and religious networks and high mobility.[34]

Just as wealth and social standing are linked together, accumulated capital and owned property simultaneously provide a certain type of safety and better living standard as well as a chance to achieve higher social status, and, respectively, to gain local influence. In the case of Tsenov, in addition to the various ways in which he manifested his wealth and achieved status, he also planned for the future of his sons and family business and to that end paid special attention to their education.[35] Furthermore, he became a trustee of the local school and actively participated in the management of other community institutions and activities.[36] Following the zeitgeist, he made donations to a number of churches and monasteries and became a churchwarden of several of them.[37] He made donations not only of money but also of land.[38] In addition, in 1791 he visited Mount Athos as a pilgrim and compiled a long list of the items and presents that he bought there at total value of 6,079 k.[39] The same document contains the names of 73 recipients of these presents, among them several members of the family, six priests, his sons' teacher Petko, and seven people who had the title *hacı*; as discussed earlier, this title indicated an important status symbol. Thus, the source is revealing not only Tsenov's piety but more importantly his high material status (he could allow himself to spend money and time to travel to and back from Mount Athos, to buy presents, and to make donations)[40] and the web of established contacts with well-to-do and prestigious people in Vratsa and its vicinity.

Without a shred of doubt, the pilgrimage of Tsenov and his whole family to the Holy Lands, undertaken in 1803–4, was a watershed in the family history.[41] This act was a clear sign of the family's prosperity and powerful status as well as an open manifestation of their desire to legitimate the achieved socio-economic position through the tradition of pilgrimage, which was both enduring and highly respected by both Muslims and Christians.[42] According to many contemporary observers, the pilgrimage was highly esteemed by all confessional and ethnic groups and the title *hacı* was a kind of "passport", which opened all doors. Moreover, this title was considered comparable to the English "lady" and "sir" or even "baron".[43] Probably the most striking illustration of the respect and prosperity that h. Tosho enjoyed is the fact that, some time during the 1850s, one of the residential districts in Vratsa was named after him "Hacı Tosho".[44] In conclusion, the main contribution to family prosperity by Tosho Tsenov, representative of the generation of the fathers, was his success in building up and legitimating the reputation of the Khadzhitoshev clan as one of the richest and most influential merchant families in Vratsa. However, it was the second generation, the Khadzhitoshev sons, who managed to expand the achieved economic power and social prestige.

Dimitraki Khadzhitoshev: the Most Distinguished Member of the Family, 1803–27

Although in the first decade of the nineteenth century h. Tosho Tsenov continued to run the family business, his first-born son h. Dimitraki (Dimitŭr) Khadzhitoshev (1780–1827) was fully integrated into the family's commercial affairs and soon became the leading figure within the enterprise. As early as 1803, we find him in the Danubian port city of Svishtov, working together with Bozhan Ivanovich, his father's partner there.[45] It seems that he acquired more responsibilities at that time because he received personal orders from different business partners and clients for buying goods on their behalf.[46] In the following years his two younger brothers, h. Tsvetko and h. Iovancho (Iovan), also engaged in the family affairs, which had now become a multi-generation business. As a result, the scheme of work organization changed: while the father h. Tosho reduced his business trips with the intention to mentor his successors and coordinate the firm from Vratsa, his sons took over his duties to visit different places in order to buy or sell goods, establish contacts or negotiate with agents, clients and partners, and sign contracts.[47] For this they relied on an extended network of agents and employees who worked in their farm and shops, collected and sold goods in the villages of the whole Vratsa *kaza*, organized transportation of wares and livestock to the big Danubian ports (Vidin, Svishtov, Oryahovo) or even abroad (Craiova, Bucharest, Belgrade), and visited some of the biggest Balkan fairs in Nevrokop, Uzundzhovo, Sliven, Pazardzhik, and Plovdiv.[48]

The preserved correspondence and ledgers reveal that while the business was growing and respectively more members of the family were involved in it, commerce remained the main source of capital accumulation. The family traded in animal products, food, and livestock, which dominated the export and domestic trade lists. During the first decades of the nineteenth century the silk trade continued to be the most lucrative business in the region, and the Khadzhitoshevs had a large share in it. As already pointed out, they established and maintained an extensive network of commercial agents from different villages and towns around Vratsa who purchased silk cocoons and premium and low quality silk on their behalf.[49] The Khadzhitoshev firm resold the silk mainly to its commercial partners from Tŭrnovo, Svishtov, Oryahovo, Craiova, and Bucharest, including a smaller part on its own account. For instance, in 1806 silk from Berkovçe was sold to Atanas Parashkevov at the value of more than 15,000 k.[50] In 1818, h. Dimitraki and his old business partners from Craiova, the firm "Kurte & Goga", established a partnership (*ortaklık*) for collecting and selling silk. It was a typical *commenda* (short-term partnership combining investment of labor and capital) where the invested capital was shared in a ratio of 1:2 in favor of the Wallachian merchants. According to the contract, h. Dimitraki would organize the collection and sale of the silk and the profit would be divided into two equal parts;[51] from this deal each party made a profit of 523 k.[52]

Other evidence that the silk trade was a profitable business is the very fact that the influential Muslims of the local ruling milieu actively participated in it. In December 1808, h. Dimitraki bought 88 *okka* and 75 *dram* of silk on credit from the Vratsa *voyvoda* (governor) h. Abu Bekir[53] at a total value of 1,587 k.[54] Consequently, it is not in the least surprising that the Khadzhitoshev operations were not confined only to the silk trade. They also made an important investment in the organization of silk production and thus paved the way for a capitalist type of manufacturing.[55] On the one hand, their agents bought silk cocoons and silk directly from the cultivators who owned and used their reeling tools. The latter, therefore, were independent producers but also dependent on the Khadzhitoshevs.[56] On the other hand, the Khadzhitoshev family was also distributing the raw material to the seasonally hired *dolapcıs*, who used either their own reeling devices or those provided by the merchants. These skilled workers were engaged in the production of premium quality silk.[57] The correspondence exchanged during the second half of the 1820s between h. Dimitraki and his trade partner in Tûrnovo Sava Khadzhiiliev provides important insights into the organization of silk production. In 1824, the two partners made their first deal for silk but Khadzhiiliev remained unsatisfied with the quality of the provided product.[58] This was probably the reason that three years later h. Dimitraki asked his partner for help in hiring skilled *dolapcıs* from Tûrnovo and its vicinity to work in the Vratsa region. Indeed, Khadzhiiliev hired 35 *dolapcıs* and a certain Neno as their supervisor. According to the deal, they would get a payment of 2 k. and 10 p. per *okka* ready product from h. Dimitraki and no other *dolapcıs* would be hired. If somebody did not do his work properly, he would bear the loss. At the same time, h. Dimitraki would hire additional supervisors to inspect their work on location. The *dolapcıs* would keep their own account books (*tefters*) and get a prepayment of 500 k., which later would be deducted from their wages.[59]

Livestock breeding and trade and the handicrafts related to them, opened doors not only to profitable businesses but also to new investments. During the first decades of the nineteenth century, the Khadzhitoshevs continued to trade in both its own livestock and in cattle bought from other people, including Muslim officials such as a certain Abdullah Pasha and the Vratsa *voyvoda* Ibiş ağa.[60] They sold the stock at the big annual fair held in Nevrokop, but also in Wallachia, Serbia or the Habsburg Monarchy.[61] It was at that time they built up a business connection with the Serbian Prince Miloš Obrenović – the richest livestock trader in the newly emerged neighboring state.[62]

Alongside the livestock business, the Khadzhitoshevs participated actively in intermediate trade in wool and hides.[63] It is difficult to say whether the share of the wool dealings within the family business increased or decreased in comparison with the previous decades. However, the sources clearly indicate that the trade in hides became a lucrative endeavor. During 1822–3, the Khadzhitoshevs collected a large number of rabbit hides delivered mainly by Muslims.[64] A big part of them – 5,667 pieces – were sold to their trade partner from Šabac, Petûr Popadich, who exported them to Trieste.[65] These hides were sold for 9,301 k., which included the net price 9,067 k., or (64 p./piece), the expenses (93 k.), and the commission (141 k.).[66] In 1826, the above-mentioned trade partner Sava Khadzhiiliev bought 10,000 rabbit hides from the Khadzhitoshev firm, while a year later Kadri aga from Lovech (Lofça) made a deal with h. Dimitraki for collecting rabbit hides and prepaid 4,928 k. for them.[67] At that period, the Khadzhitoshev company also started to collect and resell hides from various wild animals which were delivered both by local people and by other merchants.[68]

Yet it was the processing of hides where the merchant family employed a putting-out system. Similarly to the case of silk production, the raw hides would be passed to the tanners (*tabakcıs*) to be steeped and cleaned, treated with lime, and tanned. As well, these professionals worked for the Khadzhitoshevs for wages. A clear evidence of this investment in hide production is found in a letter dated 24 April 1811, in which h. Dimitraki instructed his father to keep the accounting book of the tannery (*tabakhane*) carefully by recording "how many *sahtiyan*, *meşin* [types of leather] and *çepiks* [shoes] each master delivers and how much money each receives. Write name by name legibly".[69] The preserved documents indicate that the ready products enjoyed a strong demand on the market and thus secured profits.[70]

As noted above, a significant part of the family income came from their *dükkâns*. Evguenia Davidova, having studied the property ownership of Balkan merchants during the late 1820s, pointed out that *dükkâns* and bakeries seem to be the preferred urban commercial properties.[71] The Khadzhitoshev family makes no exception to this pattern. As early as 1809, they invested 1,500 k. in buying four *dükkâns*.[72] So, in addition to their tailor shop and grocery, the merchant family owned a shop for selling *aba* (coarse woolen cloth) and one for furs (*kürk*).[73] Besides the investments in the urban properties, the family was interested in buying and even speculating in land. Scattered data from their accounting books indicate that h. Dimitraki bought pastures and forests and resold them to third parties for a profit.[74] They also invested in beehives, water- and fulling-mills.[75] In addition, they possessed barns in Vratsa and a distillery in the village of Kunino, which were rented out.[76] The Khadzhitoshevs also owned vineyards. They made efforts to rent land belonging to the Xenophontos monastery on Mount Athos and Bistritsa monastery.[77] Lastly, farms (*çiftliks*) became a new field for investment and accumulation of substantial fortunes. The family owned a *çiftlik* (approximately 3,000 *dönüm*), which was bought by h. Dimitraki in the village of Radovene[78] in 1822. Between 1824 and 1826 on the *çiftlik* a tower was constructed, a massive two-story building destroyed after the death of h. Dimitraki in 1827.[79] This *çiftlik* was inherited by his sons who sold it in 1841 to Omer ağa. In 1848, the latter sold the farm to the residents of Radovene who, eight years later, resold it to the sons of h. Dimitraki.[80]

The Khadzhitoshev family's enterprise remained active in various branches of trade, especially in purchasing honey, wax, and butter from the adjacent villages and delivering them to the partner merchants mainly in Sofia and Oryahovo.[81] They also made investments in alcohol, wine, and honey processing, and the products were sold both to local customers and to merchants from other regions.[82] They were also profitting from moneylending.[83]

During the first two decades of the nineteenth century the Khadzhitoshev family, under the leadership of h. Dimitraki, had diversified its economic activities and thus augmented its wealth, and simultaneously increased its power and sphere of influence. A preserved list with the guest names of the h. Dimitraki's wedding is indicative not only of the family's enhanced prestige but also of its networking in local society at every level.[84] The source mentions more than 100 guests among whom were high-ranked Muslim officials: the *voyvoda* of Vratsa and *molla* (judge or religious scholar) Derviş ağa, a *serdar* (military commander); several military men: *binbaşıs*, *bölükbaşıs*, and *subaşıs*; members of eight guilds (*esnafs*); the bishop of Vratsa Antim; several priests; the above mentioned teacher Petko; and a number of Christian notables.[85] Furthermore, the Khadzhitoshev family maintained both private and business relations with some of the guests.[86] Thus, it is not surprising that many individuals, including community leaders, asked h. Dimitraki to mediate between them and the local authorities.[87] Moreover, his good name and reputation became so widespread that people from Strumica and Leskovac to Craiova asked him for help or support.[88] He enjoyed the trust of local Muslim officials and business partners as well.[89] During the Russo–Turkish war of 1806–12 he even established contact with the Russian headquarters and met in 1811 with the commander-in-chief.[90]

Like his father, h. Dimitraki engaged himself actively in the management of local Christian community, school, and church affairs.[91] He diverted part of his wealth to philanthropy, including: construction, renovation, and upkeep of churches and monasteries; education of children; hiring of teachers; copying of books, etc.[92] Accumulated fortune and social prestige, as well as established contacts with both Ottoman officials and Christian notables, gave h. Dimitraki the self-confidence to play a leading part in the conflict between the local people and the Greek bishop of Vratsa Methodius. As early as 1813, the same bishop appointed h. Dimitraki as a churchwarden and authorized him to collect the church taxes in his absence.[93] However, by 1820 their relationship severely deterioreted, followed by the efforts of h. Dimitraki to remove the bishop from his post. The attempt of the archbishop of Tŭrnovo, Ilarion the Cretan, to defend Methodius escalated into a personal battle with h. Dimitraki.[94] Although this conflict had a fatal end for the latter and his efforts to replace the Greek bishop of Vratsa with a Bulgarian one failed,[95] he remains in the history as leader of the first significant anti-Greek resentment, which some two decades later grew into the so-called Bulgarian Church Movement.[96]

In short, under the leadership of Dimitraki Khadzhitoshev the family enjoyed a brief period of great prosperity and influence. He became one of the most distinguished merchants of Vratsa and the region, enriching himself through interregional and international trade in profitable commodities but also through investments in property and organizing production of silk and hides. It was he who succeeded in consolidating the family wealth, establishing important political connections and friendships, and, by doing this, increasing significantly his influence and control over the public sphere. However, with his assassination in 1827, the family's successful business expansion and increasing social power were interrupted. The Khadzhitoshev family lost not only its most active and talented member, but also part of its fortune, which was confiscated.[97] During the following decades, his brothers and sons had to rely not only on their inherited riches and prestige, but now on their own merits and networks in order to maintain their wealth and to successfully channel their power and influence. A task that, as we shall see below, was not so easy.

The Third Generation: in Search of New Perspectives, 1827–1878

The first decade following the death of h. Dimitraki seems to have been turbulent for the Khadzhitoshev family. A few preserved letters from that period are illuminating in this regard. His brother h. Iovancho, who took the lead in the family business, made efforts to solve a dispute with the ex-governor of Vidin Ibrahim Pasha and to keep the business running despite all the difficulties.[98] In 1834, he tried to secure the future of his nephew Zamfiraki (Zamfir), as an office-holder of the Serbian Prince Miloš.[99] The sources do not provide any information about the outcome of this step, but they reveal that five years later his brother Alexander also hoped to attain a post as Serbian official.[100] Thus, Alexander chose to abandon the family business for government service. In pursuit of his aim, in the 1830s and 1840s, he traveled in Serbia, Wallachia, and the Habsburg Empire[101] where he established relations with several prominent Bulgarians such as the Mustakov brothers in Bucharest,[102] Ivan Dobrovski,[103] and Anton Tsankov in Vienna.[104] Finally, in 1850 he returned to Istanbul where he was decorated by the Ottoman sultan with an order and received a sword.[105] In 1851, with the support of his patron Prince Stefan Bogoridi (Stefanaki Bey),[106] Alexander Khadzhitoshev was sent together with Mehmed Şekib Efendi to investigate the situation in the Vidin region where a revolt had broken out in 1850.[107] More importantly, he was groomed as the future *kapıkâhya* (official representative) of the planned semi-autonomous *kaymakamlık* consisting of the three *kazas* of Vidin, Lom, and Belogradchik, a project also initiated by Bogoridi.[108] The next step in his career as an Ottoman official was his appointment in Niš three years later.[109] At a time when he had acquired greater power and influence, which he used to support both personal/family interests and the demands of his compatriots, he died in Sofia in 1856.[110]

While Alexander relied on his high position and solid connections to support the family affairs,[111] his two brothers Zamfiraki and Todoraki tried to revive the family commercial activities. One may distinguish two periods in their business dealings. During the first one (1840–8) the brothers, in partnership with their relatives the Statkovich family, engaged in export of livestock to Serbia and the Habsburg Empire. At the beginning, Zamfiraki traveled with flocks of livestock to sell them abroad while his younger brother coordinated the dealings in Vratsa.[112] To secure the necessary capital for their livestock business, they sold their *çiftlik* in the village of Radovene in 1841, as mentioned previously. Furthermore, the partners borrowed money from the bishop of Vratsa Agapius and the Vratsa ex-*voyvoda* Mehmed Hurşid ağa.[113] Unfortunately, some of their deals were not successful and caused significant losses.[114] As early as 1843, Todoraki wrote to his brother that their financial situation was critical and they should sell one of their *dükkâns* to pay their debts.[115] This step did not seem to be very helpful since two years later Todoraki warned his brother again that they could not pay their creditors.[116] The situation had worsened sharply and in 1848 the partnership with the Statkovichs was dissolved.[117] It was time to look for new businesses.

During the second period (1848 till the Russo–Turkish War of 1877–8), the Khadzhitoshev brothers engaged primarily in tax farming and invested in land and commercial properties.[118] It was Zamfiraki who became active in tax farming of tithe (*öşür*) of wheat and hay; sheep tax (*beğlik*); and vineyards of Vratsa, Berkovitsa, Svishtov, Pleven, and Tûrnovo regions. He formed a coalition with his long-term business partner Mehmed Hurşid ağa, his son Kâşif bey, and Genc ağa from Lovech. Unfortunately, the sources remain silent about the relations among the partners, their capital, shares, and profits or losses. What they mention is that Mehmed Hurşid ağa bid for the farming of various taxes on behalf of Zamfiraki at the auctions in Istanbul, while the latter managed the tax collection himself.[119] In his work, Zamfiraki was supported by his two brothers: Todoraki engaged in solving issues on a local level and Alexander, with his contacts and influence, in the Ottoman capital.[120] Although Zamfiraki faced some problems with the collection of the tithe of hay in the region of Svishtov and Pleven, it seems that tax farming was a lucrative business providing good profits,[121] which he invested in property. For example, in 1857 he bought one *dükkân* in Vratsa from the heirs of his uncle h. Iovancho for 12,500 k., a distillery and a fulling mill for 2,000 k. and 25 *okkas* of copper for 1,000 k.[122] He also owned a house and a timber mill in Vratsa.[123] In 1852, Zamfiraki and his brothers inherited a house, *dükkân*, and different small chattels from his aunt Marutsa.[124] Also, as a dowry for his marriage to the daughter of the rich merchant from Sofia, Anastas Theodorov, he got a house and a *dükkân* worth of 32,000 k. in Sofia.[125] His brothers also chose to invest in property. As mentioned earlier, together they bought back their father's *çiftlik* with a water mill in the village of Radovene in 1856.[126] Two years later Todoraki alone bought a lot in Vratsa from his uncle Kostadin for 5,500 k.[127] He also owned a field and a forest in Radovene.[128] Therefore, one could rank the family among the largest local property owners.

Essentially, it was due to their good connections and accumulated experience that by the 1850s the Khadzhitoshev brothers had moved ahead in the expanding sector of tax farming and bureaucracy, increasing their wealth and influence. Similarly to their grandfather and father, they had established and maintained an extended network of formal and informal links to people of different ethnic, religious, social, and professional backgrounds. Using their powerful status, they not only formed different coalitions to guarantee their business and private interests but also tried to secure different administrative posts for their "friends".[129] The Khadzhitoshevs participated actively in all communal initiatives undertaken by their compatriots both in the region and in the Ottoman capital. They supported the teachers in the local Bulgarian school, became subscribers for books and newspapers, and took a leading part in the Church Movement.[130] It was Alexander who worked for the construction of the Bulgarian church in Istanbul and the establishment of the Bulgarian press in Svishtov.[131] It is worth mentioning that both Alexander and Todoraki withdrew from trade and devoted time to public affairs.[132] This is by no means an untypical scenario, as it appears to be the norm not only in the case of pre-industrial European merchant families but also among their Balkan counterparts.[133]

Conclusions

The members of the Khadzhitoshev family were among those enterprising Bulgarians who took advantage of the political and socio-economic changes in the Ottoman Empire and amassed their riches as traders. By the mid-eighteenth century there were already Bulgarians in their hometown of Vratsa who managed to accumulate capital in cash, precious metals and chattels, which was successfully transmitted to their offspring. Such was the case of h. Tosho Tsenov who used the inherited capital to build up a profitable business mainly as a forwarding agent. Limiting his activities to trade and moneylending, he secured relatively small but stable profits and accumulated initial wealth, which opened the doors to both prosperity and local power for his family.

The second generation entered the family enterprise early and thus formed a multigenerational business, based on a tightly interlocking network of kinship, but also friendship and business ties with people of different ethnic, religious, and social backgrounds. Although there is no preserved contract clearly illuminating the firm structure and applied scheme of division of profits, the documents suggest that the first-born

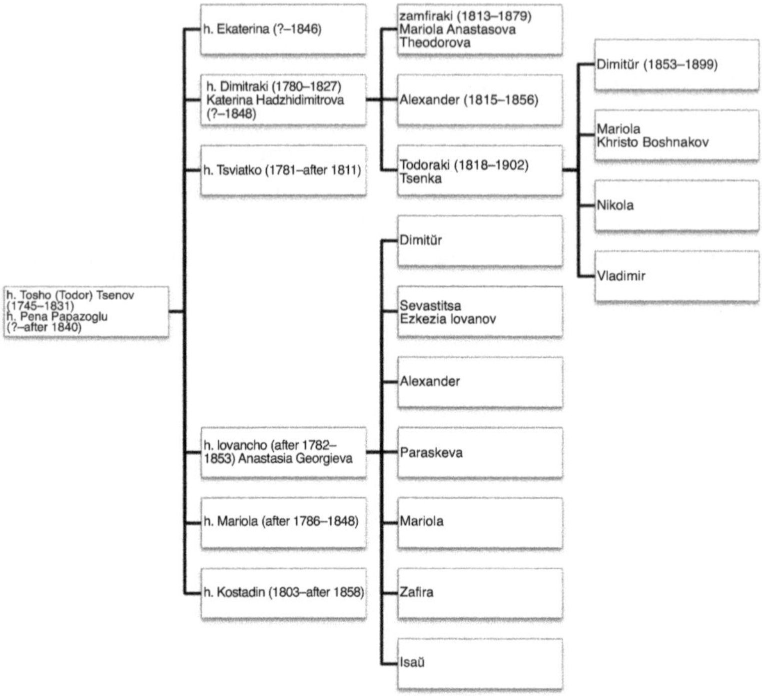

Figure 1 Genealogical Tree of the Khadzhitoshev Family
Source: Tarashoeva 2002: 512.

son took over the leading position while the other family members were subordinated to him. Thus, it was mainly due to his personal capabilities and skills to manage the business that the inherited wealth was consolidated and transferred further. Hence, h. Dimitraki applied a successful strategy to keep the lucrative trade in silk and livestock running and to expand the commercial dealings in hides, answering the brisk market demand. Furthermore, he diversified the family activities in organizing the production of the two most important trade commodities for their firm: silk and hides. Next to this, h. Dimitraki turned some of the accumulated capital into property and made profits from land speculation. In addition to his wealth, his prestige and influence had also increased. However, he overestimated the safety provided by his economic and social status and good connections. His self-confidence cost not only his life but also part of his riches. The line of growing family affluence and power was interrupted. Thus, the third generation had to rely not just on the inherited fortune and prestige, but more on their own education, abilities, and connections in order to attain desired economic and social positions. Therefore, it is not surprising that it was members of this generation who did not remain in the family business, and chose to invest in property and to become officials. So, the family wealth was not only maintained but also transformed into social capital.

CHAPTER 3

DEFINING THE PATRIMONY: NAME, LINEAGE AND INHERITANCE PRACTICES (WALLACHIA AT THE BEGINNING OF THE NINETEENTH CENTURY)

Andreea-Roxana Iancu

In 1780, the Ypsilantis Code defined and legitimated the institution of the *kamini* (Gr. *καμίνι*, Rom. *cămin*, literally "the fireplace" of the house) as ancestral eponymous land inherited only by the male descendants of the original founder's lineage: "*kamini /cămin* means the estate which is at the origin of the name (σκλιτάδα/*sclitada*) and of the lineage;" it "does not refer to all the possessions inherited by the family".[1] According to the legal text, this part of the patrimony is inalienable and therefore submitted to *protimesis* (preference), corresponding to *retrait lignager* or to *laudatio parentum*, which includes the kin, neighbors, or co-owners who should agree before any sale of a real estate.[2]

The definition of inalienable patrimony as eponymous land tenure (which gives its name and origin to a lineage) explicitly inscribes property into a logic of legitimating identity, like a birth certificate of the lineage. Thus, the *kamini* had attached a founding authority to the original estate. The lineage's identity was based not only on the right to property but also on the right of the ancientness of "birth" – an act of foundation of the first owner and the lineage's ancestor through which the *boyar* (member of aristocracy) ensured his place within the society.[3] The name of the original estate, as well as the founder's name or nickname, would then become, based on legal fiction (presumption of a fact), the patronym of his direct descendants.

This redefinition of the patrimony was taken in order to avoid lineage extinction. Nonetheless, it had the exact opposite effect on some of the big aristocratic fiefs because the text indicated that only the original (eponymous) land property was protected by the consents *(ius protimiseos)* and not all the inherited land possessions. But, outside of the economic and social effects on the aristocratic families, what are the consequences of this measure in terms of personal and lineage identity? This is the main question that preoccupies our chapter. To what extent is the idea that land belongs to individual (in terms of property) mirrored by that of an individual belonging to land (in terms of origin)? How could this ambivalence of the notion of "belonging" be used so as to legitimate the inherited patrimony? In what ways was the institution of *kamini*, as synthesis between "to be" and "to have", the very basis of a process of identity construction?

Theoretical and Terminological Framework

How could the connection – based on a genealogical construction – between an eponymous land and its owner be described? One is tempted to paraphrase Pierre Bourdieu's statement: "the one who belongs to the land and to whom the land belongs".[4] The institution of heir finds its signification through the idea of embodiment: the heir is becoming one with his patrimony and the patrimony appropriates him. The representation of this symbiosis is a mechanism that generates practices destined to keep and perpetuate the integrity of his patrimony.[5]

Maurice Godelier shows in different terms the same principle described by Bourdieu, relating it to the notion of "house" (*maison*), and defines the *maison* as a system based on modalities of inheritance. His starting point is derived from Claude Lévi-Strauss's definition of *maison* as a moral person who holds a real estate and intangible goods:[6] it is not the house that belongs to the people but vice versa "the people belong to the house, together with the tangible and intangible goods that must remain undivided and be preserved in order to be transmitted to the direct lineal descendants, men or women, provided that they are the first-born...".[7]

According to the definitions given by the three authors, the signification of the "belonging" of an heir to his patrimony is a reference to the idea of inheritance itself: the instituting power that links (im) material goods and individuals in a purpose of legitimation. This "power" is in our case the "fireplace" of the house (*kamini*) that each generation has to preserve and perpetuate.[8] One of the main expressions of this "power" is the symbolic capital represented by the name, in our specific case: the property name and the lineage or the *house* name.

The difficulty consists in defining the verb "to belong" in a way that takes into account this double meaning of property and identity. Lévi-Strauss interpreted this ambiguity as a dialectic relation between the filiation and the residency, which define societies that base their inheritance practices open to all heirs ("à maison").[9] It means that keeping the patrimony's integrity and perpetuation is a higher priority than patrilinear succession in itself.

Along these lines, the analysis carried out by Emile Benveniste may also offer an answer to this ambiguity of "belonging" as to the notion of *house*; more exactly the distinction, in terms of linguistic archaeology, between *house*-as-family and *house*-as-building. In his view, there are four circles of social belonging and he located the shift from a genealogy-based society to a society divided according to land tenure within the first circle; the name of the social unit was transferred to the physical space that this unit occupies.[10] We can find a similar shift in the dynamics of the Romanian term "*moş*" (ancestor) – "*moştenire*" (inheritance) – "*moşie*" (land possession) – "*moşnean*" (landowner), a topic discussed in the next section.

Land Belongings, Belonging to the Land: A Short Linguistic Approach

Since the beginning of the twentieth century, historians and legal historians were attracted by this terminology that could link property to its origin.[11] The starting point was the word ancestor (*moş*),[12] the root of *moşie,*[13] which was initially used to designate the inherited land, only later to acquire a broader signification of land possession, be it inherited or acquired. The owner of the land was called *moşnean*, which is also a word derived from *moş* just as *moştenire* (inheritance). Initially, *moşnean* referred to the descendant of an ancestor – landowner through inheritance, but later it came to mean any person to have gotten a land by purchase, donation, etc. The term was used in expressions such as *moşie moşteană* or *moşie de moştenire* (inherited land), *moşie ohabnică* or *moşie de ohabă* (hereditary land), *moşie de zestre* (land received as dowry), *moşie de danie* (land received through donation) and, last but not least, *moşia de baştină* (land of origin). A look at the evolution of the word *moş* in terms of representation shows the genealogical construction of a land possession, whether it belongs to a community of free peasants or to *boyars*. The properties and the people all come from an ancestor, a sort of founder, and they constitute a patrimony because of this transmission from one generation to another that is established in time.

In Romanian, belonging to or being part of a territorial community is referred to by the generic term *pământean* ("inhabitant of the land"), which comes from *pământ* (land), or by yet another term *băştinaş* (autochthon), which comes from *baştină* (place of origin). *Baştina* (*бащина*) is a term of Serbian and Bulgarian origin and its root is *баща* (father), which obviously links it to patrimony (that is the goods and the rights associated to them – *dominium* – transmitted by the father).[14]

The terminology derived from *moş* (ancestor) and *баща* draws a trajectory that highlights and legitimizes the link between land possession (*moşie*) and origin *(baştină)*, between *moşnean* (landowner) and *băştinaş* (autochthon), and between the land and personal identification in both the territorial and parental (kinship) community. In the history of the term, this link between the land and the origin of its owner is built around the notion of ancestor: founder of the patrimony, of the lineage, and of place within the territorial community of autochthons, and it legitimates two criteria in this dynamics of identity: the place and the blood. The name taken from the eponymous property is an expression of the link that it establishes. The first legal text to confirm this link is the above-mentioned Ypsilantis Code from 1780.

How is this long dynamic between identity and land property manifested in the legal practice? The following section highlights the practices of the last descendants of a few *boyar houses* to save their name and their estate through three case studies. They show how the link between the eponymous estate (*kamini/cămin*) and the lineage name would be reinforced via the preservation and transmission of inheritance.

Variations on the Topic of Succession through Adoption and Inheritance by Will

The case of boyar Ştefan Alexeanu, a great stolnic

At the end of the eighteenth century, the last descendants of the Alexeanu family had every reason to worry about the future of their lineage. At a very advanced age, none of the three sons of the *stolnic* (high dignitary) Constantin had a son "of his own flesh and blood": neither the *şătrar* (dignitary with military functions) Grigore, father of two daughters; nor his two other brothers, Constantin, *postelnic* (chamberlain) and Ştefan, ex-*great stolnic.*

The *great boyar* Matei Cantacuzino mentioned in the genealogy of his own family that the *stolnic* Constantin Alexeanu, husband of the daughter of prince Constantin Brancovan (1688–1714), originated from "a modest family compared to the grand families of Wallachia".[15] However, his ancestor Ghiorma played an essential role during the reign of prince Matei Basarab (1632–54). Coming from an obscure origin, his rise was marked by a remarkable accumulation of titles and ranks. Adopted by a freed slave, upon arrival from Constantinople, the *ban* (governor) Ghiorma married Neacşa who brought him the Alexeni estate as dowry, which later became the eponymous estate of his lineage. After having repudiated his wife by blaming her for sterility, he made a much more profitable alliance for his political career by marrying Gherghina, a widow of *great vornic* (high judge) Hrizea, kin by alliance of prince Matei Basarab's wife. Only one of his sons, Alexandru, followed a similar matrimonial strategy. He married twice: once to Marica, prince Matei Basarab's niece; once to Stanca, Dumitraşco Corbeanu's sister, who was kin of another reigning prince Constantin Brancovan.[16]

One century later, Ştefan Alexeanu would be the first in two generations to acquire the important rank of *great stolnic* (1802). He was the only one, among his brothers, to seek for a profitable marriage that would enable him to rise on the social ladder. His wife, Maria, with whom he lived for 36 years, was one of the daughters of high dignitary Scarlat Drugănescu (*great stolnic* in 1783, *great paharnic* in 1784).[17] Their union, even if enduring, would not lead to any childbirth. This is why, eight years before his death, Alexeanu asked the Wallachia's metropolitan Dositei to prepare the religious ceremony for adoption of Sultana, Marica's half-sister[18] and the last child of the *paharnic* (high dignitary) Drugănescu.[19] After this adoption, the future of Alexeanu family seemed as uncertain as before, since the adoption of a daughter does not solve the problem of lineage continuity. However, a new perspective seemed to open up by marrying their adoptive daughter to the third *logothete* (secretary of a dignitary) Iordache Lehliu.[20] The boy born from this legitimate union would have had, as single descendant, an essential role for the future of the Alexeanu family. But, the scarcity of documentation does not enable us to follow his destiny.[21]

If we analyze the succession of events, each step taken by Ştefan Alexeanu makes sense when perceived from the perspective of a strategy in response to a crisis: namely, the lack of descendants. Why was he the one who took over this task? Why, for example, did his brother Constantin not want to adopt his nephew who lived under his roof?[22] The answer lies in Ştefan's position within his family. He was the eldest son and the only one who possessed the eponymous land property Alexeni. Viewed from this angle, the adoption of his niece Sultana was the first step of a long-term succession strategy. First, he found her a husband, a low-rank dignitary coming from a *boyar* family, documented in Wallachia by the mid-eighteenth century. However, the position of his father within the Council of several princes and the kinship established by matrimonial alliances with two important aristocratic families, Cândescu and Câmpineanu, created for Iordache the necessary condition for a rapid rise. Even if the context was favorable for consolidating both his social status and his material situation, Iordache Lehliu was not driven by the ambitions of his kin. On the contrary, he proved to be prodigal and, several years after his marriage, he was heavily in debt. Moreover, he was forced to guarantee a loan by mortgaging his mother's houses and to sell the estates that were part of his wife's dowry, in order to buy back the houses sold at auction.[23]

What did Ştefan expect from this marriage? Was he looking for a future for the Alexeanu family? The immediate benefits of this alliance between the father and his son-in-law were not obvious, but we can imagine what he had to gain when the son of his adopted daughter was born. Choosing a son-in-law of a lineage with no glorious past was giving him hope that this son-in-law could easily give up his first-born son for the benefit of his father-in-law. Alexeanu had a name to defend, that of his lineage and of his land tenure.

Shortly after the marriage a boy was born. As godfather, Ştefan Alexeanu gave him his own first name, guaranteed by the act of baptism. A few years later, the spiritual filiation created by baptism,[24] acquired by a will the same legal effect as adoption; namely, transmission of the family name and the right to heritage.[25] Alexeanu found a successor by creating a spiritual link by baptism, without considering necessary the formalities of adoption. This reasoning brings forward the connection between baptism and adoption at the level of ceremony, language, and social and legal practice.[26]

In 1808, Alexeanu made his will in favor of his six-year-old grandson. In order to protect his investment, he used the institution of *fiduciary successor*, a strategy frequently used at the time especially when the heir was still minor and could not benefit from all the rights granted to a legal person.[27] He delegated the guardianship of the child to his wife. If she had died before the coming of age of the heir, the guardianship would have passed on to the bishop of Buzău, Constantin, who was her confessor, instead of the child's genitors. Designating his wife as heir was a sign of gratitude, a symbolic act dedicated to a 36-year life together. As heir, she would benefit from the heritage property all life long (as usufruct), and at the time of her death she had to bequeath to their grandson the family's patrimony.

The substitution was not enough to secure the inheritance and the successor. This is why the legitimacy of his will resides in the fact of giving his name to his grandson, together with his lineage. Alexeanu should have adopted him or used other legal subterfuges. But he preferred instead to bring together all formalities in his will in which his choice is supported by the argument of name transmission: "in order to show clearly that he is my heir, I also gave him my name Alexeanu." It would be interesting to know if the material heritage and as well as the name could have been passed on solely by a will. The answer is affirmative in case of adoption by will, which suggests the existence of a legal fiction included in the will.

In conclusion, can we consider his will as the epilogue of a long-term strategy? By all means, if we take into account the succession of previous documents that support the same reasoning. Even if there is no reference to the adoption, we can say by way of legal fiction that the spiritual filiation sealed by the ritual of baptism finds its aim in the will. The continuity of the lineage is ensured by attaching a patronym to the patrimony. Otherwise, the eponymous estate would have entered Lehliu's family, as the rule stated that the son took the name of his father.

The case of the great Vornic Barbu Ştirbei

With no children, nor any nephews from his brother's family side, Barbu Ştirbei adopted a girl by the name of Caterina (Catinca) Văcărescu,[28] a niece from his wife's side. Faced with poverty, the *great boyar* Constantin Văcărescu – descendent of the second branch of the ancient *house* of Văcărescu – looked for ways to ensure the future of at least one of his daughters. This is when family solidarity kicked in and the godfather of Catinca (the younger of the two) agreed to take her into his care.[29] Thus, what began as a philanthropic act was to prove the first step in a succession plan.

Raised by her uncle and her aunt, Catinca was a sole daughter to them. Their son-in-law was from a family of *boyars* originated by the end of the seventeenth century that belonged to the new local aristocracy.[30] Dimitrie Bibescu brought to the couple neither rank nor any important dignities or vast property as collateral for this matrimonial alliance. But Barbu Ştirbei had everything the young man lacked: an ancient and prestigious name attached to impressive material patrimony. Catinca joined her husband's family accompanied by a sizeable dowry, and with the prestige of both her birth and of her adoptive parents. In fact, the advantages this marriage brought to Bibescu would show in his rise in rank: thus, from the rank of *logothete*, he went on to become a *great logothete* and a *great vornic* under the reign of Grigorie Dimitrie Ghica (1822–8). Driven by ambition, he saw in the alliance more of an opportunity than a goal in itself. That is why he did his best to enlarge the heritage by buying the properties of his relatives or trying at all costs to get a good part of their heritage.

After having secured a husband for her in the person of *logothete* Bibescu, Barbu Ştirbei's attention was focused on a baby boy. Thus, he assumed the task of preventing the lineage from extinction. His mission became more transparent when the boy was adopted and established as Ştirbei's heir.[31] Underlying these two adoptions in a row – that of Catinca and of their grandson, Barbu – were two apparently distinct family strategies that in the long run turned out to converge into one and the same.

But what did Barbu Ştirbei, Catinca's adoptive father, gain out of this alliance? And why did he not look for a more profitable marriage for his daughter? For the same reason, as in the case of Ştefan Alexeanu; it was easier to persuade a son-in-law at the beginning of his social ascension that his first-born child to be adopted by his parents-in-law and that he was to receive their name (patronym).[32] If the husband were to come from a noble family, he would have every reason to keep his son to ensure the continuation of his own lineage. We are thus inclined to view the double adoption strategy as one stemming from the logic of succession, all the more so because it was hardly an isolated case in the age. The adoptions and his niece's marriage were the first signs pointing to Ştirbei's desire for a successor capable of taking on the destiny of his lineage. It was in his will that the successive stages of his strategy were to be deployed: as a first step, he baptized his adopted daughter's son with his first name, only to then adopt him and designate him heir.

The strategy was successful, but only after taking all legal precautions to prevent legal disputes, including the risk of invalidation. Thus, each act of the adoption must be viewed in the context established by the other two, and in chronological succession. The first is the will by which Barbu Ştirbei adopted his grandson and designated him heir (1 September 1811); this was followed by confirmation of testamentary adoption by an act signed by Ştirbei and his wife (15 September 1811): "for the name of my family not to go out, I took Barbu, one of our beloved daughter Catinca Bibeasca's, children, and gave him my name, Barbu. And I, thereby, made him a Ştirbei, my spiritual (adopted) son." Nectarie, the Bishop of Râmnic, confirmed the adoption three months later (20 December 1811) in a religious ceremony.[33]

The adopted child most probably kept the right to inherit from his progenitors, but also won the right to inherit from his adoptive parents. Although the inheritance system in force in Wallachia was an agnatic egalitarian one, in practice the aristocracy favored the eldest son who received the most important part of heritage properties and replaced his father as head of the family, after his death. Caterina Bibescu gave birth to three boys: Barbu, Gheorghe, and Ioan. By adoption, the eldest became a Ştirbei and a descendant of this *boyar house*. Yet his entry into the family of his grandparents did not mean he was separated from his brethren; they all studied in Paris. In the early 1820s, after their return to Wallachia, the two elder brothers started out on their careers as legal advisers and were soon to make a name for themselves on the political scene of the country. Their destinies intertwined around the middle of the century.

The rise of Barbu Ştirbei in the political hierarchy of Wallachia proves remarkable; he began his career as a judge, later was head of the Treasury and subsequently filled the position of editor of the *Organic Regulations*.[34] In 1832, he was working in Foreign Affairs, to be appointed Prince of Wallachia several years later (1849–53, 1854–6).

The political career of Gheorghe Bibescu is no less captivating. Until the age of 30 he successively held the position of Deputy Secretary in the Department of Justice and Secretary of State for Foreign Affairs (under the Russian occupation, 1802–12). In the 1830s, he left Wallachia for Vienna, Paris, and Brussels. 1841 is the year of his reappearance in his home country's political arena, after being elected as a member and then as Secretary of the General Assembly. In 1842, Bibescu became the elected prince of the country, after competing for the throne with his brother Barbu Ştirbei. His rise was partly due to merit, undeniable qualities, and proper training. For the rest, we must look to the marriage agreement he made with one of the oldest and richest families of Wallachia, that of the Brâncoveanus. In 1826, he married Zoe – born Mavrocordat – adopted daughter of *ban* Grigore Brâncoveanu, the last descendant of the princely lineage.[35]

The case of the great ban Grigore Brâncoveanu

Grigore Brâncoveanu had married Safta Balş, representative of a great Moldavian aristocratic family and a descendant, herself, of the prince Constantin Brâncoveanu, but along the female line. The sterility of their union forced them to look for a child among their closest relatives. Grigore's family provided them with options, but the *great boyar* nevertheless chose a niece of his wife, the 13-year-old Zoe, a daughter of Ecaterina Mavrocordat. It was 1819. The adoption was concluded five years later in Braşov.

Zoe had the name of her adoptive parents for one year only, up to her marriage to Gheorghe Bibescu. Grigore Brâncoveanu had to wait for two years to become a grandfather of a boy. Six more children were to come from the same couple. The *great boyar* with dynastic yearnings also became godfather to the first-born, giving him his first name and even attempting to adopt him. He did not succeed, though, due to a recent regulation that allowed adoption only to childless families,[36] an obstacle too small to prevent him from carrying out his plan to ensure the continuation of the lineage. He looked for creative "bypassing strategies" in the points where the law seemed vague or too restrictive. Through the document he drafted in 1828, the *ban* gave his elder grandson the name and the estate of the Brâncoveanus:

> Because the beloved son of my adoptive daughter Zoiţa is my godson, by means of the sacrament of the holy Baptism, bearing my name, I, his godfather, hereby decide to grant him the right to call himself and to sign as Brâncoveanu; may himself, his children and his progeny sign forever as Brâncoveanu in the memory of this old lineage. To certify this document, in addition to my name and this paper, I grant my godson, Grigore, my Brâncoveanu's estate. After the death of my wife and myself, let him and his offspring have the sole right of property and inheritance eternally.[37]

This is, therefore, a similar situation to those of Ştefan Alexeanu and Barbu Ştirbei. Besides the will, the godfather–godson bond created through baptism and successive adoptions are means of passing on the material and symbolic heritage. It is not only a matter of establishing a "helpful kinship" to protect the heir of legal disputes, but also of granting him all the symbolic capital represented by the name – land name, lineage name, his first name – and the prospect of a promising future on the political scene.

What was then the role of the godfather–godson bond in this context? It is a spiritual kinship that replaced the blood relation, with a concrete impact on the godson's rights. Theoretically, the spiritual bond of baptism needed to be reinforced by adoption, which also created another spiritual kinship by "imitating nature". Because the secular adoption was not possible according to the Caragea Code (1818), Brâncoveanu had to find another solution. The pluralist legal system was flexible enough to permit him to do so. Therefore, he used the simultaneously spiritual and symbolic capital of baptism for making social networks and for reference to the jurisdiction of the Church in civil law, much weaker than had been at the end of the eighteenth century, in order to get his godson's baptism recognized as an adoption and to transmit to him the lineage name and the right to signature.

Patronym and Legitimating Genealogies of Power

Did the transmission of the first name achieve the acquisition of patronym? Did it also come with the family insignia?[38] Was the title "prince of the Austrian Empire" inherited by the successors of Constantin Brâncoveanu or had it disappeared once the *great ban* died?[39] One answer comes from the godson of the *great ban* Grigore Brâncoveanu. Motivated by the ambition of finding a place in the great family of European nobility, young Grigore did his best to keep his grandfather's title, despite fierce criticism from opponents of his father, prince Gheorghe Bibescu. For such reasons, his first step was to enroll in the Austrian army.[40]

Later, when Grigore Brâncoveanu lived in France, he changed his signature depending on the circumstances. In 1858, he published in Bucharest an apologia for his father, entitled "Prince Gheorghe Bibescu Before the Public Opinion". As author of this leaflet, Grigore had chosen to state his double kinship ("of blood" and spirit) with a signature that referred, at the same time, to his biological father and to the glorious lineage of his godfather and maternal grandfather, further highlighted by the initial B, no doubt a reference to the Basarabs, the oldest dynasty of the ruling princes: "Bibescu B. Brâncoveanu". The signature is meant to reinforce the message that he delivers in the first pages. The coupling of the two princely names announces the motivation and purpose of his endeavor: a son's duty is to save the honor and good remembrance of his father by warranting the renown of one of the oldest aristocratic families.[41]

In the correspondence regarding his own marriage to the daughter of the Turkish ambassador in London, Musurus Bey, Grigore only uses the name evoking the ancientness of his lineage: "Bassaraba de Brâncoveanu".[42]

Attention should be paid to the name of Basarab, usually cited to justify claims to the throne of Wallachia.[43] Let us take, for instance, the godfather and grandfather of Grigore Bibescu-Brâncoveanu, the *great ban* Grigore Brâncoveanu. He did not use the name of his ancestors consistently, but only on some objects in order to maintain the endurance of his own remembrance and of his lineage: "Grigore Basaraba

Brâncoveanu, prince of Austria, knight of Russia and great ban of the Principality of Wallachia, from the very old and very glorious Romanian lineage."[44] The seals and the coats of arms added to the signature also attested to the illustrious history of this family.[45] The privilege of remembrance, its symbolic capital, was the most prestigious asset of family heritage; the name, invested with the authority of the past, remains the main sign of "blood" nobility.

A second text, better researched and a lot more elaborate, that also takes on the responsibility of restoring the memory of prince Bibescu, belongs to Gheorghe Bibescu, the second son of prince Bibescu: "Here is why I publish, today, the diplomatic correspondence, the political and administrative documents from the reign of Prince Gheorghe D. Bibescu. By paying tribute to history, at the same time, I pay tribute to the memory of my father."[46] This restoration was deemed necessary after the forced abdication of his father, stemming not only from a legitimate desire to make justice, but also from a fear that the dishonor could damage the image of the "Basarab–Brâncoveanu–Bibescu *house*". As heir of the two united families, the author of the biography considered it a moral duty to prove that the actions of his father were worthy of a prestigious memory.

What role does the reference to the Basarabs and to genealogical memory play? At the end of both volumes there is a "Genealogical tree of the *house* Basaraba–Brâncoveanu–Bibescu starting with the alliance of the Basaraba (the first dynasty of sovereigns) with the Brâncoveanus", which provides a specific representation of the new branch of the Brâncoveanu family (see the genealogical tree). The genealogy is not built on agnatic basis, but on matrimonial alliance (Danciu Brâncoveanu = a sister of Prince Radu Şerban; Papa Brâncoveanu = Stanca, sister of Prince Şerban Cantacuzino and of George Bibescu = Zoe Mavrocordat, adopted Basarab-Brâncoveanu); all the marriages that seal the alliance between the three families are places on the central axis of the tree. The important names, in capital letters, refer to the princes, with one notable exception, Zoe Basarab-Brâncoveanu. The central figure is Constantin Brâncoveanu (1654–1714), the martyr Prince, killed by the Ottomans. A maternal successor of the Bassarab dynasty, he had taken his father's family – Brâncoveanu – to the peak of the social and political hierarchy. Two centuries later, the alliance between the Brâncoveanu and Bibescu families seemed to reproduce the model of the union whose fruit had been the prince: Gheorghe Bibescu married also to a descendant (by adoption) of the Basarab and Brâncoveanu families. In this way, the author confers to the cognatic lineage the same authority as to the agnatic one, especially when he wanted to justify his own father's rise – through marriage – to the throne. Consequently, the idea suggested by the author through this graphic representation is that the founding event of the *house* Bibescu–Bassarab–Brâncoveanu was the marriage of his parents. Hence, he wants to reclaim his belonging to the "first dynasty of Wallachian sovereigns" by building an ascendance based on matrimonial alliances, wherein women have an essential role in the transmission of hereditary nobility and wherein adoption has the same consequences for succession as blood connection.

As to the origin of the Brâncoveanu family, the lack of attention is not surprising, as the accent falls on the cognatic lineage ancestors, whose legitimacy is highlighted once more by the genealogies of his mother's parents: Maurocordat and Balş. He added to it a few pages dedicated to the origin of the household of Balş and to his father's biography: "His father was the *great vornic* Dumitru Bibescu (1772–1831); his mother, Ecaterina Văcărescu, great-granddaughter of the Prince of Wallachia, Constantin Bassarab-Brâncoveanu, decapitated in Constantinople in 1714."[47]

If through the genealogy of the *house* of Bassarab–Brâncoveanu–Bibescu and even through that of the *house* of Mavrocordat, George Bibescu claimed the right to the title of "Prince" and, consequently, his double dynastic ascendance, then by the genealogy of the house of Balş, he endeavored to prove his belonging to old European nobility. Certified in 1815 by the Russian and Austrian chancelleries, the prestigious genealogy goes back to the seventh century, to the ancestor count Leibufe "lord of Argence and of the keep of Baux" and crosses, throughout the Middle Ages, the South of Europe (Naples, Montenegro, Albania), arriving in the fifteenth century in Moldavia and Wallachia. We will not dwell either on the arguments provided to support this version of the genealogy, or on the historical authorities mentioned to certify it. Often mystified, the Western origin of the great Wallachian or Moldavian family allowed its descendants to orchestrate ambitious matrimonial alliances with members of European nobility.[48] This practice was established in the nineteenth century, when the young *boyars* started to go study abroad.

This book is an attempt to make of Prince Constantin Brâncoveanu a hero who gave his life to protect Europe against the Ottoman menace by reminding that Gheorghe Bibescu (his father) was the first elected Prince "by the nation, for life" after his great ancestor, the martyr prince. By stating his belonging to old European nobility through the genealogy of the Balş family, alongside other arguments, this is also an attempt to recover memory and to legitimate Bibescu's own identity, his social status, both in Wallachia, his country of origin, and in France, his adoptive country. Thus, the motivation of Gheorghe Bibescu's work, organized like a monograph, seems to be more complex, addressing a diverse readership. The target audience was equally Romanian and French; the French original and the Romanian translation appeared almost simultaneously: in 1893–4, in Paris and in Bucharest.

The Bibescu family, for three generations, played an important role both in the projects of the *great vornic* Barbu Ştirbei and of the *great ban* Grigore Brâncoveanu. The descendent of a recent local *boyar* family, Dimitrie Bibescu had pushed his lineage to the highest level of aristocracy, engaging in very ambitious matrimonial politics, by systematically acquiring lands, and by investing in his sons' education. Later, his grandson would construct the genealogy of the family Basarab–Brâncoveanu–Bibescu as a functioning "système à maison"[49] by highlighting his mother's families of origin, Mavrocordat and Balş.

Conclusion: Stages of a Strategy and Redefining Inheritance

It was not by accident that we chose three *boyars* as subjects of this research. Ştefan Alexeanu, a secondary rank dignitary and owner of several lands, could not compare to the wealth, power, renown, and the ancientness of families such as the Brâncoveanu or Ştirbei. Although the *great vornic* Barbu Ştirbei rose much closer to the summit of the social hierarchy, the heights reached by Grigore Brâncoveanu, pretender to the throne and descendant of a princely family, were far beyond him. Nevertheless, these three cases representing three different positions within the aristocratic hierarchy are all marked by the same desire to prevent the extinction of their lineage, of their name, and of their patrimony.

The strategy meant to secure succession proved to be quite fragile: first, an adoption of a girl from the wife's family; second, a search for an ambitious son-in-law, but without a fame to match his ambition; third, a baptism of the couple's first born; fourth, a will, adoption or legal artifice in order to provide this child with the patronym and the eponymous estate. The plan of each of these three *boyars* was imprecise from the very start. It is very likely that there was an element of chance in it, at least in the cases of Alexeanu and Ştirbei. For instance, the death or economic downfall of the parents of their adopted daughters triggered a mechanism of family solidarity: the closest relatives had the moral obligation to take the orphans or the poor children under their protection. At times, this duty was carried out by negotiating matrimonial alliances or by concluding an official adoption; namely, the moment where charity gives room to family strategy. My arguments reside in three genealogic principles: the first name, the patronym, and the eponymous estate (*kamini/cămin*). These are the three criteria that equally define how these three *boyars* belong to local aristocracy in a context where dignity was imposed as the sole criterion of nobility.

By creating a successor bearing the same first and last name, did the last descendants of these three *boyar* families also think about the continuity of their own person inscribed in the lineage chain, as part of a moral being that represented the *house* as shown by Lévi-Strauss? People and properties are equally part of the patrimony, all linked by the principle of solidarity whose expression is the legal practice of *protimesis* as well as the commemoration of the dead. Choosing an heir with the same name and surname to replace the father represents not only a genealogic mechanism but also the principle of *universitas iuris* according to which the heritage incudes both the transmission of the role of master of the household and the set of rights and obligations that ensure the extension of the deceased person. Giving one's own baptismal name may be an attempt at reconstituting the deceased person according to an ancient tradition whereby the grandsons were given the name and surname of their grandfathers.[50] Within this logic, the grandsons represented the living memory of their grandfathers, who in their turn incarnated their forefathers.

The name seems to be the element around which the *house* as lineage and its patrimony is conceived: the baptismal name, the lineage name, and the estate name. The emphasis on the link between property and name, between residence and filiation, had a direct impact on the structure and diversity of inheritance practices despite the legal regulations introduced by the Ypsilantis Code 1780.

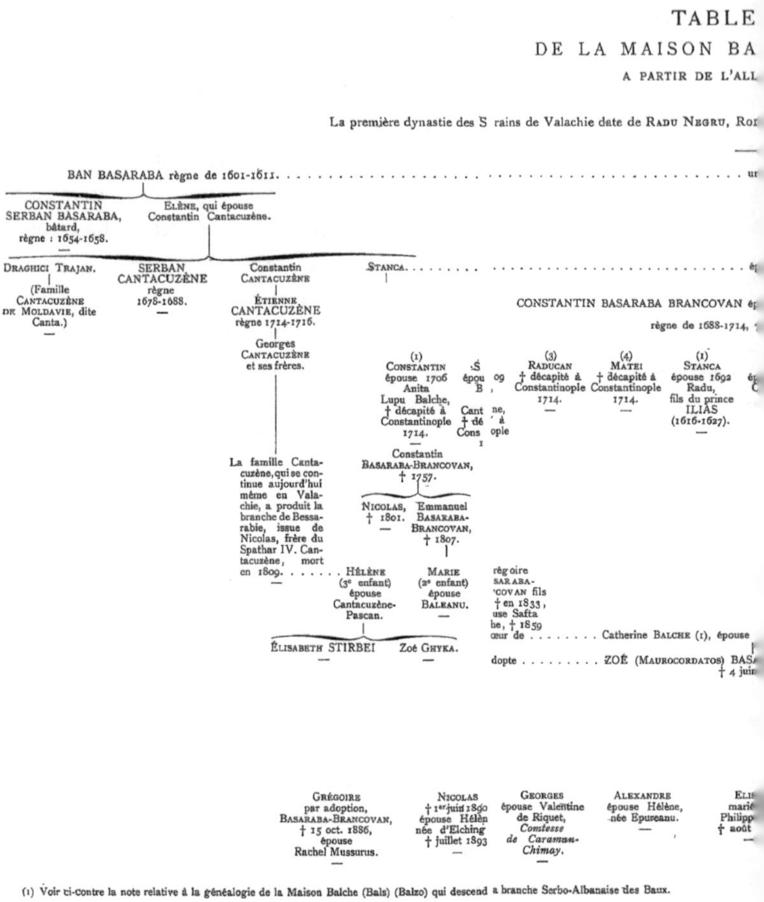

Figure 2 Genealogical Tree of the House Basaraba-Brancovan-Bibesco
Source: Bibesco 1894. http://gallica.bnf.fr/ark:/12148/bpt6k57477397.r=Bibesco%2C+Georges.langEN

;NÉALOGIQUE

A—BRANCOVAN—BIBESCO

BASARABA AVEC LES BRANCOVAN

›IR, appelé aussi TUGOMIR BASARAB, conquérant de la Valachie et chef de la famille (1290).

›ouse . . . . BRANCOVAN DANCIU

Mathieu BASARABA (1633-1654). —

David BRANCOVAN.

Preda BRANCOVAN. † 1668.

. . . . Papa BRANCOVAN † 1655.

: d'ANTONIE de Popesci, 1669-1672.

›tantinople.

(3) ILINCA ›use 1698 Scarlat ›ocordatos. —

(5) ANCUTA épouse 1704 Nicolas Rosetti. —

(6) BALASA épouse 1708 Manole Andronic. —

(7) SMARANDA épouse 1712 le boyard Balan. —

(4) SAFTA épouse 1700. . . . Georges CRETZULESCU —

Constantin CRETZULESCU.

CATHERINE épouse Vacaresco.

TH. VACARESCO —

HARICLIE épouse Ypsilanti. —

SMARANDA épouse Michel Mano. —

CATHERINE épouse de DÉMÈTRE —

JEAN BIBESCO —

Son frère BARBU, 1720.

STEFAN

STEFAN épouse E. Scanavi.

Nicolas BIBESCO, colonel. —

MARIE mariée à Banov. —

DINCA épouse Hélène Argentoyano.

DÉMÈTRE (célibataire). —

CATHERINE épouse Zimbroski.

DÉMÈTRE Bibesco par adoption épouse Zoé Glogoveano. —

ÉLÈNE, épouse le baron A. de Merentzellern. —

›OCORDATOS.

›VAN épouse. . . . . . . GEORGES BIBESCO. . . . . Marié en secondes noces à Marie Vacaresco.

GEORGES BIBESCO (2e fils) *Élu par la nation à vie*, règne de 1842 à 1848, † 1er juin 1873.

JEAN (3e fils) † 1879, épouse Anna Floresco. —

BARBU, fils aîné, † 1869, adopté par Stirbei, règne de 1849 à 1856, épouse Elisabeth Cantacuzène, † 1876.

ÉLISABETH † —

DAMIAN † —

GRÉGOIRE. — GEORGES. — ALEXANDRE. — DÉMÈTRE. — FENARETE. — ALEXANDRINE. —

›HERINE ›ct. 1866 au général Floresco. ›mai 1893. —

ZOÉ † 4 sept. 1858, mariée à Georges Cantacuzène. —

MARIE mariée à Odon, comte de Montesquiou-Fesenzac, † 1880. —

HÉLÈNE † 8 oct. 1883, mariée à Victor, baron de Courval, † 1891. —

Going back to the theoretical framework that we draw briefly at the beginning of our chapter, and observing the cases of the three *boyar houses*, we can conclude that the *house* is positioned – according to Lévi-Strauss – "in the middle of a latent conflict between the occupants of certain positions in the social structure: the father, as *taker* of his wife, sees his son as a privileged member of the lineage; the matrilineal grandfather, as *giver* of the wife [his daughter], sees in his grandson a full member of his own lineage";[51] at the intersection of these antithetical perspectives, is found the *house* as inheritance strategy. In the cases of these *boyars* the "latent conflict" takes the form of a hidden negotiation in which the symbolic content of the patrimony is becoming more important than the material one.

PART II

INSTITUTIONAL AND SOCIAL PRACTICES

CHAPTER 4

RECONSTRUCTION, RESETTLEMENT, AND ECONOMIC REVITALIZATION IN PRE-TANZIMAT OTTOMAN BULGARIA

Andrew Robarts

The questions of Ottoman state de-centralization/centralization and the emerging national consciousness of non-Muslim subjects dominate scholarly studies of state-society relations in south-eastern Europe in the early part of the nineteenth century. This chapter will (re)focus our attention on the socio-economic dimension in the history of the "early" modern Ottoman Balkans. Drawing upon research conducted in Bulgarian, Ottoman, and Russian archives as well as a reading of personal memoirs, travel accounts, consular reports, and census data, this chapter will analyze the connection between socio-economic mobility, provincial administration, and national/imperial identity in early nineteenth-century Ottoman Bulgaria. Specifically, within the framework of Ottoman provincial history, it will argue that the economic prosperity promoted by Ottoman reconstruction, resettlement, and economic revitalization policies following the conclusion of the Russo–Ottoman War of 1828–9 coupled with effective local leadership (which extended across communal lines) elided confessional and "national" differences as the primary social markers in pre-Tanzimat Ottoman Bulgaria.

An analysis of Ottoman reconstruction, resettlement, and economic revitalization initiatives during the important (and understudied) transitional period of 1829–39, sheds light not only on the legal and social status of agricultural populations in Rumelia but on the evolving conceptualization of subjecthood and citizenship in the Ottoman Empire. The basic components of the post-1829 Ottoman resettlement, reconstruction, and economic revitalization plan for Rumelia were published in the form of a declaration (*beyanname*) to the subjects of the Ottoman Empire and distributed among *reaya* populations in Rumelia.[1] The public proclamation of a set of defined rights and privileges accorded to non-Muslim subjects anticipated – by roughly a decade – the redefinition of the relationship between the Ottoman state and its *reaya* subjects as articulated in the famous Gülhane Rescript of 1839.[2]

Provincial Administration in Dobruja and Rumelia in the 1830s

During the Russo–Ottoman War of 1828–9, significant fighting along the Danubian front north of the Balkan Mountains resulted in severe and widespread destruction in the core Balkan provinces of the Ottoman Empire. The damage inflicted (both physical and demographic) in the Ottoman Balkans in 1828 and 1829 was compounded by the siege of important economic and population centers (including Silistre and Varna), the Russian military occupation of Dobruja and most of Rumelia, and evacuation operations conducted by the Russian army following the signing of the Treaty of Adrianople (1829).

Velko Kiriuv, a Bulgarian migrant traveling through Dobruja to the Russian Empire in 1830, described the devastation caused by the war of 1828–9 in the following manner: "when we passed through Dobrich on the way to Bessarabia the land was bleak and everything was deserted (*pusto razvalini*), we did not see any villages that were left intact".[3] The German Doctor Ziedlits, while traveling through Rumelia (from Shumen to Edirne) in 1829 similarly observed that "everything around here is deserted and uninhabited (*pustynia*). After traveling a few more versts we came across a village that was completely abandoned."[4]

The outbreak of Russo–Ottoman hostilities in 1828 and the Russian army's advance on Edirne (Adrianople) in 1829 disrupted economic activity in Dobruja and Rumelia and – by prompting the significant out-migration of agriculturalists and skilled laborers to the Russian Empire – drained the Ottoman Empire of vital human capital. For example, the out-migration to the Russian Empire of many skilled *reaya* workers from the towns of Midye, Vize, and Pinarhisar resulted in a marked drop in output at the important Ottoman armaments foundry (*dökümhane*) in Samakocuk (Demirköy).[5] Additionally, the targeting by Russian military and civilian officials of ship-builders, master wood-workers, and dockyard laborers for resettlement in Russian Black Sea ports severely reduced the number of naval and merchant marine vessels produced in Ottoman shipyards in the early 1830s. These losses were compounded by the out-migration of many Ottoman sailors and oarsmen who had traditionally been recruited from Greek and Bulgarian sea-faring populations along the Black Sea coast. Replacements drawn from towns and villages in the Rumelian interior lacked the necessary experience and skills – further frustrating Ottoman efforts to revitalize merchant activity in the Black Sea region following the conclusion of the war.[6]

Immediately upon the cessation of war hostilities in 1829, trusted Ottoman officials were dispatched from Istanbul to re-establish public order and security (*asayiş ve emniyet*) in the Rumelian countryside and to assess conditions for the resettlement of displaced populations. In one instance an official by the name of Halil Bey was sent to Rusçuk (Ruse) to assess resettlement conditions in and around this important Danubian port-city.[7] Special agents were also sent to the areas around Burgas and Ahyolu to assess wartime destruction and to liaise with non-Muslim elites.[8] Reports filed by these officials attested to the devastation and near anarchic conditions in post-war Ottoman Rumelia.[9] Roving bands of armed brigands (the remnants of volunteer forces organized by the Russians during the war) pillaged vulnerable peasant populations. Cossack groups (bivouacked in occupied Rumelian towns and villages to guard supply lines) plundered unarmed *reaya* populations – especially in the area around the Black Sea port of Burgas.[10]

On behalf of *reaya* populations under their charge, municipal authorities (*nahiye ayanları*) pleaded with Ottoman military officials to take action against roving criminal gangs.[11] In response to these pleas orders were issued to all Ottoman military commanders in Rumelia to investigate the reasons for disorder in the Rumelian countryside, to take measures to restore law and order among *reaya* populations, and to provide security guarantees to migrant and displaced populations who were wavering in their commitment to the Ottoman Empire and were contemplating out-migration to the Russian Empire.[12] Specific orders included the stationing of 2,000 Ottoman troops in Edirne, the deployment of Ottoman troops in vulnerable towns and villages in eastern Rumelia, and the dispatch of soldiers to escort migrant *reaya* populations returning from Russia.[13]

Agriculture had been the mainstay of the pre-war economy in Dobruja and Rumelia and the majority of Ottoman migrant and settlement initiatives in the early 1830s were focused on revitalizing this important economic sector. By the mid-eighteenth century most of the grains (especially wheat) destined for the Istanbul market were grown in Dobruja – a commercial relationship cemented by deteriorating political ties between Egypt (a long-standing grain exporting center) and the Sublime Porte. Besides grains and cereals, ships bound for Istanbul from Dobrujan and eastern Rumelian ports carried large quantities of salt, butter, lumber (*kereste*), felts, wax, and tallow. The Stranja (a mountain massif east of Sizebolu known to the Ottomans as the *Yıldız Dağları*) produced wood valued by Ottomans architects, builders, and engineers. Renowned for the high quality of its pasturage lands, Dobruja was an ideal locale for the rearing of cattle, horses, buffalo, and sheep. The Danubian Principalities supplied large numbers of sheep to the Istanbul market and Moldavian oak was used extensively in the Ottoman ship-building industry.[14]

A significant drop in grain production and the store of cereals in Rumelia was directly linked to the anxiety, skittishness, and ongoing displacement of *reaya* populations.[15] One month after the signing of the Treaty of Adrianople (and following an investigation of lands vacated by Russian occupation troops) the Ottoman Grand Vizier approved a 20,000 k. disbursement to *reaya* populations in the heavily damaged *kaza* of Yanbolu. These monies were allocated for the purchase of sheep and seeds and were intended to jump-start agricultural activity in post-war eastern Rumelia.[16]

In developing plans for the reconstruction and revitalization of post-war Ottoman Rumelia, the Ottoman state solicited the input of local non-Muslim elites. Committees (*nasihat heyetleri*) composed of respected local representatives were formed and their recommendations passed along to provincial officials.[17] In Edirne, the Ottoman *kadı* (judge) convened a council composed of the Rum Metropolitan, the Armenian Patriarch, and a senior Jewish rabbi to discuss ways to reduce inter-communal tensions and promote the settlement of displaced populations.[18] Along the Black Sea coast (around Ahyolu, Misevri, and Sizebolu), town priests (*papaslar*) and non-Muslim elites (*çorbacılar*)[19] submitted letters and petitions to senior Ottoman officials in Samakocuk.[20] Grievance letters (*arzuhallar*) sent to provincial administrators by town priests and village headmen (*kocabaşlar*) were compiled and summarized in reports forwarded to the Grand Vizier's office in Istanbul. Grievance letters were provided by local priests and headmen in the small towns (*kasabalar*) of Vasilikoz and Ahtapol. Examples of the recommendations offered in these petitions included the distribution of new and more fertile farmland to *reaya* populations, the disbursement of annual loans to re-invigorate trade in flour and cereals (*kapan-ı dakik*), the distribution of agricultural tools and supplies to a group of Bulgarian peasants in Zağra-ı Atik (Stara Zagora) and, and the provision of monies to rebuild residences and purchase farm tools to the inhabitants of Hacıoğlu Pazarcık in Dobruja.[21]

The re-imposition of order and security in the lower Balkans following the conclusion of the war of 1828–9 and the revitalization of economic activity in Rumelia and Dobruja in the 1830s entailed a coordinated and multitiered effort across and at all levels of the Ottoman state apparatus. Military and policing units intervened to pacify post-conflict zones and calm skittish populations. Governing officials and bodies distributed loans, disseminated information, and communicated, in a reasonably transparent manner, centrally generated regulations to subject populations. The "centralizing" initiatives of the Ottoman state in the 1830s were not a completely top-down affair. Provincial and municipal-level authorities solicited input from communal leaders (Muslim and non-Muslim) and were afforded a certain amount of autonomy to alter, amend, and gear central directives to local circumstances. The migration and resettlement program rolled out by the Ottoman state in the early 1830s typified the flexible and multitiered nature of Ottoman reform initiatives in the pre-Tanzimat Ottoman Balkans.

The Ottoman Migration and Resettlement Program in the Ottoman Balkans

Starting in the late eighteenth century Ottoman officials began to experiment with pro-migration initiatives that, over time, evolved into the core components of the Ottoman state's reconstruction and resettlement programs in Rumelia in the 1830s. These measures included the extension of tax exemptions and amnesties to migratory populations, direct financial assistance to settlers, and the undertaking of joint-resettlement initiatives with provincial-level Russian officials posted along the Ottoman–Russian Black Sea frontier. For example, during the opening stages of the Russo–Ottoman War (1768–74), the Ottoman Grand Vizier (Ivazzade Halil Pasha) – in an effort to forestall peasant disturbances and prevent the out-migration of productive agriculturalists in the strategically and economically important area between Galatz and Jassy – issued a *ferman* to the *kadı* of Rusçuk authorizing a five-year tax exemption for all peasants. Additionally, the *ferman* authorized the *kadı* to extend amnesty to any peasants previously charged with engaging in criminal activities.[22]

Ottoman migration and settlement policies acquired a more nuanced (and pro-migrant) character in the first few decades of the nineteenth century. From 1801–5 and in 1813, Bulgarian return settlers were offered comparatively more rights and privileges than those normally extended to *reaya* populations in the Ottoman Empire.[23] Following the conclusion of the Russo–Ottoman War (1806–12), an Ottoman servitor in the Danubian Principalities interceded with Russian civil and military authorities in Wallachia on behalf of 1,500 Bulgarian families who had expressed their desire to return to their homelands in Rusçuk and Lofça. Following extended negotiations, Russian authorities in Wallachia acceded to Ottoman entreaties to provide *bilets* (migrant travel documents) to these Bulgarian families – effectively authorizing their return migration to Ottoman Rumelia.[24]

Drawing upon all available resources, the Ottoman authorities, at times, employed more coercive or propagandistic measures to thwart the out-migration of productive agriculturalists from the Balkans. For example, the Ottoman state looked to the Greek-Rum patriarchate for support in persuading Orthodox-Christian peasants to stay in the Ottoman Empire.[25] Greek prelates were dispatched to villages on the Black Sea coast to intercede with Bulgarians contemplating out-migration to the Russian Empire.[26] In September 1829, a Russian military officer in Islimiye (Sliven) reported that two prominent non-Muslim individuals from Shumla – *Pop* Dimitrii and *çorbacı* Kosta – were distributing pro-Ottoman literature to *reaya* populations in

Aytos, Karnobat, Kazanluk, Islimiye, and Yanbolu. Displaying symbols of Bulgarian heraldry and bearing the stamp of the *ayan* of Shumla, these letters stated that although the Ottoman government was aware of the damage done and harm caused by some Bulgarian peasants during the war of 1828–9, with the advent of peace the Ottoman government would forgive and pardon all Bulgarians who committed crimes against the Ottoman state during the preceding war. Interestingly the letters distributed to the Bulgarian *reaya* population were written in Ottoman Turkish.[27] In February and March 1830, the Rum Metropolitan in Edirne traveled to Yanbolu and Islimiye to implore peasant populations in eastern Rumelia to remain in the Ottoman Empire.[28] Additionally, prominent and well-to-do Muslim-Turkish townspeople also appealed to their Bulgarian neighbors (and fellow Ottoman subjects) to remain in the Ottoman Empire and contribute to the reconstruction and rehabilitation of their Rumelian homeland.[29]

Ottoman officials encouraged *reaya* populations to communicate with their co-religionists (*dindaşlar*) in the Black Sea diaspora regarding the favorable economic and resettlement conditions in post-war Ottoman Rumelia.[30] Non-Muslim elites in Rumelia penned laudatory accounts of the Ottoman state's pro-migrant initiatives. These accounts emphasized the generosity (*cömertlik*) and empathy (*anlayış*) of the Ottoman state. Bulgarian returnees wrote letters to family members, fellow villagers, and kinsmen in the Russian Empire describing the assistance provided by the Ottoman state to resettled populations.[31] Expectations that the dissemination of the details of the Ottoman resettlement program would promote sizable return migrations from Russia were bolstered by Ottoman intelligence reports highlighting the difficulties faced by Bulgarian settlers in Bessarabia.[32]

In large measure, economic imperatives – including the repopulation of vital agricultural lands and the re-invigoration of the industrial, commercial and mercantile enterprises of non-Muslim subjects – necessitated the Ottoman state's adoption of pro-migration policies in post-war Dobruja and Rumelia. Information gathered from local populations and compiled by provincial officials contributed to the formulation of state-organized projects to promote the resettlement of displaced *reaya* populations in Ottoman Rumelia. Bulgarian return settlers were offered rights and privileges not normally extended to *reaya* populations in the Ottoman Empire such as tax-free agricultural loans, property guarantees, and input into local decision-making and governance.[33] The resettlement program rolled out by the Ottoman state in the period after the war of 1828–9 offered an array of practical and material incentives to check out-migration and lure potential return migrants from the Russian Empire. This incentive or benefits-based approach to migration and settlement signaled a departure from the types of forced settlement and coerced sedentarization operations, which defined early-modern *sürgün* operations.[34]

Pro-migrant reform measures implemented by the Ottoman state in Rumelia after 1829 included: the rationalization of the taxes imposed on peasant populations (as means to re-invigorate economic activity in the post-war Balkans); a crackdown on corrupt tax farmers (*mültezimler*); administrative reforms to improve the delivery of resettlement services; the extension of material benefits, administrative assistance, and tax exemptions to return migrants; and an offer of amnesty to any Bulgarians who had sided with the Russians during the preceding war.[35]

Lands vacated by Bulgarian out-migrants were converted into *mülk* status (effectively private ownership) and placed under the guardianship of village headmen. Income and rents from these lands were set aside and used as an incentive to promote the return migration of agriculturalists to Ottoman Rumelia and Dobruja.[36] In 1833, returnees to Islimiye were offered a two-year exemption from *cizye* (regular-levied capitation tax) and a one-year exemption from any *tekalif-i örfiye* (irregular and extraordinary tax) levies. In the same year, returnees to the village of Papaslı (near Plovdiv) received a two-year break from all *tekalif* taxes. This offer was sweetened in 1834 as Bulgarians migrants in Bessarabia were offered not only the standard two-year relief from *cizye* but exemptions from all other taxes in perpetuity in exchange for returning to their former homes in Islimiye and Yanbolu.[37] As indicated in a report filed by a Russian consular official in Islimiye, Bulgarian *reaya* were not above using the threat of out-migration to extract increased financial assistance and enhanced tax privileges from the Ottoman state.[38]

Provincial and municipal-level officials were given a certain amount of latitude to implement resettlement initiatives befitting the realities of local conditions. For example, the Grand Vizier in Istanbul authorized the *kaymakam* (governor) of Edirne to adjust his local tax assessments to reduce financial burdens on recently resettled peasant populations.

In making these adjustments, the *kaymakam* relied heavily on the input of *kocabaşlar* from the towns and villages surrounding the city.[39] In certain jurisdictions, *kadis* dismissed all legal claims (*davalar*) filed by Muslims seeking compensation for property damaged or goods seized by non-Muslims during the war.[40] In Islimiye, a group of *reaya* – in exchange for agreeing to return to their original residences – extracted funds from the local treasury for the reparation of a neighborhood church.[41] In an effort to promote the return of *reaya* from the Danubian Principalities to their former lands just south of the Danube River, the *vali* of Silistre offered exemptions from *cizye* and other taxes (*cizye ve vergiden muafiyetleri*).[42] In a similar vein, Ottoman officials posted along the southern shores of the Danube River offered to pay any debts incurred by Bulgarian return migrants during their period of emigration in the Danubian Principalities.[43]

The opening of a state wool factory in Sliven in 1836 offers an interesting example of the type of productive (and in this case proto-industrial) state-migrant collaboration produced by the pro-migration policies adopted by the Ottoman state in the 1830s. Long a center for textile production, in the 1820s Sliven textile manufacturers supplied uniforms to the reformed, European-style Ottoman army during the reign of Sultan Mahmud II. Sensing an opportunity to scale up, through industrialization, uniform and textile production, in 1836 the Ottoman state installed a Bulgarian return migrant from Russia, Dobri Zheliazkov, as the Master and Director of a new and modern (i.e. European) textile factory in Sliven – the first of its kind in the Ottoman Balkans. Zheliazkov had fled Sliven for Russia in the wake of the Russo–Ottoman War of 1828–9 and after settling in Ekaterinoslav (Dnepropetrovsk) worked in several factories in this developing and industrializing part of the Russian Empire. Interestingly, among the first pieces of machinery installed in the Sliven wool factory was a cutting machine Zheliazkov hauled back from Russia when he returned to Sliven in 1834. The overall design and set-up of the Ottoman state-subsidized wool factory was adopted from models obtained by Zheliazkov during his stay in the Russian Empire.[44]

Zheliazkov was only one of the thousands of Bulgarians, from all occupations and socio-economic "classes", who opted to return to the Ottoman Empire from Russia in the first part of the nineteenth century. While the reasons for return were varied (including fear of enserfment in

Russia, forced recruitment into the Russian army, administrative disarray in newly incorporated parts of the Russian Empire, settlement on marginal lands in southern Russia, alienation, and a longing for to return "home" to the Ottoman Empire), returned migrants from Russia, with Zheliazkov as perhaps the most prominent example, contributed to the demographic and economic revitalization of the Ottoman Balkans in the 1830s.

Return Migration from the Russian Empire to the Ottoman Empire

Ottoman Rumelia and Dobruja experienced an impressive demographic and economic revival in the 1830s.[45] Three metrics attest to this revival: the significant return migration in this period of Bulgarian agriculturalists from the Russian Empire to the Ottoman Empire in the early 1830s; economic and demographic developments in Dobruja in the 1830s; and the re-emergence and re-organization of trade fairs in Rumelian and Dobrujan market towns following the conclusion of the war of 1828–9.

An estimated 250,000 Bulgarians (or 10–15 percent of the total Bulgarian population in the Ottoman Empire) migrated from Ottoman Rumelia to the Danubian Principalities and southern Russia in the period between 1768 and the 1830s. In the early 1830s, waves of recently settled Bulgarian agriculturalists in the Russian Empire engaged in return migration to the Ottoman Empire. For example, of a group of 9,000 Bulgarians who settled in Bessarabia in 1829, 4,100 returned almost immediately.[46] In 1831, roughly 5,000 Bulgarians who had also migrated to Russia in 1829 returned. It is estimated that in the period from 1833–4, 20,000 Bulgarians engaged in return migrations from Bessarabia to the Ottoman Empire.[47] Reports filed by Ottoman provincial governors in Rumelia attest to the generalized nature of Bulgarian return migration in the early 1830s. The destination points identified in these reports for Bulgarian returnees included: Dobrujan and Black Sea coastal towns such as Ahyolu, Mesembria, Babadağ, and Hacıoğlu Pazarcık; Danubian fortress towns such as Silistre; Samakocuk, Karnobat, and Yambol in eastern Rumelia; and several villages along the northern shores of the Sea of Marmara.[48]

Ottoman decrees providing for guarantees of amnesty for any Bulgarians who had joined the Russian cause in 1828–9 and promises of assistance in resettling in the Ottoman Empire promoted considerable Bulgarian return migration to Ottoman Rumelia in the 1830s. In support of these decrees, Ottoman agents operating among Bulgarian migrant communities (mostly in the Danubian Principalities and Bessarabia) disseminated information regarding the guarantees and promises issued by the Ottoman government and generally propagandized in favor of Bulgarian return migration.[49]

Bulgarians migrating back across the Danube River from southern Russia to Ottoman Rumelia did not always return to their original village or town. Finding good agricultural conditions and generally positive economic opportunities, many Bulgarians on their way back to eastern Rumelia from Bessarabia and southern Russia stopped and settled permanently in Dobruja. For example, the population of the town of Kasapköy (between Köstence and Babadağ) nearly quadrupled in the early 1830s due to the arrival of Bulgarian return migrants from Russia. The Dobrujan village of Kamana was founded in 1831 by Bulgarian return migrants from Bessarabia.[50]

In Dobruja, Bulgarian returnees found fertile lands and a supportive local administration. For example, in 1831 in the village of Sargül (near Tulça) local Ottoman officials welcomed the return of Bulgarians from Bessarabia and encouraged (through material and economic incentives) their resettlement in Dobruja. The assistance provided to Bulgarian returnees by a pro-active local Ottoman administrator in Dobruja, Hasan Pasha, resulted in a small population boom around the Dobrujan town of Kasapköy (Sinoe, near Babadağ) in the 1830s.[51] Additionally, migrant workers (*orakçı*) from the Danubian Principalities and Danubian estuary towns were particularly welcomed by Ottoman authorities in the under-populated but agriculturally productive region of Dobruja.[52]

Trade fairs (Bulgarian – *panairi*) had flourished in eighteenth-century Dobruja and Rumelia and were an integral feature and consequence of the early-modern *Pax Ottomanica* in the Balkans. Large weekly, monthly, and seasonal fairs in Islimiye, Uzundzhovo (near Haskovo), Hacıoğlu Pazarcık, Mangalia, Karasu (Chervena Voda), Eski Juma (Tŭrgovishte), and Babadağ drew buyers and sellers from the countryside, regional traders from Rumelia, and merchants from Anatolia.[53] For example, the Islimiye fair (held every May) drew merchants from all of European

Turkey as well as long-distance traders from Smyrna, Sinope, and Trebizond.[54] At its height the large annual fair in Uzundzhovo drew 50,000 people over a 40-day period.[55] According to Nikolai Todorov,

> the well-known fairs of southern Bulgaria of the eighteenth and first half of the nineteenth century had foreign and local merchants converging by caravans to exchange their goods and carry them off, the foreigners going either to Istanbul, or Salonika, or overland to Central Europe, while local merchants shipped their goods to warehouses in Plovdiv, Sliven, and Tatar Pazardzhik.[56]

The role of inter-regional and international fairs in capital accumulation, wealth generation, and the emergence of mercantile elites in the Ottoman Balkans has been covered elsewhere.[57] There was a strict hierarchichal ordering of the Balkan trade fairs and smaller peripheral fairs (staged in Tutrakan, Pravadi and Balçık) specialized in locally grown agricultural goods. These local fairs performed an important economic function by providing an outlet for excess agricultural production.[58]

In step with measures to re-impose security and stability in the Ottoman Balkans following the conclusion of the war of 1828–9, the reinvigorated Ottoman state undertook active measures to promote regional and international trade in south-eastern Europe. This *Pax Ottomanica* 2.0 resulted in the re-emergence and expansion of the Balkan trade fair. In 1830, Islimiye staged its important trade fair for the first time since 1827.[59] By the mid-nineteenth century the autumn trade fair in Karasu was attracting roughly 35,000–40,000 visitors per annum.[60] Likewise, the annual fair in Eski Juma was revived and, over the course of the 1830s, the Eski Juma fairgrounds developed into a permanent trading complex of 1,200 stands and shops. Under the direction of the local Ottoman administrator Rashid Ağa, the Eski Juma fair attracted an international clientele – hosting merchants from Austria, England, France, Prussia, Holland, Russia, and Sweden.[61] Similarly, from the 1840s–1860s, the Eski Juma trade fair experienced a period of unprecedented growth.[62]

In Dobruja, the vibrancy of the Hacıoğlu Pazarcık trade fair was a "sure sign of the growing commercial volume of the area and of Dobruja's attractiveness, which drew not only the urban poor but those who could bring along relatively large amounts of the capital".[63]

In the 1860s, the "ethnic" composition of the most prominent merchant proprietors who annually set up shop in Bazargic included representatives from Dobruja's Bulgarian, Turkish, Armenian, and Jewish communities.[64] Additionally, the liberalization of trade between Dobruja and the Danubian Principalities (as stipulated in the terms of the Treaty of Adrianople) resulted in an uptick in the trans-Danubian carry trade in the 1830s – a development that contributed to wealth accumulation among Bulgarian merchant families with long-established factors in Wallachia and northern Rumelia. In general, as Stoianovich notes, "Bulgarian merchants began to engage in international trade after 1750, but did not achieve prominence until after the treaty of Adrianople (1829)."[65]

Conclusions

In the first decades of the nineteenth century, local and micro-historical developments (in the form of Bulgarian return migration and municipal and village-level Ottoman migration and settlement initiatives) redefined state–society relations in the Ottoman Balkans and recalibrated the trajectory of reform in the early nineteenth-century Ottoman Empire. The focus on economic prosperity and the material needs and aspirations of *reaya* populations continued into the mid-nineteenth century as initiatives tested in the provinces informed imperial-level and empire-wide reform programs. Following severe and widespread destruction in the core Balkan provinces of the Ottoman Empire during the Russo–Ottoman War of 1828–9, Ottoman Bulgaria experienced an impressive demographic and economic revival in the 1830s. This revival was the product of several factors including: sound local administration; a lack of significant inter-communal violence; pro-active economic policies; the cooperation of local non-Muslim elites; fertile agriculture land; and a geographically central location astride Ottoman–Russian trade routes. In both rural and urban settings, opportunities emerged for upward socio-economic mobility within an expansionary and revived Ottoman economic and political system.

It can be argued that well into the mid-to-late nineteenth century material interests, including wealth accumulation and socio-economic prosperity, trumped nationalism and national liberation in the political discourse of subject populations in the Ottoman Balkans. Material depredation (principally the vagaries of an arbitrary and onerous tax regime) rather than proto-nationalist sentiment fueled the widespread but uncoordinated expressions of discontent among Bulgarian populations in the Ottoman Balkans in the 1840s and 1850s. In the 1860s, the economic policies implemented in the reformed *Tuna vilayet* (Danubian province) promoted enough material prosperity to mollify nationalist aspirations among influential sectors of Bulgarian-Ottoman society.[66] It was only with the bankruptcy (literally and figuratively) of the Ottoman state in the 1870s that nationalist feelings began to outweigh material considerations among the majority of the non-Ottoman populations in south-eastern Europe.

CHAPTER 5

THE POOR MEN OF CHRIST AND THEIR LEADERS: WEALTH AND POVERTY WITHIN THE CHRISTIAN ORTHODOX CLERGY OF THE OTTOMAN EMPIRE (EIGHTEENTH–NINETEENTH CENTURY)

Dimitris Stamatopoulos

Navigating the financial world of the Ecumenical Patriarchate was captured in an interesting anecdote, narrated by Manuel Gedeon, perhaps the greatest intellectual of the Great Church in the passage from the nineteenth to the twentieth century. As a bishop of an Asia Minor province who had miscalculated the expenses of his office, he was reminiscing nostalgically about his more prosperous days as a camel owner before becoming a bishop. To become a bishop – he had already been ordained a priest – he had been forced to sell 12 of his camels and give the proceeds to the Patriarch. Recalling the failure, which had led him to this choice, he often repeated the phrase "*on iki deve sattim*" ("I sold twelve camels"). Once, on a Friday during Lent, while chanting the Akathist Hymn, when he read the fourth troparion of the seventh ode, "Entreat him, Mother of God, to inscribe your servants in the Book of Life", he said "*on iki deve*" instead of "*on iketeve*" ("entreat him"). The price he had paid to become a bishop had been high, indeed.[1]

The case of the Asia Minor camel owner–bishop is a good example of the clash between the expectations and true prospects for acquiring wealth offered by a bishop's career, especially in provinces with sparse flocks, such as those of Asia Minor. Similar experiences of inability to collect the basics for survival were recorded by another well-known bishop in the history of Balkan nationalism, Sophronious, the Bishop of Vratsa. In his case, however, his adverse finances were due largely to the successive warring in which the Ottoman Empire was involved and to the border location of his see.[2]

The eighteenth century, the century of the *Phanariots*, brought to the fore the strong class of hierarchs bound in a complex web of relationships with them. Many bishops or metropolitans owed their election to the intervention of more powerful individuals, often the rulers of Moldavia and Wallachia, or even their wives and daughters who frequently promoted their children's former tutors to the same positions.[3] The eighteenth century is precisely the period of the establishment of *gerontism*, or a system of elders (*gerontes*); that is, the establishment of a permanent Holy Synod comprised of metropolitans of the bishoprics near Constantinople, who resided in the capital and curtailed the Patriarch's power. The establishment of *gerontism* in the mid-eighteenth century and its predominance over the first period of the tenure of Patriarch Samuel Chatzeres (1763–8)[4] was linked to the diminishment of the patriarchal power (especially after the decision of Samuel to divide the patriarchal seal into four parts from which the three were always controlled by *gerontes* metropolitans) and that of the Ecumenical Patriarchate's officials, as well as to the attempt to root out corruption that plagued the Great Church at the time.[5]

Scion of a prominent *Phanariot* family, Samuel marked this transition long before becoming patriarch upon being elected to the Derkoi diocese (1746). The diocese that would rise from 51st to eighth place in the church hierarchy, resulting in its designation as "gerontic".[6] Gedeon considers this act of rapid upgrade of Samuel's see by the then-patriarch Callinicus of Karakalou as a huge concession to the *Phanariots*.[7] Bolstering the elders in the Patriarchate's administrative structure was usually interpreted as an action reflecting the *Phanariot* families' growing influence in church affairs.[8] Nonetheless, we cannot rule out the serious possibility that the establishment of such permanent Holy Synod was influenced by similar reforms imposed by Peter the Great on the Russian church in the early eighteenth century. If such a hypothesis is true, then the establishment of *gerontism* must be seen as a process of continual negotiation of the clergy's position in relation to the political and financial influence exercised by the *Phanariots*. Furthermore, the imposition of such a particular "aristocratic" clergy-laity system led to the appearance of similar phenomena of abuse mainly against the provincial hierarchs, but in these instances the protagonists were the metropolitans of Herakleia, Cyzicus, Nikomedeia, Nicaea, and Chalkedon. (The metropolitans of Derkoi, Ephesus, and Caesarea were subsequently added to this nucleus.) The reason was that these metropolitans had become *ephors*, or overseers, of all the other hierarchs who answered to their respective *geron-ephor* for their actions and, more importantly, paid a percentage of their income to him each year.

Thus, *gerontism* differentiated senior clergy into the privileged metropolitans, who lived in Constantinople enjoying close links to power centers, and those on the lower rungs of the church hierarchy. The latter, like the bishop of the Asia Minor province, desperately sought ways to repay the costs of their election by either imposing "voluntary" taxes on their flock (whose responsiveness varied) or by exploiting their role as mediators in civil, family, or inheritance disputes.

This chapter analyzes the complex process of institutional restructuring of the Ecumenical Patriarchate through exploring its finances and the concomitant internal and external shifts. The secular elements that "infiltrated" the decision-making process of the higher stratum of the clergy, in tandem with its increased financial needs, led to internal reorganization. The new concentration of power affected the income-generating system, entailing increased tax burden on the flocks. This weakening of the "pure" ecclesiastical power and prestige of the Patriarchate at the end prompted direct Ottoman involvement from the Tanzimat (1839–76) onward as well as attacks by the various nationalisms.[9] Therefore, the financial and administrative reorganization were not only intimately linked to increased secular interventions but in the end undermined the Patriarchate's ecumenical legitimacy and independence.

But in order to understand the financial dimension of the diocesan operation as well as that of the Patriarchate itself, let us look at some vital issues, such as the income of the former and the debt of the latter.

Metropolitan's Wealth: Dioceses' Income Composition

The "corps of hierarchs" that governed alongside the patriarch had to be supported and sustained, just like the priests in the villages. But there was no specific pay scale for hierarchs or priests. Their livelihood was based on voluntary offers or donations, or bequests. Alexander Helladius described the seventeenth-century reality, which, however, was also applicable to the eighteenth century:

> The Patriarch of Constantinople has today under his jurisdiction 74 metropolitans. Over 30 of them do not have bishops. The total number of bishops is 72 or 73. Together bishops and metropolitans are just 150. The patriarch raises his income as follows: from Constantinople, his city, he receives a silver *akçe* for each wedding. From his entire domain (all the dioceses under the Constantinople Patriarchate) he receives from each home twelve dinars every three years. Likewise, he receives a small gift from the priests and deacons of Constantinople when he ordains them. Additionally, every priest of Constantinople gives the Patriarch one silver *akçe* per year. Also, when wealthy Christians die, they leave the Patriarchal Church bequests such as a home, a field, sheep, cash. Furthermore, every metropolitan or archbishop ordained by the patriarch gives him a small gift. Also, every metropolitan or bishop gives the patriarch 20 or 30 or 25 piasters (*kuruş*) for the king's tax. From this money, each year the patriarch gives 6,000 piasters to the sultan on behalf of all the hierarchs so that the sultan will continue to consent to the existence of the patriarch in Constantinople and metropolitans, archbishops, and bishops throughout his domain, as a result of the Greeks' piety.[10]

Metropolitans and bishops had the same income from ordaining of priests, contributions, and weddings; priests gave one gold sovereign (*altın*) per year to their respective hierarchs. But the priests and deacons in villages faced severe survival problems. They were supported by the "Poor Men of Christ", the flock of Orthodox faithful, according to Gedeon. In some Constantinople churches the priests, deacons, cantors, vergers, and night guards withdrew a type of salary from their cash boxes. Certainly, there were more opportunities to raise income in large urban centers.

High and low clergy had also other sources of income, the so-called chance income. For example, priests hearing confession and spiritual advisors earned quite a bit from the population of the parish they served in and, if lenient, could amass an enviable fortune. Upon his death in 1879, Constantios, the spiritual advisory of the Christos parish at Galatas, left a fortune of 4,000 gold Ottoman liras, or some 92,000 French francs! His great fortune seems to have been the result of the parish's proximity to a number of brothels. Constantios' leniency towards the prostitutes who came to him for confession, which gave one the right to Holy Communion, seems to have been the main source of his great fortune. To those criticizing him for his leniency, he cited the danger of these "wretched creatures" seeking the services of another faith. And he would add: "The grocer confesses to stealing 5 and 10 grams from every kilo he sells and we allow him to repent, though he cheats his neighbour. These poor women engage in commerce. They do not remove half a gram from their wares. We should not be harsh."[11]

Another source of chance income for metropolitans and bishops was their ability to mediate conflicts. They presided over church tribunals engaged in issues of family and hereditary law (marriages, divorces, or wills).[12] They were also important cogs in the wheel of communication that could transmit information from the empire's remotest province to Constantinople – information that they made the most of. Except in cases related to the Constantinople see, it was customary for the Patriarchate to investigate a see's case independently when asked by the involved parties (assuming they have the financial ability and stature to do so) and to operate as an "appellate court" (to endorse the decision of the "spiritual court" of the first instance), or to force a see to review a case again.

Perhaps most crucial to a metropolitan's or a bishop's financial survival were not his tax-collecting abilities but rather the ability to exploit the property of the diocese or see. This raised the critical question of whether this irregular income could be invested in land, commercial property, or housing that could, in turn, become the foundation of each metropolitan's livelihood. The alienation of a large share of the land holdings of churches and monasteries after the Fall of Constantinople (1453) often forced patriarchs to merge sees.[13] The situation became even more dire when cities, villages, or bishoprics became an object of fierce disputes between metropolitans vying for their control.[14]

Calls for donations were another source of income. For a call, or a tour to raise charitable funds, to be successful, the public must have the ability to make donations.

Institutional Poverty: The Patriarchate's Debt and its Beneficiaries

Beyond the issue of personal survival, there was also the issue of institutional survival. The evolution of the Patriarchate's debt from the seventeenth century onward is quite interesting. In 1640, the clash between Cyril Kontaris and Cyril Lucaris[15] for the patriarchal throne sent the debt soaring. But in 1641 the Moldavian prince Vasile Lupu, who was of Albanian origin from Epirus (his family took refuge with other mercenaries in Arbanasi, before they moved to Moldavia), paid off the debt with his own funds. Yet this clean financial slate did not signal the beginning of a healthy management of patriarchal finances but instead boosted the rise of the *Phanariots*, a new class of lay people actively involved in patriarchal affairs who, in collaboration with powerful bishops, profited at the expense of the Common Treasury. The formation of the *Phanariot* class is, in one sense, the result of a process of increasing debt, which, of course, was passed on to the flock. To pay off these debts, successive patriarchs were forced to borrow at high interest rates from lenders who were usually *Phanariot* families. Then to pay off these loans they had to resort to heavily taxing their flock, or to exploiting the continuous transfers and elections of metropolitans and bishops who paid corresponding fees (*philotima*). The debt's unsustainability often led to the patriarch's incarceration. A pivotal moment was when Patriarch Dionysius IV Mouselimes was forced to pay Alexandros Mavrokordatos the sum of 100,000 piasters (more than 40,000 French francs).[16]

But most interesting is the fact that the rise of the neo-*Phanariots*, families that replaced the old *Phanariots* after the end of Greek Revolution, began in similar fashion.[17] Sultan Mahmud abolished all mandatory taxes the patriarch had to submit each year, such as the *peskeş* (sum paid by the patriarch on his election), as a result of the Treaty of Adrianople (1829). Yet the lifting of this enormous financial burden from the Patriarchate did not set off a period of economic restructuring but instead provided an excuse for the extended exploitation of the metropolitans by the *gerontes* and their lay supporters.[18] The following years, and especially the tenure of Patriarch Constantius I (1830–4), saw this exploitation take the form of continual elections and transfers for which the newly elected clerics had to pay *philotima* to the patriarch and the overseeing *gerontes*. The Patriarchate's debt once again spiraled upwards, reaching six million piasters by the mid-1850s from just two million shortly before 1821. Hence, the settling of the Patriarchate's debts both times set off a process of "primary accumulation" that led to a broad redistribution of wealth to the benefit mainly of those lay persons who had used this wealth to build preferential relations with key players in Ottoman politics. The exploitation of annuities from affiliated monasteries in Moldavia and Wallachia was the basic tool for the process of creating the neo-*Phanariot* families.[19]

A circular outlining the foundations of the *gerontist* system was issued during the second term of Patriarch Germanus IV (1852–3). The circular was instigated by the *gerontes* of the Holy Synod and aimed at resolving the thorny problem of a burgeoning deficit estimated at some 300,000 piasters. It set a specific timeframe for priests to repay outstanding debts to either the treasury or its lenders and provided for the bankruptcy of those who did not abide by the Holy Synod's warnings. The measure's purpose was to expedite the repayment of debts by lower prelates who often neglected to repay loans after their election. This resulted in the unchecked increase of these debts as interest, public relations expenses, and so forth accrued. Thus, in the event of a prelate's death, any debts to the treasury were lost while if these debts were due to a private lender, they had to be covered by the treasury. By implementing this decision, the Holy Synod asked for a prelate's removal in the event of financial abuses.[20]

In reality, the Holy Synod's proposal provided an administrative resolution of the problems, which were accumulated as a result of the *gerontist* system, as the largest debts had been incurred due to the demands of the *gerontes-ephors*. However, Germanus was succeeded by Anthimus VI (1853–5), who was allied to the British embassy and the neo-*Phanariot* Stefan Vogoridi. The new patriarch unequivocally stated that he faced a dilemma, as implementing the decision would be unfair to a large number of prelates while the opposite would suggest his indifference to the problem of the treasury's debts.[21] In the end, the circular was not implemented despite the evident deficits accumulated under the *gerontist* system, especially through the creation of a caste of privileged bishops within the hierarchy – many of whom no longer had any *Phanariot* descent – and despite the immense financial burden placed on the majority of bishops by the *gerontes* and their lenders.[22]

The Gordian Knot of Institutional and Personal Debts

Thus, when the nineteenth century ushered in the era of great reforms in the Ottoman state, the prelates' income (which was accompanied by the abolition of *gerontism*) and the Patriarchate's debt, emerged as crucial issues in the discussion among clergy, laity, and the Ottoman government.

The Bulgarian question was one of the issues that prompted the discussion of the clergy's pay.[23] The inability of the Patriarchate to collect dues from the Bulgarian-speaking Christians in their provinces led the Patriarchate to hire – at generous salaries of between 18 and 35 gold Ottoman liras – the metropolitans that it appointed to "Bulgarian" provinces. For the same reason, the Ottoman government's proposed pay for senior clergy was included in the *Islahat Fermanı* of 1856 (most well-known in the Western bibliography as *Hatt-ı Hümâyun*).[24] Nevertheless, the proposal was not well received by either the *gerontes* and their allied hierarchs or the lay representatives. The primary reason for this negative stance was not linked to the creation of an employment relationship between the senior clergy and the Ottoman state apparatus, a development with which many neo-*Phanariots* would be in agreement. Nor was it related to earlier proposals by representatives of Bulgarian and Greek rural populations who believed that introducing fixed salaries for clerics would eliminate overtaxing.[25] It was a common belief within the Patriarchate that the Ottoman imperial palace sought to put hierarchs on a payroll in order to place under its direct control both church property and all types of church annuities. The reason for this state endeavor was likely the enormous fiscal gaps that needed to be covered.[26]

The Millet-ı[27] Assembly (1858–60) convened at the Patriarchate in accordance with the proclamations of the Tanzimat for reconstructing the administration of the *Rum millet* and introducing laity to its governance. The result of the proceedings was the composing of a constitutional text that has remained known as the "General Regulations". The text rejected the introduction of salaries for clerics as incompatible with the Holy Canons and substituted the term "payroll" with "grant".

Replacing the concept of "payroll" with "grant" essentially meant changing the nature of the received sum: thus, instead of clerical income being in the form of pay from state coffers, it would retain the characteristics of a tax on Orthodox populations that would now have a definitive and regular form. According to Metropolitan Dionysius of Nicomedia, there was a tendency among the "laity"[28] which, with the Ottoman palace's support, aimed at addressing the issue of abuses. But in order for the Church to comply with the spirit and the letter of the *Hatt-ı Hümâyun* (1856), which provided for the establishment of a payroll for bishops, they proposed to set clerics' pay in each province, "according to the state of the population and the hierarchs' needs".[29] This income would be collected annually and equally shared by the number of families in each province. The same metropolitan believed that the measures, proposed by the reformists, did not substantially differ from the establishment of a payroll and that if implemented would greatly disturb relations between metropolitans and their flocks.[30] Interestingly, he makes no reference to the problem of the sum of clerical revenues but rather to the difficulties the metropolitans would face in collecting them, especially in urban centers.

As for the issue of patriarchal grants, the Millet-ı Assembly set them at 500,000 piasters, a sum that would be drawn from supplementary income collected from the populations of the provinces and Constantinople. But the text of the General Regulations contains a seeming paradox. Article B notes that the General Assembly decided, following the recommendation of the Mixed Standing National Council, that along with the new Holy Synod, the Council would endow the patriarchal throne with the revenues of the monasteries in the Pogoniani and Vella provinces of Epirus. This decision obviously aimed at reducing the tax burden on the Orthodox populations by controlling the revenues of the monasteries in these two provinces, which derived from the affiliated monasteries in Moldavia and Wallachia. In February 1859, the parliaments of Moldavia and Wallachia elected Alexandru Ioan Cuza as head of the two principalities, effectively clearing the way for the creation of a Romanian state. In May 1859, the Cuza government seized the revenues from tenants of monastic properties for that year because of the monasteries' accumulated debts to the principalities' treasuries. This action was certainly a harbinger of the Cuza government's future stance on the issue of the monasteries.[31] Thus the Millet-ı Assembly's political move to "endow" the patriarchal throne with revenues from monastic properties in Moldavia and Wallachia sought to reaffirm the rights of the Orthodox patriarchates over these properties.

Implementing the clerical grants became the litmus test of the implementation of all the General Regulations over the next few years. The reasons why this happened must be sought first in the economic impasse, which the Patriarchate faced after the monastic annuities in Moldavia and Wallachia were seized (and after the refusal of other Orthodox patriarchates and the monastic communities of Mount Sinai and Mount Athos to support the reform effort). Secondly, the implementation of the clerical grant would indicate the viability of the new system and whether it could successfully replace the earlier system of *gerontist ephorates*. Thirdly, and most importantly, the measure's implementation was actually a tool for transmitting the reform movement from the Ottoman center to the provinces and simultaneously an indicator of provincial populations' acceptance of the new ecclesiastic and administrative structure being imposed through the *Vilayet* Law (1864). The fact that the clerical grant's application had now become an object of the collective responsibility of provincial populations was the logical consequence of the decree establishing the metropolitan as president of the various municipal-elder councils and the mixed courts set up in the *vilayet* capitals. Whether the metropolitan's position in the provincial administrative structure meant an expansion or a curtailment of his powers was an issue that concerned the local balance of power.

In sum, the implementation of the clerical grants depended on a number of factors: the metropolitans' willingness to impose it and, chiefly, how they chose to do this; whether the Ottoman administration, central and regional, would support this effort; and, whether rural populations would balk at its imposition as it represented an added burden to the taxes already imposed by the Ottoman administration. Inevitably, this raised the issue of the degree to which each cleric could spiritually rally his flock in a particularly difficult period as Bulgarian nationalism aimed primarily at secession of Bulgarian populations from the jurisdiction of the Ecumenical Patriarchate. The secession was justified through critiques of high taxes and clergy's greed and corruption.

But the problem of the clerical grants was connected also with the issue of the Patriarchate's debt. During the tenures of Sophronious III (1863–6) and Gregory VI (1867–71), the Orthodox populations contributed the sum of 6,000,000 piasters towards paying off the Patriarchate's debts to "orphans and widows". Every Orthodox citizen contributed six piasters. The collection of these monies was overseen by a financial committee that, however, was implicated in the embezzlement of funds sent from Europe since 1872. The committee was thus suspended.[32]

Indeed, both issues – grants and debt – were inextricably entwined. The non-implementation of the grant measures in several provinces was linked to the problems with the repayment of the debts of the "National" (Millet-ı) Treasury" (as the "Public Treasury" was renamed). The Treasury's debt totaled 27,000 purses (1,350,000 piasters). According to an article in the General Regulations on the annual pay of patriarchal staff, the treasury debt, also known as the "court treasury",[33] would be subject to an audit by a special committee and repaid by apportionment by head, as in the case of the grants.

But the measure's final implementation diverged from the definition of a tax. At a joint meeting of the Holy Synod and Grand Council it was decided, according to the population ledgers (*nüfüs-i defter*) based on the land registry service (*Defter Haneyi Amire*), to apportion the outstanding amount as follows: six piasters for every Orthodox citizen of the empire under the jurisdiction of the Constantinople Patriarchate rather than per head. This meant that the burden per family would average more than 20 piasters, making the collection of the grant monies even harder. The representatives of the *Rum millet* in the provinces – metropolitans and elders – would cooperate in the collection of this emergency tax, although the final responsibility for its collection was assumed by the Ottoman administration and the collected amounts would be entered in the state budget before being handed over to the Patriarchate and entered in its records.[34] This decision provided for the direct involvement of the Ottoman administration in the collection of the outstanding amount of the debt, essentially laying the ground for the launch of a wide-ranging discussion on whether or not the Ottoman administration should become involved in the collection of church grants.

The Bulgarian side was first to react. In an article in the daily *Anatolikos Tachydromos* (*Eastern Post*), which was reproduced in

Anatolikos Astir (*Eastern Star*),[35] the Patriarchate's decision to pay off its debts "with a new tax" was roundly criticized. Noting the Patriarchate's profligacy, the article cited the strong opposition in the Bulgarian provinces from the faithful being asked to assume part of the Patriarchate's debt burden while not being allowed to participate in the Patriarchate's administration. The author took an aggressive tone against both the Patriarchate and its lay administrators: "because the wealth of many Greek families derives from patriarchs and bishops who, on passing away, bequeathed gains made at the expense of the church treasury and the people. It is to these families we must resort today to pay off the patriarchal debt in the event that a commission of competent persons is formed to discover what it actually is." The article proposed the formation of such a commission.

Commenting on the article, *Anatolikos Astir*'s editor defended the decisions of the Millet-i Assembly, noting that the Patriarchate's debt had been incurred for all Orthodox faithful and not just the Greeks. This is why, he added, that the debt's repayment should be detached from the recent emergence of the Bulgarian question. But what is most noteworthy about the Bulgarian article is that it shifted the focus of its attack from the senior clergy to the Greek families of Constantinople involved in the patriarchal affairs. This shift, which does not skirt the issue of the clergy's financial abuses, is certainly linked to the hardline in resolving the Bulgarian issue taken by specific families, especially the Karatheodores, a powerful neo-*Phanariot* family that originated from Adrianople. The Bulgarian newspaper's attack on the lay persons seems aimed at creating an internal differentiation between the laity and senior clergy that had surfaced with the issue of the debt repayment as well as the issue of grants. The Bulgarian intervention was directly linked to the debt repayment.

The Clerics' Grants between "salary", "tax", and "gift", and the Autonomy of *Rum millet*

Stephanos Karatheodores, Sultan Abdülmecid's personal physician and one of the primary proponents of the patriarchal reform at the Millet-i Assembly (1858–60), was also the person who compromised on the most significant reform. Thus, when it became evident during the tenure of Sophronius that collecting monies for clerics' grants, as set by the

Millet-i Assembly, would be impossible without the aid of the Ottoman administrative apparatus, Karatheodores switched the focus of the reforms. In what follows, I will provide some highlights of Karatheodores' views in order to contextualize the layered interests among the laics and their impact on the Patriarchate's finances.

The issue of the Ottoman government's intervention in collecting the grant monies became a point of disagreement between the Patriarchate's two collective bodies, the Holy Synod and the Mixed Council. Seeing the difficulties in collecting the monies, the Holy Synod decided to merge the church tax levied for the grants with the civilian taxes, which the state collected from the empire's populations, thus ceding the right of its collection to the Ottoman administration. This prompted a backlash from five members of the Mixed Council, who submitted a written protest (*diamartyrisis*) against the decision.[36] Karatheodores was definitely the instigator and author of this protest. Nonetheless, one should not overlook the fact that it was co-signed by *Hadji* Georgios Konstantinides, close friend of Jerusalem Patriarch Cyril, who was aligned with Russia. The three other signatories were less prominent elders of Constantinople. The political objective of Karatheodores' intervention was to avert a reaction to the Sultanate's involvement in collecting the grant monies by the Bulgarians, as had been the case with the Patriarchate's debts.

Nonetheless, while the representatives of the neo-*Phanariots* reconsidered both the way the monies were collected and the sum prelates received as compensation, this was not the case with the powerful bankers who sat on the Mixed Council and who did not sign the text of the protest.[37] For the bankers, the fact that the radical reforms put forth by the patriarch had the approval of the Grand Vizier Mehmed Emin Aali Paşa was enough to refrain from joining the first serious effort to delegitimize him.

The theoretical foundation of Karatheodores' proposal (he perceived the grant not as a salary but as a type of church tax) was that it combined two different, and contradictory in his view, means of collecting monies to pay prelates: the "tax" or duty, whose collection was under the purview of the state, and the "gift" or donation, whose collection was part of the process of raising revenue for the Church. Karatheodores believed that collection of the former was compulsory while collection of the latter should be, by its nature, voluntary, a contribution of the flock to its priest. The Holy Synod's decision to incorporate its grant monies into the other duties the Orthodox citizens were being required to pay the state automatically rendered its collection violent and forcible. Finally, for Karatheodores, the objective of earmarking state taxes was to "safely preserve the secular state" while the collection of priests' pay aimed at allowing him a dignified life. This was at the heart of the edicts of the General Regulations and implementing the Holy Synod's decision would contravene the spirit of the church's constitution.

In another document,[38] Karatheodores noted that using the state apparatus to collect the money for the priests' compensation essentially revived the proposal to establish a pay scale for the Orthodox clergy – a proposal that the National Assembly had rejected, opting instead to apply the concept of a "gift" to prelates' income. Karatheodores argued that the Millet-i Assembly had only introduced one substantive differentiation from the old system, which was predetermining the sum a prelate would receive. In this sense, he believed that Sophronius had diverged from the spirit of the decision which had been taken, and had accepted the implementation of the measure establishing priests' payroll, especially one imposed by civilian authority. For him, this was tantamount to the Patriarchate subordinating its prelates to the position of a simple employee.[39] This impressive adoption of arguments, which had been emplbyed mainly by the clergy–laity wing of the *gerontes* at the Millet-i Assembly, by its chief opponent Karatheodores on how a payroll for the Orthodox clergy would create a relationship of employment with the Patriarchate and, by extension, to the Ottoman state, altered the parameters of the dispute.

It was obvious that Karatheodores, the main proponent of reform, had made a serious concession not for reasons related to the reformist spirit of the edicts, but for political objectives set out in the General Regulations. Among these was dealing with the Bulgarians' secessionist tendencies. This meant that he continued to link the process of promoting reforms to the resolution of the Bulgarian issue, while advocating a position of relative independence for the Orthodox *millet* from Ottoman power. Conversely, Patriarch Sophronius appeared faithful to the "political line", which Ioannis Psycharis, a pro-French neo-*Phanariot*, had put forth in the past (under the patronage of Aali Pasha); namely, the only viable version of restructuring was the *millet*'s subordination to the Ottoman political model. Thus, if Sophronius appeared to be trampling the letter of the General Regulations in order to remain faithful to the radical-reformist orientation, Karatheodores, mindful of the crisis that would erupt over a homogenized tax burden on the Bulgarian (and mainly peasant) populations, was more concerned with preserving unity within the *millet* (and, by extension, the state) than with the Patriarchate's finances. For him, the reformist tendency was not to be realized by making the clergy employees of the Ottoman state but rather by reducing the tax burden on the populations.

Addressing the issue of a uniform duty, Karatheodores acknowledged that the imbalances between different regions were indeed unfair in terms of collecting revenues as each province's population density differed. (The scale varied from 25 k. per head to 10 or even as few as 7 in densely populated areas.) He believed that it would be desirable for all families within the empire to pay the same amount but that "these means were beyond the powers of the Millet-ı Assembly as had been rejected for more pressing reasons . . .". He preferred keeping the current, albeit unjust, system to the introduction of new measures.

As expected, there was a swift response to the arguments regarding "tax" versus "gift" from the supporters of reforms. The abolition of the *ephorate* system resulted in an interesting reversal: laity identified with the reformist views and effectively rejected the dominant role of the state apparatus in implementing them and took "conservative" positions, while the senior clerics who had split into reformist and non-reformist camps at the Millet-ı Assembly (due mainly to the issue of the monastery revenues) now "rediscovered" their unity by recognizing the need for the Ottoman state to intervene in securing their financial existence.[40]

The rationale was especially simple and timely: as the Patriarchate had already created a fee scale for church activity, these could not be considered either a "gift" or a "voluntary donation". This logic was succinctly replicated in the General Regulations precisely because they wanted to fix the level of prelates' income. In one sense, the Mixed Council's lay members' polemic against converting the grant to a form of wage, as the state would then assume a mediating role in collecting it, was a non-starter as it challenged another basic parameter of the Regulations: monetizing the state tax as a prerequisite to fixing these fees. At the same time, reform supporters saw the merging of the church tax with the other state taxes as the only solution for preserving a mechanism of philanthropic and educational institutions as well as for compensating Patriarchate's staff.[41]

Conclusions

The main reason for this interesting reversal of positions between the reformist laity and the conservative *gerontes* was the loss of the considerable income the Patriarchate had derived from Moldavia and Wallachia. And the effect of this reversal was the resulting linkage of all secret or public monies from state treasuries or private estates. The debt, however, could not become a profit lever for either lay members or clergy; on the contrary, it was a mechanism for binding the Patriarchate to state interests and policies that ultimately led to the loss of its "ecumenical" character.

So, it is not strange that the Ottoman involvement became more visible in subsequent years regarding the problem of the debt's management. In 1865, Patriarch Sophronious submitted a lengthy report on the state of the Church's finances.[42] He claimed that the Patriarchate incurred monthly operating expenses of roughly 70,000 piasters, including staff salaries and basic operating needs. However, its budget provided for just 15,000–20,000 piasters per month, a sum that would be further reduced following the Mixed Council's decision to cut the fees charged for church actions. The Patriarchate had already received two sizeable loans of 1,000,000 and 500,000 piasters from the Ottoman government, with the possibility of a third to meet staff payroll.

Although the reasons for the Patriarchate's indebtedness are complex, as discussed so far, we must look at the Ecumenical Patriarchate's debts as the result of the confiscation of the monastic properties in Moldavia and Wallachia in 1863 by the Cuza government. If we must identify a pivotal year for the Patriarchate's finances in the nineteenth century, it would not be 1833, the loss of the Orthodox flock in the Greek provinces, or 1870, the loss of the Orthodox flock in the Bulgarian provinces. The year 1863 was marked by the loss of considerable revenues from the exploitation of possibly even one-third of the arable lands of Moldavia and Wallachia with a direct impact on the income of the Constantinople Patriarchate, the *stavropegial* monasteries (including those on Mount Athos), and the other Orthodox patriarchates. Chiefly, though, it changed the relationship between clergy and laity within the

Patriarchate as the powerful clans that influenced the patriarchal succession also drew their income from there.

When the flow of money from Moldavia and Wallachia was cut off, the Patriarchate was forced to seek new sources of income. Contrary to what one might believe, it did not immediately turn to the Greek state – something indicative of the intentions of the ruling elite, which was still inspired by Ottoman visions. The first source to which it turned was the Ottoman state even as late as 1880 and the eruption of the severe fiscal crisis that would put its finances under international control. Meanwhile, the Patriarchate would turn towards Russia, especially during the tenure of Ioakeim III – in 1879, the dependency (*metochion*) of Saint Sergios in Moscow came under its control; while during his second tenure (1901–12) he would enjoy the financial support of both Serbia and Austria. It was only after the death of the "ecumenist" Ioakeim III that the new patriarch, and his great rival, Germanos V, would directly seek financial assistance from the Greek state. This incorporation into Greek foreign policy would peak with the election of Meletios Metaxakis, Archbishop of Athens, as Ecumenical Patriarch at the same time as the Asia Minor campaign of 1921. But the Greek army's defeat brought a quick end to that period, leading the Patriarchate to a new institutional and financial recession under the Kemalist regime.

CHAPTER 6

HEALTH AS WEALTH: COMMODIFICATION OF DOCTOR–PATIENT RELATIONS IN THE NINETEENTH-CENTURY OTTOMAN BALKANS

Evguenia Davidova

Leafing through the Vratsa trader Tosho Tsenov's commercial ledger of 1811–23, one comes across the following entry: "55 g. for the doctor (*hekim*), nails, oakum, wine, and other expenses." What is more interesting, the same (or other) *hekim* was not a stranger to payments in kind, such as brandy ("rakija") at the cost of 19 g.[1] It seems that being paid both in cash and in kind was not an unusual occurrence. In 1809, the Gabrovo merchant Sakhatchioğlu spent 85 g. on medicines for his sick son, who was studying in Bucharest, and an extra 75 g. for a *hekim* or, total 160 g., which was almost 10 percent of the family's annual expenses.[2] Another example comes from the Athenian merchant Christodoulos Efthimiou, who spent 28 percent of his miscellaneous expenses on medical needs in 1843.[3] In the 1860s, another commercial ledger marked 270 g. for a doctor and 90 g. for a pharmacist.[4] Over time, brandy as a form of transaction disappeared but medical fees and the pharmaceutical expenses went up. This trend is not surprising, as nineteenth-century medicine (and pharmacy) expanded as part of the growing service sector.[5] Healthcare spending became a visible marker of middle-class social status, and the use of medical services and social stratification were intimately related. Medical professionals in the Ottoman Empire were integrated into the local elites through bureaucratic reforms, community involvement, economic entrepreneurship and innovative marketing practices. They also contributed to Ottoman modernization by paving the way for new social practices involving both ethnic and social intermixing and new divisions.

This chapter examines three interrelated issues: the professionalization of medical service; the role of the state in this process; and the commodification of health within a specific social stratum of patients: the nineteenth-century Balkan merchants. Traders, through travel and exposure to contagious diseases, were among the first to appreciate the importance of healthcare, and who could also afford to have professional medical help and support the establishment of public health. The research is grounded in a variety of sources: commercial ledgers, wills, newspaper advertising, memoirs, travelogues, and correspondence. Commercial letters also reveal family ties and expressions of affection in the words of concern for one's health. At the same time, rumors about business partners and competitors' illnesses suggest a new approach to health as social capital and its conversion to economic capital.[6] I argue that the heightening of health awareness (and its commodification) and anxieties about diseases (and their cures), and in general new modern sensibilities, were closely connected to the concurrent expansion of trade and incorporation into the world economy, Ottoman reforms and social reordering, the institutionalization of professional education, and the proliferation of the printing press and advertising. However, all these factors that shaped new health valorization did not occur in a vacuum, but rather were intersections of existing local practices and European influences. Such major shifts in social relations and cultural values involved doctors, state, patients, and a social and institutional framework that enabled these interactions.

Healers, *Ahtars*, Doctors, and Pharmacists

Studies on modern Europe have shown that there was a strict hierarchical order within the profession: surgeon was lower than physician because surgery was considered more a "craft" than a "science". The apothecary had an even lower rank because he kept a shop and pursued "trade" and learned it through apprenticeship rather than education.[7] Similarly, social distinctions existed in the Ottoman Balkans; they were mostly among university educated versus practitioners without a formal training. Thus, healers, midwives, *ahtars* (apothecary), and *hekims* usually attained their knowledge through apprenticeship with a *hekim* and serviced a broad range of patients. In Macedonia and Thrace, for instance, particularly sought after were the itinerant *hekims* from Ioannina who acquired their fame by removing bladder stones and performing cataract surgery.[8] Most of these practitioners led a peripatetic life; they operated mostly locally and developed certain specializations.

On the other hand, the list of the subscribers of *History of the Former Dacia, or the Current Transylvania, Wallachia, and Moldavia* by Dionysios Photeinos (1818–19), reveals a hierarchical order among the *Phanariot* world, where, after the functionaries, physicians were positioned as first among the group of professions: "his excellences the doctors", "the most honorable merchants", "the most learned teachers", followed by the clergy. Moreover, among the *Phanariot* families in Constantinople, one of the strategies for increasing social power consisted of diversification – sending their youth into various fields – one son would become a doctor, another would enter the military, a third into commerce, a fourth would become clergy.[9] This "aristocratic" model of social and economic diversification trickled down and was likewise adopted by middle-class merchant families.

Often the medical profession was passed on, and the second generation – the sons – became doctors with diplomas. For example, a prosopographic study of Bulgarian medical students in Vienna in the second half of the nineteenth century demonstrated that 7 percent of them had fathers who were doctors and 1.3 percent had parents who were veterinarians, pharmacists, and dentists; more significant, 64.6 percent were from bourgeois families.[10] The cases of Spyridon Zavitziano and Moise Allatini corroborate the tendency toward professional self-reproduction; the former's father and multiple brothers and cousins were also medical doctors. Allatini, whose family emigrated from Livorno to Salonika, studied medicine in Pisa and Florence; he also followed his paternal path both in medicine and business enterprises (trade in grain, tobacco, brick factory, brasserie).[11] In other instances, municipalities or rich merchants were found to finance medical education abroad. Many young Greeks were sent in Pisa, Paris, Montpellier, Vienna, and later

Zurich and Geneva.[12] Many Bulgarians followed these same destinations for becoming physicians with diplomas.

The distinctions among healthcare practitioners were also seen among the *dükkâns* where one could buy drugs. Usually, an *ahtar*, such as Stoian of Tŭrnovo, would own a shop (*ahtarnitsa*) that combined modern pharmacy, herbal and sanitary shops with a bookstore and haberdashery. Among the inventory one finds crèmes, oils, herbs, tea, glasses. In bigger towns emerged the *spitseria* or pharmacy.[13] The pharmacy often sold powder, oil, drugs promoted as "the newest wonders" that arrived from Europe, as advertised by the apothecary Mokhosh of Rusçuk in 1866.[14] Pharmacies in Istanbul were better supplied and probably cheaper. For example, a merchant from Bucharest asked a colleague in the Ottoman capital for two bottles of "oloanov oil".[15] Actually, differences between the two types of shops were marginal.

Early pharmacies often sprang up from general trade. Three cases make this point. The Novi Sad family Barako (Baraković) had a shop selling a variety of goods first and opened a pharmacy later. The Dimić family owned two shops: a grocery and a hardware store in Smederevo and sold drugs in their grocery because the town had no pharmacy.[16] Likewise, in Gabrovo at the beginning of the nineteenth century, the Sakhatchioğlu brothers were importing for personal and commercial use almond oil, alum, mercury, "Vita" and "Antonio" balms.[17]

Most doctors also owned pharmacies, such as Antonium Utenberg from Lemberg (Lviv), who became a town doctor in Samokov in 1847 and opened a pharmacy there.[18] A document of the late 1840s reveals that another doctor in Filibe complained about his low salary, and perhaps it was his financial situation that motivated him to open a pharmacy, funded by his brother, a rich merchant and tax farmer.[19] Until 1850, anyone could open a pharmacy in the Ottoman Empire. It was in the mid-1860s that professional pharmacies with educated pharmacists were established and served larger and ethnically mixed groups. A customer ledger of Milan Genov, a pharmacist of Skopje, reveals that his clientele included 20 Christian women, among them one doctor and one maid; 83 non-Muslim males, including eight doctors and various artisans; 29 male Muslims, among them high officials such as the *vali* Hamdi Pasha, as well as barbers and a factory owner.[20] Genov's pharmacy, with a web of suppliers from Salonika to Vienna and Milano, also traded in a wide variety of commodities, including photographic plaques and cameras.[21] This intermixing of urban low and middle classes suggests that pharmacies supplied not only medicines but also cosmetic and other products as part of a growing service sector.

However, the cholera epidemic of 1865 triggered an order (1873) requiring the existence of a pharmacy and a licensed pharmacist in each district. That regulation, discussed below, had significant ramifications for the decoupling of medicine and pharmacy leading to further specialization and privileging education through licensing, and marginalizing healers and midwives from the public medical sphere.

Ottoman Government's Health Policies

Wars and epidemics, as Nancy Frieden argued, were the "classic catalysts for health reform".[22] The advent of plague and cholera stimulated the building of sanitary systems, which were usually associated with military needs and reforms. Teodora Sechel also suggested that dealing with "contagion was an economic and a political issue rather than just a medical one".[23] The Habsburg Empire established its quarantine system in the mid-eighteenth century, and Serbia and the Danubian Principalities (under Ottoman suzerainty until 1878) set up quarantine centers in 1832. Similarly, at the end of the Russo–Ottoman War of 1828–9, the Ottoman government organized sanitary control.[24] In 1838, Sultan Mahmud II established a General Sanitary Council (Conseil supérieur de santé) and set up a system of quarantines.

The Ottoman government also appreciated the importance of professional medical education. Thus, in 1827, an Imperial School of Medicine was opened as part of a larger military reform project. In 1832, a surgeon's school followed suit, and both schools were merged in 1839 as the newly established Imperial Medical School. In 1842–3, the first non-Muslim students were enrolled. Lack of civilian medical schools in the Ottoman Empire, however, contributed to a prevalence of doctors who received their education abroad. Among them, there were many minority and foreign doctors and pharmacists, especially Greeks, Jews, Armenians, Czechs, Poles, and other foreigners known under the collective term "Franks" (frenk).[25] Many physicians came from the middle classes and most of them benefitted from the early Tanzimat reforms when their families accumulated capital and were able to invest in children's professional education. The professional career of

Dr. Stoian Chomakov (1819–93) illustrates this process of social reorientation. He was born into two rich commercial families, but instead of continuing the family business, he studied medicine in Pisa and Florence and specialized in surgery in Paris.[26] Chomakov and the previously mentioned *Phanariot*'s progeny offer examples of economic capital converted into cultural (education) and social capital.[27]

The Medical Civil School was founded in Istanbul in 1867. Its main aim to produce local cadres was accompanied by a gradual shift from French into Turkish as a language of instruction and cancellation of the final annual exam.[28] A similar attempt to curb the advantages of the foreign-trained doctors was implemented through legislation in Russia almost 30 years earlier. In countries without strict licensing procedures, educated physicians supported state regulations and resented "doctors" with questionable qualifications for undermining the reputation of the profession. Legitimation by and dependence on the government created an intimate connection between the state and the medical profession.[29] Such a relationship produced even starker consequences in post-Ottoman context. A case in point was midwifery in the newly independent Greece. A couple of government decrees in the 1830s established strict regulations on midwives' work and education, both under the control of male doctors.[30]

Yet restrictions and charges against medical practitioners did not operate only "from above", but also "from below". Pertinent examples are two complaints to the Police Department in Belgrade against two different doctors in 1839. The claimants, who originated from a rural area, asked for their money back, 54 and 105 g. respectively. The second claimant complained that the doctor had no passport and medical certificate and behaved "like a charlatan". In a similar vein, a certain pharmacist, Mate Ivanović, also incurred the wrath of the population because he was selling stale and expensive medicines.[31]

As noted, in the Ottoman Empire the institutionalization of medical education began as part of military modernization and expanded during the Tanzimat (1839–76). There was, however, a chronic shortage of physicians, which was compensated by initiatives undertaken by local municipalities. For example, in 1845, the Bulgarians in Tŭrnovo, Svishtov, and Shumen requested the Polish emigrant center in Paris, known as Hôtel Lambert, a political group established in the mid-1830s with an ardent anti-Russian stance, to send them Polish doctors. This step was prompted by the arrival of two Polish physicians in the neighboring Gabrovo who enjoyed a good professional reputation. As a result, in 1846 the center sent Dr. Drozdovsky to Tŭrnovo who was charged with an anti-Russian political agenda by the center.[32] Other towns were attracting probably less politically motivated physicians through individual migration. In the mid-1840s, doctors with foreign training lived in Veles: Petrovik, a Croat from Dalmatia; Leonidas, Andreadi, Lefter, Chariton and Schnock from Greece; and Filip Poliaka from Vienna.[33]

In the summer of 1849, after the crushing of the 1848 revolutions, a group of around 5,000 immigrants arrived from Austria in the Ottoman Empire. Many of them later returned to the Habsburg Empire. According to Ottoman official information, 256 people adopted Islam, mostly Poles, among them 12 doctors and 14 engineers.[34] Apart from certain political considerations, these conversions reveal the Ottoman pragmatic goals to assimilate potentially subversive elements and to take advantage of their professional expertise.

As previously noted, since the 1850s the Ottoman government tried to regulate the process of establishing a pharmacy; in 1874, another order was issued for forming commissions in each town to check the credentials of the local doctors and pharmacists. Furthermore, the physicians were not allowed to practice medicine while owning a pharmacy whenever there was an available pharmacist with diploma.[35] Skopje municipality's records disclose a report lodged by the Kratovo's *kaymakam* in 1876 in regard to a certain doctor Kostaki who practiced without having a diploma; and there was neither a surgeon nor a pharmacist in that area. Subsequently, the Skopje *mutesarrıf* ordered rapid measures for redressing the issue.[36]

In sum, the Ottoman reforms, and particularly the municipal reform in the Danube *vilayet*, had a substantial impact on health services. The promulgation of the Municipal Law of 1867 established the crucial institution of city councils that consisted both of appointed officials and councilors elected by the local population. Those councils were charged with multiple public tasks, including social welfare, public sanitation, infrastructure construction, police, and fire fighting. Doctors were permanent members of this multiethnic local administration. The city councils opened not only pharmacies, but also hospitals and employed doctors and pharmacists.[37] Thus, healthcare was an integral part of the

Ottoman modernization policy, ranging from establishing quarantines to specialized education to licensing to municipal reforms entailing active collaboration of the local elites.

Traveling Merchants, Traveling Diseases

Cholera and plague not only stimulated state regulation but also acted as barriers to trade and threats to life that induced a great deal of fear. For instance, in 1834 the plague that began in Alexandria rapidly moved to Istanbul and the Balkan Peninsula, especially in port cities such as Salonika; in 1836–7, it reached even mountainous places such as Sevlievo and Gabrovo. The deadly disease "traveled" with commodities, following some main and secondary roads, and thus traders in wool transmitted the plague from Sofia to Karlovo; in Lovech it arrived with cotton merchants from Macedonia.[38] Letters, exchanged among traders, informed about other merchants' deaths. Such was the case of Rali Mavridi who wrote in 1849 that Petros Ioanu of Galați died by cholera.[39] Other evidence comes from a Constantinople merchant in July 1865, who communicated to a correspondent in Izmid: "But now everything is put aside and I will write about this {business} later because we are quite scared of the cholera and think only how to save our lives."[40] With another business correspondent in Bucharest the same merchant was more specific and mentioned that about 30,000 people had died.[41] Subsequently, a commercial letter from Bucharest mentioned that in one day alone (16 July 1865), 222 people died in Istanbul, mainly among the "lower classes".[42] While newspapers also provided information about such diseases and government measures, the informal way of disclosing the "itineraries" of epidemics became part and parcel of commercial correspondence along with news about commodity prices and bankruptcies.

In times when epidemics did not ravage cities, health was still one of the often-discussed issues in commercial letters. This was not just a whimsical curiosity or a polite concern, but recognition of the vulnerability of human life and the effects of health in carrying out a business. Thus, in 1858, Solomon Almaleh of Filibe, asked his long-term partner – the Istanbul merchant Khristo Tŭpchileshtov – about his health because he had heard that he was seriously ill.[43] On another occasion, Tŭpchileshtov criticized his youngest son who was studying commerce in London in 1872:

> There is a rumor here that Mr. N. Boyazoglu is severely ill. You do not write me anything about that issue and know that I have big interests invested there and I can lose 5–10,000 liras. In the future let me know about the health and behavior of my correspondents . . .[44]

Hence, health news was inextricably interwoven with information about investments and bankruptcies within a larger international framework and had a role in risk-aversion strategies. In such cases, again, health as social capital had a direct influence on economic capital. One piece of evidence, pointing to the centrality of health in the merchant's world, derived from a contract (1849) for commercial partnership between two brothers that contained a detailed article dealing with potential illness, which had a penalizing character in that it decreased the gains of the sick partner.[45] Of course, many prosperous (and not so well-to-do) traders and Ottoman bureaucrats had a personal physician.

Personalized Medicine and Support for Public Health

Foreign travelers often communicated with and gathered local information through doctors, who being educated abroad, spoke many languages. For example, Dr. Frank, Ali Pasha's personal physician, who previously served as physician in the French army in Egypt, appeared to be lavishly remunerated: according to the British traveler William Leake, he received 10,000 piastres a year.[46] Djoka, the *baş-hekim* of the Belgrade Pasha, as in the aforementioned case, served various powerful administrators, including Prince Miloš.[47] Most of these doctors not only moved from treating one high official to the next but also exercised power beyond their medical expertise. Dr. Georgi Vŭlkovich, a personal physician to Rashid Pasha, was considered by the Bulgarians in Constantinople to be an advocate to the Ottoman authorities for the Bulgarian ecclesiastical cause, and, consequently, a "very good patriot".[48] Many Greeks and Jews served as physicians to grand viziers and even to the sultan, such as Stephanos and Konstantinos Karatheodoris, Spiridon Mavrogenis. Ioannis Kolletis rose from a doctor of Ali Pasha to a leader of the Greek War of Independence, leader of the "French" party, and to the rank of prime minister in independent Greece.[49]

The above-mentioned Utenberg began as a personal doctor to Usref Pasha in Belgrade and took care of his sick wife. In 1833, the Pasha moved to Filibe and appointed him as the garrison's doctor. Later on, the Pasha moved again to Vidin, but Utenberg accompanied his wife to Samokov because of its favorable climate and became a town doctor.[50] There are multiple letters and telegrams sent by Dr. Antonaki Utenberg to local officials, such as the Prizren's *vali*, congratulating them on their new posts.[51] All these examples suggest involvement of doctors in the local power network that positioned them as intermediary voices for promoters of public health. For example, doctor Konstantin Mishajkov/Joanidi was initially appointed as a town physician in Bitola in 1845 and in the 1860s was chairing the Bitola *vilayet*'s sanitary service.[52]

The wealth of evidence about personal doctors who took care of different traders is quite consistent. For example, the Plovdiv Metropolitan Codex reveals a case of a merchant's death abroad, and his personal doctor was among the witnesses in settling the deceased's accounts (1801).[53] The quotes at the beginning of this chapter demonstrate that it is not difficult to trace expenditures for doctors within the commercial ledgers.

The precariousness of life also affected many family members who died of consumption and epidemics. Commercial correspondence attests to the interest not only in one's health but also concern about a family's wellbeing. For instance, in 1859 when the 14-year-old daughter of Tŭpchileshtov died in Istanbul, he received condolences from his partners of Eski Zagra.[54] One can read included within the news about the price of 21 barrels of alum that a certain merchant's wife Kalliopi was pregnant. He repeatedly mentioned in other commercial letters how his wife was feeling and announced a successful delivery of a boy.[55]

Many traders were engaged in containing diseases by offering donations for building modern hospitals. Aleksander Zako, a Zemun trader, gave 25 ducats for a hospital fund.[56] In 1869, in Varna a hospital was opened whose funding came from the will of Parashkeva Nikolau, a merchant who lived and made his fortune in Odessa.[57] In 1893, Ioannis Dimitriou, a rich merchant of Bitola and a Greek citizen living in Alexandria, left 10,000 English liras in the National Bank of Greece. He designated the money for the hospital "Blagoslovenie" in Bitola and the hospital's orphanage and elderly care center. He also bequeathed land to the Greek community in Alexandria for a hospital and schools.[58]

While school charity was commonplace, donations for hospitals were also a means of connecting diaspora merchants to their native places as well as an expression of individual success.

Merchants were also active in encouraging students studying abroad to choose pragmatic professions, and among them medicine had a prominent place. Promotion of the medical education was justified by arguments in support of public health, and traders engaged in recruiting doctors for various communities. Both Christian and Muslim merchants were involved in the selection of the Svishtov's doctor.[59] The previously mentioned trader Tŭpchileshtov arranged for a new doctor in his native village Kalofer.[60] Another example comes from Kazanlŭk. Dr. Khakanov was planning on moving to Galați; however, the same merchant, who did not "approve of the doctor's idea to leave the town", sent a request to Tosun Pasha in Edirne to appoint him as a municipal doctor in Kazanlŭk in 1875.The procedure was long: first a request came from the Kazanlŭk's council and went to the superior administrative centers: Filibe, Edirne, and Istanbul where the Medical Council would issue a certificate.[61] Thus, the hiring process involved various stakeholders: local city councils, which as already mentioned, consisted of Muslims and non-Muslims; higher bureaucracy at the district level; and professionals at the Medical Imperial School. With the exception of quarantines, all services that pertained to health were controlled by various commissions composed of professors at the Medical School, many of them non-Muslims.[62] Usually, hiring doctors, surgeons, dentists, and pharmacists were prerogatives of the *millet*.[63] Keep in mind the previously mentioned example of the Bulgarian request to Paris for a Polish doctor. However, whereas earlier the health issues were dealt with along community lines, with the introduction of the city councils these responsibilities were transferred to multiethnic bodies that took care of the whole population. Thus, records of the Skopje municipality reveal that a special doctor from Vienna was sought after to help stop the spreading of venereal disease among the civilians by soldiers.[64]

Yet most medical professionals were not well paid. For example, a tax ledger of the Greek community in Thessaloniki (1792–6) indicates the names of nine physicians. The book contains 19 categories of taxpayers, from 90 to 1,750 g., but the most affluent of the doctors paid 500 g. in taxes.[65] Therefore, many of them resorted to additional means to support and promote themselves.

Doctors and Pharmacists as Entrepreneurs and Agents of Modernity

Many foreign travelers described the connection between commerce and the medical profession. Physicians indeed sought to increase their earnings through trade. Ami Boue wrote that a certain Dr. Petrovich traded in leaches and cotton.[66] Petŭr Beron worked as a district doctor in Craiova between 1832–9 and simultaneously launched a commercial enterprise with his nephew in 1834.[67] Another example is the case of Dr. Pantazi Ioanu of Philippoupolis who lent "a substantial amount of asper" to kyr Lambrou for trade in "Trieste, Russia and Kasakia [sic]" in 1792. As entries in the log of 1808 attest, however, Dr. Pantazi not only lent but also borrowed 1,300 g. from the Plovdiv *abacı esnaf*.[68]

As the doctor of Samokov, Utenberg also became one of the founders of a glass factory in 1851 together with Yasim Bey. He invited Czech workers from Carlsbad but the enterprise was discontinued because of transportation and other issues.[69] He seems to have blended well into the local socio economic fabric by providing his professional skills and securing entrepreneurial partnerships with local Muslims. Other documents give witness to the fact that local *hekims* were also surety on behalf of merchants. To wit: in 1825, Dimitraki Khadzhitoshev borrowed 533 g. for four months under the surety of *hekim* Nikolaki.[70]

Doctors not only acted as silent partners in business enterprises but also employed commercial techniques to secure stable incomes. Some urban physicians developed a subscription system, such as Khrisant Bodourov, who arrived in Zagra from Istanbul to help control the cholera epidemics in 1848. He established a yearly subscription of 500 g., which included treatment and medicines, and had around 30 subscribers. After being paid in advance, he bought drugs in Istanbul and opened a *spitseria* in the town. The same system was practiced in Sofia by the Czech Doctor Naderne, a certain Turkish Hacı Bey, and the Bulgarian Doctor Kirkovich.[71] Further, a preserved contract between Utenberg and 17 Muslims in Samokov reveals that he also provided health services through a yearly subscription in 1849.[72] The book subscription system was widely spread since the eighteenth century, and doctors were among its prominent subscribers. As these examples show, physicians successfully adapted the principles of advanced payment from book to healthcare subscription system as a marketable service catering to the incipient middle classes.

Various publications attest to the growing interest in healthcare. For example, popular conversational guides touched upon the theme of health, including a standard question about whether the interlocutor was taking any medications.[73] Additionally, writing manuals included samples of respectful ways of addressing physicians.[74] Yet it was the newspapers that really brought about real change. Reaching out to broader social groups was facilitated by the advancement of "print capitalism" (*pace* Benedict Anderson). Thus, through newspaper advertising the medical professionals shaped public medical space. As noted earlier, most pharmaceutical products were advertised as European. For example, Dr. Ivan Bogorov advertised a plethora of drugs available in his pharmacy against fever, diarrhea and constipation, coughing, bed-wetting, all procured from Paris![75] Research on the nineteenth-century Bulgarian advertising reveals that advertisements for medicines were a very popular item, followed by announcements for medical services. Many ads introduced new products, such as pills and mineral waters. Advertising was seasonal: ads for curing malaria appeared mostly in spring and fall when the weather was changing.[76] It seems that both preventive and therapeutic advice guided consumption of lotions, pills, and oils. Many of those ads indicate the penetration of European proprietary medicines and use of mail order marketing.

Along the same lines, most of the Russian traveler M. Karlova's remarks are related to material markers of what she perceived as European expressions of progress and modernity, such as furniture, female attire, home facades, shops, and various commodities. For instance, in Ottoman Macedonia, "Almost everywhere the Hoffman drops [bottles] decorate the shelves of the Bulgarian and Albanian *hans* [inns] and their German labels are the only representatives of European culture." For her pharmacies, photographic shops, kiosks, and candy shops were signs of the European outlook of Bitola.[77] Karlova, like other travelers, tended to reduce progress/modernity to timid consumption of European lifestyles and products. Yet the local doctors and pharmacists who promoted modern services and commodities did not share her disdain. The Genov's pharmacy furnished local middle-class women with "brosse à dents, savon au goudron, milk soap, hair dye, crème Narziss, Ess. Bouquet perfume, viola vernis, lait virginale, one box pink poudre".[78] Earlier examples confirm not only the spread of proprietary drugs and related products but also the link between social status and conspicuous consumption. Still other documents attest to a process of self-promotion based on European competence. One example was the request by Panajot Kralević to Prince Miloš in 1836 seeking a job in Serbia.[79] He emphasized as his most precious attribute his European education and diplomas in medicine and surgery from Padua.

Descriptions of physicians' lifestyles also reveal that they brought with them not only new competences and ideas but also modern objects. Disclosed home auction items in 1839 of Dr. Bartolomeo Kunibert, a personal doctor of Prince Miloš, included pots and pans as well as a guitar, kanabe (sofa) and a varnished bed.[80] Further to the point of modernization, Dr. Moise Allatini supported the establishment of modern education and philanthropy in Salonika,[81] or to put it in Meropi Anastassiadou-Dumont's words, the representatives of the new professions were the "artisans de la modernization ottomane".[82] Whereas advertising promoted European-style marketing and consumption, some medical practitioners, incorporated into the social fabric through the Ottoman municipal reforms, also contributed to the building of loyalties and identifications with the Ottoman state among influential segments of the local elites. Others, though, participated actively in the nationalist movements.

Conclusions

Initially, wars and economic incorporation shaped state policy towards regulating public health and the promotion of institutional medical services. Doctors and pharmacists, as part of the urban educated elites, contributed to changing perceptions of health and its commodification by advancing ideas of science, progress, and modernity. While they were helping to make healthcare a serious social concern, there was also a growing and intimate connection between the new professional elites and the expanding power of the modern state, even more visible in the early years of post-Ottoman state-building processes. The emergence of modern professions and their close links to and dependence on the state had parallel equivalents throughout Europe and Russia. Yet these social transformations did not occur without exclusions, such as relegating midwives and healers into lower and/or obsolete categories.

Doctors and pharmacists were not only engaged in health education activities but also encouraged new lifestyles and reordering of old economic, social, and cultural interactions and practices. While social stratification was tangible among doctors' patients, there was also a conspicuous multiethnic mix among them. Merchants benefitted as much as patients and often acted as intermediaries in those social relationships, bridging market practices with social values. Newspapers opened advertising to a new realm of services, which provided medical market opportunities and developed a greater public awareness of the human body and health as precious social capital.

CHAPTER 7

FROM "THE SICK", "THE BLIND", AND "THE CRIPPLED" TO THE NATION OF "TOILING PEOPLE": VISIONS OF THE POOR IN THE LATE OTTOMAN EMPIRE AND THE EARLY TURKISH REPUBLIC

Efi Kanner

The Ottoman nineteenth century was marked by profound social and economic upheavals associated with the integration of the Empire into the world market. European economic penetration expanded throughout the period, economically destroying many productive groups.[1] At the same time, national movements in the Balkans, which led to the creation of new nation-states, created huge refugee flows that crowded the urban centers of the Empire alongside the ruined craftsmen. The unfavorable conditions for farmers, provoked by the formation of large estates in the eighteenth and the nineteenth centuries, also contributed to population influx in the cities.

These profound transformations led to unprecedented levels of poverty and accumulation of population in the towns and cities of the Empire, especially in the capital. Migration increased over the nineteenth century. According to Kemal Karpat, in 1885 almost 60 percent of the inhabitants of Istanbul had not been born there, and ten years later this percentage was even greater.[2]

One of the multifarious Ottoman responses to those upheavals was a policy of centralization. As has been shown historiographically, the creation of nation-states, economic modernization, and migrations are interrelated phenomena. Indeed, this is well demonstrated in the actions of the nineteenth-century Ottoman authorities that perceived the national movements and poor immigrants as centrifugal threats. In response, they attempted to strengthen state power by adopting new techniques of governance, which were attempts to control public space. Ottoman reforms undertaken during the Tanzimat (1839–76) were the culmination of this process of augmenting central government's authority.

On the other hand, literate circles within all communities in the Ottoman Empire and throughout the Balkans were acquainted with the Enlightenment and liberalism.[3] Dissemination of liberal thought in the Ottoman domains was concurrent with the emergence and empowerment of a new local entrepreneurial bourgeoisie, involved in banking and commerce and consisting mainly of Christians and Jews.

Thus, the Tanzimat reforms, despite their autocratic tendencies, marked the adoption of the concept of the social contract as a principle of governance.[4] The reforms provided an institutional framework for private property, non-Muslims' entrepreneurship, international commercial activity, and foreign investments.[5] Under these circumstances, Westernization of the whole society became the main goal of the Ottoman governments and of the elites of the ethno-religious communities of the Empire. Effective control of public space was considered a *sine qua non* condition of this.

It is obvious that in such a context, apart from the increasing scale of poverty, its perceptions were also transformed in tandem with changes of the meanings of wealth. If wealth was mainly associated with unobstructed business activity as an essential aspect of Westernization, poverty was associated with public disorder and was seen as an obstacle to Westernization and to free entrepreneurial activity. Groups hitherto well integrated into the Ottoman structures, such as beggars, emerged as a social problem. At the same time, however, the poor represented a human resource, which, if rationally managed, could lead the country to the much-desired Westernization, economically and politically. Therefore, poverty bore not only negative but also positive connotations as a potential to be developed for the country's sake. Controlling poverty was then considered essential not only for the control of the public space as a whole but also for the country's regeneration.

This chapter examines these new meanings of poverty in the late Ottoman Empire, as they were elaborated in various ethno-religious contexts. Scholars have so far shown that liberalism condemned Christian charity as being a part of the *ancien regime*'s worldview. According to the liberals, charity could not offer a definitive solution to the problem of poverty and entrapped the pauper in an eternal dependence on the benefactor's will.[6] This was incompatible with the qualities liberalism attributed to the individual. Furthermore, charity was, according to classical political economy, a hindrance to free operation of the labor market and a useless burden upon the community that had to support people who were able to work.[7] These liberal notions, familiar to the Ottoman intelligentsia, transcended ethno-religious boundaries informing new policies towards poverty, which were shaped along two main axes: education and job offers for the poor. Nevertheless, those concepts were not devoid of traditional or religious visions of poverty and wealth, in as much as Ottoman elites of every ethno-religious background invested them with the crucial objective of social cohesion (within each *millet* and in the empire as a whole).

A crucial parameter to be taken into consideration is the emergence of the concept of respectability in the nineteenth-century Ottoman Empire. This notion was articulated at the same time in the West, in the context of "moralizing the poor" and shaped new everyday ethics – new moral principles to be adopted not only by the indigent but also by the whole society. Work ethic, teetotalism, sexual self-control, and thrift were dominant among them. They were perceived as essential components of the "bourgeois selves", of potential agents of "progress" in capitalist nation-states. Hence, the concept of respectability designated poverty as a moral evil, and it was seen as a result of the individual's inability to benefit from the opportunities that market economy and "progress" offered.[8] In the Ottoman Empire the emergence of respectability as a social ideal could be related to the rise of medicine since the 1820s as a force of social reform.[9] The concept of respectability became the thread connecting policies towards poverty during that period.

For non-Muslims, *millets* and local communities or parishes constituted the main institutional framework for those policies, though they were not excluded from the state-run institutions. Institutionalization of the *millets* was a crucial aspect of the reforms aimed at a more effective control over non-Muslim subjects by the Porte. As a result of the centralization efforts carried out during the Tanzimat, the state took over many of the administrative powers held hitherto by the heads of the non-Muslim communities, and assigned them the tasks of education and philanthropy, apart from the duties concerning religion or family and inheritance law.[10] Education and philanthropy as a means of ethnic acculturation then became ways of integrating non-Muslims into the Ottoman structures and crucial tools of Ottomanism, the official ideology of the state. They became also a weapon of each ethno-religious community against the others in the context of ethnic and nationalist rivalries for economic primacy or cultural hegemony.

The politicization of tackling poverty and the expansion of philanthropy created among the Ottoman literati a perception of Ottoman society as an extended family. As such, it was connected with the predominance of the ideal of respectability across the whole society, regardless of ethno-religious groups or classes. These visions became more vibrant and politically instrumentalized following the Young Turk Revolution (1908) and especially during the rise of Turkish nationalism.

The abovementioned context determines the chronological frame of this study: it extends from the mid-eighteenth century, when the first Armenian and Greek Orthodox hospitals were created as places for incarceration of the poor, to the first years of the Turkish Republic, when the Kemalist principle of populism (*halkçılık*) was formulated. The primary material I use is the press as well as the regulations and annual reports of philanthropic or educational institutions of the Greek Orthodox and Turkish Muslims. For other communities, secondary sources are consulted, taking into account the inevitably unequal state of research on these issues for each ethno-religious group.[11]

From the Incarceration of the Poor to the Rise of Respectability

The first philanthropic institutions among the Orthodox took place from the mid-eighteenth century onwards. The communities of Izmir, Edirne, and Istanbul (actually, some guildsmen and state or church officers) created plague hospitals that were in fact quarantine sites for victims of epidemics.[12] Those initiatives expressed a general attitude towards the epidemics. In 1743, an Armenian plague hospital was built at Narlı Kapı, in Istanbul,[13] and a 1792 *ferman* granting permission for the repair of the Galata hospitals of the Orthodox referred also to a Jewish one in the district.[14] The Porte shared similar visions about epidemics: Ragip Pasha, the Grand Vizier of Sultan Mustafa III, planned to create a lazaretto and a plague hospital on the Prince Islands during the 1760s, but his death canceled those plans. The logic of quarantine made a break with the hitherto relevant Islamic practices, which consisted in the nursing of the sick by their own families.

Victims of plague were not the only category of people to be secluded in hospitals. In the 1792 *ferman,* Selim III referred also to the "blind" and "crippled" as potential hospital residents, underlining that "the sick" should be prevented "from wandering in the streets begging and annoying passersby" and that healthy beggars "should be sent back to their birthplaces".[15] All those people were regarded as "disturbing groups", groups to be removed from the public space. Subsequently, the hospitals were also used as places of imprisonment for the insane, criminals, deviants, or potential renegades.[16] Hence, plague victims constituted the starting point for the removal of wider groups from the public space and thus for its rearrangement.

Indeed, it was not the first time in the history of the region that these groups were regarded as a political problem. In Byzantium and the classical Ottoman era, the imperial authorities felt similarly threatened. What was novel in the late eighteenth century, however, was their seclusion in asylums, as a kind of penalty for the incapacity to earn a livelihood. This was considered a necessary step for the control of public space. Propensity towards the control of public space is manifested at both micro and macro levels. At the same time, in the eighteenth century, the need of the Porte to create new administrative mechanisms as substitutes for the obsolete *timar* system resulted in the emergence of institutions such as the Istanbul Orthodox Patriarchate as apparatuses for control of the Orthodox population all over the Empire.[17] It was one of the first steps in a centralizing procedure that went on until the final collapse of the Empire. In this context, the Patriarchate attempted for the first time, from the mid-eighteenth century and onwards, to gain control over the parishes of Istanbul through the control of their charity funds and activities. By that means it attempted to diminish parishes' administrative autonomy.[18] Throughout the nineteenth century, especially during the second half, the control of poverty became a bone of contention between clergy and laity, and between groups of laymen of every ethno-religious origin who aimed by that means to hold the reins within their communities.[19]

It can be argued that the rise of medicine in prestige and political importance in this same period is not coincidental. Actually, the Military Medical Academy was created as early as 1827 to be reorganized in 1839 upon European models. Around the end of the 1840s, 16 military hospitals were available in Istanbul, whereas in 1846 the first hospital for civilians was created under the auspices of the Valide Sultan. In 1856, the Imperial Medical Society was constituted under the Sultan's tutelage. At the same time, doctors emerged as a powerful group, as agents of a new applied knowledge necessary for social reform.[20] In the Orthodox communities, they attempted to modify the function of the hospitals transforming the former asylums and prisons into places for medical care and social integration. This undertaking led to the emergence of the concept of respectability because the epidemics that struck the Ottoman cities were attributed to moral evils; they were correlated to idleness, promiscuity, alcoholism. Hence, the need to protect society from those moral viruses was underlined.[21] One comes across these topics in public discourses formulated within all ethno-religious communities.

The concept of respectability became crucial for the control of public space in the nineteenth-century Ottoman Empire. Job stability, stable family life, respect for hygiene, abstinence from habits such as alcohol consumption, gambling, or visiting brothels were expected to be a basis for homogenization of society. Precepts of this kind multiplied significantly in journals and periodicals of every ethno-religious community.[22] In these discourses, the moral connotations of poverty prevailed over the socio-economic ones. Indigence emerged as a moral and individual deficiency rather than a socially rooted evil. This perception of poverty was linked to liberal individualism, the conception of the (male) individual as a rational and autonomous being and hence responsible for his and his dependents' fates.

Indeed, the institutionalization of the *millets* marked the victory of the new bourgeoisie of merchants, bankers, and technocrats. These groups assumed the responsibility to homogenize society on the basis of those liberal ideals. Christian, Jewish, and Moslem elites attempted to control their "own" segments of the public space, by spreading those principles to their respective communities. Thus, respectability as a corollary to individualism became the cornerstone of the control of Ottoman public space as a whole. Reforming the lives of the poor was the starting point for such an outcome since their conditions of life rendered compliance with those principles particularly difficult. It is in this context that in every community philanthropy and education emerged as the main means for achieving social cohesion through homogenization, a process led by their respective elites. The latter built their social prestige upon planning and financing such initiatives, a topic discussed in the next section.

"Helping the poor to rule their own fate": Education and Job Offers

To extend education to the whole society was the main concern in all communities at the time. Yet providing the poor with access to education was one of the major nineteenth-century novelties. Indeed, this became the principal criterion of its success, which explains why education was conceived to a large extent as a philanthropic activity.

A telling example of the philanthropically conceived education and its politicization among the Orthodox communities provides the conflict between the Greek-speaking elites and Bulgarian nationalists from the mid-nineteenth century onward by bringing ethnic tensions to the fore. Financing parochial schools and promoting poor children's schooling were among the main duties of the philanthropic associations. The latter were established as mechanisms of the parishes and communities, institutionalized since the 1870s.[23] These associations supplied meals for poor pupils, provided them with other basic needs for school attendance, such as books, warm and decent clothes, and paid their tuition fees.[24] According to the Ottoman legislation, non-Muslim schools were funded by the respective communities. Consequently, the only resources for the communal or parochial schools were tuition fees, and mostly, donations. Given the role of education as a means for ethnic acculturation, the importance of those donations becomes obvious. For the Greek Orthodox, ethnic acculturation was *inter alia* a weapon against

Bulgarian Exarchists; hence, the main part of Greek donations in this period was destined to the creation of schools in the disputed areas.[25] On the other hand, among the Bulgarians, donations were also necessary for the creation and operation of schools. Actually, in the middle of the nineteenth century an increasing number of beneficent actions was designated for educational purposes. Recent research evidences that schools and teachers were being financed by merchants in Odessa, Kishinev, Bucharest, and Vienna, or by philanthropic associations and municipalities.[26] It was the period when the first Bulgarian women's philanthropic and educational associations were also created. They particularly supported women's education by hiring female teachers, building schools, and supporting poor female students.[27]

Among the Jewish communities of the Empire, schools were for the most part created and funded by the Alliance Israélite Universelle (AIU) and European or local powerful entrepreneurs.[28] Certainly, the role of modern education in the emancipatory purposes of the Alliance concerned all social strata. But given the overwhelming majority of the poor among the Jewish communities of the Empire,[29] the achievement of this objective necessitated the schooling of poor children. Therefore, Jewish communities, like the Greek Orthodox ones, implemented mechanisms to attract them to school: funds to ensure free instruction for them, a supply of meals, clothing and shoes, and even in some cases a symbolic remuneration sum.[30] But the strongest motivation for schooling was the perspective of social mobility that school offered through secular knowledge based on linguistic, scientific, and technical studies. This outcome was expected to overcome the disadvantages experienced by Ottoman Jews in job and wealth distribution. For that reason technical education for boys and girls had great importance and vocational schools for poor children were opened in several urban centers.[31] This trend differentiated Jewish communities from Greek Orthodox ones which were less interested in vocational education and emphasized classical education instead, as a means of establishing of a Greek identity.

The Armenians also engaged in activities where education and philanthropy intersected. Armenian upper-class women, about whom most information is available, established self-help societies in the 1870s to create girls' schools in the Ottoman provinces, and trained young women as teachers. Aid to poor Armenian pupils (offers of clothes, etc.)

via fundraising was the unique means to achieve such a goal and develop education within the *millet*.[32] The existence of vocational schools in Armenian communities is also evidenced, though not sufficiently, as far as I know, to tell whether professional education was really promoted among the Armenians.[33]

Conceiving education in philanthropic terms was also the result of the Ottoman state's attitude towards it. Although the Ordinance of General Education (Maarif-i Umûmiye Nizamnâmesi), promulgated in 1869, stipulated compulsory primary education, the state renounced its responsibility for it. The residents of a district or a village were required to fund primary schools by their own means. The state was committed to pay only a quarter of the teachers' salaries, whereas the local councils had to raise the rest.[34] Donations became then once more essential for the operation of primary schools. The unwillingness of the state to assume responsibility for primary education, something that complicated considerably the access to it, was due to the Porte's main concern with training bureaucrats and technical experts in order to achieve its modernizing goals. Therefore, higher education became its priority.[35] Along these lines, the 1869 Ordinance provided for the creation of technical schools for boys and girls. The first technical schools opened in the Danube provinces where Midhat Paşa, one of the liberal architects of Tanzimat, was governor. Vocational education was also provided by the vocational orphanages (*ıslahhanes*) opened in the provincial centers of the Empire from the 1860s onwards.[36] The first girls' technical school was created in Yedikule (1869), and female technical education was to be further developed in the following years and included Midwifery and Nursing Schools.[37]

In spite of the differences, educational mechanisms in all ethno-religious contexts had something in common: they aimed to integrate the new generation of the poor into norms of modernity linked to respectability, such as exemption of children from breadwinning labor, new patterns of time discipline and mobility control, and new cognitive horizons. Therefore, the character of socialization of these generations changed. They were socialized through the ideals of work and social progress: the progress of the *millet* and the empire as a whole.[38] Social progress was a new notion that created new social expectations: boys – and occasionally girls – were trained as professionals (mainly teachers or skilled workers) and brought up to be independent heads of households who would inculcate the principles of work, discipline, and progress in their offspring, and contribute to the progress of the whole society. Individual welfare was connected to social welfare. In this process new "technologies of the self" were shaped. I borrow this term, coined by Michel Foucault, as "the ways in which individuals experience, understand, judge and conduct themselves".[39] The education of the poor was intended to construct a bourgeois self. While the ideal of self-made man was one of its main components, it was not the only one; the poor were for the first time perceived as political subjects. They were expected to economically regenerate their respective communities, as well as the entire Ottoman realm, and to politically defend those communities from their enemies.[40] These new social perspectives for the poor, and the promise of an upward social mobility through education, account to a large extent for the cultural hegemony of the lay bourgeois groups that headed communities and their educational mechanisms, over the clergy.

Those new norms presupposed the transformation of the family structure: the breadwinning activity should be exclusively the father's task, something that could free the mother from this duty and enable her to devote herself fully to homemaking and bringing up children. Given that these messages were first spread among literate groups, the poor obviously constituted a point of departure for the construction of "childhood" as a distinct social category and for the spread of the Victorian ideal of domesticity across the whole social scale. Indicatively enough, in some cases, parents who refused to send their children to school for any reason, or did not care about their proper school attendance or behavior, were considered a legitimate terrain of social intervention and were stigmatized as "needy", regardless of their income.[41]

This crusade for school attendance had to do with the destruction of many guilds and the state repression of beggary, which traditionally consisted of a considerable number of children. School education then could be considered an alternative apprenticeship mechanism, a substitute for those of the guild, and for beggary, both of which were no longer sufficient or socially accepted as such.

All these social interventions mark a modification in the meaning of philanthropy. Almsgiving became a secondary activity of the Greek Orthodox philanthropic associations, as their regulations and annual reports show; priority was given to education and job offers for the poor. The latter became the responsibility of new women's philanthropic associations and were institutionalized too as community regulations.[42] Women's philanthropic associations opened garment workshops to provide work for destitute women. The Ladies' Philanthropic Association of Pera (Stavrodromi) was the first one to undertake such an initiative in 1876. Its workshop developed rapidly to include several departments and employ 416 female workers in 1913, apart from the women working at home. This initiative was soon emulated by female philanthropic associations in Greek Orthodox communities all over the empire.[43] Disavowal of almsgiving, distinction between the deserving and the undeserving poor, and emphasis on the moralizing effects of work were commonplaces in their discourses and practices.[44] Indeed, to inculcate poor women with the ideals of independence and responsibility, identified with masculinity by classical liberalism, makes a break with the Victorian ideal of domesticity.

These initiatives were emulated by other ethno-religious groups, though not to the same extent. In the 1880s, the AIU opened such workshops, which offered apprenticeships and were annexed to vocational schools for both sexes. As in the case for Greek Orthodox interventions, these workshops were also invested with a moralist mission.[45] As for the Muslims, the only initiative of this kind before 1908 that I know of was the creation of a similar workshop in Istanbul in 1896 by erudite Muslim ladies collaborating with the weekly women's journal *Hanımlara Mahsus Gazete.*[46]

These interventions, which had no equivalent for men, were regarded as a deterrent from prostitution, a perspective deriving from the presumed lack of moral stamina in poor women. An equally threatening possibility was desertion from the ethno-religious body in favor of the Exarchate, Catholicism, or Protestantism. In this case poor women's children would be a literal loss to the community, whereas prostitution would be a symbolic loss – a blow to its prestige and cultural influence.

An outstanding example of the dynamics this trend generated is the Philergos Etaireia (Society of Friends of Labor), constituted in Istanbul in 1866 by prominent elite members of every ethno-religious background: Cléanthi Scalieri, president of the Masonic lodge Progress; the Jewish banker Aguste de Castro; the Greek Orthodox bankers Christakis Zografos and Georgios Zarifis; and the Armenian liberal Sakızlı Ohaness

Paşa, professor at the School of Political Science, figured among its founders, whereas Baron Goldsmith, Husni Paşa, the Police Chief, and the Crown Prince Murat were among the society's patrons.[47] The society's multiethnic membership, unusual, as far as I know, among the philanthropic associations of the time, attested to the high place of Ottomanism and liberalism in its discourse. This had also to do with the Society's masonic affiliation.

The Society was modeled upon European mutual aid societies with the aim to lend money to destitute craftsmen "without distinction of religion, sex or ethnicity", as it was constantly underlined.[48] Charity was regarded as "a route to the annihilation of [the] human race", while the Society was "helping the poor to rule their own fate".[49] This was considered, among other things, a necessary condition for the industrial development of the empire and its economic independence from the West.[50] The vision of an economically independent empire legitimized collaboration among the Ottoman ethnicities and even the absence of sex discrimination in the society's requirements for disbursing financial aid. Indeed, three women were financed by it: a limited number, however, marked a break with traditions. Encouraging women's paid work was something about which the society boasted strongly.[51]

All these steps make an exceptional case out of the Philergos Etaireia, exceptional even to the classical liberal discourses it was inspired by, envisaging a society of equality among men. This is also indicative of the intellectual profusion in the Ottoman society of the time, in a society elaborating "its own version of the Enlightenment".[52]

Ottoman Society as an Extended Family: the Emergence of a Respectable Public Sphere

Traditional and religious visions of poverty were nevertheless strong components of these novel concepts. The abovementioned undertakings were very often perceived, among other things, as religious missions. Among the Greek Orthodox elites, philanthropy was given traditional Christian meaning: it was presented as an antidote to luxury and ostentation, as a unique means for exculpating wealth. Within this discourse wealth was "a sacred gift Providence offered to chosen people in order to comfort the suffering".[53] The Ladies' Philanthropic Association of Pera presented itself as an "alerted guardian of Christ's yard watchful that no lamb is in need to be roofed and fed in another yard".[54] Apart from that, local schools were, as mentioned earlier, parochial institutions and built, for the most part, near the respective churches. Religious courses had an important place in their curricula.[55] Additionally, the educational boom in the Greek Orthodox communities from the 1870s onwards was due to the need to defend the Patriarchate's authority against the Bulgarian Exarchate. But religious studies also continued in the Bulgarian schools, even after the escalation of the conflict with the Patriarchate and the Greek elites of the *millet*. In most places, the emphasis was on education in the Bulgarian language and on separation of ethnically mixed schools but not on secularization.[56] Along those lines, religious instruction, in the sense of moral training, obtained an important place in the curricula of the AIU schools that had first targeted poor children.[57] This was also the case for Armenian education of the Gregorian, Catholic, and Protestant sects: Catholic and Protestant missions undertook extended educational and philanthropic activity, especially among the Armenians of Anatolia.[58]

Imperial – especially Hamidian – philanthropy also bore strong religious connotations. This was manifested in almsgiving during the sultan's visits to the mosque for Friday prayers, in the organization of circumcision ceremonies for poor boys, or in the construction of poorhouses and children's hospitals. According to Nadir Özbek, these were intended to disseminate a patriarchal image of the ruler, which was at the same time integrated in scientific, modernist, and positivist discourse.[59] Given the pan-Islamic policies of Abdülhamid II, these initiatives were expected to improve the latter's public profile throughout the Muslim world and to be at the same time a proof, in Western public opinion, that Islam was compatible with progress. An Islamic meaning was also given by public opinion to the fund-raising campaign for war orphans and the families of wounded soldiers in the Ottoman–Greek War of 1897, despite the fact that the Sultan was very careful not to alienate his Greek Orthodox subjects by such an initiative.[60] Furthermore, Benjamin Fortna has highlighted the emphasis on Islamic morality in the new "secular" schools during the Hamidian period, as a typical example of the "indigenization" of modern education.[61] On a grassroots level, Islam also continued to be the cornerstone of everyday local philanthropic activity, as was happening with religion in other confessional groups.[62]

Actually, these religious meanings were old vessels holding new contents. The aim of integration in the *millets* and, therefore, social cohesion within them meant also legitimization of the imperial *status quo*. In other words, philanthropic activity constituted a means of integration into the imperial order. Thus, the perception of the Greek Orthodox community as an extended family, very common in the writings of nineteenth-century Greek philanthropists,[63] corresponds to a similar conception of the "Ottoman nation" dominant in the pro-Hamidian press.[64] In this way, allegedly harmonious family relationships were intended to extend throughout the whole society. This was an attempt to exorcize any kind of social conflicts, including separatist nationalisms, but also to still the echo of labor and socialist movements.

Imperial donations in favor of various communities seem to enhance this image. Ottoman high-ranked bureaucrats, bankers, and foreign diplomats of every origin also financed associations, schools or hospitals of various ethno-religious affiliations. For example, the Russian ambassadress Ekaterina Ignatyeva put under her auspices the Greek Orthodox Educational Association of Büyük Dere. The interventions of Nikolay and Ekaterina Ignatyeva resulted also in the annual subvention of 1,300 rubles granted to this association by the Tsar.[65] The Armenian Artin Çamiç offered to the Greek schools of Arnavutköy his state-granted right over fishing in the Bosphorus.[66] The Greek banker Christakis Zôgraphos, for his part, offered 1,300 Turkish liras for the orphanage founded by Midhat Paşa.[67] Those activities and the visibility they gained in the press created the image of a large philanthropic community challenging ethno-religious segmentation. Commissions for war refugees or the victims of natural disasters, established by imperial decrees, presided over by the Grand Vizier or members of the imperial family and comprised of prominent members of all confessions could be regarded as symbolic representations of this community.[68] That this philanthropic community was headed by the paternal figure of the sultan was an additional means of legitimization of Ottoman authority and integration into its structures.

Representation of the *millets* or of the Ottoman society in general as extended families had gendered dimensions by default. The representation of the fatherly figure of the sultan as the head of the "Ottoman family" was constantly confirmed by hymns to his generosity towards the poor and all his subjects chanted in various philanthropic ceremonies.[69] Similar images were dominant in the public discourses formulated in various ethno-religious communities. Among the Greek Orthodox, the great donors (mostly bankers and merchants) were consequently proclaimed "fathers of the poor and the nation". Their benevolence was presented as a guarantee of the progress of the *millet*. The obituaries published in the press are very revealing, in that respect. The donors' benevolence was associated with their dominant position in the Ottoman economy. They were praised as self-made men distinguishing themselves in banking and commerce out of their cleverness and industriousness. Philanthropy as an act of devotion to the *millet* and the nation derived exactly from these qualities. They were also presented as virtuous and devoted husbands and fathers.[70]

This was also the case of the Jewish communities, especially in Salonica. There the hegemonic model of masculinity was epitomized in the figure of Moise Allatini, prominent merchant and philanthropist.[71] This was related to the dominance of the entrepreneurial body in the community structures. Thus, economic dominance in the city was expressed in the field of philanthropy not only within the Jewish community but also towards all the other groups. Benevolent acts reflected this group's hegemonic position in a public sphere comprising the whole city; hence, Moise Allatini was proclaimed the "father of Salonica".[72]

Philanthropic discourse was also articulated in terms of male generosity and the building civil society in Bulgarian communities. For example, the two brothers Evlogi and Khristo Georgievi, merchants and entrepreneurs, were the founders of Sofia University. Also, many local schools bear the names of male philanthropists from the late Ottoman era, such as Ivan Denkoglu in Sofia.[73]

Under these circumstances wealth was, by and large, represented as a male attribute. Such a vision of wealth as a result of male business activities was also translated into assertions of each *millet*'s primacy in the Westernization project. On the other hand, women's philanthropic role was perceived in terms of absence of breadwinning activity, of their being "unpolluted" by the brutality of the market, and thus sensitive towards human suffering. This dimension was equally highlighted in the press. In the obituaries, female philanthropists were presented as wives, sisters or mothers of the male benefactors. What was mostly praised in their case was devotion to their families, an extension of which was their concern for the poor. Female philanthropic activity was also presented as an extension of motherhood. Only rarely were female philanthropists praised as benefactors in their own right.[74] They were rather recognized as managers of male donations in favor of the poor. These distinctions are also indicative of the gendered hierarchy of the "philanthropic community", and reflect the hierarchy within the middle-class family.

The above mentioned male and female models of philanthropy corroborated the value of respectability. As such they were part and parcel of the Ottoman public sphere. The notion of the Ottoman public sphere has been already elaborated by Özbek who linked its construction with philanthropic activity.[75] What is interesting for my purpose is that the public sphere was conceived as a respectable one: not only as purged of those who rejected and/or threatened its values but also built on their very antipodes. The "unrespectable" were depicted as the "mob", a notion comprising categories from beggars and criminals to professional groups such as boatmen or porters but also the proponents of separatist nationalisms. Rejection of respectability meant hostility towards Ottoman society and its political authority and vice versa. Such an argument necessarily supported the measures taken by the Porte against the criminality of the lower strata. Measures such as correcting houses or the control of brothels and the closure of gambling houses were highly praised by the Greek press whereas Ottoman Turkish newspapers such as *Sabah* appealed for stricter state measures against begging.[76] The "unrespectable" groups were then defined not only as undeserving poor, but also as "dangerous classes" destroying the economy and the international image of the country. Discourse about them, therefore, constituted a call for further centralization of power and expression of loyalty towards the imperial order. Özbek attributes Abdülhamid's reluctance to police begging strictly, among other things, to his priority to repress efficiently separatist nationalisms.[77] Still, in the Greek press the "dangerous classes" were identified with the latter. Indicatively enough, it was not only the Bulgarians who were so identified but also the Jewish migrants to Palestine were included in this notion; the immorality attributed to them was connected with the fear of another separatist nationalism threatening the Empire's integrity.[78] Furthermore, in Greek popular literature, criminals were very often Armenians, Italian Catholics, etc.[79]

Identification of the "dangerous classes" with the ethnic other was hardly surprising taking into account that ethnic acculturation was considered a means to minimize the "other's" influence over the poor in each ethno-religious community. On the other hand, philanthropic aid to the ethnic others was intended to enhance the prestige of the ethno-religious elites involved and to ensure their cultural hegemony in the Ottoman public sphere. Influence and control over poverty was only one aspect of the rivalry among various ethno-religious groups over control of the public sphere, alongside economic antagonism.

The Poor and the Rise of Turkish Nationalism

Indeed, unequal access to the benefits of Westernization among the various ethno-religious groups of the Empire provoked rivalry between them, something that took on the character of national antagonisms in the first decades of the twentieth century. From 1909 onwards, when the initial call of the Committee of Union and Progress for cooperation of all ethno-religious communities of the Empire faded in favor of Turkification politics, the creation of an indigenous Muslim entrepreneurial class became the main goal of the state. This led to a crusade against Christian entrepreneurs. The poor were once again the central point of this politics as potential actors and objects of it. The participation of the boatmen and porters in the boycott of foreign products and Christians' shops was essential for its success. At the same time, the Young Turk policy of centralization resulted in a repressive legislation outlawing strikes and restricting labor organizations. Additionally, a new law was passed associating vagrancy with "potential criminality" and imposing a strict policing of the urban poor in order to discipline them through work.[80]

Participation of the poor in the struggle for economic regeneration of the country was considered a necessary condition for its success. A plethora of Turkish Muslim philanthropic associations were founded for that reason, aiming at educating and vocationally training the poor. Those undertakings were again often gender-centered. Many of these associations focused on women's insertion into the economically active population through education and vocational training and they endeavored to open schools for poor and orphan girls.[81] The objectives of the Osmanlı Kadınları Çalıştırma Cemiyeti Islamiyyesi (Islamic

Association for the Promotion of Women's Employment) are revealing in this respect. This Association was founded by high-ranking state bureaucrats in 1916. It was intended to "protect women by helping them to honest breadwinning through work".[82] For its part, the educational institution for women Bilgi Yurdu Müessessi (Hearth of Knowledge) founded by Ahmet Edib in April 1917, offered, apart from technical courses, courses of reading and writing, music, mathematics, history, geography and even "*savoir vivre*",[83] apparently as a means for smoother integration into the urban fabric.

Moreover, not only in Istanbul, but also throughout the Empire, dressmaking workshops operated on a commercial basis with a view to securing employment for needy women and thus strengthening local production. Poor women were once more perceived as the most vulnerable part of their community as well as the cornerstone of its very existence. These interventions were similar to those initiated by the Greek Orthodox since the 1870s. The cultural interaction between the various ethno-religious communities becomes once more obvious. This is evident even in the similarities in the structure of the philanthropic associations: in the establishment of administrative boards and the division of responsibilities between their members, in the distinction between regular and honorary members, and the publication of balance sheets. The aim of these Muslim initiatives was to politicize the broadest possible spectrum of the poor, especially women, to integrate them into the Turkish nation – a still fluid concept – mainly after 1912. Female labor, being a *sine qua non* condition of industrialization, acquired a great importance in the context of the projected economic reinforcement of the country through Muslim entrepreneurship that was expected to eliminate the Christian business class.

It is well known that persecutions of the Christian element in the last years of the Empire helped this objective come to reality, something that was completed in the context of the Turkish Republic. The new Turkish nation was perceived as the nation of the "toiling people, poor people, who work to save their lives and independence", as Kemal himself put it.[84] "Toiling people" was conceived as a classless collective subject. It was identified with the whole nation, a nation untouched by internal differentiations and conflicts. Its leading productive groups, merchants, farmers, artisans, and workers were supposed to have no distinct class interests and to cooperate harmoniously for the nation's progress.[85] This vision constituted the principle of populism (*halkçılık*), one of the six fundamental pillars of the official ideology of Turkey that were incorporated in the Constitution in 1937. Meanwhile, Christian and Jewish communities were relegated to minority status, which put an end to their role as pioneers of patriotic work ethics, a role now undertaken by the "pure" Turks.

Conclusions

The abovementioned initiatives took place in an era where "progress" and "modernization" were catchwords in the Ottoman public debate. These notions were most of the time identified with various versions of Westernization, conceived in turn as a weapon against dependence on the West. The establishment of a "modern" and independent state, economically and politically, required the mobilization of all social resources. "Helping the poor to rule their own fate" through education and job offers was inscribed in this perspective. As already mentioned, the poor were expected to consciously defend their ethno-religious community and the empire as a whole from their enemies and to work for their economic advancement. In this respect, the liberal concept of the rational and independent individual constituted the basis of Ottoman citizenship/patriotism.

Though dominant configurations of citizenship were male-centered, women's patriotic mobilization through motherhood, literally or metaphorically perceived, was another important novelty of that era. Motherhood was elevated from a biological function to a social and patriotic one. In this way the dichotomy between the public male space and the private female one was legitimized. On the other hand, the new meanings of motherhood undermined it. Patriotic expectations from women ushered them – as it did with many groups of men – into the political foreground for the first time. Women were therefore ascribed a role which, by definition, set them out of the bounds of the private sphere within which they were identified. Patriotic motherhood emerged as a classless value since it concerned women of any social origin. The female body thereby evidently acquired political connotations. It bore a new notion of citizenship, based on natural laws with which the medical discourse associated the female sex; a citizenship that, despite the various exclusions, offered women a political gravity unknown in the past.

Liberal individualism and its corollary, the concept of respectability, were the cornerstones of Ottoman patriotism and the main elements of establishing social cohesion within each ethno-religious community and in the whole Ottoman society. Through them poverty became the point of departure towards an overall social reform along the lines of new social values: domesticity, social ascension, and education. The notion of respectability and its opposite, apart from expanding the scope of both deserving and undeserving poor, also contributed to the emergence of a middle-class version of civil society. The apparent contradiction between the middle-class origin of this value and the classless character it was invested with allowed for the cultural hegemony of middle-class groups of entrepreneurs, intellectuals or scientists.

Those groups' hegemony was constructed and strengthened through educational and philanthropic activities. Those interventions constituted fields of cultural osmosis but also of competition among the *millets* and thus contributed to ethnic fragmentation in tandem with economic antagonism. Whereas religious components were strong in them, the new bourgeois values and the objective of patriotic mobilization from below marked a process of secularization of the public space and the actors within it. Turkish nationalism and subsequent Kemalist reforms accomplished this process.

PART III

TRANSNATIONAL NETWORKS AND EXCHANGES

CHAPTER 8

THE RICH IN EIGHTEENTH- AND NINETEENTH-CENTURY ARBANASI: NETWORKS OF PROSPERITY

Gergana Georgieva

Arbanasi is a small village in central Bulgaria, situated in the lower parts of the Balkan Mountains, at the very center of the Balkan peninsula. From the fifteenth through nineteenth century, it was formally defined as a village, while its actual socio-economic profile was that of a small town, more focused on trade and specialized in some crafts than on agriculture. The profile of its Albanian founders strongly influenced its economic development. Arbanasi illustrates a success story of a prosperous village that was well connected within the Ottoman administrative and ecclesiastical structures, *Phanariot*, and commercial webs within and beyond the Ottoman realm as well as in its own vicinity. Such a milieu created a stratum of well-to-do merchants and craftsmen who were both products and promoters of Arbanasi's prolonged prosperity.

Early History: Origin and Status

It is believed that the founders of Arbanasi were Orthodox Christian Albanians, stockbreeders, from the region of Epirus[1] who migrated, or had been forcibly moved, by the Ottomans in the fifteenth century; an event that overlaps with the process of conquering the Albanian lands by the Ottomans. The names of the settlement – Arnabud, Arnavutkoy, Alvanitohori – confirm that Albanian origin was one of the main markers of its early inhabitants. In addition, in later documents, such as a *firman* (1810) of Sultan Mahmud II, Arbanasi and the nearby Lyaskovets, Gorna and Dolna Oryahovitsa are called "*arnabud kariyeleri*", Albanian villages.[2]

In the early centuries of the Ottoman rule, Arbanasi managed to secure privileged status as both a *waqf* and a *dervendzhi* village, which had an impact on its economic prosperity and connections with the Ottoman capital. Arbanasi provides an illustration of the way that Ottoman notables established large land estates. The gradual expansion was a result not only of the purchase of new lands, but also of the use of illegal means for appropriation of more lands and by turning them into inalienable protected property known as *waqf*. Arbanasi became such a *waqf* (pious endowment) in the sixteenth century. Its taxes were used for building mosques, *medreses* (Islamic religious schools), *turbes* (Sufi religious centers) and other public buildings in Istanbul and Rodoschuk. Significant amounts of its money were also sent to Mecca and Medina.[3]

Meanwhile, local Christians received a number of privileges that affected the economic development of the village as well. It received a *dervendzhi* status, which gave additional benefits to its inhabitants. Residents of the *derventdzhi* villages in the mountainous areas were required to maintain the security of the pass (*dervent*), which is located nearby. In return, they were granted semi-military status and had the right to hold firearms. Because of their special duties to the state, the *dervendzhi*s were exempted from certain taxes. The claim that the village was situated in a deserted dangerous place was probably exaggerated, in order to reinforce the importance of the place as a passageway. Its residents used this pretext to secure the privileged status, tax exemptions, and especially the right to own arms, which helped them to protect their property and homes. That security attracted many newcomers.

From the middle of the sixteenth to the late eighteenth century Arbanasi experienced a remarkable economic boom that is well documented in the available sources. There was an impressive increase in the village's population. At the end of the sixteenth century there were about 1,600 inhabitants, while in the mid-seventeenth century its population reached over 2,000 people. That constant migration towards the settlement considerably affected its size and was the main cause for its growth. There is evidence that the main part of the immigrants came from the surrounding Bulgarian villages. Even the inhabitants of the nearby town of Tarnovo were attracted by the Arbanasi's economic conditions.[4] Boyan Gyuzelev claims, however, that there was a second wave of migrants from Epirus – Albanians and Greeks who were probably in contact with their relatives and fellow-countrymen in Arbanasi.[5] Thus, Arbanasi developed as a multiethnic, mainly Christian, settlement reaching around 2,000 inhabitants.

These data can be used as indirect evidence of the economic prosperity of Arbanasi. The significant population growth was a combination of natural increase and positive migration. The new settlers were apparently attracted by the economic development and the special status of the village; namely, the number of privileges and tax exemptions, the security and the economic prosperity. Although Arbanasi preserved its official status as a village (*kariye*) according to the Ottoman territorial structure, its size and characteristics more resemble a small town. Actually, its economic profile and prosperity were based mainly on commerce and crafts, instead of agriculture and stockbreeding, which were the basis of the rural economy.

Economic Prosperity: Many Livelihoods

Arbanasi had several livelihoods that characterize its economic profile: viticulture, silkworm breeding, horticulture, stockbreeding, and crafts related to processing of animal products. Different branches of trade were typical for the settlement, for example the wholesale trade of animals (*dzheleplak*). This trade in particular was very important for the economic development of the village: it contributed greatly to the prosperity and wealth and to the development of international networks. The vicinities around Arbanasi lacked arable lands for the development of agriculture, but they were very suitable for stockbreeding with its large pasture areas. That is probably the main reason why its first settlers chose the place.

Stockbreeding became the basis of the development of various crafts – soap making, furriery, meat processing. There were rich merchants (*dzhelepkeshans*) who organized the whole process of buying, fattening, and slaughtering the animals, as well as the processing of animal products. For example, a sultanic decree (1714) mentions that the population of Arnavutkoy was engaged in *dzheleplak* and the production of fat and butter.[6] That is how Dimitar Papazov[7] explains the livelihood of the village in the nineteenth century: "Many of its residents engaged in *dzheleplak*. That is, they were buying cattle for fattening: buffalo, cows, oxen, raised in large pastures (*sovats*)." He remembers the names of some famous *dzheleps* from the second half of the nineteenth century.[8] Every autumn about 500–600 animals were slaughtered in the slaughterhouses (*salhanas*) of Arbanasi, Gorna Oryahovitza, and Tarnovo. There were two *salhanas* in Arbanasi – one belonging to h. Kiro Rusovich and the other to Panayot Panonchev.[9] Products like dried meat, sausages, and smoked tongue were sent to Istanbul. The other famous product sent to the capital was bone marrow (*chervish*), used as a substitute for butter. In addition, the melted tallow was used to make candles and soap. "The village had ten factories called *kerhani* for production of soap and a few workshops for tallow candles."[10] A tax register (*temettuat defter*) of Arbanasi from 1845[11] proves also that the production of soap was one of the main occupations in the nineteenth century. According to this document, the guild of the soap makers (*sapundzhi*) had 86 members (only Christians), who constituted 37 percent of the working population of Arbanasi (232 registered Muslim and non-Muslim men). The soap makers dealt not only with production but also with trade of soap in the neighboring villages.[12] This fact explains the high income of the soap makers in Arbanasi. According to the *temettuat defter*, five representatives of the *sapundzhi* guild were among the richest people recorded in Arbanasi with incomes above 1,000 g. Some of the soap makers had more than one occupation. There is a case of a man who was registered as *dzhelep* in one source and soap maker in another.[13]

While land was not fertile for grains it was appropriate for viticulture. For example, a decree from 1639 marks the changing status of the land in the area from fields into vineyards.[14] The document is evidence for the development of viticulture in the region: people preferred to plant and grow vines even by breaking the imperial orders, which prohibited the change of the land status. This process can be traced in later documents: a *temettuat defter* from the mid-nineteenth century shows that 73 percent of the households in Arbanasi owned vineyards. Viticulture and wine were a major sector of the economy in this region. Records of taxation on alcohol also provide evidence for this massive production: taxes were paid by 62 percent of the 232 households in the village in the mid-nineteenth century.[15]

Another livelihood specific for the area was sericulture or silkworm breeding. There is evidence for its practice since the first half of the sixteenth century. In the following centuries Arbanasi was a significant exporter of silk, including Italy.[16] Harsh climate conditions, which affected the sericulture, were recorded in the marginal notes of some local liturgical books. They were considered probably as significant local events: "23 April 1767 – there was a snow and cold wind. Vineyards and mulberry trees were parched"; "May 1772 – it was a great cold and the mulberry trees were damaged."[17] Moreover, part of the immovable property of the churches and monasteries in the region of Tarnovo consisted of mulberry gardens.[18] Papazov claims that the silkworm breeding was a "favorite" occupation of Arbanasi residents because of its lucrative nature. About 500 *okkas* of thin silk were produced each year. Wearing silk clothes was part of the lifestyle of both male and female inhabitants. The *temettuat* registers from the mid-nineteenth century show that there was only one person recorded as professional silk producer,[19] while 43 people had mulberry trees registered as their immovable property along with other agricultural plots and farmlands. The total number of trees reached 116 units. So, silkworm breeding was perceived as additional income for the households.

Commercial Webs

As the previous sections have shown, commerce was one of the main activities of Arbanasi residents. They were involved not only in local but also in international trade. In his report to the Vatican from 30 August 1685, the Catholic Bishop of Nicopolis, Anton Stefanov noted that Arbanasi merchants maintained contacts with Italy, Hungary, Poland, and Russia. It is known, for example, that the merchant Dimitar Hintiliyata traded in India and Persia.[20] A document of the local *Sharia* court in the nearby Tarnovo from 1689 mentioned that 52 people from Arbanasi were trading in Polish and Hungarian lands.[21] The marginal notes in some books give evidence about trade contacts with Germany, Russia, and the Danubian Principalities in the eighteenth century.[22]

The main directions of Arbanasi's commerce were Wallachia, Moldavia, and Transylvania. Local aristocrats and princes from these regions gave special privileges to Arbanasi merchants.[23] As a result, the latter developed long-lasting contacts and established their own local offices there. Indeed, some of the Arbanasi merchants became involved in the management and organization of the local trade structure of Sibiu and Braşov.[24] All "Greek"[25] merchants in Transylvania were organized in their own company, which was granted certain privileges by the Prince of Transilvaniya George I Rákóczi in 1636. They not only received extended access to the Transylvanian markets and fairs, but also were able to establish their own council and to act as a community. According to the records of the company in Sibiu and Braşov, several Arbanasi residents sat on the board of the company in the first half of the seventeenth century.[26]

Most historians claim that there was a serious disruption in the village's development in the late eighteenth century. The raids of *kirdzhali* bands devastated Arbanasi, causing migrations of the population and it never recovered but progressively decayed in the nineteenth century. The memoires of some local people, such as Papazov and George Kardzhiev, however, prove that in the nineteenth century Arbanasi still acted as a center of commerce in the area. Kardzhiev argues that not the towns of Tarnovo and Gorna Oryahovitsa, but the nearby village of Arbanasi was a commercial center that attracted even international traders.[27] Papazov mentions the "*beratlis*" merchants as some of the richest and most successful men in Arbanasi. The term refers to the category *Avrupa tucarları* (European merchants), namely Ottoman subjects who enjoyed special privileges based on a certificate (*berat*) issued by the sultan.[28] Among their economic and legal privileges were free travel; independence from the local *Sharia* court; lower duties, and some tax exemptions.[29] The main advantage was the lower custom duties: instead of paying the regular 8 percent they were paying only 3 percent. There were at least three merchants in the nineteenth-century Arbanasi who hold *berats*: Radi Todorov Mazretov, George Anagnost, and Peter Efendi.[30]

Not only the international but also the local trade with surrounding villages was widespread in the nineteenth century. The Ottoman register of 1845 reveals three different categories of small dealers: *parchadzhi*, *charakchi*, and *cherchi*. All three terms generally refer to retailers trading in drapery. There was only one *cherchi* in mid-nineteenth-century Arbanasi: Avram, son of Christo, with an income of 675 g.[31] There were

12 *charakchi*, all of them Christians, with annual incomes between 300 and 1,035 g.; 8 *parchadzhis* with significant incomes from 600 to 2,030 g. Indeed, *parchazhis* were among the richest people in the village. As it was mentioned above, many of the *sapundzhis* (11) and coppersmiths (6) were engaged in small trade in the nearby villages; also, one could add the 10 grocers (*bakkals*) to that group.[32] Thus, we can count 48 heads of households involved in commercial activities, according to official Ottoman documents. About 21 percent of the 232 families in the village gained their annual income through retail sales. Like the urban centers, Arbanasi had its own commercial area – *charshi*, located in the center.[33] The village probably also had a fair of local importance – it is mentioned in an Ottoman document from 2 August 1868.[34]

In conclusion, the economic profile of Arbanasi demonstrates that the economic life did not diminish but actually continued to grow, and that wealth and commercial contacts had an impact on Arbanasi's elite lifestyle and culture.

Culture and Profile of the Rich in Arbanasi

Arbanasi had some distinguished characteristics in comparison to the surrounding Bulgarian villages. It was not only a multiethnic settlement but also a center that strongly supported and promoted Greek culture in the Bulgarian lands. This strong connection with Greek culture and language was a result of three factors. First, the founders of the village were believed to be (Hellenized) Albanians and maybe some Greeks from the region of Epirus. Second, Greek language and culture spread considerably in all Balkan territories of the Ottoman Empire in the eighteenth and nineteenth centuries. This Greek language dominance was a result of the influence of the Constantinople Patriarchate – the main religious institution of all Orthodox Christians in the Ottoman Empire, whose high officials were mainly Greeks and Greek was the main liturgical language in all Ottoman Balkan territories. In addition, a net of well-developed Greek schools spread there, too. Most people learn to speak, read, and write in Greek. Thus, the Orthodox Christians accepted the Greek culture as an elite, high culture of their community. In fact, Raymond Detrez claims that the development of Greek culture is possible even without the presence of a strong ethnic Greek majority[35] because it developed also as part of the traditions of the Orthodox

Christian communities. Third, Greek was the language of commerce: all merchants had to know Greek in order to manage their business contacts and contracts. Hence, Greek became the *lingua franca* of the Ottoman Balkans in the eighteenth and nineteenth centuries.

In the nineteenth century the Hellenization of Bulgarian society reached impressive dimensions. Moreover, some towns became nuclei of Greek culture and traditions. They strongly supported the Constantinople Patriarchate and its elite. Arbanasi and nearby Tarnovo were two of those focal points.[36] The Bishop of Tarnovo actually used Arbanasi as his second residence.[37] Moreover, many high clergymen from the Patriarchate, Mount Athos, Jerusalem, and Antioch visited the village.[38] Because of its prosperity, Arbanasi was also a stop for many mendicant monks.[39]

The dissemination of Greek culture and the connection with the Patriarchate, together with good commercial relations, were probably the reasons for the development of a close connection between Arbanasi and the Wallachian aristocracy. After the seventeenth century Wallachian and Moldavian rulers were chosen from among some *Phanariot* families from Istanbul, and closely connected with the Patriarchate, so the Greek line was visible and strong there. Wallachian princes supported the Greek school in Arbanasi and frequently donated to its churches. Some Wallachian aristocratic families even built their own residences there.[40]

Greek was the language of religious, educational, and private spheres. There is no doubt that Greek was the main liturgical language in all churches of Arbanasi till 1878.[41] The only school was the Greek school, which developed and modernized in the nineteenth century; it was in the early 1870s that Bulgarian language and grammar were introduced there. It is very indicative that the home language of all families in Arbanasi was Greek.[42] Kardzhiev recounts his father reading and singing in the church only in Greek.[43] Many others, like Konstantin Jireček, who visited the village, claim that even in the late nineteenth century the language of the residents was Greek.[44]

After the *kirdhazlis* raid in 1798 many Arbanasi residents migrated and the ethnic composition of the village changed considerably. The empty houses were occupied by new settlers from the surrounding mountainous villages. Even after these considerable changes, the tradition of Greek language and culture was preserved. Kardzhiev asserts that the new residents spoke Greek as well as the old ones.[45] This fast adoption was a result not only of the privileges associated with the language but also with the understanding that Greek culture was an elite culture. Panteli Kisimov, who was born in Tarnovo, remembers that all peasants from the surrounding villages were called "*vulgaros*" – common people, while "every Bulgarian who knew Greek considered himself *evgenos* – noble."[46]

There are several categories of people that can be listed decisively among the rich of Arbanasi. Some indirect evidence has been provided in the inscriptions that mention names of church-founders and donors. Giving examples of Bulgarian presence in the village, Papazov lists the names of a number of donors: the iconostasis of the church "St. Demetrius" was made with the help of "God's servants Dimo and Lada" (note from 1794); the names of Nikola and Kiratsa on the icon-lamp from the same church (inscription from 1763); another inscription in the church "St. George" says: "The Church was renewed in time of the churchwardens Nedyalko and pop Stamo"; some names of the church donors in the inscription of "The Nativity of Christ" include: Tsonyu, Stoyko, Lada, Nedyalko, Stanko (1832).[47]

The Muslim and non-Muslim pilgrims were also among the distinguished citizens of the village.[48] Usually after gaining some wealth, people decided to acquire prestige and elevate their status within the community by making a *hajj* to the Holy places. There are only two references to pilgrims in the *temettuat defter* of 1845: h. Ismail son of Mustafa[49] (*dzhambaz*, horse dealer) and Yorgo son of h. Iliya[50] (grocer). Obviously, they both were related to the commercial estate of Arbanasi. Other historical sources, however, added several other names of Arbanasi's pilgrims – all of them merchants or grocers.[51]

In this context mention must be made of a list of sponsors who supported the publication of the book of Ivan Simeonov[52] *Odigos tis evsevias* (*Guide of Piety*), published in Istanbul in 1850.[53] Among them, 35 residents of Arbanasi are mentioned.[54] These people definitely belong to the more affluent stratum of the village that also supported education and churches. The comparison with data from the above-mentioned Ottoman *temettuat defter* (1845) proves that some of the subscribers were among the richest people, like the well-known Kiril Dimitrov Rusovich and the two *dzheleps* Hristo Atanasov and Yanko Dobrev.[55]

In fact, the priests of Arbanasi were also wealthy people such as priest Marin, as discussed below, who owned a substantial immovable property. Growing in Arbanasi, Papazov heard many stories about the wealth of the village's residents:

> Many times I have heard of the greatest treasures of its residents: about their expensive long furcoats . . . the luxurious silk dresses of their wives . . . the pearls, golden coins, and a high-priced jewelry with diamonds, sapphires, rubies, emeralds, opals, agates. Even the French fashion passed through Arbanasi.[56]

He claimed that old earrings with diamonds and dresses made of silk, whose fabric costs 2,000 g., had been preserved at the homes of some wealthy inhabitants.

More information is preserved for some prominent families in Arbanasi, whose members left traces of their activities in numerous historical sources. In what follows, I give brief information about two of them and their contributions to schools, churches, and modern lifestyles.

George Anagnosta and His Family

There is historical evidence for three generations of this family: pop Simeon, his son George Anagnosta, and grandson Dimitar (Dimitraki) Popsimeonov. Pop Simeon was a priest in Arbanasi in late eighteenth–early nineteenth centuries and a teacher at the first Greek school in the village.[57] His son – George pop Simeonov, known as George Anagnosta (1789–1881), was well known in the region because of his public activities, prestige, and special position among the Orthodox Christians. For 24 years he was an official representative (*kaza vekil*) of the Tarnovo *kaza* before the Sublime Porte.[58] There are many letters addressed to him from the *chorbadzhi* of the nearby towns of Gabrovo and Dryanovo.[59] Papazov says: "his voice was always heard in Constantinople and his requests were not ignored". When in 1845 Sultan Abdülmecid celebrated the circumcision of his son, each region sent two representatives to the capital: Tarnovo was represented by the Christian George Anagnosta and a certain Muslim.[60] From 1826 to 1869 the former was a regular member of the Tarnovo's council (*meclis*), and in 1854 he received the medal "Medzhidiye" for his service to the Ottoman state. Some marginal notes in a manuscript in his library mention that he received a fixed state pension "till the end of his life, even after the liberation of Bulgaria".[61]

Papazov mentions that Anagnosta was respected for his loyalty, honesty, and fairness by the community. He remained in the collective memory as "very strict morally and religious" man. Anagnosta had a strong opinion on many disputes and issues of the Orthodox community in Tarnovo. He strongly supported the official Patriarchate's position in order to preserve "the prestige of the religious power". At the same time, he did not hesitate to fight against the arbitrariness of the Metropolitan Hilarion of Crete.[62]

Meanwhile, the main source of income for George Anagnosta was his trade. Kisimov wrote in his memoirs: "surprisingly he died in extreme poverty, despite his semi centennial high status (*chorbadzhiystvo*),[63] a proof of his kindness and honesty, rare among people of that rank".[64]

Anagnosta and his son Dimitar were known not only for their wealth and local leadership but also for the private library they established. Well-educated, fluent in Greek, both father and son collected books with various content. Unlike the rest of the private libraries in Arbanasi, Anagnosta's library was preserved after the *kirdhalis'* attack (1798) and later stored away at the National Library in Sofia.[65] The activities of these two men are proof of their commitment to society. Besides the fact that they both supported local culture and intellectual life,[66] they also had some sense of historicity. The marginal notes in their books became one of the most valuable sources for the history of Arbanasi.

The Papazovs/Sakelarovs Family

The family had several prominent members whose activity is recorded in various historical documents. Dimitar Papazov, the best chronicler of Arbanasi, was among them. The first known representative of the family, priest Anastas, served at the church "The Nativity of Christ". An educated man and a prominent priest, he received the rank *sakellarios*, i.e. first among the priests.[67]

Priest Anastas had several sons who are registered in the *temettuat defter* (1845): Marin (priest), Ivan (tailor), Nestor (grocer), and Tanas (furrier). Two of them are enlisted also as contributors to Simeonov's book *Odigos tis evsevias*. Most evidence is preserved for priest Marin who, as his father, served at "The Nativity of Christ" and taught at the Greek school. Among his students were the future revolutionaries Thoma and George Kardzhievs and their father, h. Kirola (Kiril) Rusovich and "other prominent residents".[68] Due to his experience and knowledge, he was invited later to serve as a teacher at the Greek school in Tarnovo.

Dimitar Papazov himself was his uncle's student. He remembers priest Marin not only as a strict teacher but also as a representative and imposing figure, and a well-known member of Arbanasi's elite. The priest possessed an impressive amount of profitable real estate: vineyards, fields, meadows, shops, and a mill in Arbanasi and the surrounding villages, as well as a huge house with bathroom, spacious courtyard, and well-maintained garden.

The preserved evidence confirms not only the existence of an economically strong social stratum in Arbanasi, but the presence of an elite consciousness expressed through the characteristics of their profile and by their activities. They were well educated; owners of big estates but also of large private libraries. Many people (Kiril Rusovich, George Anagnosta, priest Marin) held strong positions on social and religious issues and actively participated in the debates within the Christian community. Some of them occupied official posts not only in the village, but also in the *kaza*'s administration, which attests for the recognition of their prestige within the community. Many of them promoted various social activities and financially supported the publication of books and the renovation of churches and schools.

Conclusions

Arbanasi presents a successful model for a village prosperity that stimulated economic and social entrepreneurship. It based its economic prosperity on the development of certain livelihoods and the establishment of strong connections with several powerful centers within and beyond the Ottoman Empire. Arbanasi received substantial privileges and tax exemptions from the Ottoman authorities, i.e. the established *waqf* and *dervendzhi* status which created advantageous conditions for its economic prosperity. The development of international commerce was based also on the close ties and privileges given to Arbanasi by the Transylvanian and Wallachian elite. The relations with the Danubian Principalities created a tied network whose members made numerous donations and provided support for religious and educational institutions. There was a constant exchange of money, ideas, and people between Arbanasi and the Wallachian capital Bucharest. The relations with the high clergy of the Constantinople Patriarchate and other Eastern Orthodox churches were also important for the position of the village. Arbanasi gained prestige as a center of the Patriarchate's politics in the Balkans. So, this mountainous village situated at the very center of the Balkan Peninsula was not just a small isolated settlement. It was connected with distant economic and power centers through a network of ties with secular and religious, Christian and Muslim elites. Meanwhile, it was well connected with the nearby area as well. In the sixteenth and seventeenth centuries, Arbanasi benefited from positive migrations that supported its economic prosperity. After the *kirdzhalis* attack in 1798 the ethnic structure of the settlement changed, but it preserved its economic profile (focused on commerce and several crafts) and the traditions of its cultural development. The new settlers from the surrounding area adopted the old traditions in livelihood. Moreover, they accepted Greek as a main language in the religious, commercial, and private sphere.

CHAPTER 9

REDRAWING STATE BORDERS: PROSPERITY TO POVERTY IN OTTOMAN AND POST-OTTOMAN BITOLA (MONASTIR)

Dalibor Jovanovski

In his work dedicated to Bitola, the French historian Bernard Lory wrote that before World War I this city surpassed Skopje in importance and was the second most significant city in the Ottoman Balkans.[1] What Lory wrote was true, but where is Bitola now and why is that so? Together with Thessaloniki and Skopje, Bitola was one of the three *vilayet* centers in Ottoman Macedonia. However, the wars that devastated the Balkans from 1912 to 1918 led to the evident decline of the city. Moreover, the new border established in 1913 between the Kingdom of Serbia and the Kingdom of Greece, along with Serbian rule, caused this once thriving Ottoman center to lose its significance. Today the other two ex-*vilayet* centers are flourishing. Skopje, once the center of the Kosovo *vilayet*, nowadays is the capital of the Republic of Macedonia and its economic, cultural, and political center. Thessaloniki, the largest city in the Ottoman Balkans, and the center of the eponymous *vilayet*, today is the main economic, political, and cultural center of Northern Greece. A railway and a modern highway connect these two cities, which are a part of the European corridor 10. On the other hand, Bitola is a city in the south-western part of the Republic of Macedonia that does not enjoy its previous importance.

The aim of this chapter is to trace Bitola's prosperity during the Ottoman period and to discuss the reasons that led to its decay. I will argue that its inclusion in the nation-state system and subsequent geographic marginalization through the new border regime led to significant demographic, economic, political, and cultural changes that contributed to its decline. The research is grounded in consular reports, Protestant missionary materials, and Serbian newspapers. The chapter will first analyze Bitola's administrative history, economic prosperity, its multiethnic composition, communications, and urban infrastructure during the Ottoman rule; second, the focus will shift to the political entanglements of the late nineteenth century, the Balkan Wars and World War I, and the inclusion of Bitola into the Serbian state.

Administrative History

The growth of Bitola commenced during the second decade of the nineteenth century. In 1816, Sultan Mahmud II made Bitola the center of Rumelia. Writing about this step of the Ottoman sovereign, Lory and Aleksandar Popovic emphasize that the sultan's motives for this action were not clear.[2] The Serbian intellectual Jefto Dedijer noted that the turmoil in Albania at the end of the eighteenth and the beginning of the nineteenth century and the Greek Uprising of 1821 influenced the decision that Bitola would become a significant administrative center in European Turkey.[3] Bitola became a military and administrative base for launching all the operations to re-impose central Ottoman power in parts of Albania and Epirus.[4] The Bulgarian historian Gergana Georgieva considers that the transfer of the center of the Rumelian *eyalet* from Sofia to Bitola was caused by the activities of the *karjalee* (brigands).[5] This meant that Sofia was not secure enough for the management of the territory but Bitola did not have that problem.[6] Finally and officially, Bitola became the seat of the Rumelian *eyalet* in 1836.[7] In 1841, it was a center of the Third Ottoman Army.[8] This was significant for the development of the city's economy, especially crafts, because the needs of the army were immense. These steps of the sultan's government stimulated the beginning of the swift development of this Macedonian city and the increase of its influence upon its hinterland.[9] In discussing the administrative division of the European part of the Ottoman Empire, we should not forget the *Vilayet* Law of 1864,[10] which abolished the *eyalets* as an administrative unit. At the beginning, Bitola was a part of the Thessaloniki *vilayet*, but in 1873–4 it became a center of the same named *vilayet*.[11] In fact, Bitola had commenced its development during the time of the Tanzimat (1839–76), the top-down reforms that were intended to modernize the state, strengthen its centralization, and prevent its further decay.[12] Writing about Bitola, Mark Cohen considers that this city became a showcase of the Ottoman adoption of European standards.[13] Naturally, its new administrative position and the security that the city provided, compared to the rest of the region, attracted people from its vicinity and from more distant places.[14]

Economy

Besides the transformation into an administrative center, Bitola's economic development also contributed to its prosperity. Its whole economic and social life revolved around Bitola's *bazaar* (market).[15] It was the place where crafts and trade thrived and stimulated further economic development.[16] However, at the end of the century, due to the penetration of better quality products imported from Europe, and the beginning of industrialization in the city, the number of crafts decreased.[17] The growing need of the Ottoman state for capital and money led to the adoption of the Muharem Decree (1881).[18] Consequently, after 1881, the goods from Western Europe commenced to penetrate into Ottoman Macedonia. The local crafts could not withstand the competition and began gradually to vanish. On the other hand, the upper class Bitola tradesmen began to invest in industry. The penetration of capital from European countries created a greater competition, and Bitola traders invested their capital in construction of smaller factories. Thus, several factories emerged: manufacture for candies and *lokum* (Turkish delight) in 1883; brick factory (1895); brewery (1890), and several hydraulic mills.[19] The predominant construction of food factories and light industry is due to the fact that the residents of Bitola did not have enough financial means to build larger industrial capacities. Lory mentioned that Bitola possessed a modest industry for a city with 50,000 residents.[20]

Communications and Urban Infrastructure

The expansion of the *bazaar* and trade was not possible without the improvement of communication and transport connections to the city's surroundings and the other centers of the Ottoman Empire. The last two decades of the nineteenth century were perhaps the most important period in the development and establishment of Bitola as an economic, cultural, and administrative center of the Ottoman Balkans, especially in Macedonia. From 1875 to 1885, a number of roads were constructed that connected Bitola with neighboring cities.[21] Other roads were built to connect Bitola with other centers in European Turkey. The train connection with Thessaloniki, the main economic center of the European part of the Ottoman state, was completed in 1894. This fact is of particular interest because it enabled Bitola to become a real trade center for the area from Durres and Shkoder to Vardar, and from Pelagonia to Epirus.[22] Many merchants from neighboring towns depended on their regional trade offices in Bitola.[23]

The rise of Bitola as an administrative center inevitably led to its increased urbanization. At the end of the 1830s, Kose Ahmed Zekiriya, Monastir's governor, commenced the urbanization of the city in accordance with European standards. At that time, a new quarter was constructed with military barracks.[24] However, the construction of the barracks that were supposed to represent the new spirit of reforms, ended in 1839.[25] Later in this military quarter were built a hospital, military depots, pharmacies, baths, and a military school, which was attended by the founder of modern Turkey, Mustafa Kemal Ataturk. This was only the beginning of the process of construction that intensified at the end of the nineteenth century. In 1894, the new railway station was gradually connected with the city center through Hamidie Street. Several years later, the construction of a theatre was commenced.[26] Thus, the transformation of Bitola into a significant administrative and economic center in the European part of the Ottoman Empire turned the city into a place with a number of elementary schools[27] and banks,[28] and the European states began to open their diplomatic offices there.[29] The peak of Bitola's boom was achieved just before the beginning of the Balkan Wars.

Political Entanglements

However, not everything was ideal. The beginning of the twentieth century meant the beginning of a very hard period for the city. The struggle led by the IMRO (Internal Macedonian Revolutionary Organization)[30] for autonomy of Macedonia reached its peak on 2 August 1903 when the Ilinden Uprising began in Krushevo, a small town in the vicinity of Bitola.[31] The Bitola *vilayet* became the theatre where a large number of severe battles between Macedonian insurgents and Ottoman forces were fought. The beginning of the insurgents' actions brought anxiety among the population. The insurgents destroyed telegraph and railway lines.[32] They were soon repaired but the consequences remained. Bitola, as a city, was not in danger of being attacked by the rebels who did not have the capacity to do it. The insurrection was suppressed by the end of 1903, but the period that followed was full of uncertainty and instability. The tumultuous times reached another peak five years later, when in 1908 the Young Turk Revolution started.[33] Being at the center of these actions, Bitola, illustrated the tensions that burdened the empire.

The aspirations of the Balkan Christian states towards the Ottoman territory in the Balkans were not a secret. Serbia, Greece, Bulgaria, and Montenegro looked at the Ottoman territories as their unredeemed historical lands. However, none of them could independently realize their desires for territorial expansion. The Ottoman state was not strong enough to oppose a power like Italy, but was powerful enough to counter every Balkan country separately. It was for these reasons, that in 1912, the afore mentioned Balkan countries signed several agreements to expel the Ottoman state from the remaining territories in the Balkans. Bitola, according to the Serbo–Bulgarian agreement, was supposed to belong to Bulgaria, but the Greeks and the Serbs also desired the city. The beginning of the First Balkan War on 8 October 1912 determined the destiny of the city. The victorious Serb army swiftly approached it.

At the beginning of the war, Muslims were intolerant towards Christian citizens. However, the advance of Serbian forces to the city changed that attitude. The Muslim leaders even asked the more prestigious Christians to join their petition addressed to the retreating Ottoman armies to stop and defend Bitola.[34] The city had already become a place where Muslim refugees arrived, while trade began to suffer greatly.[35] After the great victory over Ottoman forces near Kumanovo, Serbian armies arrived near Bitola. After three days of intense battles in November, the Serbian army entered the city as victor.[36] Bitola obtained a new master. The Christian population welcomed the entrance of the Serbs in Bitola.[37]

Establishing the Serbian Authority: Discourses and Practices

The Serbian occupation of the city seemed, perhaps, temporary to some. Yet not only the initial steps and decisions of the Serbian authorities, which I shall discuss below, but also Serbian diplomacy showed no intention to remain there only temporarily. Thus, a comment on the Serbian military victory near Bitola in Belgrade's most influential daily newspaper, *Politika*, emphasized that Serbia should obtain what was conquered with blood, and that this outcome should be accepted by the Balkan Allies.[38] Serbia and Greece introduced a border regime even before the London Peace Treaty (1913) was signed. After 10 December 1912, one needed a passport to travel between the territories conquered by the Serbs and those by the Greeks.[39] In addition, in January 1913, the newly appointed customs manager arrived in Bitola.[40] The renaming of thc Bitola's main Avenue Hamidie to King Peter[41] certainly was not for temporary use. Initially, Serbian occupation and governance of Bitola received a positive response by some people due to the fact that certain issues were put in order for a short period of time.[42] Furthermore, simultaneously with the implementation of the new administration of the city that commenced immediately, and as part of the whole process, Serbs started to print a newspaper in Serbian language. This newspaper is an interesting source for learning how the Serbian authorities viewed their mission in the city.

From the very beginning of their rule in Bitola, the Serbs wanted to commence a process of de-Ottomanization of the city. At the end of 1912, a step towards achieving this goal was the decree of Serbian King Peter I for the organization of the liberated regions, wherein interim governance based on military law was implemented.[43] Serbs thought that the entrance of their army into Bitola meant not only the end of a despotic regime, but also a break with a number of habits and traditions that existed within such a regime.[44] According to Serbian views, in the parts of Ottoman Macedonia conquered by Serbian forces, only Skopje and Bitola satisfied certain European urban standards.[45] Thus, it is not surprising that Serbian administration in the newly conquered territories was interested exactly in the administrative organization of Bitola and its surrounding area. Bitola and its vicinity were organized into a particular district, and the city itself was divided into seven districts.[46] This division of the city was kept from the previous period because it was considered that in such manner security of persons and property would best be preserved. Several months later, the city was divided into five districts: Dragor, Varosh, Voivoda, Belgrade, and Sveto Nedelski.[47] The ideological aim of the new administration is evident in the names of some of the districts. At one of the first sessions of the new Municipal Council, wherein representatives of all ethnic and religious communities participated, the city regulations and an elaboration of the city plan were discussed.[48] Along these lines, a decree was issued by the headquarters of the Bitola district that banned construction of houses without adequate permit; its aim was, as it was written, to regulate house-building processes.[49] This decree demonstrated that the new authorities wanted to have control of both private and public life.

Water supply to the city was also one of the priorities of the new authorities because both the local population and the Serbian soldiers stationed there suffered from the polluted water.[50] Therefore, it was necessary to construct a water pipeline and to bring water from Pelister Mountain. For that purpose, the Municipal Council prepared a special study.[51] However, the problems with water did not mean that the authorities did not pay sufficient attention to other issues, such as the green areas of the city. In February 1913, the council issued a decree to arrange the city parks. Thus, the arrangement of the Kerim-pasha garden commenced.[52] The city authorities also discussed the construction of an electricity generation plant for electrification and lighting of Bitola.[53] Later on a tax for city electricity, street cleaning, and garbage collection was introduced.[54] Moreover, the local authorities intended to show that their management satisfied the population of Bitola. A rally was held in May 1913, at the same time when the crisis of relations among the Balkan Christian Allies was at its peak. However, a large number of Bitola citizens did not support the organized manifestation.[55]

The peace between the Balkan allied states and the Ottoman Empire was not yet concluded, but Serbian newspapers had already announced that Narodna Banka (People's Bank) would open a branch in Bitola and that Belgrade Zadruga would follow suit.[56] The plans for opening Serbian banks in Bitola show that the Serbian authorities wanted to implement economic control of the region and to integrate it within their economic and financial systems.

The Balkan allied armies defeated the Ottoman army on all fronts. No one any longer considered a possible return of Ottoman rule in any part of the Balkans. However, military successes brought to the surface some problems that were hidden before. Territorial division among the allies proved to be very difficult. On the one side stood Bulgaria, which achieved great victories on the Thracian front; on the other side was Greece, which conquered Thessaloniki; on a third side was Serbia that governed Bitola, but had to withdraw from the Albanian coast due to Austrian pressure. In that way Serbia was not able to fulfill the Bulgarian requirement designated by the treaty of February 1912 – to retreat from the undisputable territories. The Serbs were not willing to do that. Bulgaria also faced problems with Greece, particularly in regard to former Ottoman territories in Macedonia. Not surprisingly, Belgrade and Athens negotiated an alliance and the agreement was signed on 19 May 1913. Military confrontation between the recent allies was about to commence. The Second Balkan War and the Bulgarian defeat determined the borderline and Bitola remained under Serbian rule.

The new borderline entailed the beginning of a new process of decay of the former *vilayet* center, one of the most developed cities in the European part of the Ottoman state. If someone were to read Bitola's community newspaper from January 1913, one would think that the city would have an ideal future. According to an article in this newspaper, Bitola possessed all the natural conditions to become an important industrial and trade center.[57] It was preordained to become the most important center, according to the newspaper *South Serbia*. The plain between Florina, Prilep, Resen, and Bitola would contribute to such prosperity.[58] Yet was this really possible? The Serbian Prefect of the Bitola district Alimpich noted:

> The creation of autonomous Albania, and particularly the retreat from Florina and the whole Florina region and giving it to the Greeks, without doubt, will have a very bad influence on the future of Bitola because it will become a border city without any ties to Thessaloniki, as was the case recently with Vranje. For this reason it

> is necessary as soon as possible to commence the construction of the railway line Veles-Prilep-Bitola-Resen-Ohrid and to start an industry that does not exist in Bitola at the moment.[59]

Alimpich's thinking was pragmatic. Bitola as a city on the new borderline had lost economic contacts with Florina, Thessaloniki, Kozani, Kastoria, Korche, and Elbasan, with which Bitola, during the Ottoman period, had developed extensive trade relations. The new border prevented Bitola from having contacts with two thirds of those districts that previously enabled its economic influence over a larger economic area. Furthermore, "the state borders, which should not have become the economic borders, prevented any business collaboration. They become unsurpassable barriers to trade exchange and traffic, as long as the city itself remained on the border limited to its own economy and to the nearest vicinity."[60] So, political frontiers cut off economic ties from the past.

Besides the new border between Serbia and Greece, there is another cause for the impoverishment of Bitola, and it is again connected with the new situation after the Balkan Wars, and that is civil rights, although they can be interpreted in a different manner. Serbian authorities started to increase limitations on civil and personal liberties. In February 1913, the Prefect of the Bitola District, Branislav Nushich, issued a decree limiting the civil freedoms previously announced in the official Community Newspaper. Indeed, that decree banned several rights, such as public gatherings and sitting in cafes, but also, and more importantly, it added the requirement of a special permit in order to enter and exit the city, and prohibited idleness with a threat of expulsion from the city.[61] In wartime, these types of orders are common, but the control over idleness, exit and entry seems to have had its purpose.

Several consular reports offer interesting information that refers to the attitude of the new authorities towards the local population. According to one report, Serbian policy had three basic and interrelated goals: first, to create an impression that in the occupied territory all Macedonian Slavs were Serbs; second, the fast assimilation of a larger number of the non-Slav population; and third, the forced migration or destruction of Muslims and the confiscation and sale of their property to immigrants who were supposed to settle in Macedonia.[62] This observation of the

British vice-consul explains the intentions of Alimpich, the Serbian Prefect of the Bitola district. In the above mentioned report, Alimpich also wrote about the religious diversity in the city. He noted that in Bitola there is neither a Serbian church nor a Serbian clergy and therefore it was necessary to create them as soon as possible.[63]

In the already mentioned report by the British vice-consul, we can find out which of the steps undertaken by Serbian authorities caused additional impoverishment of the local population in the city and its vicinity. Thus, with the intention of putting economic pressure on the population that was very close to the Bulgarian Exarchate, the new administration forbade travel from the city to villages, and among the villages, and trade to a great extent was suspended.[64] The remarks of the British consul in Bitola about the attitude of Serbian authorities towards those residents that did recognize the ecclesiastical jurisdiction of the Bulgarian Exarchate concur with the reports of the last Exarchate's Metropolitan in the city.[65] Likewise, the residents of Bitola who were attached to the Constantinople Patriarchate were also subjected to pressure through the attempts to take over their funds that supported schools, hospitals, and other institutions. Concerning the schools, especially during the time of the annexation of the city by the Kingdom of Serbia, we should mention that the staff in schools was "imported" from the northern part of Serbia.[66] It is certain that the most painful experience was reserved for the Muslims who paid the price of the five-centuries-long rule over the region. Besides different limitations, they were subjected to forced labor every Friday;[67] actually, during the great prayer. Moreover, all communities were subjected to great taxes and customs fees and this increased their emigration.[68]

This observation of the British diplomatic officer in Bitola seems quite plausible. However, reading the Serbian sources from that period, we get different information. Indeed, Marko Novakovich, the Prefect of the Bitola district, proposed to the Serbian Minister of Internal Affairs some steps that could improve the situation in Bitola and its vicinity. Among other things, he thought that the most important issue that should be solved was the agricultural one. By giving the peasants land, they would become more integrated into the new state and that would prevent some subversive activities.[69] He also proposed ways to improve the economy of the towns and villages in this region. Novakovich thought that it was desirable to permit the transfer of all properties that were not part of a *chiflik* and, therefore, the people who had a lot of money could freely buy land from the Turks.[70]

The Muslims were frightened by the entrance of the Serbian forces in Bitola. The Protestant missionaries wrote: "Our Turkish neighbors came here this morning, in great fear, because they imagined that the Servians would do to the Turks as Turks have done to Christians under similar circumstances. It was late in the afternoon when these people were convinced that they would be in no danger whatever in their homes and returned there."[71] However, the security of the Muslim population was really a great concern. Turks and other Muslims, until the final expulsion of the Ottoman authority from the Balkans, with the exception of the wider vicinity of Istanbul and Adrianople, massively migrated to Asia Minor. This can be seen even in the composition of the Municipality Council of Bitola where the number of the Muslims significantly decreased.[72] It seems that the majority of Ottoman clerks left Bitola together with their families. The new authorities did not have posts for them. On 27 August 1913, King Peter I announced in a proclamation to the Serbian people that the territories Serbia gained at the conference in Bucharest (the peace treaty was signed on 10 August 1913 there), were annexed to his kingdom.[73] Thus, the Serbian language became official. On 14 March 1914, Serbia and the Ottoman Empire signed another peace treaty; its Article 4 stipulated that those persons who wanted to obtain Ottoman citizenship would have a three-year period to do so.[74] We can suppose that a part of the Muslim population was interested in obtaining Ottoman citizenship because otherwise they would become Serbian citizens.

The Muslims were not the only ones who deserted Bitola due to the new government and the new border. As already mentioned, Serbia used the allied war in June 1913 to settle scores with supporters of the Bulgarian Exarchate. Serbian authorities arrested more than 600 citizens of Bitola from 30 June to 2 July 1913 and they remained in jail until 26 July. When it became clear that Bulgaria would lose the war, some of them were released.[75] Simultaneously with their liberation, other residents were called to sign a statement that they accept the new *status quo*.[76] Avksentie, the Metropolitan of the Bulgarian Exarchate, was arrested by the Serbian police, and forced to leave the town.[77] One group of Exarchate teachers was also forced to leave Bitola although they were born in Macedonia.[78]

Thus, politics played a great role in the outmigration of segments of Bitola's population. The Greek historian Asterios Kukudis noted that the pro-Greek circles in the town, i.e. a large number of Vlachs from Bitola, wished Bitola to become a part of Greece.[79] This did not happen, and the city, as mentioned before, officially became a part of Serbia by a decision of the Bucharest Peace Treaty. The Greek prime minister Eleftherios Venizelos, returning from Bucharest, visited Bitola to calm down the pro-Greek oriented citizens who did not easily accept that fact. He proposed to them, as a consolation, to move to Florina where the Greek state could help the establishment of the so-called "New Bitola".[80] His advice was followed by some who moved to the Greek territory, and a good part of them were influential members of the Patriarchist community.[81] Their migration, without any doubt, was a loss for the city's prosperity.[82]

The Protestant mission that existed in the city for more than 40 years,[83] and had its own school, commenced to face some challenges, too. Two members of the mission visited the Serbian capital city where they met the prime minister and minister of education. The Serbian politicians emphasized that they would like to cooperate with the mission in Bitola to cultivate loyal citizens.[84] However, actually, the situation was developing in another direction. Generally, the Serbian authorities did not create problems,[85] but the members of the mission felt a certain pressure to close their school.[86] The local authorities commenced to insist on the use of the Serbian language in the school.[87] That did happen and the Protestant missionaries in Bitola were required to teach both in English and Serbian.[88] Indeed, an article by D. Arangyelovich, university professor and member of the Serbian Parliament, published in the community newspaper, argues that in Bitola the teaching was in Serbian language because the city became a part of Serbia, and, therefore, the official language was Serbian.[89]

The above mentioned examples show that the new border and the behavior of the Serbian authorities forced some of the residents to leave Bitola or to start thinking about leaving. In a letter to the magazine *Missionary Herald* the Protestant clergyman William P. Clarke expressed the emergence of nostalgic feelings: "People long for the past – and yet that was bad enough."[90] Bitola, which until recently was a center of the *vilayet*, now became a border city of the Kingdom of Serbia. However, the Balkan Wars and the new border between Serbia and Greece did not mean the end of the sufferings of Bitola and its citizens. A new catastrophe approached.

Bitola during World War I

The beginning of World War I on 28 July 1914 marked a period of great suffering for the city that just a few years ago had been the second center in importance in Ottoman Macedonia. At the beginning of the war Bitola was far from the battlefields. The remoteness from the front did not mean that it would not face the consequences of the military activities, however. During the second half of 1914, a number of ill and injured Serbian solders arrived in the city,[91] and Bitola became a large medical center.

In 1915, the conditions in the region changed. The relations between Serbia and Bulgaria were strained more and more. When Bulgaria joined the war on the side of the Central forces against the Entente whose ally was Serbia, Bitola became part of the great European battlefield. At the end of 1915, Bulgarian and German military forces advanced towards Bitola. Their approach forced a closure of a number of stores; some people deserted the city because the supply of basic goods was diminishing.[92] When the French, Russian, and British consuls left the city on 2 December,[93] it was clear that Bitola would get a new master. On 6 December 1915, the allied Bulgarian–German forces entered Bitola and, within a three-year period, Bitola had again changed its ruler. The Bulgarian administration replaced the Serbian one. Although initially the population welcomed the Bulgarian army with sympathy,[94] as the Serbian forces were welcomed in 1912, the period that followed is perhaps the most difficult one in the modern history of Bitola. The bombardment of the city that was carried out by French planes on 23 January 1916 was just a hint of what was going to follow.[95]

During Bulgarian rule in those parts of Macedonia that belonged to the Kingdom of Serbia, according to the Bucharest Peace Treaty, the Sofia government sent an expedition to Macedonia, Kosovo, and Eastern Serbia. The reports and impressions of this expedition present some interesting data. For example, according to Dimitar Mishaikov, under Bulgarian administration the Bitola district was divided into six districts with 78 communities, 17 of which were within Bitola.[96] The population of the city, according to Dimitar Gadzhanov, was around 36,000.[97] The

Bulgarian authorities printed a newspaper with the name of the city (scripted in Bulgarian version) "Bitolya". The newspaper was issued only once on 6 January 1916, though.[98] The Bulgarian authorities prepared plans for a railway connection from Bitola to Veles and in that way with Skopje, which were imposed by the military needs. In February 1916, the Bulgarians and Germans commenced the construction of the narrow railway line from Gradsko to Bitola.[99] The construction, although intended for military use, progressed relatively well and quickly. However, the occupation of the city by the forces of the Entente in November 1916 prevented the completion of this railway connection, which reached only the village of Berantsi (14 kilometers north of Bitola).[100] This was the first concrete attempt to connect Bitola by railway with Gradsko and Skopje and Europe.

On the other hand, however, there were real problems in Bitola. The Bulgarian authorities did not differ a lot from their predecessors. During the Bulgarian rule, a certain number of influential citizens who did not sympathize with the authorities were interned. Among them were Todor Christoboulos; the medical doctors Christidis, Duma, Adzari, Naka; Petar Nechov, Aleksandar Altiparmakov, Nikola Stojchev.[101] These respected persons were a part of a larger group of citizens who were expelled to Bulgaria.[102] Writing about the behavior of the Bulgarian authorities in Bitola, Laffan, a British writer, noted that people were satisfied with the Germans who paid for everything they took.[103] However, this was not true for the Bulgarians. Whereas Laffan's position was hostile to the Bulgarians, the famous Bulgarian archeologist, later Prime Minister Bogdan Filov, was part of the already mentioned scientific team that visited Macedonia in 1916. This outstanding intellectual also wrote that the Bulgarian administration was completely corrupt.[104] There was also another member of the Bulgarian expedition, Ljubomir Miletich, a native from Macedonia, who besides other Macedonian cities also visited Bitola: his impressions were not positive either. According to him, people starved, while the wheat that they needed so much, was expensive. The starvation was a result of military activities, interruption of the import of flour via Thessaloniki, and requisitions for the armies.[105]

The military situation in the vicinity of Bitola gradually changed. In September 1916, the Entente forces approached the city. Severe battles were carried out in the nearby area. The French planes again bombed the city, and refugees arrived from neighboring villages where the battles between the warring parties were taking place.[106] Very soon, the Entente armies arrived in front of the city, and the Bulgarian and the German troops withdrew very quickly. Their withdrawal was followed by a big fire in the barracks that endangered the city. That was followed by general plunder, in which the starving and impoverished citizens took part.[107] This phenomenon was not surprising, considering that hunger ruled over the city. Every opportunity was used in the battle for survival and plundering was not considered a crime. On 16 November 1916, the Entente forces entered and soon established order in the city. The Serbian army returned with them and gradually re-established their administration. The entrance of the Entente troops was considered by the commander of the Serbian army, Zhivojin Mishich, as an entry into the most important city in southern Serbia.[108] Serbian authorities, most probably, wanted to present the arrival in Bitola as the beginning of the liberation of Serbia. Even some newspapers, like the *New York Times*, pronounced Bitola the temporary capital city of Serbia.[109]

However, the Entente troops in Bitola did not bring anything better than the situation in the previous period. As a result of military actions, the situation of the population was desperate, and starvation was rampant. The basic needs for products were not met, and this was particularly true in the case of flour, one of the most needed products.[110] Serbian authorities, together with their allies, took decisive steps to solve the starvation problem. The city that before the end of the Ottoman rule had had several steam mills, at that moment suffered from lack of flour. In November, a large quantity of flour arrived from Thessaloniki. Naturally, the allies blamed the former rulers of Bitola – the Bulgarians – for the devastation and impoverishment of its inhabitants.[111] Not surprisingly, some influential citizens who were very close to the previous authority, such as Metodi Altiparmakov, a brother to the previous mentioned Aleksandar, Evrem Rizov, Naum Rizov, the city mayor Atso Dorev, Petar Robev, the pharmacist Tashko Filipov, were forced to withdraw together with the Bulgarian armies. After regaining power the Serbian authorities had their own plans for those residents who remained in the city after the Central forces left Bitola. Some Serbian documents reveal, as was the case with the Bulgarian authorities, the intent to expel some teachers who taught in Bulgarian schools.[112] The expulsion or internment of those who were not desirable was not limited only to people who worked for or had contacts with

Bulgarian authorities and were originally from Bitola. The Bulgarian administration sympathized with the Protestant missionaries and encouraged their activity. However, after the Serbian army had returned to Bitola in November 1916, the authorities expelled the family of the missionary Clarke and the priest Mishev.[113]

The withdrawal of the Bulgarian and German military units from Bitola did not mean an end to the troubles of the population. The proximity of the front line meant a threat for destruction and that is exactly what happened in spite of the fact that Bitola was proclaimed an open city.[114] From November 1916 to September 1918, the Central forces constantly bombarded Bitola[115] and multiple buildings were destroyed, people were exposed to an ongoing risk to their lives. For example, on 4 August 1917 Bitola was bombarded with firebombs that caused considerable damage. The president of the Bitola's municipality noted: "Bitola has lost its most beautiful and most planned part, the fire swallowed one third of the city, the most beautiful part of the city ... The owners of a number of houses and huge warehouses turned into paupers and wanderers over night. Would this beautiful city ever recover again?"[116] In this situation, poverty became a common phenomenon. Living with bombs dropping while people were having their meals became a regular occurrence.[117] Life in cellars became an ordinary habit for people in Bitola, just with one goal – to survive.[118] Nobody was safe any longer.

That is why it is not surprising that the residents wanted to leave the city temporarily and to get shelter in other places that were far from the front. This period marked a vast migration of the Jewish population to Florina and Thessaloniki. However, some Serbian reports present another reason for the migration of Jews from the city. Haim Asreti, a Jew from Bitola, proposed that Bitola's Jews resettle in Thessaloniki and he sent his men to promote the idea.[119] According to Serbian information, it achieved a certain success.[120] Most probably the Jews from Bitola migrated to Thessaloniki, which was a part of the Greek state, as an easier way to emigrate to America or some other place.[121] Even departure from the native city was better than the hell that the citizens suffered each day due to bombing and military actions.

The breakthrough in the Macedonian front by the Entente armies meant an end of Bitola's sufferings. On 25 September 1918, Bitola could breathe again. After the end of World War I, Bitola was proclaimed a hero city, or "Verdun of the Balkans".[122] That was no satisfaction for a city that was destroyed. The loss of human lives and material destruction were huge.[123]

After the end of World War I, Skopje became the capital city of the Vardar Banovina and was revived again, while the situation in Bitola worsened.[124] The great damage suffered by Bitola from the border change of 1913 and the military activities that commenced in 1912 and ended in 1918, is well expressed in the words of Teodosi Robev:

> The economic progress of Bitola, which from day to day with a quick and sane step strengthened and increased its influence in all nearby regions, was ended with the wars in the Balkans, and thus the damaging consequences are felt even today in all fields of economic activities of the city. The lengthy wars, starting from 1912 until 1918, which with small exceptions were waged very close to the city, had destroyed not only the city and its vicinity, but also everything that had been achieved up to that time, and also wiped out all other economic assets that could survive and develop in peaceful, long lasting, and stable circumstances.[125]

Four years after World War I ended, despite the efforts to revive Bitola, it was still ruined due to the bombing during the war.[126]

Conclusions

One aspect of the devastating impact upon the population of the new borders and the wars from 1912 through 1918 can be illustrated through official statistical data. According to the census held by the Serbian authorities in 1913, the population was 48,370.[127] In 1921, the authorities of the new state – the Kingdom of Serb, Croats and Slovenians – organized the first census of the population and at that time 28,420 residents lived in Bitola.[128] Within nine years, the city had lost 20,000 citizens. This is the best proof of the damage that Bitola suffered from the new borderline, shifting rule with opposing political goals, and the military activities. Joël Kotek wrote that borders brought good or bad consequences for cities.[129] In the case of Bitola, the new border and the wars brought a decay of the once important Ottoman administrative, economic, military, and cultural center.

If a hypothetical citizen of Bitola, who survived all the circumstances in the period between 1912 and World War I, were asking himself what had happened to the city, he or she would be perplexed by his complex identity: on 1 October 1912 he was a citizen of the Ottoman Empire and the capital was Istanbul and Bitola traded with Thessaloniki and lived in the same state with the inhabitants of Adrianople, Bursa, Tirana, Ioannina, Beirut, Damascus, Izmir, Jerusalem, Jeddah. By 10 August 1913, after the Bucharest Treaty, Bitolans lived in the state of Serbia, with its capital Belgrade together with the citizens of Nish, Leskovats, and Vranje. Several years later, on 1 December 1918 after the creation of the Kingdom of Serbs, Croats, and Slovenians, the capital was the same, Belgrade, but now the residents of Bitola lived together with the citizens of Split, Sarajevo, Podgorica, and Ljubljana. Thessaloniki was replaced by Zagreb and Ljubljana.[130] Bitola, economically linked to Thessaloniki and Durres, could only go down, which is what did happen. The inclusion of Bitola within the Kingdom of Serbs, Croats, and Slovenes meant the commencement of a process of de-Ottomanization of the city despite the fact that even today in Bitola there are buildings that are reminiscent of the Ottoman past. The Muslim population in the city is smaller compared to the Ottoman period, while those who were Vlachs by origin, but felt Greeks, migrated to Greece, and Jews were eliminated during World War II, as was the case with their compatriots in other parts of the Balkans. The city lost its Ottoman character, but this is not an exception with respect to other parts of the Balkans. The inter-religious and inter ethnic tolerance is what has remained even though the city is now mainly populated by Macedonians.

CHAPTER 10

WAR, DYNASTY, AND PHILANTHROPY: KAVALA AND THE KHEDIVIAL RELIEF CAMPAIGN DURING THE BALKAN WARS (1912–13)

Eyal Ginio

The collapse of the Ottoman administration in the city of Kavala (in present-day eastern Macedonia in Greece) at the beginning of November 1912 was sudden, quick, and devastating for the civilian population there. Writing his memoirs in Judeo–Spanish (Ladino) about 15 years later, Itzhak Florentin, a Jewish resident of Kavala, could recall that the Ottoman military and civilian officials departed from the city in a hurry anticipating an imminent Bulgarian entry to the city. The city's population, consisting of Greeks, Muslims, Bulgarians, and Jews, was left to its own devices. Those who could afford it paid large amounts of money to secure a place on one of the ships, flying the flag of a neutral foreign country, which could transport them and their families to the safe haven of Istanbul or Izmir. All the others had to rely on their own means to secure their needs. As the Bulgarian army and administration were not in a hurry to implement their rule over the city, chaos prevailed. Many had to cope with a dearth of the most basic commodities and even with hunger. In those dark days of political vacuum, the panicked local population found some solace and salvation in the dispatches of food arriving from Egypt. This emergency food, Florentin recalled, saved the locals from starvation and reflected the commitment of the Egyptian khedive towards the town where his family originated.[1]

Kavala witnessed economic ruin, social dislocation, and human destruction during the First Balkan War (October 1912–May 1913). As this port city was situated relatively far from the main theatres of war in which the coalition of four Balkan states (Bulgaria, Serbia, Greece, and Montenegro) defeated the Ottoman army,[2] local armed bands dominated the warfare in and around the city until the arrival of the Bulgarian regular forces. This may explain the harsh conditions and atrocities, which Kavalans suffered at the hands of Bulgarian irregulars, as mentioned in Florentine's testimony. This human tragedy was not limited to Kavala, as many other Muslim communities suffered a similar fate following the retreat of the Ottoman army. However, the case of Kavala is significant in one sense: while similar upheavals led many Muslims (and Jews) living in the Balkan provinces to flee to Istanbul or to Salonica in desperate search of assistance, thousands of Kavalans turned their eyes to Egypt and to its khedive to receive aid. Florentin's memoirs suggest that their pleas were amply answered.

This chapter aims to elucidate the formation of this special bond between Kavala and the khedivial family and its ramifications for the scale and nature of the philanthropy offered to the city's inhabitants during the Balkan Wars. Basing my discussion on the contemporary Egyptian press and accounts of the war and memoir literature, the chapter discusses war relief against the background of the reshaping of philanthropy and its political aims in khedivial Egypt, reflecting both long-standing Ottoman practices and new perceptions of philanthropy. It likewise perceives political legitimacy and sovereignty as being reconstructed during the khedivial period as part of the processes of modernization and the shaping of the nation.[3] After all, caring for the weaker members of society mirrored the elite classes' national obligation under the aegis of patriotism. Similarly, Jay Winter has argued that in such charitable activities, like child welfare in World War I-Britain, "collective virtue and national interest clearly coincided".[4] During the Balkan Wars, the Egyptian dynasty engaged in expansion of the traditional notion of the "deserving poor", those perceived as entitled to philanthropy,[5] by including the Kavalan war victims. This inclusion,

I would argue, aimed at strengthening social mobilization, khedivial image branding, and national sovereignty.

War, Philanthropy, and State Formation

War and philanthropy are often presented in the literature on twentieth-century wars and societies as a means of studying the shaping of the modern state and civil society. In her study of the shaping of philanthropy in pre-WWI Germany, Jean Quataert argues that with the modernization of warfare in the nineteenth century, the ensuing increases in the targeting of civilians, and the advancement of the principle of general mobilization, philanthropy towards war victims became one of the major venues of action for civilians.[6] For those non-combatant groups of society (women, children, "left-at-home men")[7] distributing philanthropy to those deemed deserving victims of war became a major mode of demonstrating their loyalty, contribution and attachment to the national cause and, in this manner, affirming their status as playing a meaningful role in the national community. The various activities of civilian benefactors and volunteers reflected a new understanding of the bond between the state and its citizens. Their philanthropy created a new arena for displaying the well-off elite's commitment towards the less-fortunate members of the community, while keeping social boundaries and hierarchies intact.[8]

Similar perceptions of philanthropy developed in the late Ottoman period and in khedivial Egypt, where elite members invested in new forms of public philanthropy and welfare towards the "deserving poor".[9] By offering assistance to those deemed deserving, the different groups of war victims, the state and society, through the work of non-governmental organizations, acknowledged their obligation towards less-fortunate members of society. Philanthropy, especially during wartime, enabled elite groups to manifest their contribution to the war effort and to emphasize their belonging to the national community by contributing some of their wealth to those suffering the most from the circumstances of war. In addition, different elite groups used philanthropy towards the suffering victims not only to assist the state in its obligation to take care of the war victims but also, sometimes, to shape their own alternative discourses and agendas. By assisting their less fortunate brethren, such elite groups could display their national commitment and loyalty to the national cause and strengthen social legitimacy and bonds inside the society. The proliferation of such voluntary associations in the major Ottoman cities indicates that during the Balkan Wars these organizations were able to promote and pursue their own agendas while supporting the national cause.[10]

However, the choice of the incumbent khedive, 'Abbas Hilmī II (r. 1892–1914),[11] to concentrate his philanthropy during the Balkan Wars on Kavala presented a different case that merits our attention. Those defined as deserving poor were not selected from among the nation's poor, but rather from a faraway destination, situated outside the state's boundaries. Their main connection to Egyptian society was based on the distant origins of the khedivial family that had reigned over Egypt since the beginning of the nineteenth century. In this sense, it seems that the case of Kavala reflected the continuity in seemingly bygone dynastic policies of establishing pious endowments and iconic constructions to gain political benefits.[12] However, this is not to claim that khedivial philanthropy towards Kavala reflected only such traditional philanthropy. As I will show, the khedivial family was able to insert its personal benevolence within a social mobilization of broader philanthropic activities and to popularize the benevolence towards the population of the Macedonian port city, by soliciting, for example, public subscriptions for the benefit of the city's victims.

More telling is the arrival of a small, but still significant, wave of refugees from Kavala on board Egyptian and neutral vessels at Alexandria. This was the only category of refugees fleeing the atrocities in the Balkans that could claim permanent shelter in Egypt.[13] Indeed, the attention to the needs of the civilian population of Kavala extended beyond the boundaries of the khedivial family and developed to what could be described as an "Egyptian relief campaign" towards the city. The shaping of this new form of "popular-dynastic" philanthropy stands at the center of this chapter, as I explore how Kavala changed during the Balkan Wars from a distant *lieu de mémoire* ("site of memory"),[14] commemorating the khedivial family's origins and its symbolic departure for Egypt into a popular target of the Egyptian elite's benevolence, representing the devastation of the Balkan Wars to an Egyptian audience. It seems that the transformation of the Kavalan war refugees into the "deserving poor" is intimately related to the construction of Kavala, the *lieu de naissance* of the Egyptian dynasty, into a major *lieu de mémoire* serving the dynasty to commemorate its origins.

Kavala as a *lieu de mémoire* of the Khedivial Dynasty

Ottoman rule over Kavala began in the late fourteenth century, after the city was taken by the local warlord Evrenos Bey, being in the service of the Ottoman dynasty. Becoming a major road-station along the Via Egnatia (the Ottoman *Sol Kol*, "The Left Arm") during the mid-sixteenth century, Ottoman governors embellished Kavala with some significant constructions, such as the huge aqueduct supplying the city with drinking water from Mount Pangas.[15] However, by the time Mehmed Ali was born around 1770, Kavala was "no different from numberless other equally undistinguished ports of the Ottoman empire", to quote a modern scholar of nineteenth-century Egypt.[16] This was about to change as the tobacco industry developed in the nineteenth century, turning Kavala into a major center of tobacco industry and commerce. Furthermore, Mehmed Ali, while serving as the Ottoman governor of Egypt, constructed some major educational institutions and restored the sixteenth-century aqueduct and the citadel. The significance of Kavala for the ruling khedivial dynasty was prominent during the family's rule over Egypt.[17] Foreign travelers and observers were equally impressed by the Egyptian constructions in Kavala and with their relations to the Macedonian city. Konstantin Georgievich Mostras, the Russian consul in Izmir, authored the *Dictionnaire géographique de l'Empire Ottoman* (1863), wherein he observed that Kavala was "patrie de Méhémed-Ali-Pacha, vice-roi d'Égpte, qui l'a considérablement embellie".[18]

This investment of wealth in charity away from Egypt needs explanation. Ehud Toledano emphasizes the lingering connection between Mehmed Ali and the Ottoman center to the extent that a distinct group of "Ottoman-Egyptian" governing elite was formed and ruled Egypt. This privileged group was clearly demarcated from the bulk of Arabic-speaking Egyptian society, as its members:

> spoke Turkish; shared the values and heritage of Ottoman culture; were mostly, though not exclusively Muslims; came from various parts of the empire, though some were born in Egypt, and from various ethnic backgrounds; were committed to serve in Egypt

> under an Ottoman-Egyptian dynasty; held office either in the military or in the bureaucracy; tended to be well-off and gradually came to hold agricultural land.[19]

The continuous bond of the Egyptian rulers to the Ottoman state was also reflected in philanthropy. Mehmed Ali's reign over Egypt was characterized by the establishment of institutions intended to care for the poor and needy of Cairo, Alexandria and other major urban centers, such as shelters, hospitals, orphanages and foundling homes, poorhouses, and insane asylums. These institutions mirrored the ruler's (and his household's) benevolence towards the weaker elements of society and were founded within the Islamic rubric of obligation towards society's vulnerable members. Yet these reformed and centralized institutions, perceived as modern forms of benevolence, often took the place of traditional forms of philanthropy, such as religious endowments and other means of charity. The new institutions reflected aspects of a modern state apparatus and philanthropy, as well as the government's goal of instilling public order through the control, confinement, and punishment of those deemed "undeserving poor". The poor relief offered by the khedivial dynasty was centralized, standardized, and secularized through the mediation of increasing welfare bureaucracy.[20]

It seems evident that philanthropy enabled Mehmed Ali, and his descendants who ruled Egypt, to demonstrate their modernity and ability to efficiently control the local population and thus to claim hereditary rule. Furthermore, during the second half of the nineteenth century, as the members of the Turkish-speaking elite increasingly interacted with the Arabic-speaking locals, investment in philanthropy towards "the deserving poor" probably played a major role in securing legitimacy for khedivial rule. Indeed, Mine Ener indicates that during 'Abbas Hilmī's rule, *waqf* profits were directed toward political purposes, including the nationalist cause.[21]

However, such Egyptian-based calculations were absent from their policy towards Kavala as traditional forms of charity continued to play a major role in strengthing the links between the Egyptian ruling family and their city of origin. When donating funds to Kavala, the need to use philanthropy to better control and modernize society probably was not an issue, as the city served the dynasty only as a distinct *lieu de mémoire* telling the narrative of the dynasty's origins. Indeed, it is clear that the khedivial interest in Kavala revolved around the city's role in the shaping of the khedivial dynasty. Rarely did this interest also have a political aspect; following the city's conquest by Bulgarian forces in November 1912, some voices in the Egyptian press raised the question of annexing Kavala and the nearby Aegean island of Thasos (Taşöz) to Egypt.[22] Since only as recently as May 1902, the incumbent Ottoman sultan had been able to oust agents of the Egyptian khedive from Thasos, one of the main sources of revenues that supported the pious endowment founded by Mehmed Ali, such a scheme was not totally inconceivable.[23] Yet such political claims seem to be only anecdotal.

Kavala's unique position may explain the seemingly unreasonable choice to establish a pious endowment there rather than in Cairo or Alexandria. The choice was to represent the inhabitants of Kavala as the deserving poor entitled to the charity of the Egyptian khedive. While charity towards the poor could strengthen Mehmed Ali's ability to control Egypt better, in Kavala, public philanthropy could assist the khedivial family to present and to venerate its own family history.

The significance of Kavala was constructed in history essays that began with Mehmed Ali's experiences in his natal town and fondly presented the city as a major site commemorating the roots of the royal family in the legendary land of Alexander the Great and the Ptolemaic dynasty. Egyptian historiography during the khedivial period was a product of an attempt to connect modern Egypt to the legacies of pre-Islamic dynasties, some originating in Greek lands, which controlled Egypt and endowed it with some of its most visible relics of the past. The historical references suited the agenda of Mediterranean identity in Egyptian royalist historiography that prevailed in the 1920s and 1930s. The story of how the myth of ancient Egypt was incorporated into modern Egyptian national ideology is complex and controversial. Egyptian authors mythologized Kavala as the breeding ground of the ruling dynasty. An illustrative example is Mehmed Ali's biography written by Ilyās al-Ayyūbī, a Palestinian who served as the head of the translation section in the Egyptian Senate House, and a protégé of King Fū'ād (r. 1917–36). The opening pages of the book were dedicated to Kavala, its historical significance since classical times and its role in molding the skills and abilities of the young Mehmed Ali. For the author, Kavala and Macedonia were connected to Alexander the Great and his successors, the Ptolemies, who governed Egypt and endowed it with some of its most significant institutions. Mehmed Ali, the founder of the khedivial dynasty was born in Kavala and became "the successor of Alexander the Great and the Ptolemies, his countrymen [*muwātinīhi*] on the sublime throne of Egypt".[24] This type of narrative characterized the royalist school of history, as developed mostly under King Fū'ād's tutelage and his wish to cultivate historical scholarship in Egypt sympathetic to the monarchy and its devotion to Egypt's modernization.[25]

Whereas the city's history provided a secular genealogy of power, the construction of buildings relied on religious mechanisms of philanthropy and legitimacy. The most salient example of benevolent investment in the construction of Kavala as the dynasty's birthplace was the pious endowment founded by Mehmed Ali in 1813 in support of his newly established and later on enlarged *külliye*, or complex of educational and charitable buildings, for the benefit of the inhabitants of Kavala. Heath Lowry and İsmail Erünsal studied the various endowment deeds and their stipulations in order to narrate the shaping of this pious complex.[26] Later expansion of the endowment and the establishment of other new constructions underlined the khedivial family's attachment to Kavala. Probably in 1846, during his only return to Kavala – in the course of an official visit to sultan Abdülmecid in Istanbul – Mehmed Ali constructed mausoleums on his parents' burial sites.[27]

Even after Mehmed Ali's death in 1849, the reigning khedival (later royal)[28] family of Egypt maintained a strong connection with Kavala. This bond proved to be a lasting one even when the ruling dynasty "Egyptianized" and became part of an Egyptian elite at the turn of the nineteenth century.[29] The khedive 'Abbas Hilmī, who ruled Egypt during the Balkan Wars, visited Kavala in 1908–9 and again in 1911. During these visits, he initiated some restoration and construction work in the city; other projects remained only on paper due to the Balkan Wars.[30] Even the demise of the Ottoman rule and Kavala's annexation to Greece after the Second Balkan War (July 1913) did not sever the connection between the khedivial family and the city. However, interest in Kavala clearly shifted from philanthropy towards the local Muslim population (which was removed from the city in 1923 in the framework of population exchanges between Turkey and Greece) to the safeguarding and maintenance of different sites that had witnessed the early stages of the khedivial family. Under King Fū'ād, the house where Mehmed Ali was born was made into a small museum; in 1934, the Greek authorities built a statue of Mehmed Ali riding his horse. The statue still stands in a small square adjacent to Mehmed Ali's house. It was designed to create a commemorative itinerary comprising the main points linking the Egyptian monarchy to Kavala. Until his deposal in 1952, signifying the end of the royal regime, King Farouk served as the last royal director (*mutawallī*) of the endowment.

After the removal of the royalist regime in Egypt, the republican governments showed interest in what were perceived to be assets of the Egyptian nation. The Egyptian Minister of Religious Endowments took over as director of the endowment. In the early 1960s, following the confiscation of Greek private property in Egypt, the Greek Ministry of Finances ordered the seizure of all property that belonged to the endowment in Kavala. In 1964, a formal agreement was concluded between Greece and Egypt, according to which Egypt sold some of the property to the Greek municipality of Kavala. A final settlement was reached in 1984, according to which the Egyptian government safeguarded its ownership rights to two properties: the house of Mehmed Ali and the *imaret* (literally, public kitchen; the popular name given to the whole complex), which was leased later to a private Greek company that turned it into a luxurious hotel. All of these pious acts and constructions commemorated the "Egyptian" aspect of Kavala and narrated the origins of the khedivial family.[31] The assistance offered to Kavalan refugees during the Balkan Wars should be regarded as part of this lasting bond between the khedivial family and its city of origin.

The Balkan Wars as an Opportunity to Display Egyptian Patriotism

The Balkan Wars dominated the Egyptian press as daily reports were published in an attempt to first introduce the battlefields and then to provide details regarding major events. Following Montenegro's declaration of war on 8 October 1912, the first Balkan state to take such a step, *al-Garidah*[32] (*al-Jarīda*; "*The Newspaper*"), the organ of the national Egyptian movement,[33] dedicated its first page to reporting the outbreak of hostilities and declared its confidence in the Ottomans' ability to safeguard their territorial assets in the Balkans and their honor. It also elaborated on the assumed determination of the European powers to keep the *status quo* in the Balkans unchanged while insisting on the Ottoman implementation of administrative reforms, especially in the European provinces. *Al-Garidah* was especially intrigued by the Ottoman response to employing such reforms in both its European and Anatolian provinces. Did the term "Anatolia", the editorial article wondered, mean only those provinces situated in "Northern Asian Turkey" (*shimālī Turkiya Asya*; i.e. Anatolia), or "all of the Ottoman provinces in Asian Turkey", including Syria and Iraq? – an option clearly preferred by the journal.[34] At this early stage of the war, the Egyptian press took upon itself not only to narrate developments on the battlefields, but also to introduce the Balkan lands to its readers.[35] By providing maps, images, descriptions of landscapes and historical sketches, it endeavored to familiarize these faraway lands.[36]

As the scale of the military rout and the loss of territories unfolded, the Egyptian press turned to discussing the causes of the swift Ottoman defeat. In tandem, the press reported different campaigns of public subscription for the benefit of the Ottoman Army and the Ottoman and Egyptian Red Crescent organizations. By doing so, the Egyptian press also supported and made public such initiatives. Already in late October, a General Committee of "Assistance to the Ottoman State" (*I'ānat al-Dawla al-Āliyya*) was established in Cairo to gather donations for the Ottoman war effort. Headed by two princes, Prince Muhammad 'Alī Bāshā,[37] the khedive's younger brother, and Prince 'Umar Tūsūn, it soon established branches all over Egypt.[38] Often coordinating its efforts with the Egyptian Red Crescent, which was also directed by Prince Muhammad 'Alī Bāshā,[39] its main mission was to raise Egyptians' awareness of the events in the Balkans and to urge them to contribute money towards the war victims. Many of the fundraising campaigns were based on public ceremonies.[40] *Al-Garidah* perceived these benevolent activities as stemming both from a movement of patriotic fervor (*al-ghaira al- wataniyya*) and from Islamic compassion (*al-shafaqa al-islāmiyya*).[41] In a similar manner, the departure of Egyptian Red Crescent medical expeditions were accompanied by public gatherings in which speeches exalting the contribution of the khedive were made.[42] Clearly, such acts of philanthropy and assistance were meant to be publicly displayed and celebrated. Nadir Özbek defines similar initiatives performed during the Hamidian period (1876–1908) as "ceremonial occasions" designed to attain political ends. The development of mass media enabled the sultan to diffuse his image as a benevolent ruler.[43]

The Egyptian media served the khedivial family to claim a similar position by daily reporting the ruling family's deeds for the benefit of the Ottoman state during the Balkan Wars. The daily press also published official and overtly optimistic announcements, spread by the Ottoman Commissariat in Cairo, even in early November 1912 when the dimensions of the defeat were evident.[44] Donations in support of the Ottoman cause were collected all over Egypt. For example, *al-Muqattam* (named after a range of hills near Cairo), a daily newspaper with a pro-European leaning, reported in its issue of 25 November 1912 on the collection of considerable sums of money in provincial cities, such as Mansūra and Damanhūr. Prince Muhammad 'Alī Basha, mentioned above, attended the popular gathering that took place in Mansūra and offered his patronage to the subscription.[45] The Egyptian press regularly published lists of the donors' names and the amount of their donations, thus enabling those who contributed heavily to the subscription to demonstrate their commitment and generosity publicly. The press perceived the mobilization as a patriotic movement (*haraka ahliyya*).[46] Its leaders were members of the khedivial family.

Such public campaigns positioned the khedivial family under the public spotlight. Senior members of the ruling family, both men and women, offered their sponsorship and headed such gatherings, benefitting from the opportunity to display their benevolence and to present their political agenda. For example, Muhammad 'Alī Bāshā delivered the main speech in a gathering that took place in Zaqāzīk, a provincial town situated in the eastern part of the Nile Delta and a center of the cotton trade. In his speech, he utilized key terms, such as "human act" (*'amal insānī*), evoking humanitarian interest to characterize the mobilization of the Egyptian masses to assist the Ottoman state in its time of severe need. At the center of his lecture stood "the Egyptian nation" and how its both patriotic and religious connections with "our master (*mawlānā*), the sultan", kept their vitality through the efforts of the khedive. This envisioned triangle – the Egyptian nation, the Ottoman sultan, and the khedive – were connected to each other through the war relief emphasizing their common destiny and solidarity. The British, the colonial power that had real control over Egypt, were totally absent from this bond. Prince Muhammad 'Ali carefully chose his words to underline both Egypt's independence and its subordinate relations with the Ottoman Empire.[47]

What were the motives behind these relief campaigns? Notwithstanding humanitarian concerns, philanthropy during the Balkan Wars served the donors to achieve political gains and to claim moral superiority. International relief campaigns played a major role during these conflicts, as different international associations sometimes competed with each other in an attempt to dominate the "philanthropic arena". The Egyptian government and non-governmental associations joined this "race". It should be remembered that since 1882, Egypt was subject to British rule in which "a façade of Egyptian control was kept up in the shape of a Khedive, licenced to rule by an Ottoman Sultan, who has accepted to play the game according to rules set by the British".[48] Therefore, caught up in its own concerns regarding its ability and legitimacy to rule over Egypt, the Egyptian political elite was eager to gain some prestige at home through ambitious campaigns of assistance offered to Ottoman war victims. This was an attempt to assert some form of sovereignty.[49] It is true that during the reign of ʻAbbas Hilmi II, there were some significant points of contention with the Ottoman sultan, like the above mentioned ownership of the Aegean island of Thasos, or the activity of the Ottoman opposition on Egyptian soil.[50] However, Egypt's position during the Balkan Wars was very clear, as its political elite and press identified with the Ottoman cause, envisioning the ongoing war as a modern crusade launched against all Muslims, including Egypt. Therefore, while Egypt was regarded as a neutral state during the Balkan conflicts, the political elite did not conceal its overt support for the Ottoman cause.

Kavala as an Object of War Relief

Indeed, the Egyptian ruling family and various governmental and non-governmental organizations became involved in the Balkan Wars using different arguments, such as a humanitarian interest in alleviating wartime suffering, patriotic zeal, and Islamic solidarity. The wartime relief offered to the inhabitants of Kavala provides a case in point. Assuming that the city was known to the Egyptian reader of the press, its fate was explored in much more intimate language. Through the media reports, Egyptian readers became receptive to appeals for offering assistance to the inhabitants of Kavala. Only in the case of Kavala was this solidarity translated into offering permanent shelter for the city's refugees.

Kavala's exceptional position in the philanthropy extended to Muslim refugees during the Balkan Wars is evident also when compared to the writing on the city in Turkish as published in Istanbul. The fate of Kavala and its Muslim population during the Balkan Wars played some role in the Ottoman culture of defeat. Scenes of massacres that took place in the city and in its vicinity were disseminated to Ottoman readers through the press and the publications of different philanthropic associations that mushroomed during the Balkan Wars.[51] However, from the vast Ottoman literature on the defeat in the Balkan Wars, it becomes clear that Kavala played only a secondary position in this literature of mourning and revenge. For Ottoman authors, Kavala did not share the bravery and determination of Edirne, nor the shame of capitulation without a fight, as did Salonica. However, its image in Egypt was different, as Kavala became the main symbol of the defeat and the catastrophe that befell the Muslims in the Balkans. Furthermore, Ottoman philanthropy during the Balkan Wars was mainly distributed through sectarian categories and mechanisms.[52] While Ottoman discourse during the war underscored the shared destiny endured by all Ottomans, assistance was still offered in the framework of, and according to, mainly religious categories. For the Egyptian press, "their" victims were clearly the inhabitants of Kavala. Those refugees were singled out as the most deserving targets of khedivial philanthropy. One of the main reasons for Kavala's elevation to representative of the Ottoman defeat in the Balkans was the arrival of thousands of refugees from this city in Alexandria. In this manner, their narratives of atrocities became visible also for Egyptian audiences.[53]

While already during the war of 1877–8, rented Egyptian ships took part in transporting refugees from the Balkans to Anatolian ports,[54] the assistance offered to the Kavalan refugees during the Balkan Wars stemmed from the khedive's initiative. The first refugees originating from Kavala arrived in Alexandria, the main Egyptian port, after the signing of a temporary armistice with Bulgaria at the beginning of December 1912. Those first refugees, called by the Egyptian press "Kavala's refugees" (*muhājirū Kawala*) or just the *mankūbūn* ("those afflicted with disaster"), arrived on board a Romanian ship in early

December. They numbered 367 refugees and were first sent to the quarantine station for medical examination. All their needs were covered by the khedive and his household. Men, women, and children received food, clothes and means of surviving until they could earn their own money. Their presence was perceived as permanent; they were not temporary guests. Some of them were later settled on a *çiftlik* owned by the khedive in Dolmen.[55]

Of interest here are the intimate bonds forged between the khedivial family and the Kavala refugees. It is clear that the khedivial charity towards them was based on personal and intimate giving. The khedive himself handed over his donations, displaying the personalized nature of provision for the war victims. Once discharged from quarantine, the refugees were housed in one of the khedive's palaces in Alexandria – *Qasr Ra's al-Tīn* ("The Cape Fig Palace"), which was constructed in the 1840s by Mehmed Ali. Thus, the khedive accommodated them in his own house, sharing with them his private accommodation.[56] The arrival of these refugees on board the Romanian ship was the first convoy to Alexandria. Other refugees followed, constructing their own small colony in the city. The refugees benefitted from the khedive's personal concern and attention. Indeed, the Egyptian press reported that the khedive spent the whole day with them tending to all their needs. Only in the evening did he return to his newer palace – al-Muntaza, constructed in the early 1890s.[57]

At this stage, the Egyptian press already followed the scheduled arrival of the khedive's own yacht, *al-Mahrūsa*, carrying, it was rumored, more than 2,000 refugees from Kavala. When the yacht did arrive, the press reported on the debarcation of another convoy of 525 refugees who were dispatched to the quarantine. Apparently, many of the refugees chose to disembark from the ship when it made a stop in Istanbul.[58] All of the refugees' needs were taken care of by the khedivial household.[59] As the *Qasr al-Tīn* was already overwhelmed with refugees, another palace, owned by the widow of Muhammad Rāthib Bāshā and situated next to the Mahmūdiyya canal in Alexandria, served also to accommodate the refugees.[60] Indeed, according to the Egyptian press reporting from Cairo, the generosity of the Alexandrian widow illustrated Alexandria's mobilization to assist the refugees. Clearly, palaces, and not refugees' camps, were deemed appropriate to accommodate the Kavalan refugees. Following the khedive's footsteps, a certain merchant, Sālih Effendi al-Qādi, established a committee to provide the refugees with all their needs.[61]

In 1913, Tawfīq Tannūs published in Alexandria his account of the Balkan Wars. His book was one of several publications that attempted to explain the recent events in the Balkans and their ramifications to Arabic-speaking audiences. The author regarded the Egyptian mobilization to assist the Ottoman victims of war as representing "the Egyptians' noble heartedness and compassion" (*karam al-misriyīn wa 'atfihim*) towards the Ottoman Empire. For him, Egypt provided the most significant assistance enabling "to allay the calamities and the disasters that befell on the poor and the wretched".[62] While the author underlined the contribution of all sections of the Egyptian population to the Ottoman Empire, it is clear that the khedivial household led the campaign.

Among the beneficiaries of khedivial philanthropy, the Kavala refugees had a special share. More than any other party of war's victims, they were singled out as the group entitled to the personal charity of the khedive and his family. In their case, the ruling family's dynastic narrative came to be bound together with the Egyptian discourse on the Balkan Wars as representing a deliberate attack on the Ottoman Caliphate and a modern crusade against Muslims, resulting in the formation of a distinct group of deserving poor.

Conclusions

Providing charity accords the donor legitimacy and the gratitude of those benefitting from his charity. Launching relief campaigns in favor of those suffering from dearth can provide a suitable common cause, strengthening inner bonds and marking communities' boundaries. Being subject to British rule since the early 1880s, philanthropy was one of the main arenas in which the khedivial family could still display its independent political and social agendas and mobilize the Egyptian public towards well-defined aims chosen carefully by the khedive. Offering humanitarian assistance to the Ottoman army in the military fronts, especially through the services of the Egyptian Red Crescent, could equally indicate Egypt's position as an enlightened and "civilized" nation capable of affording relief in distant lands where Muslims came under threat. Indeed, the Balkan Wars offered ample opportunities for the khedivial family to demonstrate its concern and commitment towards Muslim civilians living in the Balkan provinces of the Ottoman Empire. However, such a public campaign needed a meaningful and well-known symbol that could represent the suffering of civilians, urging Egyptians to come to their assistance.

Kavala offered an appropriate such symbol. Benefitting from 100 years of khedivial charity, the Macedonian town played a major role in the khedivial narrative of the dynasty's origins. Philanthropy, newspapers, and official historiography, all preserved the bonds between the Egyptian ruling family and Kavala. The suffering of the city's population during the Balkan Wars enabled the incumbent khedive, ʿAbbas Hilmī, and his family to place the city at the center of their well-publicized campaign of war relief and to unleash a public campaign mobilizing the Egyptian population around a target well related to the ruling family. Furthermore, the significance of Kavala was reflected in the khedive's personal assistance to the refugees fleeing the city. Khedive ʿAbbas Hilmi and his close family relatives based their aid on face-to-face encounters with the refugees, tending to all their needs. The assistance offered to the inhabitants of Kavala represented the ruling family's concern towards Muslim victims of war, while putting a major *lieu de mémoire* of the khedivial family under the public spotlight.

PART IV

DISCOURSES OF SOCIAL AND NATIONAL VALUES

CHAPTER 11

NATIONAL INTERPRETATIONS OF MISFORTUNE AND WELFARE: THE PARADIGM OF THE INTELLECTUALS OF THE BULGARIAN REVIVAL

Eleonora Naxidou

This chapter examines how the notions of individual and collective misfortune/welfare were interwoven in national ideology in the Balkans during the second half of the nineteenth century, focusing on the Bulgarian paradigm. It compares the discourses among the diaspora intellectuals and activists in the Ottoman capital. Both groups copiously used metaphors of wealth and poverty to advance political ideas for achieving national independence. Such an approach is mainly related to the political facet of nationalism and the present analysis pays more attention to this dimension while keeping in mind its economic, social, and cultural/ethno-cultural aspects. Therefore, the examination of national interpretations of misfortune and welfare offers a window into the eclectic use of nationalism and classic liberalism, which modernity, as complex phenomenon, embraces.

Theoretical Background

Before spreading eastwards, nationalism in its current form initially emerged in western and central Europe in the second half of the eighteenth century as a product of the Enlightenment and the principles of the French Revolution and Romanticism.[1] Not constituting "a clear systematic body of doctrine",[2] though, "nationalism rarely travels alone. It always works with other ideologies, other kinds of political ideals, and these may be of the left as much as of the right."[3] At the same time, "while nationalism may always need a 'host' ideology, it is also possible that other ideologies find a useful 'host' in nationalism".[4] Indeed, during the first period of its development, at least until the beginning of the twentieth century, nationalism was intertwined with classical liberalism,[5] which was also inspired by modern ideological trends and middle-class values and interests.[6] Absolute individual freedom and self-determination, the core liberal ideals, were likewise applied to the nation by many liberal thinkers.[7] This association was produced by modern political and socio-economic changes, which gradually transferred the ruling power from the monarch to the people, making the latter the legitimate and sole source of authority within the state. Simply put, this means that the new viewpoints perceived the right to govern as emanating from the will of the people rather than from any divine or dynastic privilege. It was at this point that the concept of national community was employed in order to provide an appropriate explanation to the justified question of how the term "people" might be understood. The nation was identified with the citizens of a political formation entitled to self-rule, and, therefore, with the state itself.[8] This was also how the main doctrine of nationalism, which states that national and political entity should be congruent, came to be derived.[9] The outcome of this relationship is described as liberal nationalism that promotes freedom and self-governance for the nation as essential factors for progress and welfare.[10]

In this context, the proponents of liberal nationalism supported the right of sovereignty for the people/nation in the already established European states, such as England and France. In the case of multiethnic political entities, however, such as the Habsburg and Ottoman Empires, liberal nationalists, among whom Giuseppe Mazzini stands out, propagated revolution for liberation from foreign/alien domination, whose oppression was perceived as responsible for national decline and misfortune. For them, in order for the nation to flourish, freedom was essential.[11] Similarly, the aspiration for political emancipation from the Ottoman dominion and the concomitant creation of independent nation-states, mostly by means of armed uprisings, predominated in the Balkans. Within this framework, the present chapter aims to show how Bulgarian intellectuals/national leaders during the period of the Revival[12] conceptualized the interplay between liberal and national ideals. Furthermore, although their liberal orientation was prevalent, elements from other political ideologies were also integrated in their interpretations, such as federalism, and socialism/communism, which mostly addressed social and economic issues.

The Liberal Face of Bulgarian "Political Nationalism"

Bulgarian nationalism was a product of the modern ideological and political trends originating in western and central Europe, as well as the significant socio-economic changes that occurred in the Balkan provinces of the Ottoman Empire throughout the nineteenth century: growth of trade, emergence of an upcoming urban class,[13] economic incorporation, Ottoman reforms, and Russian influence, in particular Slavophilism and Pan-Slavism.[14] In addition to its cultural expressions, which aimed to cultivate the distinct ethnic character of the Bulgarian people, the Bulgarian national movement soon made demands for the abolition of all forms of foreign domination, which had until then been enforced upon the Bulgarian nation. Namely, the Bulgarians sought emancipation from the Greek-controlled Patriarchate of Constantinople and the creation of a separate church on a national basis.[15] They also wanted liberation from the Ottoman rule and the establishment of an independent nation-state. The first goal was accomplished in 1870 with the establishment of the Exarchate by the Sultan's decree without the Patriarch's consent,[16] and the second one in 1878 with the Treaty of Berlin at the end of the Russo–Turkish War (1877–8).

It was the national leaders/intellectuals of the diaspora who promoted the political agenda mostly in the late 1860s and 1870s, although there were some earlier manifestations related mainly to the pursuits of Georgi Rakovski.[17] Being settled mostly in the Danubian Principalities, Serbia, and Russia, these leaders formed groups with differing and/or opposing views and plans with regards to accomplishing their political aspirations. Among them the pro-Westerners and the firm adherents of revolutionary action who were called the "Young" (*Mladi*) founded various committees in Bucharest where the most active and influential community resided. In the 1860s, the most important organizations of the Young were the following: the Vŭrhovno Narodno Bŭlgarsko Taino Grazhdansko Nachalstvo (Higher National Bulgarian Secret Political Leadership) formed by Rakovski; the Taen Bûlgarski Centralen Komitet (Bulgarian Secret Central Committee), which published the newspaper *Narodnost* (Nationality); the Bŭlgarski Revoliucionen Centralen Komitet (Bulgarian Revolutionary Central Committee) under both Liuben Karavelov, who was the editor of the newspapers *Svoboda* (Freedom) and *Nezavisimost* (Independence), and Vasil Levski.[18]

Despite the differences between them, they all based their national programs on liberal ideals, thus endorsing liberal nationalism. The main belief these men shared, presented in their writings and propagated through the press in order to instigate a Bulgarian armed uprising, can be summarized as follows: subordination of the nation to foreign power was slavery and equaled misfortune and backwardness, whereas independent national governance was the unique political system that could provide the necessary conditions for progress and prosperity. The twofold argument they employed in order to support their claims was, on the one hand, to characterize the Ottoman administration as a barbaric and tyrannical yoke under which the Bulgarian people suffered innumerable hardships and, on the other, to exalt the benefits of freedom and national self-determination.

One of the earliest proponents of such political aspirations, Georgi Rakovski (1821–67), did not actually propose any form of political structure after achieving liberation and only vaguely alluded in his work to the merits of freedom as such. He was more prone to emphasizing the sufferings of the Bulgarians under Ottoman domination and calling for immediate revolutionary action to be taken. He insisted that there was nothing more real or notorious in the world than the criminal acts of the Turkish rule, as evidenced by the ruin and devastation wherever they set their foot. He also painted a picture of an indifferent Europe just sitting back and watching the Muslim infidels shedding the blood of their Christian brethren in the most beautiful corner of the continent; the Europeans could hear the victims' desperate and sorrowful cries but did nothing to help. Rakovski stressed that the Christians were aggrieved under the heavy Turkish yoke, as they were deprived of their freedom, homeland, and basic human rights.[19]

In an impassioned manner Rakovski expounded that without civil rights, a man is not a man in the image of his Creator, since God created him to be free and independent, and to dominate all other creatures on Earth with the might of his mind. He went on to bemoan that a man who knows no freedom is equal if not inferior to animals, which labor in misery and in servitude to their masters because of their inability to speak out.[20] He therefore urged the Bulgarians to take up arms in order to regain the precious freedom that their ancestors had enjoyed and to restore their celebrated name.[21] "One strong blow will chase away from our lands the bloodthirsty Muslims and ensure us a glorious future", he declared.[22] Overall, his ideas are summed up in the following verses from his poem *The Forest Traveler Herald* (1866):

> The Turkish yoke, four centuries endured
> let us smash heroically
> Our dear, beloved homeland,
> let us bravely free
> so that our nation may be reborn.[23]

In the late 1860s (1867–9) the newspaper *Narodnost*[24] served as a platform of the Bulgarian Secret Central Committee, as previously mentioned. It also adopted the "Turkish yoke versus national liberation" reasoning. The almost five centuries of Ottoman domination were perceived as a long period of pain and suffering for the Bulgarians who under these adverse conditions had sunk into complete illiteracy instead of having developed their education, as had other people.[25] Many examples of Turkish arbitrariness, injustice, oppression, military abuse, financial exploitation, theft, and anarchy were highlighted.[26] Turkish authorities, it was claimed, were totally indifferent to the welfare of their subjects, their only interest being tax collection.[27] Living under a regime that did not respect a person's life, property or honor,[28] Bulgarians were deprived of all their political rights, which reduced them to the position of slaves.[29] It was assumed that had the Bulgarians protected their own kingdom, church, and schools, they would have developed a robust political life and become one of the European powers.[30]

Another article presented a parable of the fates of a good and a bad merchant, using economic example and language to promote political goals. The shrewd merchant keeps his balance sheets in check and is able to make future investments on an annual budget. In the same way, advised the story, the Bulgarian people need to have a clear picture and a balanced account of its political developments, so as to make sound plans and moves for the future in order to avoid having the same fate as the bad merchant who ends up becoming lost in darkness.[31] In the same article, the Turks with the collaboration of the Greeks had seized the Bulgarians' "national capital", meaning their political and ecclesiastical autonomy. The Bulgarians were urged to claim it back and to demand the restoration of their kingdom because loss of freedom and sovereignty was the greatest misfortune that could befall a nation.[32] In order to set an example for the Bulgarians, reference was then made to how other states had handled their national affairs. The Romanian national liberal party that had initiated the revolution in 1848 as a reaction to the detrimental policies of their administration was mentioned as an example, which although unsuccessful, triggered a series of events that led not only to the unification of Wallachia and Moldova, but also to autonomy and constitutional government.[33] It was in this way that the writings in *Narodnost* encouraged the Bulgarians to rise up against the Turks, stating that this was the only sure way to take their fate in their hands, as done by the Greeks, the Serbs, and the Romanians.[34]

Vasil Levski (1837–73), who is often referred to as the Apostle of Freedom,[35] belongs to the same revolutionary milieu. Unlike the other national leaders presented here, he was not engaged in journalism and did not generally put his ideas on paper. Rather, he was mostly a man of action. His views on the situation at the time and his visions for the future of Bulgaria were mainly made known through his correspondence and the few texts that he actually penned. Levski considered the Bulgarians to be slaves under the Ottoman despotic and inhumane rule.[36] He advocated for a Bulgarian democratic republic through revolution, as the only way to escape the Turkish tyrannical regime.[37] Bulgaria, as he envisioned it, was to be governed by the people rather than the king.[38] It would encompass all the lands where Bulgarian people lived, stretching across Bulgaria, Thrace, and Macedonia,[39] and it would be a true "Temple of Freedom"[40] where unity, fraternity, and equality would exist between the Bulgarians and the other nationalities. Bulgarians, Turks, Jews and others would have equal rights irrespective of faith, nationality, civic state, or any other distinction. They would all adhere to the same laws to which they would have agreed.[41] Levski was not only opposed to Turkish absolutism, but to all autocratic systems of governance. He declared that in the century of freedom and equal rights for all nations, all peoples were entitled to live free and with dignity.[42] Levski believed that the time had come for the Bulgarian brothers in Serbia, Montenegro, Romania, and elsewhere to rise up and fight for democracy, as did the organizations "Young France", "Young Russia", and the like.[43]

Liuben Karavelov (1834–79), one of the most prominent intellectuals and revolutionaries of the Revival, described the hardships endured by the Bulgarians during the Ottoman era in a similar vein. For four and a half centuries the Bulgarian people had been living enveloped in a fog, suffering and dying under the cruelest of tyrannies. Their homeland having been plundered, they were forced to migrate to Romania and Serbia to make a living.[44] They were beaten and skinned like animals and endured pain greater than any human could bear with patience.[45] For these reasons, Karavelov was convinced that the Bulgarians could never develop friendly relations with the Turkish authorities, as the happiness of the former depended on the misfortune of the latter. As long as the Turks controlled the Balkan Peninsula, the Bulgarian people would suffer.[46] Karavelov categorically rejected the proposal put forward in 1867 by the Bulgarian Secret Central Committee in Bucharest for the transformation of the Ottoman Empire into a dual Turko–Bulgarian state.[47] For him, only a madman would think that the Bulgarians and Turks could ever co-exist since the only "virtues" that the Muslims possessed were bloodthirsty fanaticism and sheer hatred against infidels.[48] The Turks, being Muslims, could not be seen as humans because the Quran definitely opposed every attempt at human progress.[49] Finally, claiming that the Bulgarians had drunk enough from the cup of misery, Karavelov, like the other revolutionaries, urged his people to take up arms against the Turkish yoke.[50]

Karavelov firmly believed in the sacredness of both individual and national freedom.[51] Freedom, he claimed, was like a fast-flowing river washing away all the dirt and grit.[52] If it were a self-governing nation, oriented towards industry and culture, Bulgaria could have a glorious future, as it had the most fertile and productive lands of the Balkans stretching as far as the Aegean, the Black Sea, and the Danube, which provided the Bulgarian people with the means to become rich and mighty in this wide area.[53] According to him, Bulgarian liberty should be pure and unblemished because the Bulgarian soul and spirit were great and sincere.[54] Being deprived from living under the "sun of freedom" and in spite of the commendable efforts and remarkable skills of Bulgarian intellectuals, Bulgaria could not move forward, let alone keep pace with European progress and education. Under these conditions, the Bulgarians could not, indeed dared not, dedicate themselves to the welfare of their country. The lack of freedom brought with it both moral and material poverty, which meant there could be no advancement in arts or sciences.[55] Moreover, industry, trade, and economy in general could not flourish, leaving the young, educated people unemployed and without career prospects or the means to maintain themselves.[56]

In sum, Karavelov likened freedom to a goddess who should be worshiped to the highest degree. It was through liberty that humans attained the highest level of civic life, self-respect, and enlightenment. Freedom could lift man to the heights of knowledge. The mind of a free man knows right from wrong and enables him to subjugate nature. For Karavelov, only people who enjoyed civic, social, ecclesiastical, scientific, national, and individual independence could be considered to be complete human beings.[57] He declared that there were no greater blessings in the world than freedom and human self-knowledge, and that the former is the outcome of the latter.[58]

Karavelov envisioned a liberated Bulgarian state that would be both prosperous and progressive: on the one hand, organized on the basis of one nation or at least one race that had common ethics, customs, traditions and religion; and on the other, governed by liberal principles, as was the case of America (meaning the United States), Switzerland, and Belgium.[59] Opposed to monarchy, he claimed that all royals, the Sultans included, were tyrants who were enemies of the people and looked only after their own interests. Monarchical regimes strove to perpetuate people's ignorance by keeping them illiterate. Even though the monarchs were responsible for the poverty and misery of their subjects, it was the foolish and blind loyalty and immature allegiance of the people that kept them in power.[60]

Karavelov also combined his national and liberal ideals with federalism. Being a keen adherent of co-operation among the Christian Balkan peoples against the Turks, he fervently promoted the idea of the creation of a liberal Balkan federation that would ensure the individual liberty and the national rights of all members. Although he wavered as to who the participant nations should be, he stood firm on the model of governance of such a political union. The Serbs, the Bulgarians, and quite likely the Romanians and the Greeks would participate on equal terms and enjoy autonomy. While keeping their own judicial system based on national ethics and traditions, their own educational system, and their own literature, they would also be represented in the Supreme Federal Parliament.[61] Karavelov was convinced that the real nature of freedom was not to abolish the Turkish or German tyrants and replace them with national leaders who had similar absolutist attitudes and conduct. For him, the government should exist for the sake of the people and not vice versa.[62] In sum, all of Karavelov's designs were aimed at establishing peace, freedom, and equality in the Balkans.[63]

Hristo Botev (1847/48–76) was another distinguished journalist, poet, and revolutionary of the Revival. He expressed similar views about foreign rule and national emancipation, which were interwoven into an even broader ideological canvas. Various ideologies were blended together to form his particular worldview: nationalism – national self-determination; liberalism – individual and national freedom; federalism – the creation of a Balkan federation; and socialism/communism – abolition of domestic oppression by the ruling classes and the clergy; and friendship and collaboration among the peoples. This amalgamation of ideas means that Botev's work contains obscurities and inconsistencies that make it difficult to describe and interpret. Nevertheless, his primary goal, like the others mentioned here, was to achieve Bulgarian liberation from Turkish domination through an armed uprising. "Freedom is precious" was the motto of his newspaper *Duma na Balgarskite Emigranti* (Account of the Bulgarian Emigrants), which he published in Braila in 1871. According to Botev, Bulgarians had suffered savage acts of cruelty under the barbarian Turkish yoke for 500 years.[64] He stated that Bulgarian history was full of bitter sorrow and the people's lives were appallingly hard. With vivid imagery he described that their hands and feet and their minds and will were bound by heavy iron chains that rusted with their bitter tears and blood.[65] They were both physically and morally paralysed, he explained, due to life filled with intimidation, theft, and corruption under the Turkish administration. The Bulgarian people, living like slaves or cattle, possessing nothing – not even their own heads – would never reap the fruits of their labor because the slothful, yataghan-wielding Turks, who cared naught for education or science, took everything.[66] Botev was also strongly opposed to Ottoman reform and the proposed dual Turko–Bulgarian monarchy. For him, the two races had nothing in common; not only were their character and customs incompatible but also their morality and worldviews. Revolution was for him the sole means of liberation.[67] "Freedom or death", he declared.[68]

Like Karavelov, Botev was convinced that the best solution for the Eastern Question was the creation of a South Slav or Danubian free confederation consisting of five or six members: Serbia with Bosnia, Herzegovina and a part of Old Serbia; Greece with Thessaly and Epirus; Romania incorporating some Austrian and Russian territories; Montenegro, which would be either united with Serbia or expanding into northern Albania and part of Herzegovina; and Bulgaria with Macedonia and Thrace. All participating countries would enjoy complete independence; a council, comprised of an equal number of representatives from each member-nation, would hold supreme political and legislative power. It was also proposed that Constantinople would become a free commercial city under the protection of the Great Powers.[69]

Botev's assertion was that political freedom was essential for the nation's welfare. He declared that liberty was the necessary condition – just as an eye needs light and an ear needs sound[70] – for each individual and every nation to prosper and promote their moral and material wellbeing.[71] It was imperative for the Bulgarians to gain their freedom because of their distinctive national physiognomy, their national principles.[72] In addition, their characteristic diligence and potential for political and cultural growth[73] made them resemble a young person capable of developing mind and character.[74] Then, as a nation, they could become the "Germans of the south", or the "English of the east".[75] Moreover, being a proponent of socialist/communist ideals, Botev lent a social dimension to the issue of liberty, which will be discussed in the next section.

The Social Dimensions of Liberal Nationalism

Many of the proponents of national independence criticized not only external but also internal oppressors, such as the Bulgarian *chorbadzhi,* for contributing to the people's misfortunes. Some even went as far as to demand that they give up their authority.

Rakovski, for example, had no sympathy whatsoever for the Bulgarian notables. They had attained their social status not because they descended from the medieval Bulgarian aristocracy, but because they were the heads of the local communities. They had been designated by their compatriots to represent them and to collect taxes for the Turkish authorities.[76] Although initially the *chorbadzhi* had been respected members of their society, gradually they became avaricious and corrupt, abusing their brethren, especially the poor, simple villagers, for their own profit. As representatives of the Turks and lackeys of the Greek high clergy, they had drained further the already impoverished folk.[77] In his works, Rakovski recounted numerous instances of injustice. In Vidin the local governors exploited the people by demanding higher taxes than required by law, which they extracted with the help of the *chorbadzhi*.[78] In Liaskovec, as well, instead of protecting the rights of their co-nationals, the *chorbadzhi* grew even richer at their expense.[79]

Levski, likewise, held the *chorbadzhi* responsible for the miserable situation of the Bulgarian people. They were to blame for the lawlessness, corruption, and misappropriation of power.[80] He nevertheless solicited their cooperation in the armed revolt against the Turks on the grounds that all patriots should participate to whatever extent they could for the common good.[81]

In his work, Karavelov stated that Bulgarians everywhere bitterly complained about the behavior of the notables who were worse than the Turks and the *Phanariots*.[82] He asserted that in the past the majority of the *chorbadzhi* had forsaken their nationality for personal interest. They had betrayed their nation by changing their names and taking on other nationalities, such as Greek, Romanian, Russian, and even Gypsy.[83] From personal experience, he stated with certainty that the Hellenized Bulgarians (*Graecomans*) had humiliated and dishonored their compatriots more than the Turks or *Phanariots* did.[84] How, he wondered, could anyone be considered a Bulgarian who was ashamed of his origin, who could not string five words together in his mother tongue, and who had no relationship with his family?[85] With a bitter irony he commented that, despite this disgraceful situation, Bulgarians' welfare depended on these notables simply because of the power that they held.[86] Therefore, he declared that Bulgarians should dispense with their notables who shamed them. As for the Bulgarian ecclesiastical hierarchy (the Exarchate was established in 1870), he suggested that they should reform and abandon the Byzantine/*Phanariot* mentality.[87]

While Rakovski was opposed to the Bulgarian *chorbadzhi* in general, Karavelov vaguely implied the elimination of their authority, focusing his critique mainly on certain obvious groups. In addition, both writers supported the creation of a national Bulgarian church despite the fact that the notables, whom they despised, were actively involved in this. Yet they expressed hostility towards the Hellenized clergy of the Patriarchate of Constantinople whom they blamed for manipulating and exploiting the Bulgarian flock.

In contrast, Botev spoke out more consistently against the social distinctions and discriminations that existed, and envisioned a revolution that combined both the national and social dimensions. He explained that the main reason for the Bulgarians' subordination, first to Byzantium and later to the Ottoman Empire, was first and foremost because the Bulgarian kings, aristocrats, and clergy were corrupt and immoral and sided with the Byzantines at the expense of the welfare of their own people.[88] In the first issue of his newspaper, *Duma,* he wrote that the Bulgarians hated the notables and clergymen perhaps even more than the Turks. He described them as "byzantine dirt" because, as keepers of the keys to the Turkish chains, they had betrayed and ruined their own people.[89] It was for this reason that he was skeptical about the autonomous Bulgarian Church, which was established in 1870. He could not see how it would contribute to the people's wellbeing. Although the matter appeared to have been solved for the clerics, it would only be solved for the people once they got rid of the clergy.[90] In his view, religion and priests were the biggest enemies of freedom and progress.[91] Being a declared opponent of the clergy, whom he characterized as global parasites of humanity, he directed his anticlericalism against the hierarchy of the Bulgarian Exarchate, which had failed to do its duty in protecting and caring for the people's welfare.[92] He did admit, however, that the Exarchate was useful in maintaining the unity of the Bulgarian nation.[93] For example, he lauded the late Bishop Dionysius of Lovech, describing him as a patriot who strongly defended the national interests and as one of the best and most dignified high priests.[94] Thus, in his own words, Botev called for "revolution, which will clear the Balkan Peninsula not only from the Turks who consider us as merchandise and livestock but also from everything that can harm our true efforts for complete and absolute human freedom".[95] Having branded the Bulgarian elite and clergy as among the people's oppressors, Botev invited the members of the diaspora to lead the liberation struggle. After all, they were, according to him, the rightful heirs of the outlaws (*haidouti*) who had turned against the Turkish authorities.[96]

Ecclesiastical Liberation as National Welfare

While the Bulgarian liberal activists of the diaspora sought a political solution to the national question, the national leaders residing within the Ottoman Empire and mostly in Constantinople, fought for ecclesiastical independence. Nevertheless, as previously mentioned, most of these national activists, such as Rakovski, Karavelov, and the newspaper *Narodnost*, did support the efforts of the latter through their writings.

In the 1860s, the demand for the establishment of a separate church provoked a serious conflict between the Bulgarians and their traditional ecclesiastical authority, namely the Patriarchate of Constantinople. In the course of this dissension, differing groups with opposing views concerning both the content of their claims and the strategies to achieve them emerged among the Bulgarian leadership. The radicals, nicknamed the "Young" by their contemporaries,[97] were more concerned about the national aspect of the issue. They were headed by the representative of the Bulgarian community of Philippoupolis (Plovdiv) in the Ottoman capital, Stoian Chomakov, and Petko Slaveikov, the editor of the newspaper *Makedoniia*. Both were opposed to any compromise that did not foresee the creation of an independent national church with jurisdiction over all the Bulgarian population in the Balkans, including those living in Macedonia and Thrace. Being adherents of an all-inclusive or maximalist nationalism, the radicals favored the perpetuation of the Ottoman rule in the European territories because they considered it the most suitable for the cultivation and consolidation of the Bulgarian national character and for the thwarting of the assimilationist policies of rival nationalisms. Moreover, they believed that gaining Bulgarian autonomy through a separate *millet*[98] within the imperial environment would facilitate national and territorial unification and was, therefore, preferable to creating a small state that would not encompass the entire nation within its borders.[99]

It was within this ideological framework that a different version of liberal nationalism developed. Misfortune was attributed to the subordination of the Bulgarians to foreign/Greek ecclesiastical administration, whereas prosperity would be gained with ecclesiastical emancipation. It was maintained that Bulgarian socio economic and cultural progress was not so much impeded by the Ottoman regime but more by the absence of a separate ecclesiastical organization that would enable Bulgarians to enjoy some sort of political autonomy as well.[100] This autonomy would be broader because the clergy controlled not only the religious aspects of people's lives, but also the moral, civic, and financial activities of their flock, such as education, tax collection, legal secular cases, and representation before the Ottoman administration.[101]

This rationale was based on the view that although the Bulgarians inhabited a land rich in natural resources that had enormous economic prospects, they could not develop their potential as a people. No matter how fertile the soil was, or how bountiful the forests, or how great the mineral wealth and so on, these resources remained idle and unexploited due to the fact that they were under the dominion of a foreign clergy that oppressed the resourceful, intelligent, and diligent Bulgarians.[102] The sufferings that the Bulgarian people endured under the spiritual domination of the Patriarchate of Constantinople, which identified Orthodoxy with Hellenism, were enumerated within this context: all high ecclesiastical posts were assigned to *Phanariots*/Greeks who sought to deprive Bulgaria from her rich, intelligent, and noble elements,[103] and whose aim was to turn the Bulgarian people into a stupefied, passive flock by destroying their body and soul.[104] Being forced to support the enormous Church expenses and the escalating patriarchal debt that was due to the mismanagement and abuses of the *Phanariot* high priests, the Bulgarians also fell victim to economic exploitation.[105] Finally, pressure was put on them to abandon their nationality and Hellenize. The main ways for achieving such assimilation were: prohibiting Bulgarians to use their language in church or education, attempting to inspire Greek national ideals into Bulgarian children at school, and compelling them to adopt Greek names.[106]

In sum, it was assumed that due to the Greek ecclesiastical "yoke" the skills of talented Bulgarians could not bear fruit nor could science and art develop, and thus the Bulgarian nation could only be in a state of ignorance, stagnation, and apathy. This was well expressed in Chomakov's allegory of blooming nature: if and when liberation was to be achieved, the powerful seeds that the Bulgarian people possessed would grow into the tree of genius that would blossom in the fields.[107] Then the Bulgarian people would be able to reap the fruits and gather ideas, and experience the public life and material wealth that would empower them as citizens not only for their own benefits but for their government as well.[108]

Conclusions

In the case of the Bulgarians, political nationalism emerged in the 1860s and 1870s within a circle of activists of the diaspora who were not only acquainted, but most of them were also related to each other, or occasionally were associates. For example, Levski was a member of the first Bulgarian legion, which was formed by Rakovski in Belgrade (1862) with the aid of the Serbian government,[109] whereas with Karavelov he founded the Bulgarian Revolutionary Central Committee (1870). Kasabov, the editor of *Narodnost*, assisted Rakovski with the publication of his newspaper *Dunavski Lebed* (The Danube Swan), which appeared in Belgrade (1860–1).[110] Botev was a friend of Karavelov and co-editor of his newspaper *Nezavisimost* (1872–4) before they fell out for both ideological and personal reasons.[111]

All of them were strongly influenced by the principles of the Enlightenment, the American and French Revolutions, as well as the rebellious turmoil that reigned in central Europe and the Balkans resulting from the rise of national movements, which served as a paradigm for the Bulgarian revolutionaries.[112] The personal ties and ideological orientation that they shared meant that their ideas bore strong resemblances, the most significant of which was their adherence to liberal nationalism. They all believed that the supreme value and prerequisite for human welfare was individual and collective freedom, which they perceived in two ways: as national liberation and the establishment of a system of governance based on the will of the citizens/nation in a newly created nation-state. Each advocated one main aspect of national liberalism: Rakovski was focusing on civil rights, Karavelov and the *Narodnost*'s editors on constitutional government, and Levski on democratic republic. Moreover, each one, in his way, expressed hostility against the Bulgarian notables, whom they identified with the ruling class. Botev, due to his leftist inclinations, envisaged a more radical socio-political change, making an attempt to combine national/liberal with communist ideals. Although not clearly stated, he seems to propagate a national revolution to overthrow both the political and social order.[113] While both Karavelov and Botev incorporated national sovereignty into a federal context, Levski was the only one who took into account the existence of other nationalities within the borders of a future Bulgarian state and promoted equal rights for them, too. Hence, eclecticism of ideologies is characteristic of their worldview.

During the same period, liberal concepts emerged into another context that associated freedom of the nation with ecclesiastical emancipation. The Bulgarian national leadership within the Ottoman Empire agreed with the assessment of their counterparts in the diaspora concerning the deplorable situation of the Bulgarian people. However, the agents they blamed for this regression where not the same – the Patriarchate, not the Sultan – and thus they proposed quite a different solution.

Essentially, however, the two approaches were not disparate because ecclesiastical independence was understood as a mode of political autonomy within the imperial structure. One merely constituted a more modest political program, which foresaw a gradual deliverance from Ottoman rule, whereas the other was directed toward the same ends in a more radical manner. It was without a doubt that the overriding objective of both approaches was to rid the Bulgarian people of misfortune and to provide welfare for the Bulgarian nation.

CHAPTER 12

"PEOPLE'S WELFARE" AS NATIONAL SECURITY: SERBIAN LIBERALS AND DISCOURSES ON ECONOMIC DEVELOPMENT IN PRE-INDEPENDENCE SERBIA (1850s–1870s)

Momir Samardžić

The gradual transformation of Balkan societies and states, as well as their economic structures, has been a process conditioned by a number of interrelated internal and external factors, which have had a lasting impact on their further development. The history of the modern Serbian state was marked by the efforts of rulers and ruling elites to provide the necessary conditions for the development of capitalism through reform legislation and the creation of an appropriate institutional framework. This process represents a constant in the history of Serbia, but a constant that is characterized by different levels of intensity in the modernization effort. However, when faced with complex internal and external factors, the state failed to make a decisive step towards successful economic development through effective intervention.

The aim of this chapter is to analyze the specific aspects of the social transformation of the modern Serbian state in the period before it gained its independence from the Ottoman Empire (1878). Particular attention will be paid to how liberalism and nationalism reinforced each other and how debates and political decisions about institutional reforms were framed within a political rather than a comprehensive economic modernization, which thereby influenced not only the discourse about economic development, but also the development itself. The concepts of rapid economic development adopted by Serbian economists, intellectuals, and politicians were influenced not only by knowledge and experience, but also by ideas and ideologies adopted during their education at European universities. From the late 1840s until independence, Serbian students were particularly under the influence of liberal political ideas. These ideas influenced several generations of Serbian intellectuals' concepts of economic development and were adopted mainly through the texts of interpreters and refracted through the social and economic reality of the German states, whose economic theorists had the greatest influence. They were then applied to the reality of the predominantly peasant Serbian society. This eclectic compilation of liberal and protectionist attitudes, in tandem with the goal of "national liberation and unification" as a unifying factor, shaped the Serbian intellectuals' perception of development, which shifted together with the changing socio-economic development. In this context, the concept of "the people's welfare" was often used in public discourse and became a tool for liberals of different generations to achieve political rather than economic goals.

Specific Features of the Serbian Developmental Path

Modern Serbia emerged in a very sensitive geo-strategic position on the border of the Habsburg Monarchy and the Ottoman Empire. In the nineteenth century it was primarily an agricultural country with a dominant small peasant landholding[1] that excluded the possibility of a "second serfdom" or refeudalization by introducing capitalist means of production into agriculture, which was characteristic of the agrarian economies of the European east and south-east.[2] The struggle for political independence after creating a vassal Principality of Serbia within the Ottoman Empire (1830) was not followed by changes that would transform an underdeveloped agrarian economy into a developed one based on the development of manufacturing and further industrialization.[3] The most perceptive analysis thus far of the development and structural deficiencies of the nineteenth-century Serbian economy by Marie-Janine Calic emphasized a number of elements that characterize the specific path Serbia followed into modernity: the preservation of a system of peasant family economy within the cooperative (*zadruga*), consisting of a family community or extended family characterized by indivisible common property, cooperative economy, and collective legal responsibility. This system was resistant to the pressures of various economic conditions preventing an agrarian revolution as a precondition for further development and industrialization, and thus causing permanent low non-agricultural sector growth and lack of a chain reaction, which would stimulate the development of other sectors. Essentially, Calic identified structural barriers to economic development in the relationships between and interdependence of cultural traditions, socio-economic structure, and regulatory policies, thus emphasizing the responsibility of the state and its wavering policy in the areas of social reform, education, and social policy.[4]

In the first decades of the nineteenth century the dynamics of Serbian social development were decisively influenced by contacts with the West, the process of gradual incorporation into the modern capitalist system, and the process of modernization, intertwined with nation-state building and the construction of national identity. Although the beginning of constructing a national identity was associated with the impact of ideas of the Enlightenment on the Serbian ethnic community in the Habsburg Monarchy, its development differed from the development of the national movements of other ethnic minorities in the Monarchy. It was decisively determined by the uprising of the Serbs in the Ottoman *Sanjak* of Smederevo and the creation of a vassal principality. The early creation of the state contributed definitively to the construction of the nation and its identity through a specific synergy of vernacular mobilization and bureaucratic incorporation.[5]

Nevertheless, the concept of a nation of the Serbs was solely genealogical/ethnic and it determined all the fundamental characteristics of its equivalent organicist, nationalist ideology. As already mentioned, its main objective was "national liberation and unification", which was the ambition to overthrow Ottoman suzerainty and achieve territorial expansion, thereby bringing together all the Balkan territories of the Ottoman Empire thought to be populated by a majority of inhabitants of Serbian ethnic origin. The method for achieving this goal was war, seen also as a catalyst for national homogenization.[6] Moreover, this preoccupation with the idea of national unity dictated the dynamics of internal development by "suppressing the harmonization of the relationship between the state and society into the background, and giving the process of the country's internal modernization a one-sided character". Consequently, any orientation toward the development of the existing state solely within its existing territorial framework and neglecting the need for "national liberation and unification", was seen as a betrayal.[7]

Our analysis takes into consideration these dynamics of the Serbian nation-building process and Calic's arguments, as well as Gale Stokes' thesis that "in the era of transformation" countries "must face the pressures of exogenous change, whenever it comes, with a given set of social arrangements".[8] Moreover, since "no major social change occurs outside of the world context: and though the strengths and weaknesses of individual states and societies are largely determined by internal causes, it is the way these characteristics of societies interact with the world system that determines the direction, intensity, and speed of further internal change",[9] it is clear that the specificities of the Serbian developmental path should be sought in the complex interrelation of different internal and external factors, which had a decisive influence on structural obstacles to economic development. Within this process, the last decades of the history of the nominally Ottoman Serbia were marked by the entrance of a group of intellectuals into the political life of the country, specifically the group influenced by liberal political ideas during their education abroad.

Serbian Liberalism as a Paradigm of Social Contradictions

The above-mentioned thesis of suppressing the "harmonization of the relationship between the state and society" was a result of the social structure inherited from the Ottoman period that would set limits on the possibilities for future change. Even in the 1840s, this structure was perceived as "an essentially classless system" with "only one class, a highly undifferentiated peasantry",[10] and since there was no developed, numerous, and influential middle class as a political factor, the existing social vacuum was filled by the state, which then became the dominant element and the most developed institution. But, a modern state with the principle of separation of powers, a legislature, a judiciary, and centralized bureaucracy was only one of the forms of modernization taken from the West, which according to Stokes, "occurred in a social situation that was almost completely unprepared for it", and, "whereas it operated using the same forms as its models in the West, the actual content of political activity was more consistent with the status of traditional societies than with the more legalistic societies from which the state forms were copied".[11]

The reign of Prince Miloš Obrenović (1830–9) is often described in terms of governance of the vassal principality as an Ottoman *pashalik*. Its paternalistic concept was replaced in the 1840s and 1850s with the autocracy of an oligarchy, a restructuring of the public administration, a gradual construction of a bureaucratic state with an organized government and judiciary, and a certain concept of economic and educational policies. The construction of a system according to a cameralist governmental pattern, which included a strong ruler and centralized bureaucratic administration alienated from its subjects, led towards the perception of the people's underdeveloped political consciousness and its inability to participate in the country's administration, as well as the claim that the principles of parliamentary government and civil rights were inappropriate for Serbia's political and social structure. These positions were the basis of the construction of conservative political thought in Serbia, and were the main reasons for cooperation among rulers, bureaucracy, and conservative intellectuals.[12]

At the end of the 1840s, upon the return of the first state scholarship holders from their studies abroad, a resistance began against the centralized bureaucratic state and the absolutist government as well as calls for the introduction of basic civil rights and parliamentary democracy. As a socially undifferentiated agricultural country of small landholders without a developed civil society, and, consequently, without a liberal political tradition, Serbia did not have the basic preconditions for a more profound adoption of liberal ideology. Nevertheless, Serbian students believed that the adoption of liberal political institutions could be a precondition for the country's social and economic transformation and conflicts among political groups with different views on the resolution of existing political, social, and economic issues were perceived as a clash of conservative and liberal political forces.[13]

According to one of the oldest and widely accepted periodizations, Serbian historiography divides Serbian liberals into three groups: "the liberals of 1848", "the liberals of 1858", and "the liberals of 1868".[14] Dimitrije Matić and Kosta Cukić ("the liberals of 1848"), Heidelberg students and professors at the Belgrade Lyceum, secured their place in the history of Serbian liberalism by criticizing the police state and arguing that people had to be aware of certain rights, thus promoting the freedom of the individual, constitutionality, and the rule of law. The leaders of the next generation, Jevrem Grujić, Milovan Janković, and Vladimir Jovanović ("the liberals of 1858") were their students.[15] However, the ideology linking not just all generations of intellectuals considered as liberals by historiography, but also liberals and their opponents the conservatives, was nationalism, which was particularly important in the political activities of the generation entering the political arena in 1858. Liberal political ideas, or liberalism as a political philosophy seeking to explain the legal and institutional implications of popular sovereignty, were combined with nationalism as a dominant ideology, and, under the influence of the revolutionary democracy of German and Italian nationalist movements, became powerfully influential in Serbia at the end of the 1850s. In its Serbian version, within a society that constructed its collective identity above all on a negative perception of the Ottoman suzerain, liberalism replaced the principle of freedom of the individual with the ideal of collective liberty. National and political liberation were viewed as synonymous; national independence was "a link in the chain of other freedoms" and mutually dependent with the expansion of political freedoms.[16] An important consequence of this was the elite's focus on political modernization and the reform of institutions, especially constitutional restructuring as the culmination, as well as the framework of political system reform. However, the need for comprehensive modernization was neglected, which inevitably led to deviations from the assumed models and to the failure of political reforms, without a deeper essential impact on social changes.[17]

Considering that ideas of national sovereignty, political freedom, and equality fit in well with the agrarian social structure of Serbia, the generation of 1858 focused on the Assembly (Skupština) as an institution of customary law, consisting primarily of peasants; an institution that was both a part of historical tradition and a relic of the local governmental system from the Ottoman period. In an egalitarian society without significant social differences, the existence and tradition of the patriarchal family cooperatives (*porodična zadruga*) and municipalities (*opština*) were the basis of a local governmental system and a most important stable form of social community. Similarly, the survival of the institution of the Assembly contributed to the perception of the Assembly not only as a permanent and necessary authority, but also to the role of the people in political decision-making, which was crucial for the development of Serbian parliamentarianism.[18] Stemming from the belief that Serbs have a natural propensity for democracy, liberals found inherent democracy in the existing social institutions: the family cooperative, the municipality, and the Assembly, thus reconciling their own liberalism and nationalism. For the Serbian liberals, introduction of parliamentarianism was a return to their roots.[19] Furthermore, as Diana Mishkova stresses, "their attempt to attain a synthesis between tradition and modernity ensued from their effort to 'condense' the historical time needed for the implementation of modern forms of social organization, economic and political freedom in particular, and most of all the nation-state".[20]

The peculiarities of the reform movement of 1858 also point to the fact that the "group of liberal-minded people" included clerks, traders, teachers, and officers, but also wealthy peasants and priests. Those educated in Russia during the 1850s, such as Panta Srećković and Alimpije Vasiljević, as well as Russian-educated representatives of the Serbian church hierarchy were also considered to be liberal-minded intellectuals. Above all, nationalists, much like the German and Italian liberals, were focused on national unification, were more "national romantics, and less progressives", and focused their struggle on winning political freedoms as a precondition for national liberation. Bearing in mind the ideological context of the roots of the reform movement of the 1850s, we can talk about the Serbian intellectuals' liberal nationalism, rather than about national liberalism.[21]

After the overthrow of Prince Aleksandar Karađorđević and the oligarchy in 1858, the liberals' attempt to build a modern parliament on the foundation of the Assembly as an institution of customary law consisting primarily of peasants failed. In 1859 and 1860 laws were adopted legalizing the Assembly for the first time, now as the National Assembly, but solely as an advisory body and without any real influence.[22] Some of liberals' ideas were realized under specific historical circumstances with the adoption of the Constitution of 1869 after the assassination of the autocratic Prince Mihailo (1868). Serbia became a constitutional monarchy, and a representative system and a principle of division of power were adopted for the first time, while at the same time preserving the centralist state and strong executive government.[23] As a German scholar, the creator of this moderate liberal Constitution and leader of the "liberals of 1868", Jovan Ristić always had inclinations towards right-wing liberalism, disliked the idea of the populace interfering in politics, and was far from believing in the inherent democratic potential of the Serbian peasant. Under the influence of the Prussian constitutional system, the centralized state and strong executive power were preserved.[24] Yet the new Constitution institutionalized a pattern of the previously nominal participation of peasantry in political life through the National Assembly, and thus created conditions for the articulation of public opinion and the confrontation of different political ideas and agendas, and, in doing so, confirmed the thesis that a social structure existing before the creation of a modern state had a strong influence on its subsequent political directions.[25]

Furthermore, a group of intellectuals, called "the young conservatives" by the older historiography, is also considered to be part of the liberal political tradition by contemporary Serbian historiography.[26] They opposed Ristić's version of moderate liberalism based on the Prussian model with their own vision of a political state order based on the English and French models. However, this was an early model from the 1830s and 1840s, which was supposed to bring power to a narrow class of the intellectual elite and, thus, had little in common with the democratic ideas of European liberalism of the 1860s. They also advocated for a more consistent transfer of experiences and achievements from Western Europe which would lead to internal modernization, and "whose inseparable elements they considered to be strict legality, personal and political freedoms, as well as a responsible government". Although they were also nationalists, as the generation educated during the 1860s, they had different perceptions of social transformation for the Serbian state and society and emphasized internal political change as the most important goal and as a precondition for successful economic development and national unification.[27]

For almost three decades, generations of reform-oriented intellectuals sought to find answers to the challenges of modernization that had been imposed by more developed European countries on the Serbian peasant society. Of those belonging to the moderate liberals of the 1840s, Cukić and Matić had by the 1860s become part of the ruling conservative political elite. At the time the Constitution was adopted, liberal nationalists of the second generation had their doubts concerning their previous thesis about the "inherent democracy" of the Serbian village. The Constitution of 1869 was the work of Ristić, a man close to conservatives in the 1850s, who pragmatically seized the moment and took the lead of the reform movement and, after coming to power, gradually moved away from liberal principles and took a stand towards further social changes that could be considered conservative.

Bearing in mind these aspects of Serbian liberalism as an "interesting anomaly" typical not only for the liberalism of the Balkan nations,[28] Mishkova concludes that "the lasting achievement of the liberals' intervention in the Serbian political scene was the creation of a modern political system and the instalment of the nation-state as the only legitimate form of supreme political power".[29] In this context, debates on the paths for economic development can be analyzed as a paradigmatic example of the way in which different external influences were refracted through a specific social reality and influenced the perception of reform-oriented intellectuals educated abroad.

Influences of European Economic Thought

The predominant focus on the struggle for national liberation and unification, the creation of a strong state and liberal political reform show, among other things, a remarkable influence of Western political ideas. But to what extent was the Serbian intellectual elite aware of the limitations imposed by the level of economic development on political development, and far-reaching nationalist ambitions and territorial aspirations at the time? It would be misleading to conclude that awareness that economic development was a significant component of the nation-state and the guarantor of its security was not present. But, it is also indisputable that, while focusing on the struggle for political reforms, the Serbian liberal intellectual elite neglected the need to develop a comprehensive program of economic reforms. The theory and practice of Serbian liberalism manifested itself primarily as political and national, while economic issues were neglected.[30] As outlined by

Latinka Perović, it seemes that even after the formation of political parties during the 1880s, none of them had a well-formulated economic program.[31] This statement refers not only to the ruling political and intellectual elite, but also to the educated individuals and political groups within the opposition. As well, there was no shortage of serious debate on the need for and paths of economic reforms. These discourses raise some questions such as: What ideas and trends of European economic thought were reflected in the attitudes of Serbian economists and intellectuals with a certain level of education in economics and to what extent? How were these ideas interrelated with their perception of Serbian economic development? Is there a connection between theoretical considerations and practical economic policy, and what were the differences between promoted concepts and their implementation?

New knowledge was affected both by existing incentives and by cultural models and belief systems that decision-makers possessed, and was, as Heino Heinrich Nau argues, essential for economic development.[32] In the Serbian case, since the cameralist concept involved complete control over economic activities, during the course of the organization of the state apparatus, the economy, infrastructure and other related activities came under the jurisdiction of the Ministry of Internal Affairs until the administrative reforms of the early 1860s. The abandonment of the cameralist concept was connected with the education of Serbian students in European universities beginning in 1839. Thus, it does not come as a surprise that the entirety of Serbian economic thought in the second half of the nineteenth century was mainly modified European economic thought, adapted to Serbian conditions.

The future intellectual elite was educated over a broad geographic area, from Moscow and St. Petersburg to Berlin, Heidelberg, Vienna, and Paris.[33] Serbian students, therefore, felt a strong and varied impact from European economic thought, including the classical British–French liberal economy and the so-called older German historical school, or the influence of German economic thought, in general. According to Obren Blagojević, it is not possible to make clear differentiation based on different economic schools of thought. Rather, the powerful influence of certain economic thinkers can be discussed, but this is in no way exclusive, so "among the majority of Serbian economists we can sense different, sometimes even contradictory influences, even liberal and interventionist at the same time".[34]

Classical liberal economic thought reached Serbian economists later and mostly not through the original works of its founders, but through their translators: Claude Frédéric Bastiat, Jean-Baptiste Say, John Ramsay McCulloch, and others. Moreover, Serbian students learned about French and English economic thinkers through German economic textbooks that had grown from the tradition of cameralism.[35] The influence of classical economic theory was, with varying intensity, present in the 1850s, 1860s and early 1870s, but it was disproportionate to its importance in the history of European economic thought. Although the impact of liberal economic theory could be felt, the political and economic circumstances were not favorable for its growth, while the opposite was the case with German economic thought, which advocated state interventionism and economic protectionism as a precondition for the development of domestic industry.

According to Blagojević, the strong influence of German economic theorists, as well as of the American theorist Henry C. Carey, is understandable for two interrelated reasons. First, the similarity to the historical situation in which the German school of economic thought had been created: the unfinished process of national unification and an economy that needed government intervention for faster development. Second, was the fact that the most important economic writers and professors of economy at the Belgrade Lyceum studied in Austria and the German states.[36] As Stokes emphasizes, "almost every political economist in Belgrade in the 1850s . . . studied political economy under Karl Rau", a professor at Heidelberg and "one of the foremost exponents of classical economic theories in Germany" in the nineteenth century. This included Kosta Cukić, Dimitrije Matić, Vladimir Jakšić, Milovan Janković, and Vladimir Jovanović.[37] In Vienna, Jovanović attended the lectures of Wilhelm Roscher and Čedomilj Mijatović was a student of Lorenz von Stein, while Stevan Popović was also a German student. As professors, Cukić and Mijatović relied to a large extent on the knowledge formulated under the influence of their professors when writing their textbooks, but they went a step further.[38] Mijatović in particular, who relied on Stein and Rau, also accepted in his books theses of certain liberal economic theorists, such as Bastiat, and of Carey, a defender of interventionist state policy.[39] Jovanović was a student of Rau's son Ludwig at the Hohenheim Agricultural Academy, and Rau's book was a part of his library. He translated Roscher's *Die Grundlagen der*

Nationalökonomie,[40] used it for lectures at the Great School, and later published it as a book. He also particularly respected Bastiat and his theory of harmony of interests because he thought it could be applied to the Serbian reality of an egalitarian social structure facing the challenges of capitalist development.[41]

The influence of German authors and their concept of "national economy" (*Nationalökonomie*) was essentially determined by the role assigned to the state in their writings. The specificity of their reception is particularly evident as the three mentioned – Cukić, Mijatović and Jovanović – are regarded by Serbian historiography as representatives of liberal political thought, regardless of significant ideological differences and subsequent political evolution. Similar to the German states, in the processes of political integration and economic development in the area which, in comparison to Western European economies, could be seen as "backward", "less developed", or "underdeveloped", the role of the state was a necessity, but, as Iván Dénes outlines, not an absolutist state, "but a state that could be the instrument of social development and national integration – a liberal constitutional nation-state".[42] Due to the specifics of the development of Serbian society and the process of the construction of national identity, their national liberalism, or liberal nationalism, was reflected in a paradigmatic way in everyday public discourse through the concept of the "people's welfare".

The very concept of "welfare" was part of the conceptual legacy of the absolutist state whose legitimacy was based on concern for the welfare of its subjects, a commonplace topic in the cameralist literature of the time. In the context of the construction of the Serbian nation, its organic, ethnic/genealogical foundation and specific features of a still significantly egalitarian peasant society, the "people's welfare" ("general welfare", "welfare of the state"), i.e. the benefit for the largest part of the population, meaning the peasantry, took on a specific meaning in the public discourse and conceptions of political and economic development of the liberals of 1858. It represented, at least nominally, a goal and a basis for a concept of economic development under the supervision of the state. This primarily relates to the positions of the "liberals of 1858", the liberal nationalists, who were aware that the main consequence of economic liberalism was a society of economic inequality, which needed to be avoided. According to Jovanović, "when we say the wealth of the people, we do not mean the wealth collected in the hands of individuals, but the wealth of all classes of citizens, that wealth when each, according to his or her needs, has what is necessary for pleasurable comfort, when he has no debt and has more than he needs for pleasure".[43] As the Serbian nation-state was an Ottoman vassal, the entire discourse on development, both politically and economically, was a part of the struggle for independence, and a preparation for territorial expansion at the expense of the suzerain.

Indeed, due to these specificities of Serbian society and the process of nation-building, the importance of the Assembly as an institution of customary law consisting primarily of peasants, as well as the role of the peasant army in the creation of the state, concern about the "welfare of the people", nominal or real, was an integral part of the demagogic discourse of the autocratic Prince Miloš, the oligarchic elite in 1840s and 1850s, and the absolutist reign of Prince Mihailo during the 1860s. Construction of the bureaucratic state apparatus, centralization, and state intervention, as well as Cukić's first textbook of political economy designed mainly to educate future government officials, suggests a similarity, at least nominally, with the late cameralist character of the state's economic policy. A specific indicator of the superficiality and only nominal application of a cameralist governmental pattern, where a ruler wishing to maintain the government should take into account the well-being and welfare of his subjects, was ever more apparent in the alienation of the bureaucratic state apparatus which was reflected in the increasingly rare convening of the Assembly. Although without real power, decades of its institutional presence and the fact that it was always convened at the time of the most important political decisions, even if only to approve them, contributed to strengthening the perception of its necessity within the system of government. Peasant representatives at the Assembly had an opportunity to express their wishes and comment on the work of the government, and thus had a fictitious idea of their own importance and of the ruling political elite's interest in their needs. For example, under the influence of the young liberal intellectuals, the Assembly decided in 1858 to depose Prince Aleksandar Karađorđević and to accept the return of the former Prince Miloš Obrenović. This act was also one of the most important consequences of this narrow, bureaucratized implementation of the newly formed state apparatus' mechanisms and an example of neglect of the importance of the Assembly.

Roads of Economic Development: Ideas vs. Practice

Despite all the efforts to introduce the basic theoretical knowledge of economic thought of their time, authors of textbooks, professors of economic subjects at the Lyceum (from 1863 the Great School), and intellectuals with expertise in economics had to deal with the issues related to the acceleration of economic development and to achieving the "people's welfare". This raises the question of the impact of foreign economic theorists on the concepts of development of the Serbian state as defined by Serbian economists, intellectuals, and even the ruling elites. According to Blagojević, even though all important economic writers were under the influence of German economists, the impact of Western economic theory had been largely limited to textbooks.[44] When faced with the real issues of the state's economic development under specific social circumstances, Serbian economists and intellectuals thought and acted independently of schematic theoretical concepts, and their different visions of economic development could be observed in response to the question of the extent to which was appropriate and desirable to follow the western and central Europe's paths of economic development.

The late 1840s and the early 1850s were marked by significant projects: the opening of an arms factory, a smeltery, and textile manufacturing as the first industrial enterprises in Serbia, followed by the opening of an agricultural school in the newly established first experimental farm on the hill of Topčider; the construction of the first steam mills.[45] Focusing predominantly on production for military purposes, and the fact that the government was engaged in the early 1850s in improving export trade transport infrastructure and negotiating the place of Serbia on the first trans-Balkan railway route or construction of a commercial road to the Adriatic coast, clearly indicate the importance of economic development within a broader conception of "national liberation" and territorial expansion within the territory of the Ottoman Empire thought to have a population of Serbian ethnic origin.[46] Paradigmatic for the history of a state whose most important foreign policy goal was national liberation and unification, the most important and oldest industrial plant was an arms factory.

Characteristic of the beginning of the 1850s, as well as of the period immediately after the Crimean War (1856), and after the return of the

Obrenović dynasty (late 1850s–early 1860s), was the dynamization of the public debate on economic issues. The essential feature of these works had been the pursuit of ways to achieve the people's welfare, or the search to understand the causes of underdevelopment in the Serbian economy in order to resolve the developmental enigma. Industrial development was not set as a primary goal of economic development in most of these works during the 1850s. Attention was primarily focused on the issues of improving agriculture and animal husbandry, and on trade. The problem was further complicated by the fact that, along with the decay of family cooperatives, there was a process of monetization in the village, accompanied by borrowing and spending to a large extent on non-productive purposes. Thus, in addition to an extremely low level of agricultural production, in the mid-century a high percentage of indebtedness was one of the most important and the most salient problems discussed among the public.

Starting from the assumption that the people's prosperity depended on the development of agriculture and animal husbandry as preconditions for increasing export trade and the development of manufacturing and further industrialization, the state was expected to solve the existing problems. In the 1850s, contemporaries saw as the most important problems: a low level of agricultural production, the decline of crafts, non-existent industry, an underdeveloped financial market, and a weak commercial exchange. Measures for overcoming the present situation, suggested by Jovanović and others, were: encouraging population growth; educating the peasants and encouraging their desire for a higher quality of life; intensifying labor; providing capital by establishing credit support for agricultural development; opening specialized schools; establishing experimental farms; sending state scholarship holders to foreign agricultural academies; publishing professional literature; and developing transportation infrastructure for stimulating trade. Liberals considered the improvement of agriculture "as the most important of people's occupations" and "the most reliable and important source of state welfare", with the state playing the key role.[47]

Kosta Cukić authored a textbook on national economy,[48] the main source of basic knowledge on the subject for decades, wherein he paid special attention to the question of agricultural development, ignoring some ideas of his teacher Rau, such as the development of industry and the financial market. In contrast, Jovanović and his supporters, who were advocates of major reforms at the end of the 1850s and throughout the 1860s, suggested a number of measures necessary to overcome structural deficiencies in the Serbian economy and to accelerate economic development. For Serbian liberals of the late 1850s, a decisive factor was the issue of peasants' overindebtedness as an essential part of starting agricultural development and preserving the "people's welfare". This indebtedness was also a concern within the context of the necessary preservation of peasant life within a family cooperative as the basis of the peasants' alleged inherent democracy. A special committee was formed by National Assembly, which had been newly established after the 1858 coup d'état and which had been influenced by the liberal intellectuals involved in the coup. The committee concluded that the necessary preconditions for overcoming peasant indebtedness were: securing the necessary capital with low interest rates; facilitating market access to agricultural production through the development of transportation infrastructure; reforming the judiciary and the tax system; and creating a legal framework that would allow the development of agriculture, manufacturing, and trade.[49] Likewise, particular emphasis was placed on the necessity of preserving "political unity" (which was, in reality, national unity), or preventing the negative influence of internal political conflicts from affecting the village, the consequence of which would be "losing national harmony, and rending and weakening national and state power". Agricultural improvement represented the strengthening of "the internal force" necessary to achieve the ultimate goal of state independence.[50] Therefore, the peasants' welfare was framed within political terms: national unity and sovereignty.

Another essential component, dependent on agricultural development, was trade, because "to raise, develop, disseminate, protect and secure trade, is the most important and the most difficult task of any government; everything else is easier".[51] These ideas were based on the gradual commercial rise of Belgrade, a border town on the crossroads of important water and land routes, as well as in data showing a constant rise in the export trade surplus.[52] In the late 1850s, after the Crimean War opened the Ottoman Empire to foreign capital, a vigorous debate about the necessity of, and ways to, enhance trade was launched among the Serbian public. A special Committee for the Improvement of Trade in Serbia, formed in 1855, identified the uncertainty of business operations as the most significant obstacle and called for the legal regulation of trade operations by: adopting commercial code; establishing special commercial courts; establishing a state bank that would provide cheap loans; opening specialized trade schools; and developing transportation infrastructure to facilitate the distribution of goods.[53] With a general belief that "only those *individual*s [my emphasis] who, through trade and industry, achieved strength and prosperity for themselves – and through them the entire nation – were capable of making great sacrifices for the sake of their own happiness and that of their country", the Committee was, in fact, a representative of the interests of wealthy Belgrade retail importers.[54] Their request for the legal regulation of commercial operations was directed against the existing legislation that permitted the free practice of trading to everyone (hence the peasants) and was an integral part of the attitude of conservative political circles who, in the spirit of cameralist tradition, advocated for the police regulation of all aspects of economic life, from agriculture to trade, including land cultivation regulations, and performing any commercial activities only with prior approval of the government.[55]

Meanwhile, in the context of resolving the problem of peasant overindebtedness, or agricultural improvement as a precondition for the development of villages, at the end of the 1850s liberals fought against the paternalistic approach of conservatives towards the village, thus advocating economic freedom as a way of improving the peasants' position. Free trade was perceived as a problem of internal market development, and transportation infrastructure as its necessary precondition. Construction of good roads, regulation of the Morava River that flowed through the central fertile areas, introduction of steamship transportation and ships, development of postal service, irrigation of certain regions, were part of the measures necessary for the expansion of commerce that would, according to the opinion of the liberals, encourage farmers to intensify agricultural production, which would result in surpluses for the market and the development of trade.[56]

In contrast to ideas for improving the "people's welfare" was a social and economic reality in which economic activity was directed predominantly by the state. Since the road to modernity must be paved from above through reform legislation, the state needed to create an institutional framework to facilitate economic growth and to establish the legal and institutional preconditions of capitalism. In the Serbian case, though, reform legislation played a role that was contrary to its intentions. It contributed to the preservation of the social structures inherited from the Ottoman period, and prevented the rapid development of agriculture necessary to transform the agrarian sector and the development of a modern market-oriented economic structure. Numerous legal regulations in different areas created a situation in which various branches of the economy blocked one another. Given the restrictions on domestic trade by a series of government regulations and the restrictions on the freedom of crafts by a special law (1847), along with the above mentioned agrarian social structure and self-sufficient, small peasant property that was legally protected and uninterested in market production, it is not surprising that the internal market, one of the most characteristic indicators of rapid economic development of a country, was sluggish. Although from the mid-nineteenth century monetary exchange was increasingly replacing exchange in kind and market development was gradually undermining the existing social order, reform legislation did not achieve the desired effect, and the laws adopted were not sufficient to trigger a decisive step on the road towards comprehensive economic and social modernization.[57]

After the failure of the efforts of the early 1850s, especially those related to raising the agricultural population's level of education, the state tried to speed up economic development in the 1860s. Although Cukić's attempts as finance minister to introduce direct taxes ended without success, he was able to found the Uprava fondova (Funds Administration) in 1862 as the first Serbian monetary institution. Furthermore, he made preparations for the establishment of the National Bank, initiated the coining of the first Serbian money, and also worked on mining improvement.[58] At the beginning of his reign in 1860, Prince Mihailo said that "work on the material welfare of the people will be one of the most important goals", but economic policy was actually the weakest point of his reign. According to Slobodan Jovanović, the cause of this was a financial policy, which prevented economic development due to the continuously rising costs of organizing a People's Army (almost one-quarter of the state budget before his assassination). Preparations for the war for liberation from the Ottoman Empire dominated a major part of Mihailo's reign.[59]

The rise to power of a number of moderate liberals after the assassination of Prince Mihailo (1868) marked the beginning of a period characterized by accelerated economic development that remained largely confined to cities. The establishment of Prva srpska banka (First Serbian Bank) in 1869 by private and mainly foreign capital was a way of solving the problem of capital necessary to support commerce, and the government began to establish district savings banks in an attempt to resolve the issue of peasant indebtedness. The liberals' belief in the critical importance of education for economic development contributed to the establishment of a new agricultural school and of various associations in order to initiate the development of Serbian industry and the general level of agricultural production by connecting knowledge and capital. In 1873, the government passed a law supporting industrial enterprises, and attempts to start manufacturing were engaged, but without significant success. At the time independence was gained (1878), the only industrial plant remaining was the arms factory in Kragujevac.[60]

The dynamization of economic life after 1867–8 stimulated public discussions about the prospects for economic development. But this time, even though the importance of improving agriculture, which was basically at the same level as it had been in the 1850s, was not neglected, the focus was on the question of supporting industrial development, and with it the connected construction of the railways as the most obvious symbol of the economic rise of the West. For the most significant representatives of this generation of Serbian liberals, the railway had, as Jovanović wrote, a "special, almost cult meaning" as "a symbol of progress, its materialization and its driver",[61] and as "proof that the Golden Age is really before us".[62] In the fall of 1867, Mijatović was the first to begin advocating in the press the necessity of constructing a railway as soon as possible as a precondition for Serbian economic development. Although educated in Germany, Mijatović stood out as a proponent of free trade and an opponent of protectionist policies. He accepted a number of Adam Smith's theses as "the true basis and foundation for the current development of the science of political economy" and did not believe that they were completely opposed to the views of the German theorists.[63] He belonged to a generation of liberals educated during the 1860s, out of whose circles would emerge the leaders of the Progressives in the 1880s, a generation that had different perceptions of the economic foundation of national freedom, which was closer to the spirit of liberal economic theory.

Mijatović viewed the railway as a precondition for faster economic development and believed that it would immediately allow not only the concentration of capital, people, knowledge and skills, but would further open a larger market for agrarian products and increase production "and would finally improve the transformation of the nation."[64] In a later debate (1871), while referring to the opinion of the Populists (the Serbian version of the Russian *Narodniki*) that the construction of a railway would postpone fulfillment of the task of national unification, he stressed that a country without modern transportation links as a symbol of overall progress cannot pretend to a "cultural mission" in areas where those links exist, because possessing modern transportation is one of the most important forms of displaying "civilizational superiority".[65]

A critique to this statement was provided by Mijatović's colleague Stevan Popović, supported not only by Srećković and Vasiljević, members of a group of liberals educated during the 1850s, but also by Živojin Žujović, an intellectual with an ideological orientation bordering between liberalism and socialism. Popović, like many Serbian economists, was educated in Germany and adopted views that, regardless of political liberalism, called for state intervention and economic protectionism. Popović was also particularly influenced by the economic ideas of Carey, which were close to the German historical school.[66] It was precisely by referring to Carey and in response to Mijatović's support for the construction of a railway, that Popović argued that the state should implement a protectionist policy that would prevent free export of domestic raw materials and the import of foreign industrial products, thus ensuring the development of the domestic industry. In this sense, he viewed the railway as a great danger that would thrust "a sharp knife into the heart of the people's future", prevent further Serbian economic development, crush the already humble beginnings of a domestic industry, open the door to Austro-Hungarian colonial expansion, and cause "hunger and displacement of the people".[67]

The position of Popović and his like-minded liberals was characteristic for a portion of the reform-oriented intellectuals educated during the 1850s, especially those who, like Srećković and Vasiljević, had been educated in Russia. They were, above all, nationalists, and like the German and Italian liberals, they were focused on national unification and directed their struggle towards winning political freedoms as the precondition for national liberation. While adapting the economic dimension of the liberal ideology to the Serbian reality, they preferred the views of German economic theorists over the Anglo-French classical liberal *laissez faire* economy. Essentially, they were not against the railway, but were afraid of the possible consequences. They believed that its construction should be preceded by a series of state measures that would lead to a strengthening of the economy and to the development of internal transportation, so that the construction of a railway would be launched when it became necessary for the Serbian industry and not for its foreign trade, which was based on the export of raw materials.

As I have discussed elsewhere, the debates about the construction of railways brought no real impact on the country's economic policy before independence.[68] It seems that differing opinions among the reform-oriented intellectuals, later labeled by historiography as liberals, point to the contradictions of a society faced with developmental challenges and to the diverse perceptions of the preconditions for overcoming the structural deficiencies of a predominantly agrarian economy. Mijatović, who had received his education during the 1860s, did not belong to the generation of liberals who, as part of their nationalism, enthusiastically believed in the alleged democracy of the Serbian village, but rather he belonged to a generation of intellectuals, future Progressives, whose ideological roots were later found by contemporary Serbian historiography to be akin to the aristocratic liberalism of post-revolutionary Western Europe.[69] In addition to foreign ideological influences, perceptions of political and economic development among the younger generation were influenced by the reality of Serbian society, with an accelerating process of capitalist economic transformation causing the disintegration of traditional social structures.

In this sense, agrarian legislation provides a telling example of development perplexity, and of the barriers against economic development created by state measures with demagogic aims, while at the same time it was conditioned by the necessity of preparing for a war for independence. Starting from the idea of indivisible and non-transferable collective property of the Serbian family community from the Ottoman period, from 1836 onwards the state legally protected the existential minimum necessary for the survival of the peasant, and then was gradually redefining and increasing the minimum. In 1865, the government added to the house, garden, two oxen and one cow (1836), the area of two days ploughing, and in 1873, along with a law supporting industrial enterprises, the Assembly adopted the act known as the Law on six days ploughing, which determined the new existential minimum and prohibited any sale or alienation of one's home site or garden.[70]

During the voting period for the new law on supporting industrial enterprises, the peasant majority in the Assembly wanted to resolve the old problem of overindebtedness and impoverishment of Serbian villages by reinforcing a social security mechanism of a protection of land minimum and by enlarging it. Peasant deputies insisted on this from the time the first National Assembly was formed. Once a liberal, Srećković defended the proposal in the Assembly by saying that "the peasant is our brother and we must keep him safe, because tomorrow he will carry a gun and will fight for the liberation of our brothers" and it "makes no sense to create a proletariat at home when we need to liberate our brothers from slavery".[71]

The proposed legal solution was called "the Law of the people's welfare",[72] and tersely expressed the essence of the Serbian peasants' specific perception of ways to solve their existential problems. The new law further limited credit possibilities, but the Assembly did not consider that to be an obstacle to faster economic development, although a lack of capital was in fact the decisive cause of the slow development in Serbian agriculture.[73]

At the same time, debate in the Assembly indicated the formulation of different attitudes towards the issue of preserving the "people's welfare". The Assembly's minority believed that these restrictions on the disposal of land limited personal liberties, which was contrary to the Constitution. Starting from the premise that peasant indebtedness was a consequence rather than the cause of the village's increasing impoverishment, some Assembly members argued that a low level of economic development was a consequence of irrational cultivation and low productivity. The Assembly's minority opinion was written by Milan Piroćanac, after the independence leader of the Progressive Party, who stated that, "we are attempting to eliminate capital from agriculture and we go to kill the industrious one who toils for the sake of the idle and the reckless" and that "people may be equal in their rights, but never in their abilities, so all provisions meant to legalize this equality are harmful to overall development".[74]

Agrarian legislation primarily aimed at preserving the minimum land as a way of maintaining a "system of economic freedom for small land holders because of the people's welfare and national moral strength in the coming struggle for liberation and unification",[75] was perceived as misleading. The younger generation of Serbian intellectuals considered that accepting the demands of the peasantry, as the survival of equality at the expense of equality in poverty would essentially mean preventing the country's economic development and committing it to a policy of underdevelopment. In comparison with the generation of liberal nationalists who observed the wealth of the people as "the wealth of all classes of citizens ... necessary for pleasurable comfort"[76] and not the wealth of individuals, the difference was essential.

Conclusions

Having neither a moderate level of underdevelopment, nor well-defined economic activities and market forces, nor a social framework open to change, Serbia did not possess the objective conditions for faster economic development. In real economic life, theoretical concepts were confronted by specific developmental challenges, and the Serbian intellectual elite, consisting of economists and politicians, dependently or independently of their theoretical knowledge and beliefs, acted in accordance with their own generational perception of the obstacles to economic development. Their pursuit of political solutions to socio economic issues was based not only on theoretical knowledge, but also on perceived limitations of the state, and on pragmatic political measures to win the support of the Assembly consisting primarily of peasants. Consequently, the economic discourses primarily demonstrate a lack of understanding of developmental necessities, or the inability to perceive them comprehensively.

Within a given set of exogenous circumstances, activities of reform-oriented politicians and intellectuals were decisively influenced by the dynamics of internal social development, and by the ever-present idea of achieving state independence and national unification. By adopting nationalism, as a dominant ideology and as a generally recognized system of social values, as a unifying element, different generations of intellectuals who were inclined towards the liberal tradition shaped their own perception of pathways to economic development, and were consistently guided by the assumption of the state's leading role as the predominant social institution. In the decades covered by this chapter, the evolution of the perceptions of these intellectuals was decisively influenced by their education abroad, by the dynamics of internal developments, and by external theoretical and ideological influences. The concept of the "people's welfare", that is benefit to the peasantry as the largest part of the population, became an intersection of developmental disputes in the public discourse of Serbian liberalism. As a concept derived from the late cameralist heritage in economic literature, the "people's welfare" in liberal nationalists' political and economic discourse in the late 1850s represented – at least nominally – a goal and a basis for the concept of economic development under the supervision of the state. Such a vision presented an attempt to avoid a society of economic inequality, which would be dangerous for the fulfillment of the ultimate goal of Serbia – "national liberation and unification". The negative attitude towards a larger role for the peasantry in political life – and even towards the very concept of the "people's welfare" that could be seen before the wars for independence (1876–8) in the opinions of the generation of future Progressives – faced its historic defeat during the 1880s under the attack of radicalism, which demagogically relied on nationalism and the alleged "traditional values" of the patriarchal Serbian village.

In the end, the various factors conditioning the structural deficiencies of the Serbian economy were mutually connected and influenced each other, and the measures implemented by the state were not enough for an innovative step forward due to the preservation of the quasi-feudal structure of the Ottoman period. On the one hand, lies the issue of preserving the welfare of the Serbian village, destined to bear the biggest burden of the future war for independence, and, on the other hand, lies economic development, which included the dissolution of this village's traditional social structure. Together they proved to be a question of squaring the circle, the Gordian knot of the Serbian developmental enigma.

CHAPTER 13

RICCHI E POVERI: IMAGES OF WEALTH AND POVERTY IN NINETEENTH-CENTURY BULGARIAN LITERATURE

Nikolay Aretov

Siete ricchi di idee e poveri di soldi.
Franco Califano

Literature has its own way to engage in a discussion of money and everything related to it. While literary texts are often used as a source of economic information, many researchers have been questioning the reliability of such a "source". This chapter is trying to outline some questions concerning the topic of money or wealth representation, and then to offer a few representative samples that deal with money, wealth, and poverty by shedding light on the mechanisms through which literature does this.

Without discussing some key problems for the humanities, this text gives an account of: a) the variable and uncertain boundaries of literature that separate it from the nonfictional written discourses; b) the elusive and uncertain meaning of every text since it is constructed every time by its readers and interpreters; c) the indirect relations between reality and literature and various factors that determine these relations; and d) a certain skepticism of generalisations, especially of the national specificities. Finally, without stating it too explicitly, this text accepts the well-known assumption that nonfictional discourses are not and could not be indifferent recorders and observers of objective facts and developments. Because there are some long-lasting processes without clear chronological markers, mentioning instances outside the indicated period that mark either previous manifestations or further developments, seems acceptable. The general objective is to outline a typology of the observed phenomena, which also presupposes a relaxed chronological approach.

The meaning of the *opposition "wealth–poverty"* changes over time; it was not so culturally important in the earlier periods as it has been in modern times. When it comes to literature, one should ask, what did money and wealth mean at a particular moment, and by what means were they presented in a text? Often there are direct statements and reasoning on this matter, as well as characters marked as "rich" or "poor." Sometimes this opposition was the main feature of these characters. From a certain point it is relatively easy to detect *plots* concerning accumulation, stealing or, more often, waste of wealth. And yet, what is wealth in literature, and not only in literature? The object of possessing money, gold, or other attributes of luxuriant life varies in different cultures and periods.[1] Alternatively, possessing capital may not necessary be associated with lavish life; for instance, real or fictional plots concerning the frugal lifestyle of big businessmen are popular in Protestant cultures. The limit beyond which possessed property began to be perceived as wealth is relative and flexible. It is also determined subjectively: the criterion is different across time and culture, for example, consider variations from Versailles at the time of Luis XIV, to Henry Ford's Detroit, to an Ottoman Balkan village, and to early twenty-first-century Ethiopia.

What are the markers of wealth in literature? How do they evolve over time? What is each author's attitude towards these markers and to what extent does it form them? Are there any readers' reactions that are different, even opposite, to the author's intentions? Gold and money are the two unequivocal markers of wealth that partly overlap, but they also differ. Gold, especially in earlier periods, is also a marker of power and even of beauty, and thus the attitude towards it could be positive on a different ground.

Literature, following the evangelic pattern traditionally treats money negatively, seeing in love for money first of all the root of all kinds of evil

(1 Timothy 6:10). From such a perspective money is also something static, it is accumulated or absent, but usually it is fruitless. Money may trigger certain, often negative actions, or change people who come into contact with it. This approach tends to position money as treasure, often as cursed treasure; this is something slightly different from narrations about "our" treasure that is usually an object of abduction in the Bulgarian national mythology.[2] There is also a hedonistic variation of the treasure motif in folklore and popular literature; namely, characters finally find the treasure and live happily ever after. This option, however, is not so typical for the Bulgarian culture of modern times.

A second approach represents money and wealth as capital. This approach, let me call it modern, is not so overtly negative. It seems to me that (Bulgarian) literature avoids it; it is more typical for other forms of discourse – philosophy, sociology, and journalism – where attitudes toward capital are not so dominantly negative. For all of them, treasure often represents just a frozen capital that can be reactivated by the economy. This approach also often tends to evidence a negative attitude towards money, but perceives it as something dynamic and as a means for social climbing; it represents money in other semantic fields and other plots. Unlike treasure, capital is dynamic and productive; it produces not only corruption and evil, but also useful revenue. Capital serves as an investment tool to build lucrative rational structures, and not only to provide prestige and luxury or just a comfortable life. Furthermore, capital can be created through conscious and purposeful efforts while treasure is generally inherited, located/discovered in some way, usually all at once, normally as a result of a crime, by a mere chance, or by a purposeful search that is quite different from a typical business activity.

Attitude toward money as capital is more characteristic for Protestants (and Israelites), to a lesser extent for Catholics, and least of all for Orthodox Christians. At any rate this is the general suggestion of Max Weber's *The Protestant Ethic and the Spirit of Capitalism*, a seminal work despite various objections raised by its critics.

Confessional, Historical, and Social Contexts

The evolution of the representation of wealth and poverty is a function of the *social environment* within which the particular texts emerged, with its economic base and social structure and, last but not least, with its dominant mentalities. And vice versa, by examining the attitude towards money recorded in literature, and readers' responses, one could gather information on the economy and especially on the mentalities of a given society. One has to bear in mind the capacities, and not so rare efforts, of writers to influence society by representing wealth according to their own ideas, political affiliations, utopias. Often these writers experienced influences from the foreign cultures adopted by them during their study abroad. The overall picture that literature presents and imposes on readers is always slightly (or even not so slightly) distorted.

A better understanding of the problems in the Bulgarian and Balkan context requires distinctions between several partially overlapping *oppositions* and developments such as: ours (own) – alien (foreign); Bulgarians – Greeks and other aliens; town – village; traditional – modern; educated people – simple-minded people. Very often each pole of these oppositions is somehow associated with wealth, money or its absence. One of the poles is clearly marked; the other is neutral. It is important to understand what is perceived as an exception in a specific context, and what as a norm.

Pre-modern ideas dominated in Bulgarian nineteenth-century society and they associated "ours" and the norm with the village life, with traditions and customs, and very often with poverty and uneducated people. Modernizers, the marked element of the opposition, come usually from outside and are juxtaposed against traditional rich men. The aim of the civilizers is actually to get hold of "our" "treasure", which is not always material. It could consist of women, books, faith, alphabet, etc. And suddenly, one unexpected idea can be heard, articulated in sotto voce: as a matter of fact "we" are the rich ones, "we" possess something valuable, and the aliens are trying to take it away from "us". And they often succeed in this, at least temporarily, and that provokes reactions in return.

Currently, many tend to think that communist ideology imposed positive attitudes towards poverty and condemned wealth. But such a viewpoint existed earlier. It is based on the Christian doctrine, and it is particularly characteristic of Orthodox Christianity. Similar juxtapositions can be observed in other Balkan cultures, at least in Greek (and maybe in Turkish), which are less influenced by communist ideology. These two ideologies – Christianity and communism – managed to coexist in some particular but yet indicative cases in the twentieth century.

This happened in states where communism was not an official ideology. The novel *Christ Recrucified* (1948) by Nikos Kazantzakis is one significant instance in which the Gospel's message is successfully combined with modern social perspective.

Ideologically, Orthodox Christianity does not mark positively luxury and splendor as does Catholicism and does not stimulate entrepreneurship as does Protestantism. The literature of Orthodox Christianity presents refusal of wealth and voluntary poverty as virtues. Voluntary renunciation both of wealth and joy of life is typical for all Abrahamic religions, and not only for them, but in Catholicism this is prescribed mostly to monks and hermits, and not so much to laypeople. The major criticism of Catholicism by Protestants pointed to the lavish lifestyle and affluence of its clergy. The same criticism was also heard in the nineteenth-century Balkans, articulated in sotto voce, first by Greeks, then by others, among them Bulgarians who emphasized the alien ethnic origin of the high clerics, mainly Greeks. Both the Protestants in the West and the Orthodox in the Balkans at that time highlighted the gap between the principles of Christianity and the actual practice of the high clergy as an important argument in their dissent. Within the Balkan context, Protestantism was presented as something negative. It was also a label often used by clergy when wanting to discredit its critics.

Scholars tend to associate notions of wealth and poverty in Balkan Slav cultures with a long absence of "native" aristocracy and with some forms of community life and work such as the *zadruga*.[3] Guilds of craftsmen and traders in towns were also strictly regulated by Ottoman laws and, at least in early modern times, they rather hindered economic prosperity.[4] The accumulation of wealth was often the result of closer ties with government, or so thought many contemporaries and subsequent generations.

Strict regulations during Ottoman rule also rather limited accumulation of wealth through business; the main factors for becoming rich were the *timar* system, and later – corruption, connections with government, and tax farming, which was also linked to corruption. All these means were well known all over the world, but their importance in the Ottoman Empire was especially significant in the time of its decline, according to many historians. Here the idea that wealth by default has to do with venal use of power or with connections in the government was, and still is, relatively more widespread.

Islam, which adheres more strictly to the general high standards of Abrahamic religions, disapproves, or at least qualifies negatively, the lending of money at interest and requires believers to periodically give a significant portion of their earnings to charity (*zakāt*, one of the Five Pillars of Islam). In the ethical plan all this seems perfect, but it rather held back economic development. One should bear in mind a specific condition in the Ottoman Balkans: an intersection of the *Sharia* with the customary law of Christians, and the gradual modernization of different *millets* and their legal regulation.[5]

Members of the higher (and richer) classes among Greeks, and to some extent also among Vlachs, Moldavians, and Serbs, succeeded partly in retaining their status and wealth. Similar cases could hardly be found among Bulgarians, at least not in statistically significant numbers. Quite often accumulation of wealth in the Ottoman Empire by "our" persons was seen as an alienation from the "native", from the origin, from Bulgarian roots. Enrichment along with rising social status was associated with losing mother language and bonds with "our" people and even with family. The most representative instance is the popular short story "God, Don't Let a Blind Man See Again" (1894) by Aleko Konstantinov. The sarcasm in the title, referring to a proverb, is obvious, but behind the indignation deriving from the unacceptable conduct of the parvenu, one could also trace a fear of wealth as such and even of modernity.

The conflict between aristocracy and the third estate is absent in Bulgarian society. Despite some not so persistent claims of a few persons (like Aleksandar Eksarh), the traditional aristocracy vanished after the Middle Ages. Members of the bourgeoisie, having acquired the ideology of the third estate from abroad, did not have to fight for rejection of feudal privilege by birth, at least not within their own nation. This great conflict was widely echoed in the literature of eighteenth- and early nineteenth-century European societies. Even if this conflict was pre-formulated as a clash between traditional and new elites, it still remained relatively weak among the Bulgarians, even compared to the Danubian Principalities, Poland, Hungary, and others. However, some manifestations of this phenomenon can be found in disputes about the First Bulgarian Constitution (1879). In these deliberations the idea of an upper chamber of Parliament (Senate), in which representatives of the traditional elite should be members by right was rejected in favor of elected representatives from the bourgeoisie, which was gradually gaining prestige, education, and wealth.

In the Balkans and Bulgaria even capitalism itself was somewhat specifically defined as "communal",[6] stimulating cooperative ownership (by granting monopoly rights), restricting accumulation of wealth, and imposing protectionist measures. This phenomenon is associated in at least two aspects with collective mentality (and even with national or ethnic psychology). On the one hand, the communal perspective is a result of existing attitudes, and, on the other, it shaped and strengthened people's attitudes.[7] Some economic historians conclude that the establishing of the new Bulgarian state (1878) pulled Bulgarians out of the large and not very demanding market of the Ottoman Empire and its large purveyance for the army; as a result, at least initially, this had a negative impact on trade and emerging industry,[8] although the change stimulated the processes of modernization of economy and society as a whole. And yet a very popular, but not entirely indisputable study by Ivan Hadzhiyski suggests that the Bulgarians' had a cautious attitude towards market and modernization in everyday life in the nineteenth century.[9]

The lack of an aristocracy, the strict Ottoman regulation, some characteristics of Orthodoxy, and the development of capitalism determined the predominantly negative perception of wealth and clearly visible egalitarian attitude in Bulgarian society that persists even today.

Medieval Background

However, medieval sources depict a picture that is quite motley. Rare instances of positive representations of wealth, mostly as attribute of the King and power, can be traced in medieval Bulgarian literature. An excerpt of the important compilation *Shestodnev* or *Hexaemeron* by John the Exarch (ninth–tenth centuries) is often quoted in this context:

> Just as when a lower class and poor person – and a foreigner as well – coming from afar towards the outer buildings of the Prince's palace, is amazed when he sees them; and approaching the portals he marvels at them, as he asks to be let in. And when he enters he sees both sides, decorated with stone and wood, and painted. And when he enters further into the courtyard, and sights

> the high palaces and the churches decorated lavishly with stone and wood and paint, and inside with marble and bronze, silver and gold – he will not know what to compare them with, because in his own land he hadn't seen such a thing, just miserable straw huts! And he will stand in awe at such things, as if he has lost his senses. But if he should manage to see the Prince himself, seated in the pearl-embroidered robes, wearing his necklace of gold coins around his neck and rings on his hands, grilled with a purple belt and with a gold sword hanging at his hip – and his *boyars* with gold necklaces, belts and rings ...[10]

One can find here a blend between wealth, power, and beauty. Of two relatively durable associations, the first *wealth–power*, is primordial and still valid, while the other, *wealth–beauty,* comes and goes, is not always openly stated. Both associations vary in different periods and cultures. The quoted fragment is often used to represent the medieval Bulgarian state, but it is an exception, as there are a few similar descriptions in other texts from that time. Thus, it is more representative of the way later times and ideologies depict the past and its material and spiritual wealth.

Folklore and Popular Beliefs

The real presence of wealth in the everyday life of medieval and early modern times was obviously another story. Travelers visiting the Ottoman realms were often astonished by the combination of poverty with the sumptuous golden adornment of the poor villagers. William Hunter, a British traveler of the late eighteenth century, for example, exclaimed: "Look at the children with hats, ornate with coins while they and their parents are suffering from lack of food ... Stupidity and vanity had never been manifested more convincingly to my mind!"[11] In such texts, though, it is difficult to distinguish what was really seen from the effects of preconditioned perceptions and stereotypes.[12]

Folkloric texts, as far as one can assume that records transmit authentic voices and messages, seem to be divided regarding the valuation of wealth. Let us leave aside the important and widespread presence of golden adornment in marriage rituals. Some positive references to gold, ostentatious splendor, and booty, associated with the

King or the Hero (such as Prince Marko) can be traced side-by-side with texts eulogizing poverty and condemning or ridiculing wealth (mostly in prose works). Initially, the distinction was more within the genre; later, after the 1870s and especially in the twentieth century, it gained a "social" meaning. Usually, the epic genre defines the "our" and requires attributes of power, which later could be interpreted as "wealth"; something similar could be traced in fairy tales. Narrations about tricksters have different functions, and, in later times, are interpreted as social criticism.

Wealth and affluent life have various manifestations in folklore. Gold cups, thrones, lavish clothes, are often markers for affluence and social prestige. And yet idiomatic phrases and *paremia* (proverbs), such as "bread and milk", "honey and butter", side-by-side with the famous baked lambs, a food enjoyed by the noble robbers (*haidouti*) and insurgents, also mark an easy life obviously different from reality, but desired, and hint that the food of kings and heroes in real life and even in folklore was not so magnificent.

The traditional and universally widespread motif of the poor lad who succeeds in winning the hand of the King's daughter, or of the poor maiden (variation of Cinderella) who gains the heart of the Prince, was also present in the Balkans. But both of them were not seen originally as an instance of social mobility. It seems that these are later interpretations that are only partly connected with the initial meaning. Earlier, they revealed mostly initiation rites for entering into the social group of adults, and for delimiting the endogamous community.

The most popular Bulgarian trickster is Hitar Petar (Sly Peter). He is connected with his Turkish analog Nasreddin Hoca and has variations in other Balkan cultures; especially popular is the Macedonian Itar Pejo or Itroman Peyo. All these characters could be seen as embodiments of the epigraph "rich in ideas and poor in money", which is a widespread mental formula, a stereotype, very productive in most cultures and ages. Another characteristic is that the trickster's attitude towards money and wealth is not necessarily negative. Indeed, he appreciates money and wants to acquire it; the intent to help the poor is not obligatory, and maybe this was highlighted a little bit later for ideological reasons.

Indirectly associated with the opposition "wealthy–poor" is the traditional and widespread figure of the beggar, the beggar-singer, and especially the wandering blind man, all creators and performers of specific folk songs.[13] These songs were not linked directly to the opposition "wealth or poverty" but the presence of the beggar figure in the culture (which has to do with Russian *yurodiviy*, wacky) reveals a particular positive meaning of one specific variation of the image of the poor man.

Another character of the poor man, typical in Balkan folklore (Bulgarian, Greek, Serbian) is the *gurbetchiya* (migrant worker) who grieves for his native land and for his family from whom he is separated due to harsh economic conditions. These reasons, however, are still heard in the background in today's popular folk songs ("Oh, Tell me, Little White Cloud"). Folk songs focus also on the homecoming of the migrant worker and the presents that he has brought, or promised to bring, and in some sense, on the small fortune that he has gathered with hard work (or by luck). Such songs are often ballads with supernatural elements: for example, the man who comes back but appears to be dead ("Last Night Ralin from Gurbet Came Back"). One possible interpretation of this motif associates it with the disastrous effects of separation from the "own" and its search for a fortune, even though small, sought by honest means. Another interpretation, at least as likely, finds mythic figures and meanings in such songs.

Treasure-hunting legends are another widespread genre with several sub-divisions. The focus is always on a hidden treasure, and the story is about its accumulation (often by robbery), specific signs that mark it, and about the maps, rites, and taboos that help the quest. The overall treasure-hunting plot could be separated into three parts. The first deals with the accumulation, the second depicts the hiding process and the signs that lead to it, and the third focuses on the finding or the failure of the quest. The hiding part is usually the most elaborated, the accumulation is often only mentioned, and the finding is represented through narrations about other treasures that were found by somebody else. Thus, the treasure itself is not presented directly; its finding, in turn, is often followed by an unhappy ending.

Plots and Ideological Interpretations in Literature

The poor man: sympathy and idealization

From its very beginning, modern Bulgarian literature in the strict sense of the term prefers the *poor and underprivileged* to the rich and prosperous. This happens for various reasons. The poor is a bearer of evangelic virtues, he is a victim who generates sympathy and is also a potential herald of positive changes for society. Indeed, association between these two notions – poor and underprivileged (or victim) – is not mandatory, but it is often implied. Rarely other interpretations can be found, such as that of an individual's responsibility for his poverty; the potential of poverty to generate antisocial and criminal behavior; or the way that poverty deprives people of some virtues. The short story "Uncle Stoichko's Willow" (1912) by Elin Pelin is practically the only text in the Bulgarian literary canon that displays an animosity towards a poor man. In the story, he cuts a tree containing a storks' nest because the storks stole his old and greasy hat.

In general, the poor is "ours", and is opposed to the "alien" who is the bearer of negative qualities, especially perfidy. This is a tradition that began at least with the *Slavo-Bulgarian History* (1762) by the monk Paisius of Hilendar, a text now placed at the beginning of every survey of modern Bulgarian literature. Here the opposition "wealthy–poor" was not foregrounded, but the reader of later periods usually draws this conclusion.

Bulgarian literature tends to focus on poor men in a Bulgarian ethnic environment while rich men appear to be foreigners. A positively marked image of the evangelically poor and simple Bulgarian (as opposed to the sly Greek) is an element of the opposition "town–village". It is not necessarily ethnically marked and was, indeed, shared with Greek authors. According to *Modern Geography* by Daniel Philippidis and Grigorios Konstantas, the Bulgarians were "simple, hospitable, pious, physically strong, hard-working, industrious, tireless, calm and peaceful". This opinion was shared by other Greek writers from the Enlightenment.[14] Attributing an ethnic sense of belonging to the opposition may have started with the monk Paisius but, until the 1830s and 1840s, it was not predominant.

Petko Slaveykov (1827–95) – a very popular Bulgarian poet, journalist and political activist – introduced the image of the poor man and poverty in his lyrics, especially in his satiric verses. Some of them were variations or translations of or inspired by the works of other Balkan poets who shared similar ideas. Scholars have traced the links that connected "The Song of my Small Coin" (1871) to a poem with a similar title by the Greek poet Ilias Tantalidis, and have also found connections between the "Ode of the Empty Purse" (1883) and a poem by the great Serbian poet Jovan Jovanović Zmaj. In all of them, poverty is idealized and combines an irony towards the rich man with the gentle self-irony towards the impoverished poet.

The evolution of one poem, entitled "Bad and Nasty Not to Be" (1875), by Slaveykov is significant. It ends as follows:

> Now I'm free from everything
> Hungry, thirsty, naked and barefoot,
> Thus it shows that I'm from the people,
> And submissive, and not bad.

The character was poor by origin; drinking had also contributed to his miserable situation; but the satire was aimed at his submissiveness. However, this poem became very popular in a later variation (1901) published posthumously by his son Pencho Slaveykov, the most important Bulgarian poet of the next generation. To a great extent the son turned the meaning of the satiric poem upside down by transforming the character into an idealist and patriot:

> After a life of a people lover,
> With miseries so many,
> It shows that I'm from the people,
> Hungry, thirsty, naked and barefoot.[15]

The oeuvre of Petko Slaveykov actually offers a wider range of representations of poverty and wealth. This poet was anything but a hermit and moralizer; on the contrary, he loved and praised earthy pleasures. He also was one of the writers who popularized Benjamin Franklin's writings among the Bulgarians, presenting them as an embodiment of the spirit of bourgeois enterprise. To a great extent Slaveykov shared the ideas of Franklin and this could be traced even in the poem "Bad and Nasty Not to Be". However, the next generations have preferred to keep his image as champion of poor people and, in the background, of the jolly bohemian.

The journalist, poet and prose writer Lyben Karavelov (1834–79), the poet Hristo Botev (1848–76), the memoirist Zahari Stoyanov (1850–89), all authors and political activists that are now an essential part of the Bulgarian literary cannon, have actively promoted their variations of the poor man as part of the revolutionary ideology from the mid-nineteenth century on. They launched the notion of the poor man who was not as rich in "ideas" and slyness as the traditional trickster, but who was rich in energy for making changes that would destroy the existing *status quo* and build a new, better, and more just social order. At least this idea was suggested in their literary works and journalism. Memoirs describing the revolutionary decade (1870s), which became an integral part of the literary cannon, and especially *Memoirs of the Bulgarian Uprisings* (1884–92) by Stoyanov, indeed diverged from the idealized image of people devoted to the Revolution. However, that well-known feature remains backgrounded in later interpretations of these works.

The Bulgarian literature from the first half of the twentieth century seemed to prefer the poor and suffering man to the poor rebel. Even the so-called proletarian literature and its greatest poet of that period Hristo Smirnenski (1898–1923) did not shift from the suffering man to the rebel but rather tried to combine their representations. It was not until later that the ideologues of so-called *socialist realism*, using some earlier texts, forged the cliché about the ideological evolution of the poor proletarian into the conscious revolutionary.

In some plots the figure of the underprivileged poor man presupposes another universally widespread figure – the *noble robber* – who takes from the rich and gives to the poor (Robin Hood; Arsène Lupin, gentleman cambrioleur). Popular literature exploits images such as Le Comte de Monte-Cristo. In Bulgarian and Serbian contexts this kind of figure is associated with the *haiduks* from folklore. Similar characters, such as Greek *klephts*, and to some extent Croatian *uskoks,* are familiar; all of them belong to a rich tradition shared in the Balkans and worldwide.[16] The image of the *haiduk* in literature and its ideological interpretation as a champion of the underdog and fighter for freedom was introduced by Georgi Rakovski, a revolutionary activist, journalist, poet, and continued by his followers. Folk texts did not exactly follow the same trend; even in the verses of Botev, a follower of Rakovski, the word *haiduk* had both positive and negative connotations.

Rich is Evil

Authors such as Karavelov, Botev, and Stoyanov always associated the character of the rich man with evil that appeared in different, but connected forms: cruelty to the poor, cynical perspective on life, rejection of one's "own" (family, language, ethnicity), negative effects of modernity. This association was most overtly demonstrated in "Three Pictures of Bulgarian Life" (1875), published by Karavelov at the time when he was in conflict with the younger radicals accusing him of abandoning revolutionary ideas. In another short story – "Hadji Nicho" (1870) – the character was an accomplished criminal committing all kinds of sins and dark deeds starting from small school and grocery frauds, to reselling stolen cattle, to hiring a killer and committing national treason. All these deeds were typical for the *chorbadzhi* in the writings of Karavelov. An extreme variation of such an image, presenting the rich man as a degenerate who almost lost his humanity, is offered in another short novel "Mommy's Boy" (1875); it has been part of the literature curriculum of the Bulgarian schools for many years.

Botev's social criticism and rejection of wealth extends even to the rejection of modernity as something alien; for instance, in his famous article "The People – Yesterday, Today and Tomorrow" (1871). This paradox – a radical revolutionary who rejects modernity itself – has not so far received significant attention by literary critics.[17]

Serbian culture seems to be more prone to presenting wealth and luxury, maybe even lavish waste, as something not always negative. In Serbian and Greek culture, at least in the twentieth century, representations of poor and primitive men as carriers of some "primordial" folk merits, who eagerly wasted what little they had, are more typical and their gestures are portrayed more positively. *Zorba the Greek* (1946) by Kazantzakis, and some films of Emir Kusturica and his Balkan followers, are the most obvious among more recent instances.

The rich man is often also a *miser*, but classical variations of this image (Shakespeare, Molière, Pushkin) have only rare analogies in Bulgarian literature. As a whole, Bulgarian society tends to appreciate thrift. Misers, of course, were subjected to ridicule, but they are also seen as bearers of traditional (patriarchal) values.

Hadji Kosta, the comic champion of traditions in the most popular Bulgarian comedy of all times "The Phony Civilization" (1871) by Dobri Voynikov, was a typical miser. But here, and in many other Bulgarian texts from that time, lavish waste was presented maybe as more dangerous than miserliness. One of the two main satiric characters of the most popular short novel of Karavelov, "Old Time Bulgarians"

(1867), was also a miser. The attitude towards him was more negative compared with the other character that was shown as generous, especially when it comes to his own pleasure and social prestige. But both of them were portrayed as caricatures.

The miser is portrayed more distinctively in the dramatic works of "the father of Serbian drama", "Serbian Molière" Jovan Sterija Popović (1806–56), such as "The Miser", "Matchmaking and Marriage". He also deals with well-known plots about marriages of convenience as a means of acquiring wealth and social advancement that are not so characteristic for Bulgarian culture. Marriage between a poor aristocrat and a rich girl from the bourgeoisie or vice versa was impossible in Bulgarian society where aristocracy was absent. Unequal marriage there had a more material or ethnic meaning.

In the above mentioned Voynikov's comedy and in the similar play "Fudulesku" by Todor Peev, also written in the 1870s but published much later, "our" Bulgarian characters were rich, while the foreigners were those who sought to seize their wealth. But somehow this aspect remained in the background, and kidnapping beautiful daughters of the Bulgarians came to the fore. Meanwhile, in Peev's drama, ethnicity is complicated: the kidnapped "our" girls were in fact daughters of a mixed marriage between a Bulgarian man and a Romanian woman; they all lived in Romania and the kidnapper was also Romanian. This kind of plot was familiar to Romanian society in the nineteenth century when Greek men were seeking marriages with noble and/or wealthy local maidens.

Ambivalent Perspectives: the Parvenu, Ambitions, and Self-Interest

Social mobility, associated with education, high social status and wealth (*nouveau riche*), was presented ambivalently; if not presented as suspicious, it was at least satirized. This was the case with the most popular book in the Bulgarian literary canon *Bay Ganyo* (1895) by Aleko Konstantinov. Writers and intellectuals as a whole insisted on presenting themselves as poor; this was emphasized in some comic short stories of Konstantinov ("Lucky man", "Passion", "Happy New Year"). Images of ambitious young men (not to mention women) eager to climb the social ladder, such as Balzac's Eugène de Rastignac or Stendhal's Julien Sorel, are rare in nineteenth-century Bulgarian literature. When they appeared later, for example, Boris Morev from the novel *Tobacco* (1951) by Dimitar Dimov, they were depicted negatively and finished their lives tragically.

In Bulgarian culture, money is seldom interpreted as capital, as something useful in the spirit of "Protestant ethic", and even less as something positively valued for bringing prestige to its owner. However, translations were an organic part of nineteenth-century Bulgarian literature and ideas about money as capital could be found in some translated texts. The most significant instance is the widespread reception, beginning in the 1830s, of Franklin and his "Poor Richard's Almanack".[18] There were several translations of his famous aphorism: "An empty sack cannot stand upright."

Some variations of positive attitude towards money, capital and the self-made man who creates his own fortune can be found in the literature of the Enlightenment, which was blurred to some extent in the Balkans, and especially in Bulgarian culture. It was more common in Greek culture, and some important elements can be found in Serbian culture, more precisely in the oeuvre of Dositej Obradović, "Counsels of Common Sense" (1784), and also in his interesting autobiographical narration, "The Life and Adventures of Dimitrije Obradović Who as a Monk Was Given the Name Dositej" (1783–8).

One would expect that modernity and capitalism should change the situation. How did this really happen and to what extent?

Wealth, Power, and State in Modern Times

Before the establishing of the Principality of Bulgaria (1878), government and authority, like rich men, were seen mostly as foreign, especially by the ideologues of nationalism. The Sultan and his Sublime Porte were somewhere in the distance and hardly occupied the minds of his Christian subjects before the spread of nationalism, which started before the mid-nineteenth century at first with vague calls for secession from the Ecumenical Patriarchate, perceived as Greek and corrupted.

Since the Ottoman Empire had no conscription for Christians, the state manifested its presence mostly through tax collection. The so-called "blood tax" (*devşirme*) was presented in folklore before 1878 but also in later literature and historic works as being especially hard and cruel duty. The perception of the state as alien and cruel, collecting excessive taxes and working for the rich, remained after the emerging of the new Bulgarian ("own") principality. This negative perception was transferred to the new tax collectors who were depriving poor peasants of their modest belongings. The most significant example is probably the short story "Andreshko" (1903) by Elin Pelin, a writer who was not a follower of the communist ideology. On the contrary, he became a personal friend of Tsar Boris III. In "Andreshko", the state with its taxes, wealth, and injustice form a semantic field set in opposition to the poor, which has the right to reject it. This is an idea that is still alive and widespread.

Indeed, a rich man is not synonymous with a man entitled with governmental power. These two types were even opposed later in plots dealing with rich men pulling the strings of the government. Nevertheless, the literature of the late nineteenth and the early twentieth centuries often merged these representations and offered up a gallery of job seekers and members of parliament and government, in comedies such as "The Job Seekers" (1900) by Ivan Vazov, "Golemanov" (1927) by Stefan Kostov, or "The Cabinet Minister's Wife" (1929) by the Serbian writer Branislav Nušić, to mention only a few of the most popular ones. To be part of the government meant to be rich or at least to have the opportunity to become rich; this was the predominant conviction shared by public opinion and literature. In the current social debate one could come across some very timidly articulated opposing notions. For example, one conservative and rather problematic viewpoint held that political power should be entrusted to the hands of rich men because they have proved an ability to accumulate and manage capital; moreover, they would not be tempted to misuse the entrusted power.

Wealth is not always so Evil?

The negative attitude towards rich men and the accumulation of fortune that dominated poetry and fiction included some attempts, adopted from non-fiction, to encourage and stimulate economic activity, including the accumulation of capital. One instance was the travelogue "Several Days Stroll in Bulgarian Places" (1868) by Ivan Bogorov. The author himself was active, though not so successful, in business. Numerous textbooks for traders and accounting manuals were translated and published at that time with this goal.[19]

Indeed, a noteworthy number of intellectuals were descended from relatively rich families: for example, the journalist and translator Nikola Mihaylovski and his brother the poet Stoyan Mihaylovski; the poet, writer, painter, and minister Konstantin Velichkov; and the well-educated revolutionary Todor Kableshkov. Nevertheless, they preferred not to highlight their origins. Literary critics and culture in general, often favored stories about the intellectual with a humble origin from the ordinary people (*narod*). This ideal initially spread among the Russian *raznochintsi* and later became a socialist stereotype.

Paradoxically, after the establishment of the new Bulgarian state, some of the significant authors who became either part of the political elite, or at least became well-to-do people had demonstrated negative attitudes toward wealth in their youth. Stefan Stambolov, later regent, prime minister and powerful politician, was accused of all sorts of financial misappropriations, though he was the author of the poem "We do not want wealth" ("Bulgarian March") from the 1870s that became a very popular song. Similar, to a certain extent, was the case of Vasil Drumev, later Metropolitan Kliment of Tŭrnovo, prime minister and a leading figure in political life. Drumev created one of the most glaring caricatures of rich men, moreover, rich men who were philanthropists, in the novel "Student and Benefactors or What is Another's is Another's" (1864–5).

A slightly different attitude towards the rich, though a specific type of reasonably rich patriarchal figures, could be traced in the oeuvre of Ivan Vazov, usually referred to as "The Patriarch of Bulgarian literature" and "The People's poet". In the novel *Under the Yoke* (1894), he drew a portrait of *chorbadzhi* Marko, whose prototype was Vazov's father. The same perspective can also be noted in the documentary, semi-documentary, and fictional writings of Ilia Blaskov. They offered a positive image of relatively rich peasants (or inhabitants of small towns) who followed all the traditions of the patriarchal order, but who did not separate themselves from the "people", living the same life and willingly helping the poor. This trend would later be extended by Tzani Ginchev, Todor Vlaykov, and the so-called *Narodniks.* They were populist writers (with a positive connotation of "populist" here), meaning literature coming from and addressed to the ordinary people.

Nevertheless, negative images of wealthy men who were alienated from their "own" milieu and who abused their poor compatriots can be easily identifieded in the writings of all of the above mentioned authors. The long poem "The Pile" by Vazov is a telling instance. It recounted a specific rite condemning the bad *chorbadzhi* Tzeko. Scholars have established that the poem followed real events and the ethnologist Dimitar Marinov described in detail the rite and its occurrences in different locations.[20]

Money was also represented in plots that were more distant from the charged ethical meaning of the opposition "wealthy–poor". "The Life and Sufferings of the Sinful Sophronius", a very valuable autobiographic text, written at the beginning of the nineteenth century, represents the earliest manifestation. In his private life, Sophronius acted as a modern man, including where money was concerned: his ordination was associated with a bribe (something usual for that time), he accumulated some money, took part in a dubious sheep trade, and managed to collect money for printing *Nedelnık* (Sunday Evangelic Interpretation) (1806), the first new Bulgarian printed book. Apparently, for Sophronius, money was more capital than treasure. But this attitude was introduced too briefly, and even timidly, in the plot.

Money was presented more directly in the short novel *It Was* (1883) by Vasil Popovich.[21] Here also the ethical meaning was slightly different from the dominant ideas of the time. A small capital has been accumulated by honest means, but its later appropriation by wealthy men is represented pointedly negatively. The positively marked character was associated with education and a modern attitude towards money: he was a teacher who cleverly invested his savings, while the antagonists were *chorbadzhi* – a retrograde social type – and their fortune was not as much a result of trade and investment, as of brutal appropriation of others modest savings. The conflict between traditional and modern notables (and wealthy men) gained prominence later in twentieth-century Bulgarian literature; from Petko Todorov to *The Value of Gold* by Gencho Stoev, but often, writers abstained from plunging into details of the financial aspect of this conflict.

The presentation of money as capital, and not always negative, has hardly increased in the twentieth century, at least not in the texts that find their place in the canon of Bulgarian literature. On the contrary, narrations that, at least according to dominant interpretations, revealed the misfortunes caused by wealth to men and women, gained popularity and prestige. The most indisputable instance was the short novel "The

Gerak Family" (1911) by Elin Pelin from which several generations of Bulgarian schoolchildren were supposed to become aware about the evil generated by money.

> The wealthiest man in the village was the old Yordan Geraka. Brisk and industrious, he had been working his whole life and had managed to double and triple the property inherited from his father. Gifted with a practical mind and an aptitude for trade, he had succeeded in accumulating money and rising as a notable man among the peasants. He was gentle and had a kind heart. And although he was a little miserly, he was not strict in his accounts and helped people and cared for the affairs of the village. That is why everybody loved and respected him.

But a little further, the readers learn that: "Quarrels, misunderstandings, and brawls, crawled out like snakes from nowhere in the house and poisoned the tender peace of the home."[22]

Similar ideas could be traced also in the oeuvre of one of the most emblematic writers of *socialist realism* – Georgi Karaslavov, who speaking about his short novel *Tatul* (Datura, 1938), openly confessed: "The conception came from my conviction about the grave harms that private property generates; so, I was only searching for some kind of event that would serve to reveal these harms and their disastrous impact on human beings."[23]

Conclusions

According to one popular saying, whatever we are talking about, we always end up talking about money. Is the contrary also true? Do we also, when talking about money bear in mind anything else? Do we think about "our" and alien, power, social prestige, and the desire to shift or to keep our position in the social hierarchy, among other things?

The observations in this chapter have illustrated that the discourse of idealizing poverty and satirizing wealth dominated Bulgarian culture. The poor were seen as bearers of evangelical and/or traditional "popular" virtues, and also as those most charged with energy for revolutionary change. The association "wealth–power" was strong and held true not only for the nineteenth century but also holds true now, while the association "wealth–beauty" is still relatively weak.

Deliberate ideological suggestions can easily be noticed; initially, they did not correspond to the mindset of the reading audience but gradually began to influence it.

The discourses that invert this dominant hierarchy that favors the poor are oppressed: they are used in a rather shy way in literature and are more typical in nonfictional genres. The presence of some plots and motifs known from other cultures was achieved through translations and was still not so widespread and accepted. Also, there is a noticeable absence of some narratives and ideological elements that are widespread elsewhere. One can hardly trace any kind of phenomena specific to Bulgaria or the Balkans; research finds mostly universally known elements that differentiate only by the degree of their representation.

Due to lifestyles and mentalities, shaped by economic reasons, rather than by the impact of Orthodoxy, ideas and literary texts vaunting self-made (rich) men similar to those articulated by Ayn Rand are missing or at least doomed to be marginal in twentieth-century Bulgaria and the Balkans.

CONCLUSION

Evguenia Davidova

Until recently, a wealth of research on nationalism and political discourses dominated the historiography of south-eastern Europe. Yet one finds a paucity of literature about social interactions and quotidian practices in comparative perspective. It is difficult to locate studies on both abstract interpretations and concrete social manifestations and perceptions of key analytical categories such as wealth and poverty.[1] Their polyvalent quality stimulates the creative use of known and fresh primary sources as well as different conceptual lenses to illuminate various forms of social order, well-being, and civic engagement – described within a dynamic intersection of society, state, and modernity. As Michel Mollat, in his pioneering work on poverty, reminds us, "Poverty is an idea as well as a composite of complex, shifting, hard-to-grasp social realities. There is no obvious or constant relation between the concept and the reality."[2] This collection similarly provides a broad understanding of the social meaning of wealth and its interconnections with poverty in the modern history of the Balkans.

One of the common themes that appeared in each chapter (under a different guise) concerns the formation and transformation of elites and middle classes. Some contributions investigated strategies for wealth accumulation and social prosperity of local elites (Razhdavichka-Kiessling, Georgieva). Minority notables and local Ottoman administration in tandem, contributed to the economic revitalization of pre-Tanzimat central Balkans (Robarts). In contrast, the ever-changing administration in Bitola during the Balkan Wars was unable to retain the city's prosperity (Jovanovski). Other chapters discussed the secularizing role of non-Muslim and Muslim elites through philanthropy (Kanner). Charity also provided an opportunity for claims on political legitimation of the Egyptian khedivial dynasty during the Balkan Wars (Ginio). Although Orthodox ecclesiastical elites were similarly engaged in philanthropy, they underwent internal power shifts due to secular interventions that involved wealth redistribution (Stamatopoulos). Respectively, the Bulgarian revolutionaries and liberal intelligentsia leveled sharp critiques against those developments in the 1860s and 1870s (Naxidou). In the Serbian context, foreign-educated elites, both in power and opposition, addressed economic development mostly through political means (Samardžić). In independent Greece, the new bureaucracies impacted the legal relationship of women to their property (Doxiadis). Legitimation of traditional political elites, such as the *boyars* in Wallachia, was also reinforced through legal changes (Iancu). The incipient professionally trained groups, such as doctors and pharmacists paved the way for new market services and values (Davidova). Ambiguous representations of social elites enlivened diverse plots in the Bulgarian and other Balkan literatures (Aretov).

The role of the centralizing and modernizing state loomed large at the foreground and background of each contribution. While some depicted attempts to modernize Greece (Doxiadis), the Serbian principality (Samardžić), and the Serbian state (Jovanovski) in the form of institutional de-Ottomanization, other chapters addressed the Tanzimat's ramifications that boosted economic prosperity (Razhdavichka-Kiessling, Kanner, Davidova); yet another set of contributions discussed similar processes even in the pre-Tanzimat period (Robarts, Iancu). Still, the late Ottoman government was also engaged in direct financial intervention (Stamatopoulos) and in promoting political legitimacy through Ottomanism (Kanner), while Egypt expressed Ottoman loyalty for political reasons (Ginio). Most political and literary discourses employed a profusely metaphorical and literal lexicon of wealth and poverty to convey both social cohesion and divisions (Naxidou, Samardžić, Aretov). And yet the promise of the modern state of social inclusion vis-à-vis the reality of diverse forms of inequality and exclusions (women, minorities, peasants, workers) was a persistent thread in most chapters.

A related topic that resurfaced in different chapters both by conspicuous presence and prominent absence is the role of women during the period under investigation. Whereas Doxiadis dealt with the gradual loss of legal identity and economic agency of Greek women, Kanner showed that middle-class women in the late Ottoman Empire achieved some significant inroads in the "respectable public space".

Liberalism emerged as another recurring theme. As Samardžić, Naxidou, and Kanner elucidated the subject, there was no single channel of transmission of liberal ideas (and concomitant institutions) from Europe. Various liberal notions of citizenship were creatively appropriated in the debates about nation, state, and socio-political legitimation (Doxiadis, Jovanovski, Kanner). Implicitly or explicitly expressed, liberal middle-class values shaped the process of commodification of healthcare (Davidova), literary plots (Aretov), and philanthropic acts (Ginio).

Most chapters engaged in analyzing various forms of social, interethnic, multiconfessional, and cultural exchanges through networks of solidarity (Georgieva, Iancu), through urban interactions (Jovanovski, Ginio, Kanner), economic activities (Razhdavichka-Kiessling, Robarts, Doxiadis, Davidova, Stamatopoulos), political engagement (Naxidou, Samardžić), and literary representations (Aretov). Thus, the volume as a whole portrayed a dynamic picture of mobile people, property, commodities, diseases, services, ideas, and their attendant values.

It was the central contention of this collection that wealth – and its antithesis, poverty – were socially embedded and functioned in various and changing local, regional, national, imperial, transnational, and transimperial contexts. At each of these levels, both categories served as boundary delimiters, be it ethnic, religious, communal, social, institutional, cultural, national, class, and gender. It was the possibilities for human actors to permeate, transgress, and redraw these formal and informal boundaries that most absorbed the contributors. It is our hope that this volume will encourage new comparative studies at the intersection of society, state, and modernity.

NOTES

Introduction

1. Walker 1864: 34.
2. Lefebvre 1991: 26 ff.
3. Werner, Zimmermann 2006: 32.
4. Eisenstadt 2000: 3.

Chapter 1 Women, Wealth, and the State in Greece (1750–1860)

1. Varika 2004a: 299.
2. Norton 1981.
3. Michailidis-Nouaros 1984: 11; Alexakis 1980: 205.
4. Alexakis 1996: 36.
5. Varika, 2004a: 123; Tomara-Sideri, Sideris 1986: 155.
6. Watson 1998, Vol. 2, book 24, Ulpianus, On Sabinus Book 32; On Sabinus Book 31, 238. This concept that "the man bore the burdens of the marriage" was included in the 1946 Greek Civil Code. Kaklamanaki 1979: 84.
7. Valassis 1970: 532, 541.
8. Kalpourtzi 2001: 83.
9. GAK Mykonos, F18, No. 069, 7 February 1764; GAK Mykonos, F96, No.72, 17 May 1806, among many.
10. IEEE Naxos, No. 3592, 21 November 1765.
11. Pharmakopoulos 1886: 83; Hughes 1978: 277; Dincer 2012: 316.
12. Kasdagli 1999: 225.
13. Doxiadis 2011: 263.
14. Ibid., 45.

15. GAK Mykonos, F96, No. 95, 28 September 1807.
16. IEEE Mykonos, No. 22597, 12 November 1761; IEEE Naxos, No. 3954, 3 July 1783; among many. Women also inserted similar clauses. IEEE Mykonos, No. 22612, 21 February 1780; GAK Mykonos, F4, No. 031, 25 December 1781; GAK Mykonos, F4, No. 042, 26 July 1785; IEEE Naxos, No. 5274, 31 December 1812); IEEE Naxos, No. 3954, 3 July 1783.
17. Doxiadis 2011: 271.
18. Zepos 1976: 78; Whittle 2005: 90.
19. GAK Mykonos, F18, No. 083, 20 March 1797.
20. IEEE Naxos, No. 5553, 1 June 1815; IEEE Naxos, No. 6505, 7 November 1826; IEEE Naxos, No. 4101, 10 February 1788; GAK Mykonos, F3, No. 081, 8 May 1755; GAK Mykonos, F96, No. 121, 29 March 1811; GAK Mykonos, F16, No. 51, 9 July 1772.
21. Weisner 1993: 92.
22. Kampouroglou 1969: 252, 254.
23. Gerber 1980: 235, 237; Shatzmiller 1988: 36–58.
24. Asdrachas 2003: 288.
25. IEEE Mykonos, No. 22585, 9 August 1817.
26. GAK Mykonos, F16, No. 57, 15 October 1788.
27. IEEE Mykonos, No. 22565, 23 March 1810.
28. Koukou 1989: 231.
29. A. Laiou 1992: 234.
30. S. Laiou 2007: 243; Gradeva 1997: 55.
31. Erickson 1997: 5; Lanza 2007: 23; Hardwick 1998: 53.
32. Churches 2004: 58; Erickson 1997: 23.
33. IEEE Naxos, No. 6172, 23 October 1822.
34. A. Laiou, 1992: 237; IEEE Mykonos No. 22281, 24 August 1806.
35. IEEE, Mykonos, No. 22357, undated; IEEE Mykonos, No. 22352, 10 October 1809.
36. Kuehn 1991: 197–211.
37. IEEE Mykonos, No. 22321, 16 November, 1808; IEEE Mykonos, No. 22326, 22 January 1809; GAK Mykonos, F16, No. 74, 23 January 1809; IEEE Mykonos, No. 22558, 22 October 1817.
38. IEEE Mykonos No. 22537, 22 May 1817; IEEE Mykonos, No. 22540, 30 May 1817.
39. S. Laiou 2007; Gradeva 1997.
40. GAK Mykonos, F117, No. 419, pp. 162–3, 12 October 1828.
41. GAK Mykonos, F18, No. 058, 18 April 1754.
42. Armenopoulos 1971: 273.
43. GAK Mykonos, F96, No. 34, 4 November 1803.
44. Maurer 1976: 697, 699.
45. IEEE Mykonos, No. 22518, 16 June 1818.
46. Koukou 1989: 207–8.
47. Chouliarakis, Vol. A, Part I, 1973: XX.

48. Katsoulis, Nikolinakos, Filias 1985: 141.
49. Bastea 1999: 2; Houmanidis, Vol. B, 1990.
50. Todorov 1983: 335.
51. Bikelas 1868: 292.
52. Finlay 1971: 119.
53. Ibid., 125.
54. Sfyroeras 1970: 39.
55. Kalligas, Vol. E, 1876: 252.
56. Meijer and Meijer 2002: 227; Mirow 2004–5: 184; Tarchila 2012: 153; Saraceno 1990: 427.
57. Pantazopoulos 1965: 215, 236; idem, 1988: 579–80; Zepos 1954: 15; Svoronos 1972: 103.
58. Pantazopoulos 1965: 160, 179.
59. Kalligas, Vol. A, 1878: 153; Argyriadis-Kervegan 1998: 40, 43.
60. Geib 1990: 67.
61. Pantazopoulos 1988: 572, 577.
62. Desan 2004: 142, 175; McMillan 2000: 38.
63. Erickson 1997: 24; Wright, Ferguson 2004: 5; Morris 2005: 92, 388; Staves 1990: 28.
64. Morris 2005: 389.
65. Staves 1990: 98, 167; Pateman 1988.
66. Phillips 1988: 595; Stone 1990: 368, 382; Bonfield 2002: 123; Shanley 1989: 103; McMillan 2000: 152.
67. Desan 2004: 12.
68. Maridakis 1922: 166.
69. Kalligas, Vol. B, 1878: 597.
70. Maridakis 1922: 131, 135, 148.
71. Papagianni 1997: 140; Kalligas, Vol. D, 1930: 177.
72. Paparrigopoulos, Vol. 8, 1875: 160.
73. Kalligas, Vol. D, 1930: 110.
74. Paparrigopoulos 1875: 186; Radulescu 1962: 849–50; Maridakis 1922: 302.
75. About 1992: 151.
76. Miller 1905: 192, 265; Carnarvon 1869: 34, 47, 54, 109; Geib 1990: 74; Bartholdy 1993: 28, 131.
77. GAK Efeteio, Vol. 121, No. 18259, p. 683, 17 June 1860; GAK Efeteio, Vol. 121, No. 18270, p. 783, 4 June 1860.
78. GAK Efeteio, Vol. 121, No. 18265, p. 753, 22 June 1860.
79. GAK Efeteio, Vol. 121, No. 18307, p. 1207, 25 June 1860.
80. GAK Efeteio, Vol. 121, No. 18299, p. 1131, 30 June 1860.
81. GAK Efeteio, Vol. 120, No. 18132, p. 777, 25 May 1860.
82. GAK Efeteio, Vol 121, No. 18389, p. 1973, 28 September 1860.
83. GAK Efeteio, Vol. 121, No. 18385, p. 1941, 28 September 1860.
84. GAK Efeteio, Vol. 121, No. 18257, p. 645, 21 June 1860; GAK Efeteio, Vol. 120, No. 18166, p. 1121, 4 June 1860.

85. GAK Efeteio, Vol. 121, No. 18276, p. 847, 25 June 1860.
86. Hughes 1978: 281; Kelleher 2010: 37.
87. Hughes 1978: 282.
88. Cassia, Bada 1992: 177–8.
89. GAK Leonidio, No. 2552, 21 September 1843.
90. Alexakis 1996: 35.
91. Psychogios 1995: 178.
92. Maropoulou 1994: 113, 123; Couroucli 1983: 327.
93. Kalligas, Vol. D, 1930: 76.
94. Doxiadis 2011: 61, 266.
95. Samiou 1992: 59.
96. About 1992: 57, 141; Varika 2004a: 60.
97. For Greek monetary policy see Lazaretou 2005: 202–36.
98. GAK Leonidio, No. 201, 10 June 1848; GAK Leonidio, No. 515, 12 November 1849.
99. GAK Leonidio, No. 2041, 15 July 1842.
100. Friedl 1962: 55.
101. Doxiadis 2011: 70.
102. idem, 2007: 75–97.
103. Varika 2004a: 77.
104. Nikolopoulos, Kakoulidis, Vol. B, 1860: 214.
105. Wiesner 1993: 124.
106. Varika 2004a: 77.
107. Vranousis 1953: 374. Although his work is usually translated as "Rights of Man", Rigas used the Greek word for human (*anthropou*) instead of man (*andros*).
108. Sakkis, Vol. A, 2001: 89.
109. Koppa 2002: 172.
110. Bakalaki 1994: 79, 80.
111. Ibid., 82, 84.
112. Ibid., 78.
113. Varika 2004a: 57.
114. Ibid., 78.
115. Hionidou 2005: 475, 476.
116. Nikolopoulos, Kakoulidis, Vol. A, 1859: 328.
117. Ibid., 463, 464, 872.
118. Ibid., 222.
119. Gobineau 1999: 201.
120. Varika 2004a: 234–6.
121. Ibid., 230.
122. Varika 2004b: 267.
123. Hionidou 2005: 474.
124. GAK Leonidio, No. 383, 20 September 1848.
125. GAK Leonidio, No. 161, 1 May 1850.
126. GAK Efeteio, Vol. 119, No 17775, p. 77, 30 January 1860.

127. Hionidou 2005: 477, 483.
128. Liata 1984: 51; Hionidou 2005: 480. Compare that a seven- or a five-member household's annual expenses were roughly 506 and 101 dr. in 1855 and 1853, respectively. Psychogios 1995: 113–14.
129. Hionidou 2005: 478.
130. Varika 2004a: 46, 50.
131. Ibid., 302.
132. Katsoulis, Nikolinakos, Filias 1985: 284.
133. Kyriazis 1995: 273.
134. Senders Pedersen 2005: 27.
135. Varika 2004a: 321.
136. Sakkis 2001: 39.
137. Varika 2004a: 72–4.
138. Nikolopoulos, Kakoulidis 1859: 391.
139. Svoronos 1972: 90; Mamoukas, Vol. 9, 1941: 108.
140. Nikolopoulos, Kakoulidis 1860: 875–7.
141. GAK Leonidio, No. 109, 15 April 1847.
142. Thiersch, Vol. B., 1833: 53.
143. Leontidou 1992: 106, 107.
144. Maridakis 1922: 83, 92, 166; Triantafyllopoulos 1918: 11, 12, 16, 17, 21, 35.
145. Symeonidou-Alatopoulou 1979: 339.
146. Lambiri-Dimaki 1985: 166.
147. Kaklamanaki 1979: 82, 95.
148. Handman 1994: 249; Kyriazis 1995: 281.

Chapter 2 People of Wealth and Influence: the Case of the Khadzhitoshev Family (1770s–1870s)

1. Wallerstein, Kasaba 1983: 336–54; Islamoğlu-Inan 1990; Stoianovich 1992: 1–77; Göçek 1996; Ianeva 2011b: 35–48.
2. Stoianovich 1992: 42–4.
3. Ianeva 2000: 99–119; idem, 2011a; Davidova 2007: 64–75; idem, 2013; Lyberatos 2010: 55–85.
4. For such examples see Davidova 2013: 33–6, and the cited there literature.
5. Vŭzvŭzova-Karateodorova, 1984: 8–10.
6. Vŭzvŭzova-Karateodorova 1984; Tarashoeva 2002.
7. Many researchers have used materials from this archive: Dimitrov 1976: 135–70; Ianeva 2000: 99–119; idem, 2007: 54–63; Markova 1976: 90–7, 141–5; Marinska 2011: 222–6.
8. Tarashoeva 2002: 25, n. 16.
9. Vŭzvŭzova-Karateodorova 1984: 367.
10. There are several minor mistakes in the sums; the correct total sum is 54,180, k. Vŭzvŭzova-Karateodorova 1984: 367–72.

11. Popgeorgiev 1904: 7–8; Kharizanov 1977: 57–70.
12. Vŭzvŭzova-Karateodorova 1984: 27–8, 371.
13. In his accounts Tsenov indicated their own livestock as "*damızlık*". Ibid., 368–70.
14. Many of them are listed in an account from 1789 where Tsenov recorded the remaining capital invested in livestock after the partners split. Ibid., 373.
15. Ibid., 369.
16. Probably he is the same Hüseyn Bayraktar mentioned in the letters sent from Georgi Drokhna to Tsenov and Vasilev in 1786. Ibid., 29–30.
17. Ibid., 367–71.
18. In December 1786, Tsenov and Vasilev made efforts to buy wool on behalf of the Drokhna brothers from the village of Zlatitsa. Two months later, the brothers ordered more wool from Koprivshtitsa. Ibid., 30–1.
19. Ibid., 26, 30–1.
20. Ibid., 367–72.
21. Ibid., 371.
22. Ibid., 372–3.
23. Ibid., 373–4.
24. Ibid., 373–4.
25. Kostadin was a nephew of the above-mentioned Drokhna brothers. His name is mentioned also in the correspondence between Tsenov and his partners Michal Goga and Michal Kurte. Ibid., 42–3.
26. Ibid., 40.
27. Ibid., 379.
28. Later, two additional people were sent to Vratsa in order to expedite the delivery of wool. Ibid., 41–3.
29. Ibid., 42–4.
30. Ibid., 43.
31. In his letter (15 June 1802) to Tsenov, Kurte informed him that he was ready to buy all collected wool at a price of 23 p. and asked him to coordinate his work with h. Osman ağa, the same person with whom he had worked the previous year. Three years later Kurte asked Tsenov to buy silk on his behalf at a price of 20–2 p. His commission would be paid separately. The advanced payment would be done through a trusted person, sent by Tsenov, and the ordered silk would be delivered to Osman ağa in Oryahovo. Ibid., 44–5, 69.
32. Ibid., 379–80.
33. Ibid., 38, 378–9.
34. For more about the "first generation" of Balkan merchants – that of "the fathers" and their mixed economic activities – see a recently published book by Evguenia Davidova that offers a comparative analysis of the origin and development of the Orthodox merchant stratum within the Ottoman province Rumeli. Davidova 2013: 9–43.
35. An account from 1785 until 1803 shows that he hired the teacher Petko to teach two of his sons. Vŭzvŭzova-Karateodorova 1984: 375, 377. One of

them – Iovancho – finished his education in Zemun. Kharizanov 1976: 249–50.

36. Vŭzvŭzova-Karateodorova 1984: 246–7; Kharizanov 1976: 239–43, 251.
37. Vŭzvŭzova-Karateodorova 1984: 33, 55, 61, 65–6, 74; Kharizanov 1976: 175.
38. In a letter (6 April 1852) sent by the churchwardens of the Hilandar monastery to h. Iovancho Khadzhitoshev and other Vratsa notables, the monastery refused to sell the vineyard, donated by Tsenov. Tarashoeva 2002: 246.
39. Vŭzvŭzova-Karateodorova 1984: 375–8.
40. The pilgrims often gave money to monks for praying for them and their relatives, for copying of indulgences or holy texts, and for buying different church-related items and gifts. Giurova and Danova 1985: 13–14; Vŭzvŭzova-Karateodorova 1984: 549–52 (An account, written by Tosho Tsenov and other persons who visited the Holy Mount and the monasteries there with an attached list of the donors.)
41. Vŭzvŭzova-Karateodorova 1984: 50–1, 56–7.
42. A published part of his account, kept during the journey to the Holy Lands, reveals some of the expenses: money spent for traveling, food, donations, presents, and different wares. Tsenov and his family spent more than 5,000 k. on presents and goods alone. Giurova and Danova 1985: 317–19.
43. Ibid., 14–15.
44. Kharizanov 1976: 160.
45. Vŭzvŭzova-Karateodorova 1984: 49.
46. In their letter (7 October 1803), Mitko Utak, Dimitŭr Tsenov, and Nikolaki pop Sakelariyî asked h. Dimitraki to buy 5–6,000 *okka* wax at market price. They informed him that the *ayan* of Oryahovo also had wax and asked h. Dimitraki to buy some and send it directly to Bucharest. Four days later, h. Dimitraki got a letter from a certain molla Hasan Skenderli from Sofia who asked him to buy and send 1–2,000 *okka* wax. Ibid., 52–3.
47. Regardless of the war between Russia and the Ottoman Empire (1806–12) and the dangerous roads in 1808, h. Dimitraki and a certain Osman Pasha and Mancho traveled together to Sofia. From September 1808 to January 1809, h. Tosho was in Oryahovo and intended to cross the Danube and enter Wallachia. In the autumn 1809, he went to Istanbul. Two years later (1811), we find him in Sofia and then in Oryahovo, his brother h. Tsvetko in Craiova, while the youngest h. Iovancho was traveling between Vratsa and Plovdiv. Ibid., 88, 90–1, 104–19, 392–6.
48. In the ledgers of h. Tosho and h. Dimitraki, many people are mentioned as herders and farm helpers who worked on the family farm or were seasonally hired. Ibid., 401–3; 461–3; 471–2. Others worked as agents who collected on the Khadzhitoshevs' behalf livestock, raw materials, and food. Ibid., 452–3; 487–90; 512. The Khadzhitoshevs also hired skilled workmen who worked at home. Ibid., 104, 422, 455–6, 459. There were also employees

who worked in the family *dükkâns* or directly supported the work of their masters. Ibid., 75, 99, 214, 482, 486, 501–6.

49. Ibid., 384–6, 421–9, 482–4, 537.
50. Ibid., 79–83, 386–7.
51. Ibid., 524–5.
52. Ibid., 472–4. It seems that the merchants from Craiova were dissatisfied with that deal, as is revealed in a letter sent by another Craiova merchant Atanas Lilovich to h. Dimitraki (23 August 1818). Ibid., 178.
53. Popgeorgiev 1904: 16; Kharizanov 1976: 148–9.
54. Vŭzvŭzova-Karateodorova 1984: 390.
55. For a brief review of proto-industrialization in European and Bulgarian context, see Ianeva 2000: 99–119.
56. Vŭzvŭzova-Karateodorova 1984: 384–6, 423–9, 438–9, 516–17.
57. A document of 1806 mentions somebody explicitly indicated as "our *dolapcı*" who provided 7 *okka* at value of 12.10 k. Ibid., 384. Another one illustrates that in 1812 the Khadzhitoshevs hired 19 *dolapcıs* who were sent to the adjacent villages with 20 *dolaps*. Seven of them worked in more than one village while one *dolapcı* but with two *dolaps* was sent to another village. Ibid., 422; Account with the sums paid to the *dolapcıs*. Ibid., 455–6.
58. Ibid., 233.
59. Ibid., 301–2, 304, 537.
60. Ibid., 387.
61. Ibid., 109, 111, 159–62, 177, 245, 388, 484, 489–90, 526, 528.
62. Ibid., 269–70.
63. Ibid., 429–31, 449–51, 498–504.
64. Ibid., 499–502.
65. Ibid., 206, 498.
66. Ibid., 498, 526.
67. Ibid., 286, 344, 542.
68. Ibid., 257, 486, 498–502, 504, 540.
69. Ibid., 104.
70. Ibid., 286, 299, 532, 537.
71. Davidova 2013: 36–40.
72. Vŭzvŭzova-Karateodorova 1984: 391–2.
73. In 1811, h. Dimitraki set up a partnership with a certain Tseno, a furrier from Sofia, for opening a common shop in Vratsa. According to their contract, the former would provide his *dükkân* and 3,000 k. capital, while the latter would send two apprentices to Vratsa and invest capital of 1,000 k. Ibid., 105, 107, 109–10, 408, 503–6, 517.
74. In 1822, h. Dimitraki bought a forest in Peshtane for 1,350 k. and resold it for 1,500 k.; in Drenovitsa he bought another land for 330 k. and resold it for 590 k.; and bought a third plot in Varbitsa for 1,100 k. and resold it for 1,780 k. Ibid., 283, 479–80, 509–10.
75. Ibid., 461–3, 478, 490, 495.

76. The distillery in the village of Kunino was also rented out. Ibid., 463, 511, 520; Testimony, dated 20 September 1853, reveals that the barns were rented out and the rent was paid in kind: one *şinik* per ten. Tarashoeva 2002: 279.
77. Vŭzvŭzova-Karateodorova 1984: 97–8, 338, 470.
78. Marinov 1894: 439, 441; Kharizanov 1976: 153; Tarashoeva 2002: 421, 423, 425–9, 431–2.
79. Vŭzvŭzova-Karateodorova 1984: 226–7, 234–5; Marinov 1894: 439, 441, 445.
80. Tarashoeva 2002: 439.
81. Ibid., 400, 413–14, 467, 494–7, 521–2.
82. Ibid., 439–42, 468–70, 518–19.
83. Ibid., 386, 388–9, 463.
84. On 18 August 1812, h. Dimitraki married Ekaterina Khadzhidimitrova from Tŭrnovo. As her family name suggests, she was a member of a notable family. His brother, h. Iovancho, also married a woman of a notable Sofia family – Anastasia – the daughter of Georgi Nikolov Pazarbaşı, a warden of the market in Sofia. The Khadzhitoshevs maintained good business relationships with her family.
85. Vŭzvŭzova-Karateodorova 1984: 553–5.
86. Ibid., 104, 110, 409–10, 441.
87. Ibid., 261, 263, 329, 355, 359.
88. Ibid., 188, 196, 203–4, 261, 263, 265, 355, 358, 360.
89. Ibid., 91, 104, 113, 174, 291, 359.
90. Ibid., 103, 107–12.
91. Ibid., 125–6, 216, 325, 361.
92. Ibid., 126, 208, 216, 265, 337, 525.
93. Ibid., 142–4.
94. Ibid., 214–15, 223–5, 227–9, 236, 243–5, 256, 265–7, 269, 280–2, 531; Markova 1976: 90–6.
95. The correspondence reveals that h. Dimitraki made efforts to replace Methodius with Gavrail Bistrichanin. He was born in Vratsa but immigrated after the war of 1806–12 to Wallachia where he became an abbot of the Bistriţa monastery. Vŭzvŭzova-Karateodorova 1984: 325–6.
96. Markova 1976: 95–6.
97. Marinov 1894: 441–4; Markova 1976: 94–5; Kharizanov 1976: 153–4.
98. Tarashoeva 2002: 23–6, 29, 33.
99. The sons of h. Dimitraki: Zamfiraki, Alexander, and Todoraki were pupils of Konstantin Ognianovich. The latter was born in Serbia, but worked as a teacher in the Bulgarian school in Vratsa (1822–7). During this period he became a close friend of the Khadzhitoshevs. Probably through him h. Dimitraki got in contact with Prince Miloš. Later his son Alexander continued his education in Serbia where he maintained a relationship with Miloš Obrenović. Ibid., 2–3, 27–8.

100. Ibid., 31.
101. Ibid., 30–1, 34, 36, 44–9, 61.
102. Ibid., 62, 192. For the connection between Dimitŭr Mustakov and Miloš Obrenović, see Racheva 2008: 200–38.
103. Danova 2008: 175, 525–6.
104. Tarashoeva 2002: 272, 280, 284.
105. Ibid., 225–6, 234.
106. Stefan Bogoridi (1775–1859) was a high Ottoman official of Bulgarian origin. He was a grandson of the prominent writer Bishop Sophronius of Vratsa. For his support to Alexander Khadzhitoshev, see Tarashoeva 2002: 239–40, 313.
107. Dimitrov 1972; Pinson 1975: 103–46.
108. Dimitrov 1972: 49–50, 77, 159–64, 179–81; Pinson 1975: 132–3.
109. Tarashoeva 2002: 321.
110. According to the family legend, he was poisoned in 1856 in Sofia on his way to Niš. Ibid., 463.
111. Ibid., 287, 292, 326, 334.
112. After his marriage in 1845, Zamfiraki settled in Sofia where he ran together with his cousin Dimitraki and Isaî Georgievich *dükkâns* and helped his father-in-law while his brother Todoraki took over the deals abroad. Ibid., 50, 52–4, 68, 70–1, 78, 92, 419–25.
113. Ibid., 41, 56–7, 439.
114. Ibid., 69, 72–6.
115. Ibid., 65–6.
116. Ibid., 97.
117. The revolutions of 1848–9 blocked access to the markets in Austria. However, it seems that the main reason for the dissolved partnership was the insolvency of the partners. Along these lines, in the same year the Khadzhitoshev brothers sold the shop of their mother in Vratsa in order to cover their debts. Moreover, for the same reason Zamfiraki had to pawn his wife's jewels and even to sell some of them. The Statkovich brothers also owed money to Zamfiraki's father-in-law and the teacher Zakhari Krusha, which they could not pay back. Tarashoeva 2002: 167, 172–5, 178–9, 181, 210.
118. Ianeva 2007: 54–63; Ianeva 2011a: 85–7, 116–19, 154–7, 176, 262–3, 279–80, 308–11, 328–9.
119. Tarashoeva 2002: 171, 188, 194, 225, 227–8, 232, 235, 236, 261, 274–7.
120. Ibid., 236, 261, 264–5, 275, 284–7, 326, 388, 409–10.
121. Davidova 2013: 148–65; Lyberatos 2010: 57–71.
122. Tarashoeva 2002: 429–30. The will of his uncle, written in 1852, a year before his death, shows that his fortune amounted to 24,550 k.; it consisted of a house, shop, half a garden, a vineyard, forest, three pastures, two distilleries, and a large dish. He also had debts of 10,260 k. due to eight creditors. Ibid., 247–8.

123. Ibid., 194, 198, 396–7, 399–400.
124. Ibid., 189–90.
125. Ibid., 86, 91, 204, 209, 213–16.
126. Ibid., 425–9, 431–2, 434–9. The sources do not shed light on the fortune which h. Dimitraki left after his death. Besides the already mentioned farm in Radovene, a granary, and a garden, his sons and wife also got the family house and his shops in Vratsa. Ibid., 279, 286–7, 291–3, 332.
127. Ibid., 430.
128. Ibid., 432–3, 413–14.
129. Ibid., 167, 194, 206, 216, 242, 253, 303, 319–20.
130. Ibid., 179–80, 218, 263, 277, 300, 303–6, 335–6, 377–8; Markova 1976: 141–4.
131. Tarashoeva 2002: 240, 279–80.
132. He was a member of the local council (*meclis*) and of the town's municipality council after the establishment of the Bulgarian Principality (1878). Ibid., 345, 364–7, 369–74, 376–8, 380, 382–6, 390–4, 396–7, 463.
133. Braudel, Vol. 2, 1982: 478–82; Davidova 2013: 79–100.

Chapter 3 Defining the Patrimony: Name, Lineage and Inheritance Practices (Wallachia at the Beginning of the Nineteenth Century)

1. Rădulescu 1957, § 3, 100.
2. Norm that stipulates the right to purchase and redeem land by those who had a relationship of solidarity (family, indivision, neighborhood) with the vendor.
3. This refers to the eponymous ancestor who is also the mythical founder whose traces cannot be always documented. Klapisch-Zuber 1986: 112; idem, 1990: 41–5; idem, 2000.
4. Bourdieu 1980: 257.
5. Ibid.
6. Lévi-Strauss 1979: 47.
7. Godelier 2010: 138.
8. For a similar signification of the notion in ancient Greek society, see de Coulanges 1927. Paul Stahl also mentions the "fireplace" as administrative unit of a household. P.H. Stahl 1986: 19.
9. Lévi-Strauss 1979: 51.
10. Benveniste, Vol. 1, 1966: 293.
11. Iorga, Vol. 2, 1937a: 153; Filitti, n.d., XI; Giurescu 1920; H.H. Stahl, Vol. 1, 1998: 54–70.
12. Scurtu 1966, see "moş".
13. H.H. Stahl 1998: 215–16; Fotino 1925: 88.
14. Condurachi 1919: 8; Fotino 1925: 87; Petriceicu-Haşdeu 1893, Vol. III, see "baştină".

15. Iorga 1902: 51.
16. Stoicesu 1971: 105–6.
17. Filitti 1919. See Drugănescu family.
18. BAR, mss. roum. 611, f. 134.
19. Marica, wife of Ştefan Alexeanu, and Sultana were born from two different marriages of their father Scarlat Drugănescu. Filitti 1919: 4–5.
20. Grecianu, Vol. 1, 1915: 10. Within the ladder of ranks, he would rise as far as *paharnic* (1852). Cernovodeanu, Gavrilă 2002: 113.
21. BAR, mss. roum. 612: "Testament de Ştefan Alexeanu" (22 January1808), f. 179v–180.
22. In 1803, Constantin Alexeanu made his will designating his wife sole legatee without mentioning the existence of a descendant. Six years later, Maria Alexeanu made a will in favor of her adopted son, Amandache, a cousin coming from the family of her mother. BAR, mss. rom 612, f. 32v–34.
23. Filitti 1919: 5–6.
24. Radulescu 1962, *IL*, ch. 195, 192–3.
25. A document written in 1591 suggests that this form of adoption could have been preferred in an ancient legal practice: "I, Radu *postelnic* [...] state [...] that, as I had no child of my own flesh and blood who could give alms for me and remember me, I took this child (my cousin) in my arms, I baptized him and gave him the name of Socol [...]. And, after baptizing him, I gave him all my possessions", *Documente privind istoria României,* B, XVI Century, 6, Vol. III, 1952: 15.
26. Iancu 2004: 237–77.
27. The legal term refers to an inheritance with a condition to be passed on to the next generation. Sachelarie, Stoicescu 1988, see "diată".
28. Lecca 1899: 534, 571–2.
29. Iorga, Vol. II, 1969, n. 265, 113; Badea-Păun 1997: 194.
30. Iorga 1906: 9–10.
31. BAR, mss. roum. 4025, f.3–5v; Iorga 1906: 347–52.
32. The relationship established by adoption is lineal. Radulescu, 1962, *IL*, cl. 195, 192–193; idem, 1955, *LC*, ch. 3, § 22, 124.
33. BAR, ms. roum. 4025, f. 3v.
34. The fist Constitution that brought the two Principalities of Wallachia and Moldavia in administrative unison. Politically, it established the modern principle of the separation of legislative, administrative, and judicial systems.
35. About Grigore Brâncoveanu, see Berindei 1989: 280.
36. Radulescu 1955, *LC*, ch. 5, § 2a), 2b), 136.
37. Vîrtosu 1938: 437.
38. Iorga 1937b: 177–86. In his description of Grigore Brâncoveanu's funeral, Heliade Rădulescu also refers to titles of nobility that the *great boyar* had inherited from his forefather, prince Constantin Brâncoveanu: "Prince of the Holy Empire and knight of Saint Stanislaus". Vîrtosu 1938: 443; Cernovodeanu 1989: 127, 131.

39. Iorga 1902: 411–12; Iorga 1937b: 177–86; Badea-Păun 1997:196–7. Starting with the second half of the eighteenth century, certain *boyars* showed themselves to be very open to Western influence and to the idea of hereditary nobility. This attitude can be observed especially through their political choices of services provided to the Austrian or to the Russian Empire. In exchange, they expected a title of nobility. Hereafter, the presence of these titles was rather fleeting, unable to impose a real concept of hereditary nobility. Georgescu 1972: 91; Cernovodeanu 1994: 86. One of the best-known cases of rise to nobility is that of Nicolae Rossetti. Grecianu 1903: 219 and passim; Rosetti, Vol. I, 1938: 19; Urechia, Vol. VIII, 1897: 469; Iorga, Vol. VIII, 1904: 55.
40. Badea-Păun 1997:197.
41. "After informing myself of my father's reputation, without managing to understand by now how all this slander reconciles with all I know of him, his talents, his character and his patriotic love, I started conducting serious and objective research on his political life to discover – in a positive way – if the fault needs to be looked for in the feebleness of his love or in the passions of others." Brâncoveanu 1858: 3–4.
42. BNF, Fond Bibesco, carton 47, dossier 3: "Copie d'une lettre adressée par S.A. le Prince Grégoire de Brancovan à S.A. la Princesse Michel Sturdza, Princesse régnante de Moldavie;" "Lettre de S.A. le Prince Grégoire de Brancovan à Maître Mocquard", Amphion, Haute Savoie, 1873.
43. Gorovei, Rădulescu 1990: 220–37.
44. Vîrtosu 1938: 431–2.
45. Iorga, 1904, Vol. VIII, 67: "Stephanus Bassaraba de Brancoveanuis", 69.
46. Bibesco, Vol. I, 1893: 1.
47. Bibesco, Vol. I, 1893, 33; Vol. II, 1894: 537.
48. On fake genealogies, see Pippidi 1980: 282.
49. Godelier describes a "système à maison" based on the principles of both descent and alliance, a system that creates kinship groups that are called "maison". "At this level, the system is cognate, but with a tendency to privilege the paternal line [...] Instead of opposing masculine to feminine descent (or radically opposing descent and alliance), he uses all these kinship relationships to maintain the existence of a household and to preserve its name and place." Godelier 2010:136–8.
50. P.H. Stahl 1981: 47–62.
51. Lévi-Strauss 1979: 53.

Chapter 4 Reconstruction, Resettlement, and Economic Revitalization in pre-Tanzimat Ottoman Bulgaria

1. Gülsoy 1993: 45.
2. The Gülhane Rescript is frequently referred to as the Ottoman "Bill of Rights" and its proclamation in 1839 is generally considered to mark the beginning of

the Tanzimat era in Ottoman history. Drawing upon European models, the thrust of the Tanzimat reforms included a move towards a contractual relationship between sultan and subjects, elevated rights and equality for the empire's non-Muslim subjects, the rationalization of the empire's tax regime, the desacralization of education, and property rights. For more on the Gülhane Rescript in the context of the shifting understanding of the relationship between the Ottoman state and its subjects in the mid-nineteenth century, see Salzmann 1999: 39–45; Abu-Manneh 1994: 173–203.

3. *Fakiisko Predanie* 1985. Written down in 1888 by the well-known Bulgarian man of letters Balcho Neikov, *Fakiisko Predanie* is a compilation of oral histories (as told to Neikov) recounting the lives of the ancestors of the famous Bulgarian revolutionary Stefan Karadja. In the Ottoman time, Faki was an important fortified transportation hub in eastern Rumelia. *Predanie* can be translated as "legend" or "tradition".
4. "Vospominaniia Doktora Zeidlitsa", 1878: 429.
5. BOA –HAT 727/34628 (6 March 1830) and BOA – HAT 747/35272 (1835). This drop in production continued a trend, which had begun in the 1760s. In 1814, the displacement of many of the skilled factory workers employed at an important Ottoman weapons manufacturing facility in Islimiye resulted in a shortfall in the plant's monthly output of armaments. BOA –C.AS. 600/25315 (9 July 1814). For more on output levels in the Samakocuk foundry in the eighteenth century, see Agoston 2005: 175–6; Genç 2000: 213–14.
6. The pre-war population of the important Black Sea port-town of Sizebolu dropped from roughly 4,000 before the war to 1,500 in 1830. Ovcharov 1999: 93–5.
7. BOA –HAT 1042/43127 (16 August 1831).
8. Gülsoy 1993: 46.
9. Favored terms used by Ottoman officials to describe circumstances in post-war Rumelia included: *tevhiş* ("a making empty and desolate like a wilderness"); *tahliye* ("an emptying or vacating"); and *hengame* (uproar, tumult). Bulgarian historians tend to use the term *zapustiava* (desolate, wild, or deserted) when describing the situation in Dobruja after the war of 1828–9.
10. Gülsoy 1993: 28.
11. BOA – HAT, 1042/43120 (2 May 1830). In Ottoman archival documents, these bandit gangs are alternately referred to as *erbab-ı fesad* or *eşkiyalar*. Individual brigands were identified by local Ottoman officials according to their gang affiliation (i.e. *Pantolar* or *Velendirler*). The leader of one of the largest bandit gangs (Alexander Velendir) lent his name to both his specific gang (active in the region around Islimiye) as well as to general brigand-like activity in the Rumelian countryside. BOA – HAT 1027/42792 (16 February 1830).
12. BOA – HAT 1085/44179 (3 May 1830) and BOA – HAT 1085/44180 (7 May 1830).
13. BOA – HAT 1044/43169 (28 June 1830); "Report from Russian Consul in Islimiye Vashchenko to Russian Field Marshal Dibich-Zabalkanski" RGADA,

f. 15, d. 707, ll. 1–13 (28 April 1830). According to Vashchenko, by April 1830 Ottoman authorities had been able to impose a certain amount of law and order in eastern Rumelia – persuading some Bulgarians (who had been making preparations to leave for Russia) to have a change of heart and stay in the Ottoman Empire. "Instructions supplementaires á Monsieur Vashchenko, consul á Slivno", RGADA, f. 15, d. 707, ll. 1–13.

14. Gradeva 1999: 181; Wilkinson 1971: 77–8; McGowan 1981: 12, 26; Ovcharov 1999: 93–5; "Dobruzha", Vol. 10a, 1893: 830; Karpat 1994: 484.
15. BOA – HAT 1085/44179 (3 May 1830).
16. BOA – HAT 1076/43944-A (October 1829).
17. Gülsoy 1993: 44.
18. BOA – HAT 1052/43332 (26 November 1829).
19. While *çorbacılar* were often employed by Ottoman provincial authorities to assist with tax collection and the resolution of legal disputes, the social status of the *çorbacı* in early nineteenth-century Rumelia is best understood as that of the representative (or headman) of a village or, in the most general usage, as a "rich peasant".
20. BOA – HAT 1044/43169 (28 June 1830).
21. BOA – HAT 1068/43745-C (1830). BOA – HAT 1085/44179 (3 May 1830), and BOA – HAT 1038/43008-F (1830). For more examples of peasant petitions submitted to Ottoman officials in the period immediately after the Russo–Ottoman War (1828–29), see BOA – HAT 1048/43239-G (12 July 1830); BOA – HAT 1066/43722-H (1830); BOA – HAT 1068/43745-C (1830).
22. BOA – C.MTZ 11/534 (1769–1770).
23. Chilingirov 1917: 10.
24. "Otnoshenie V.I. Krasno-Milashevicha P.V. Chichagovu o Sbore Dizhmarita s Zadunaiskikh Pereselentsev Valakhii" (9 August 1812) and "Otnoshenie V.I. Krasno-Milashevicha General-Maioru S.F. Zhelukhinu o Sbore Dizhmarita s Zadunaiskikh Pereselentsev Valakhii" (24 August 1812), in Kryzhanovskaia, Ruseev 1957: 73–5.
25. This despite the fact that the *kadı* of Midye accused the Rum Metropolitan of Edirne (Yerasimos) of working with Russian forces to promote the out-migration of Bulgarians in 1828. BOA – HAT 1052/43332 (26 November 1829); Gülsoy 1993, 32–3. It is worth noting here that the pro-Ottoman initiatives of the Patriarchate were, perhaps, a bit self-serving as both the Ottoman state and the Patriarchate stood to lose financially from the out-migration of tax-paying Orthodox *reaya*.
26. Doinov 1981: 308.
27. RGVIA, f. 14057, op. 16/183, d. 50, ch. 1, ll. 49–53 (16–20 September 1829).
28. BOA – HAT 1027/42792 (16 February 1830) and BOA – HAT 1068/43742 (29 March 1830). During these tours, a trusted state official was attached to the Metropolitan's retinue to observe his actions and record his words.

29. *Fakiisko Predanie*, 155. Bulgarian chronicles ascribe the qualities of "moderation" or "temperance" (*umereni*) to those Muslim-Turkish townspeople who appealed to their Bulgarian neighbors to stay in the Ottoman Empire.
30. BOA – HAT 43944-A (October 1829), Meshcheriuk 1965: 18; Titorov 1903: 28.
31. BOA – HAT 1044/43169 (28 June 1830), BOA – HAT 1047/43226 (1 October 1830) and Gülsoy 1990: 35.
32. Meshcheriuk 1965: 187.
33. Chilingirov 1917: 10.
34. Alternately defined as a system of "deportation", "coerced or compulsory resettlement", or "population transfer", the Ottoman *sürgün usülü* focused primarily on the deportation of populations from central and south-eastern Anatolia and their forced resettlement in northern Rumelia.
35. BOA – HAT 1080/43991 (6 April 1830). Those local officials in Rumelia who did not "buy in" to administrative reforms and pro-migrant policies were dismissed. BOA – HAT 1066/43722-G (19 April 1830).
36. Gülsoy 1993: 69. These set-asides were often time-limited. Examples exist of *çorbacılar* writing to fellow villagers in the Russian Empire notifying them that after an absence of five months they would forfeit the right to their lands and their crops. Gülsoy 1993: 72. Also, some lands vacated by departed migrants were distributed to returnees and internally displaced Muslim-Tatar agriculturalists. BOA – HAT 776/36417 (13 September 1830) and "Consul v Slivno G.V. Vashchenko Poslanniku v Constantinopole A.I. Ribop'er" (27 June 1831), in *VPR,* Vol. 17, 1960: 98.
37. Gülsoy 1990: 34–5.
38. BOA – HAT 922/40086-C (1831).
39. BOA – HAT 1027/42792 (16 February 1830).
40. Gülsoy 1993: 42.
41. Ibid., 53.
42. BOA –HAT 778/36443-A (20 January 1834).
43. Traikov 1981: 162.
44. Todorov 1983: 276–84.
45. A development remarked upon as early as the fall of 1830 in a report issued by the *muhafız* (military commander) of Varna to the Ottoman Grand Vizier. The *muhafız* noted the significant revival of trading activity in Ismail, Galatz, Tulça, and Hirsova. BOA – HAT 1038/43008 (20 October 1830).
46. Titorov 1903: 24.
47. Meshcheriuk 1965: 196–7.
48. BOA – HAT 747/35272, BOA – HAT 776/36417, BOA – HAT 778/36443-A, BOA – HAT 1038/43008, BOA – HAT 1038/43008-A, BOA – HAT 1039/43027, BOA – HAT 1042/43136.
49. Traikov 1981: 160–1.
50. Chilingirov 1917: 180, 202.
51. Ibid.,180.

52. BOA –C. IKTS. 40/1966; BOA – C.MTZ 6/261.
53. On regional and international trade conducted by merchants from Chervena Voda, see Gradeva 2006: 1–20.
54. "Report from Russian Consul in Islimiye Gerasim Vashchenko to Russian Field Marshal Dibich-Zabalkanski" (28 April 1830), RGADA, f. 15, d. 707, ll. 1–13.
55. The only disruptions to this trade fair prior to the outbreak of Russo–Ottoman warfare in the early part of the nineteenth century were due to periodic outbreaks of epidemic disease in the last two decades of the eighteenth century. Manolova-Nikolova 2004: 98.
56. Todorov 1983: 427–8.
57. Ibid.; Stoianovich 1960: 234–313.
58. Davidova 2013: 23; Tonev 1980: 277–8; Karpat 1994: 484; McGowan 1981: 20, 24. The importance of local fairs is well described in the oral histories compiled in *Fakiisko Predanie*, 148, 278.
59. RGADA, f. 15, d. 707, ll. 1–13.
60. Tonev 1980: 277.
61. Ibid., 277.
62. Davidova 2013: 136.
63. Todorov 1983: 462–3.
64. Ibid., 462–3.
65. Stoianovich 1960: 310.
66. For more on this period in Bulgarian and Ottoman history, see Robarts 2008: 61–74.

Chapter 5 The Poor Men of Christ and their Leaders: Wealth and Poverty within the Christian Orthodox Clergy of the Ottoman Empire (Eighteenth–Nineteenth Century)

1. Gedeon, Vol. 3, 1939: 255.
2. See his autobiography, Sofronii Vračanski 1989.
3. Gedeon, Vol. 3, 1939: 266–7. Instances where individuals in positions of power have influenced the election of priests include the Grand Vizier Köprülü Mehmed Pasha's demand to Patriarch Gregory for the appointment of his friend Chrysanthos of Eudoxias as bishop to a certain small diocese in 1867. The rise of a new social class with enormous political and cultural influence, the *Phanariots*, was actually a consequence of the first military defeats of the Ottoman Empire in the wars with Habsburg Austria (Treaty of Carlowitz 1699, Treaty of Passarowitz 1718) and the appearance of another great opponent in the North, Russia, which delegitimized the power of the Moldavian and Vlach Princes. On the *Phanariot* class, see *L' Epoque Phanariote*, 1970; Zervos, 2 Vol., 1990. This Greek-speaking aristocracy ideologically gathered around the Patriarchate and exercised a host of commercial and civic functions, managed to control the

promotion of leaders in the Danubian Principalities and to occupy important posts in the Ottoman administration. The *Phanariotes*, a social group guaranteeing the maintenance of Ottoman legitimacy in border states vital to the empire, and the influence they had over internal political issues, may be considered a pivotal factor in defining the Orthodox *millet* as *Rum*. For this crucial issue, see Stamatopoulos 2006: 253–73.

4. Konortas 1998: 127–34.
5. For background on the establishment and structure of *gerontism,* see Papadopoullos 1952: 39–60, especially 57–60.
6. Gedeon, Vol. 3, 1939: 228–9.
7. Ibid., 229.
8. Konortas 1998: 144–6.
9. Stamatopoulos 2003: 355 ff.
10. Helladios 1714. The work was devoted to Peter the Great.
11. Gedeon, Vol. 4, 1939: 297–8.
12. Stamatopoulos 2010: 91–118.
13. The joining of Trikala, Gardiki, and Peristera under the Larissa metropolitan in the sixteenth century is a good example; of these, Trikala and Gardiki reemerged as independent sees in the eighteenth century while Peristera remained only in name with a titular bishop. Gedeon, Vol. 4, 1939: 300–1.
14. One example is the clash over the Servia bishopric between the Metropolitan of Thessaloniki, who had control over it, and the Archbishop of Ohrid who sought to expand his jurisdiction south. The city of Naoussa was also contested by the Archbishop of Ohrid who sought to wrench it from Veria's control. The attachment of villages to a see was often done with an eye to a monastery with considerable revenues. In 1636, Patriarch Cyril Kontaris annexed Sarakinitsa, a village under the jurisdiction of the Dryinoupoli, and made the Goura monastery a *stavropegion* (directly dependent on the Ecumenical Patriarchate). But the new patriarch, Neophytos III, and the Holy Synod decreed that both the village and the monastery would come under the Dryinoupoli. Gedeon, Vol. 4, 1939: 303–4.
15. Hering 1968.
16. Gedeon, Vol. 4, 1939: 331.
17. The period of the history of the Ecumenical Patriarchate from 1830 until 1860 could be considered a transitional one. Elements of the previous period survived through procedures of transformation, such as the function of the Holy Council of the elders/*gerontes* and the collaboration of its members with powerful seculars. The former, however, no longer came from the great families of the *Phanariots*, which had prevailed before the Greek War of Independence, mainly through the control of the thrones of the Danubian Principalities. These families, after the outbreak of the Revolution (1821), were politically tarnished, financially devastated, and the majority of them left Constantinople. In the vacuum, new dynasties emerged, concentrated around powerful personalities of neo-*Phanariots* (as cleverly named by Manuil Gedeon): Stefan Vogoridi, of Bulgarian origin; Nikolaos Aristarchis, of Armenian origin; and Ioannis Psycharis, of Greek origin.

This ethnic composition of the political elite of the neo-*Phanariots* was not accidental, since the Greek Revolution had deteriorated the terms under which the *Rum millet* was treated by the Ottoman authorities. For the complicated relations of continuity/discontinuity between *Phanariot* and neo-*Phanariot* world, see Stamatopoulos 2013: 45–57.

18. Gedeon, Vol. 4, 1939: 332
19. Stamatopoulos 2003: 37–44.
20. F.O.78/1087, No. 716, Stratford Canning to Earl of Clarendon, Therapeia, 20 September 1855, appendix 1.
21. Ibid.
22. Stamatopoulos 2003: 57–8.
23. For details of the hermeneutical schemes on the Bulgarian Schism (1872), see Stamatopoulos 2008–2009: 105–25; idem, 2008: 243–70.
24. Filippides 1946: 6–7. For the decisive role of the Tanzimat reforms to the administrative reconstruction of the Ecumenical Patriarchate, see Stamatopoulos 2006: 253–73. See also the classic works of Davison 1963; Braude & Lewis, Vol. 2, 1982; and some important works by Turkish scholars like Bozkurt 1989; Ortayli 1994; idem, 1996.
25. Markova 1976; idem, 1989.
26. Sokolov 1904: 731–2.
27. The word usually used in the Greek sources is "National" Assembly, translating a posteriori, and wrongly, the word "*millet*" as "nation".
28. That means the reformist wing of the Millet-i Assembly, which undertook to reform the administrative structures of the Patriarchate.
29. I.A.Y.E. / 1859, File: aak A, No 31, P. A. Zanos charge d' affaires of the Greek Embassy to the Greek Foreign Minister A.G. Kountouriotes, appendix 2, Pera 11 July 1859.
30. I.A.Y.E. / 1859, File: aak, No. 31.
31. For developments on the monastic issue during this critical period in the unification of the two principalities (1859) under Alexandru Cuza, see Jelavich 1959: 103–20.
32. Gedeon, Vol. 4, 1939: 330.
33. Anthimos Alexoudis 1901: 406–7.
34. *AA*, No. 161–203, 24/5 November 1864. See the publication of the order issued by the Vizier Mehmed Fuad Pasha (21 August 1864). To pay off the public debt but also the provincial (court) treasury debt, an audit committee was formed. Holders of bonds from both debts were called on to submit their titles to the committee within 61 days (18 December 1864) so that interest payments would not be halted. The notice by the Metropolitan Dionysius of Crete, president of the Mixed Council, was published in *AA*, No. 168–218, 16/28 December 1864.
35. *AA*, No. 162–205, 31/12 November 1864.
36. The fact that both the draft and final text are kept in the archive of Alexandros Karatheodores, son of Stephanos, reinforces the belief that his father instigated

the protest. AKA, file 01/31, No. 1497, 1499. The text was also published in *Armonia*. *AA*, No. 226, 16/28 January 1865.

37. The pro-reform council members were Christakis Zographos, a supporter of the then Patriarch Sophronius and a close friend of the powerful banker Georgios Zariphes, and Constantinos Adosides. *AA*, No. 245, 24/5 April 1865.
38. AKA, file 01/40, No. 1463. The text is signed by "a member of the Orthodox contingent", which evidently is Karatheodores himself. The document titled "Observations" is undated.
39. AKA, file 01/40, No. 1463.
40. Assigning the collection of monies to the Ottoman administrative apparatus would relieve the metropolitans from their dependence on powerful local *muhtars* (administrative officials) and *çorbacıs* who held sway over money collected for the clergy's compensation. Such a development would alter the relationship at local level by weakening the local notables and would subordinate those used to a tradition of community self-administration to the Ottoman central authority. The *Vilayet* Law (1864) was in a similar vein. Thus, the efforts to impose the new measure on grants would simultaneously create local councils and *muhtar-gerontes* that would place local elders' power under the state's direct control. Converting the *muhtar-gerontes* into state employees would result in the corresponding subordination of the Orthodox clergy as employees of the Ottoman state. *AA*, No. 228, 23/4 January 1865.
41. *AA*, No. 226, 16/28 January 1865. Transferring authority to the Ottoman state aimed at preserving the financial health of philanthropic and educational institutions would also legitimize control over its internal operations, a problem that would be raised in a particularly intense manner during the 1880s under the form of the "Privilege Question". Recent research has shown that awarding of privileges by the Ottoman state to religious functionaries of the *millets* occurred through *berats* that, however, were intended to confer individual rights, which is to say that they did not necessarily presuppose recognition of the Orthodox or Armenian Patriarchates as institutionalized mechanisms of the Ottoman state; or, to put it in modern terms, as public legal entities. On the question of progressive concessions of privileges to the Ecumenical Patriarchate, see Konortas 1998: 123, 315–61; Exertzoglou 1992: 65–84.
42. *AA*, No. 228, 23/4 February 1865.

Chapter 6 Health as Wealth: Commodification of Doctor–Patient Relations in the Nineteenth-Century Ottoman Balkans

1. Vŭzvazova-Karateodorova 1984: 434–5.
2. RIM-Gabrovo, Inv. no. 399, 18.

3. Liata 1984: 63.
4. BIA-NBKM, f. 6, IA 27538.
5. Porter 1987: 34–5.
6. Here I am referring to Bourdieu's definition: "Social capital as made up of social obligations ('social connections')." Bourdieu 1986: 243.
7. Porter 1987: 18–19. For a recent revisionist approach, see Lindemann 2010: 16–17.
8. Stefanov 1980: 11.
9. Philliou 2011: 12–14; 28–9.
10. Nazarska 2011: 40.
11. Anastassiadou-Dumont 2003: 20–6; Nahum 2003: 52–62.
12. Trompoukēs 2000: 75.
13. Mazhdrakova-Chavdarova 1985: 19.
14. Gavrilova 1999: 175.
15. BIA-NBKM, f. 6, IA 833.
16. Popović 2000: 323, 355.
17. Tsonchev 1996: 404.
18. BIA-NBKM, f. 628, a.e. 2, 30–1; 37.
19. BIA-NBKM, f. 70, a.e. 135, 3–9.
20. DARM, Skopje, f. 725, box 2, n. 8, 1906–1908, 443 pages.
21. DARM, Skopje, f. 725, box 1, 54–5, 89.
22. Frieden 1981: 27.
23. Sechel 2011: 58–9, 71.
24. Promitzer 2011: 101–7.
25. Yildirim 2003: 127.
26. Todev 2003.
27. Bourdieu 1986: 252–5.
28. Stambolski, Vol. 1, 1927: 140–1, 308.
29. Frieden 1985: 31, 108.
30. Doxiadis 2011: 167.
31. Prpa, Vol. 1, 2003: 382–3; 396–7.
32. Smochowska-Petrowa 1973: 69–70.
33. Stojanovski 1999: 87.
34. Paskaleva 2000: 229–37; Smochowska-Petrowa 1973: 106.
35. The pharmacists were also required to understand prescriptions in French and Italian and to have a basic knowledge of math and chemistry. *Dunav*, No. 903, 28 August 1874.
36. DARM, Skopje, f. 10, box 7, 1.10.7.2/3.
37. Sahara 2011: 31–48.
38. Manolova-Nikolova 2004: 33–5.
39. Danova 2004: 412–13.
40. BIA-NBKM, f. 6, IA 8987, 66.
41. BIA-NBKM, f. 6 IA 8987, 71–4.

42. BIA-NBKM, f. 7, a.e. 19, 132.
43. BIA-NBKM, f. 6 IA 383.
44. BIA-NBKM, f. 6, IA 8999, 115–16.
45. BIA-NBKM, II A 7907; Davidova 2013.
46. Leake 1967: 223.
47. Popović 2000: 262.
48. BIA-NBKM, f. 112, a.e. 97, 37–8.
49. Doxiadis 2011: 139.
50. BIA-NBKM, f. 628, a.e. 2, 37.
51. BIA-NBKM, f. 628, a.e. 7, 1; a.e. 8, 1; a.e. 3, 1.
52. Bojadžievski 2003: 56–8.
53. Snegarov 1946: 246–7.
54. BIA-NBKM, f. 6, IA 5128.
55. Danova 2004: 410–413, 438–9, 444.
56. Prpa, Vol. 2, 2004: 485.
57. Stefanov 1980: 73.
58. DARM, Skopje, f. 868, box 3, 1–4.
59. The expenses varied, though, if the municipality were to hire an older and more experienced physician, it would offer 15–16,000 g. annually and a prepaid house with five-six rooms. BIA-NBKM, f. 6, IA 8988, 64–5.
60. BIA-NBKM, f. 7, a.e. 1429, 41.
61. BIA-NBKM, f. 6, IA 9002, 343–4.
62. Yildirim 2003: 129, 142.
63. Ibid., 127.
64. DARM, Skopje, f. 10, box 2, 1.10.2.2/2.
65. Chekimoglou 2005: 157.
66. Cited in Manolova-Nikolova 2004: 226.
67. Stefanov 1980: 109.
68. Apostolidis, Peev 1931: 112.
69. BIA-NBKM, f. 628, a.e. 1, 21.
70. Vŭzvazova-Karateodorova 1984: 533.
71. Gavrilova 1999: 197.
72. BIA-NBKM, f. 628, a.e. 37, 5.
73. BIA-NBKM, IIB 6441.
74. Chrēstidis 1837: 19.
75. Stefanov 1980: 77.
76. Ilchev 1995: 78,117, 166, 186; Lindemann 2010: 261.
77. Karlova, 3,1870: 731; 4, 1870: 179.
78. DARM, Skopje, f. 725, box 2, 45, 181.
79. Džambazovski 1979: 125.
80. Prpa, Vol. 1, 2003: 296–8.
81. Molho 2005: 89–90, 95.
82. Anastassiadou-Dumont 2003: 5.

Chapter 7 From "the Sick", "the Blind", and "the Crippled" to the Nation of "Toiling People": Visions of the Poor in the Late Ottoman Empire and the Early Turkish Republic

1. For the destruction of many Ottoman guilds as a result of the European commercial penetration see the testimony of Alexandros Paspatis, a prominent Greek Orthodox doctor of the time. Paspatis 1862.
2. Karpat 1985: 104.
3. Svolopoulos 1980: 441–57; Kitromilides 1996; Özcan 2013: 27–8.
4. Lewis 1961; Davison 1963.
5. Özcan 2013: 19–20.
6. Duprat, Vol. 1, 1993: 11–16.
7. Checkland and Checkland 1974: 15, 22.
8. For the rise of this notion in Victorian England, see Thompson 1988.
9. Anastasiadou-Dumont 2003; Kanner 2004.
10. Davison 1963: 114–35.
11. Whereas studies on philanthropy in Muslim or Jewish communities are prolific, relevant research for the Armenians is, to my knowledge, rather limited.
12. Paspatis 1862: 4–5; Gedeôn 1886: 138–46; Hasselquist 1766: 20; Howard 1791: 64.
13. Barsoumian 1985: 179; Kévorkian, Paboudjian 1992: 96.
14. Gedeôn 1886: 245–7.
15. Ibid.
16. Paspatis 1862: 11, 15.
17. Konortas 1998: 217–27.
18. Kanner 2004: 95–105.
19. For the Greek Orthodox, see Kanner 2004: 111–29, 177–206; for the Armenians, see Libaridian 2011: 94–5; for the Jews, see Dumont 1985: 225–30; Benbassa 1993: 20–7, though this dimension does not appear very clearly in these pages.
20. Anastasiadou-Dumont 2003; Kanner 2004.
21. Paspatis 1862: 15–21, 36–41, 70.
22. For the Greek Orthodox, see the daily newspaper *Néologos*, 24.1/5.2.1875 and the weekly periodical *Savvatiaia Epitheorēsis*, 11/23.11.1878, 783–4. Many public lectures against alcoholism were also delivered by the Istanbul Hellenic Literary Association; see *Periodiko tou En Kônstantinoupolei Hellēnikou Philologikou Syllogou* (1913–21). For the Muslims, see the weekly periodical *Hanımlara Mahsus Gazete*: "Kadınların Para Kesesi", *HMG* 12, 28 Eylül 1311 / 1895, 3–4; Matmazel Talya, "Çocukların libasi ve muhâfaza-i Sıhhatı", *HMG*, 58, 4 Nisan 1312 / 1896, 5; Çakır 1996: 25–6. For the Jews, see Rodrigue 1990; Abrevaya Stein 2004: 123–53. For the Bulgarians, see Kenderova 2003: 194–5.
23. Kanner 2004: 190–206.

24. *Kanonismos tēs En Phôtēra yper ton Aporôn Mathētôn Adelfotētos,* 1874; *Kanonismos tēs En Therapeiois Agathoergou Adelfotētos*, 1874; *Kanonismos tēs En Xyloportē Arôgou tôn Aporôn Mathētôn Adelfotētos "Ennea Mousai"*, 1887.
25. Kanner 2004: 321–2.
26. Davidova 2013: 140–1; Daskalova 1997: 60.
27. Daskalova 2006: 413–17; Cholakova 1994: 142–73.
28. Rodrigue 1990: 38–43, 47–70; Molho 2001: 186; Benbassa 1993: 25–6, 28–9; Land 2006.
29. Dumont 1985: 291–7.
30. Molho 2001: 170, 176; Benbassa 1991: 209.
31. Rodrigue 1990: 100–11.
32. Rowe 2008: 53–55; Ekmekçioğlu, Bilal 2006: 123, 152.
33. Kévorkian, Paboudjian 1992: 92, 96.
34. Ortaylı 2004: 325–6.
35. Ibid., 326.
36. Maksudyan 2011: 493–511.
37. Çakır 1996: 220–1; Kurnaz 1996: 85–8.
38. Regulations and reports of the Greek Orthodox schools and educational associations are clear, in that respect. *Kanonismos tēs En Phôtēra*, art. 26, 12; *Ta egainia tôn en Vathyrryaki sholeiôn*, 1871: 33–4; *Logoi kai euthynai tēs en Megalô Reumati tou Vosporou Eforias*, 1889: 11. For such an orientation in the Jewish schools supported by the Alliance, see Molho 2001: 157, 170; Benbassa 1991: 212–13, 219–23. For this dimension in the Ottoman state-run schools, see Somel 2001: 6–8, 60–4, 244–70. In the Armenian case, see Eroğlu 2003: 34, 51–2.
39. Rose 1996: 135.
40. For this discourse in the Greek Orthodox communities, see Kanner 2004: 368–70. For a similar tendency, as far as the Hamidian education is concerned, see Deringil 2003: 289–333; Maksudyan 2011: 498–503. For the Armenians, see Eroğlu 2003: 51–2.
41. See, for the Greek Orthodox *Néologos*, 27.7/3.8.1871; *Ta egainia tôn en Vathyrryaki,* 24–7; *Logodosia tēs epi tēs anegerseôs tou en Ypsomatheiois Kentrikou Parthenagogeiou*, 1875: 23. For such problems in the relations between parents and schoolteachers of the Alliance schools, see Benbassa 1991: 222–3.
42. *Kanonismos tēs en Stavrodromiô Hellēnikēs Orthodoxou Koinotētos*, 1876, ch. VI, 45–6; *Apologismos pepragmenôn tēs en Chalkēdoni Philoptôchou Adelfotētos tôn Kyriôn*, 1904: vii; *Philoptôchos Adelfotēs tôn Kyriôn Megalou Revmatos,* 1907: 10; For the Ladies' Philanthropic Association of Kum Kapı (Kondoskali), see *Néologos,* 19/31.5.1887.
43. *Apologismos pepragmenôn tēs en Chalkēdoni Philoptôchou Adelfotētos tôn Kyriôn; Philoptôchos Adelfotēs tôn Kyriôn Megalou Revmatos.* For such initiatives in the Greek Orthodox community of Salonica see "Hē en Thessalonikē Philoptôchos Adelfotēs tôn Hellēnidon Kyriôn", *Hēmerologion Skokou* 22 (1907), 193–5; for Trabzon, see "Kanonismos tēs en Trapezounti Adelfotētos tôn Kyriôn Merimnēs",

art. 2, 2, 1904. For comparable activities among Greek Orthodox women of Ayvalik, see Karachrēstos, http://www2.egeonet.gr/aigaio/Forms/fLemmaBodyExtended.aspx?lemmaID=3440.

44. See *Ekthesis Pepragmenon tēs en Stavrodromiô Philoptôchou Adelfotētos tôn Kyriôn*, 1876: 27; *Apologismos pepragmenôn tēs en Chalkēdoni Philoptôchou Adelfotētos tôn Kyriôn*, vii.
45. Molho 2001: 170–3; Benbassa 1991: 224; Rodrigue 1990: 71–80.
46. *HMG*, 53, 22 Şubat 1311 / 1896, 1. So far, I have not come across any similar initiatives among the Armenians.
47. *Philergos Etaireia. Ekthesis*, 1873: 4, 23; *Philergos Etaireia. Ekthesis*, 1874: 4.
48. *Armonia*, 26.4.1866.
49. *Philergos Etaireia. Ekthesis*, 1873, 9; *Armonia*, 9.3.1867.
50. *Armonia*, 16.3.1866.
51. *Néologos*, 23.12.1872/4.1.1873.
52. Faroqhi 2000: 342.
53. *Néologos*, 20.8.1868.
54. *Ekthesis Pepragmenôn tēs en Stavrodromiô Philoptôchou Adelfotētos tôn Kyriôn*, 1885: 43–5.
55. Kanner 2004: 215.
56. I am grateful to Evguenia Davidova for this information.
57. Rodrigue 1990: 80–5.
58. Eroğlu 2003: 48–50; Maksudyan (forthcoming).
59. Özbek 1999.
60. Özbek 2005: 70–4.
61. Fortna 2000: 369–93. See also Somel 2001: 167, 172.
62. For the philanthropic activity of the Muslim merchants of Salonica, see Papamichos-Chronakis 2011: 68.
63. For instance, *Ekthesis Pepragmenôn tēs en Stavrodromiô Philoptôchou Adelfotētos tôn Kyriôn*, 1896: 6.
64. Özbek 2005: 71.
65. *Ta egainia tôn en Vathyrryaki sholeiôn*, 9, 27–8.
66. *Logoi kai euthynai tēs en Megalô Reumati*, 18.
67. *Néologos*, 20.8.1868.
68. See, for instance, the commissions for the assistance of the wounded soldiers and the refugees of the Russo–Turkish War, *Néologos*, 12.12.1877/4.1.1878, 7/19.1.1878, 10/22.1.1878, 3/15.2.1878, 7/18.2.1878. For the commissions for the assistance of the victims of the earthquake in Sakız ada and Çesme, see *Néologos*, 7/19.3.1881, 27.3/9.4.1881, 30.6./12.7.1881, 12/24.8.1881, 16/28.12.1881.
69. Kanner 2004: 362.
70. Ibid., 374.
71. Papamichos-Chronakis 2011: 25.
72. Ibid., 85–6, 105.
73. I express again my acknowledgement to Evguenia Davidova for this information.

74. This was particularly the case of Eleni Zarifi, the widow of the prominent Greek banker Georgios Zarifis, called the "mother of the orphans" by virtue of her donation to the Orphanage (Kanner 2004: 321) and of Fakima Modiano, a widow of the Jewish banker of Salonica Saul Modiano (Papamichos-Chronakis 2011: 170). Among the Bulgarians, women's donations were quite negligible and mostly local.
75. Özbek 2005.
76. *AA*, 2.3.1868, 27.1/8.2.1871, 1/13.3.1871, 18/30.9.1879. For the Ottoman Turkish press, see Özbek 2009: 786–8.
77. Özbek 2009: 790.
78. *Néologos*, 8/20.11.1881, 3/15.5.1881.
79. Kanner 2004: 319.
80. Özbek 2009: 795.
81. See the regulations of *Teal-i Vatan Osmanlı Hanımlar Cemiyeti Nizamnamesi,* 1909, articles 1, 8 and 16, and of *Osmanlı- Türk Hanımları Esirgeme Derneği Nizamnamesi,* 1913, article 1 in Çakır 1996: 324–7.
82. *Osmanlı Kadınları Çalıştırma Cemiyeti Islamiyyesi Nizamnamesi,* 1913, article 2 in Çakır 1996: 335.
83. Çakır 1996: 49.
84. Lewis 1961: 458.
85. Kemal's speech in the Economic Conference of Izmir (17.2- 4.3.1923), ibid., 460.

Chapter 8 The Rich in Eighteenth- and Nineteenth-Century Arbanasi: Networks of Prosperity

1. Kiel 1985; Dimitrov 1988: 40–1; Gyuzelev 2004: 50–7.
2. Balaschev, Ihchiev 1909: 144–56.
3. The village was part of the *waqf* of Rustem Pasha, the Grand Vizier of Sultan Suleyman I, together with the nearby Lyaskovets, Gorna and Dolna Oryahovitsa. The establishment of the *waqf* happened before Rustem Pasha's death (1569). Mutafov 1979: 84.
4. According to a grievance (*arzuhal*), forty people moved from Tarnovo to Arbanasi in 1660. *Podbrani osmanski dokumenti,* 326–7.
5. Gyuzelev 2004: 56.
6. Refik 1938, doc. No. 76.
7. Dimitar Papazov was born in 1863, graduated law in Belgium, and worked as a judge, lawyer, and professor. He also served as deputy mayor in Sofia. He belonged to the famous and rich Arbanasi family Papazovs, known also as Sakelarovs. Interested in the village's history, Papazov wrote one of the most detailed and comprehensive studies about Arbanasi, mixing memories with historical information. BIA- NBKM, f. 588.
8. Papazov 1937: 76.
9. BIA-NBKM, f. 784, a.e.1, 13.

10. Papazov 1937: 74.
11. *Temettuat defters* were initiated in 1844–6 by the Ottoman central authorities, which try to record name, occupation, property, taxes, and estimated annual income of all taxpayers in the Anatolian and Balkan provinces. This initiative was related to the other administrative and military reforms implemented in the nineteenth century. Today 17,747 *temettuat defters* of both Balkan and Anatolian provinces are preserved at the Başbakanlık Osmanlı Arşivi in Istanbul.
12. An example is the father of a Bulgarian revolutionary, Toma Kardzhiev. He was first "*charakchi* – a dealer of dry goods". When the family moved from Arbanasi to Russe, he became a soap seller and traveled in the adjacent region. BIA-NBKM, f. 784, a.e. 12, 1.
13. Christo son of Tanas –BOA, ML. VRD.TMT.d 12698, p. 5, No. 6. See also Simeonidis 1850: 373–81; Papazov 1937: 56–7; Stoyanov 1978: 212–13, No. 1749.
14. Tsvetkova 1966: 64, 65–6, doc.II.
15. BOA, ML. VRD.TMT.d 12698.
16. Papazov 1937: 74.
17. Ibid., 65; Kostov 1959: 116.
18. Snegarov 1940/1: 49–53.
19. BOA, ML. VRD.TMT.d 12698, p. 18, No. 37.
20. Maslev 1991: 131.
21. Dimitrov1988: 40–1.
22. Papazov 1937: 33.
23. Maslev 1991: 59.
24. Kostov 1959: 20–1.
25. Orthodox Christians from the Ottoman Empire.
26. For example, Evstatiu Platzgu was a chairman; Christo Datibani, Costa Zotu, Isar Hotu were members of the board. In 1644, Zotos Nikokiritsis Alvanitohori was a president of the Company; in 1646, Panos Ioannou was a juror. In 1698, two other traders were elected as jurors. The Greek company in Brasov also had Arbanasi merchants among its residents. Maslev 1991: 131.
27. BIA-NBKM, f. 784, a.e. 1, 2.
28. Masters 1992: 579–97.
29. Papazov 1937: 77.
30. The latter is registered in the *temettuat defter* from 1845 as Peter son of Kiro, a grocer with an annual income of 600 g. BOA, ML. VRD. TMT.d 12698, p. 13, No. 10.
31. BOA, ML. VRD.TMT.d 12698, p. 14, No. 14.
32. One can find different kinds of drugs there; many groceries had also cafes. Papazov 1937: 76.
33. BIA-NBKM, f. 784, a.e. 1, 3.
34. *Opis na osmanoturski documenti,* 307, No. 1106.
35. This thesis was presented in the Bulgarian–Greek conference in Sofia (June 2014).
36. Gyuzelev 2004: 55.

37. Konstantinov 1893: 15, 49; Irechek 1974: 305.
38. Dimova 2011: 471, No. 113.
39. Vachev 2008.
40. For more details, see Gyuzelev 2004: 50–7.
41. In the early 1870s, the teacher Panayot Antonov tried to introduce Bulgarian language as an alternative liturgical language at the churches. There was an incident, which proves that he faced a strong resistance. Antonov had a fight with one of the influential Arbanasi residents – Kiril Rusovitch – and was publicly humiliated. Papazov 1937: 13.
42. Papazov 1937: 29, 60.
43. BIA- NBKM, f. 784, a.e. 1, 4.
44. Irechek 1974: 306.
45. BIA-NBKM, 784, a.e.1, 3.
46. Papazov 1937: 89.
47. Ibid., 89.
48. A brief description of the departure of pilgrims from Arbanasi to Jerusalem in 1754 is preserved in a marginal note in one of the books in George Anagnosta's library. Dimova: 2011, 472, n.18.
49. BOA, ML. VRD.TMT.d 12698, p. 2, No. 12.
50. BOA, ML. VRD.TMT.d 12698, p. 4, No. 3.
51. h. Kirola Rusovich from the merchant family of Rusoviches (mentioned also in the *temettuat defter* as Kiro son of Dimo, a tailor); BOA, ML. VRD. TMT.d 12698, p. 18, No 29; George h. Ilioglu owner of a candle shop in the *charshi*; h. Statitsa owner of a grocery shop; h. Dimitar Raynooglu owner of a grocery store. Papazov 1937: 56–7, 73–5.
52. Ivan Simeonov Balabanov, a nineteenth-century Bulgarian intellectual, was strongly Hellenized and he signed his books as Joannis Simeonidis. Ivanov 1931: 214.
53. It was a compilation of popular religious texts. Its author, Ivan Simeonov, was a teacher in Tarnovo. Many citizens of Tarnovo, Arbanasi and surrounding area contributed financially to its publishing. In his memoires Kardzhiev claims that the book was one of his father's favorite instructive readings at home. BIA-NBKM, f. 784, a.e. 1, 4.
54. Ioannis Nidelku; Dimitrios Yanuli; priest Atanas; priest Nikola; priest Christo; priest Margarid (*abadzhi*); deacon Dionisiy; h. Teodosi, monk of the Monastery of the Transfiguration; George Simeonov (George Anagnosta); Dimitraki Georgiev; h. Ivanov (furrier); Hristo Nikolov (furrier); Yanko, a cousin of pop Nikola (grocer); Petar Kirov (grocer), also called Peter Efendi; Ivan Protopopov; Ivan Pophristov; Stefan Christov Chamurov; Vangel Bakardzhiya; Anastas Varbanov; George Ivanov; George Panitza (grocer); Ivan Stoykov (soap-maker); Nikola Hadji Kostov; Hristo Atanasov (*dzhelep*); Kiril Dimitrov Rusovich; Atanas Sakelarov; Yakov Konstantinov; Yanko Dobrev (*dzhelep*); Michal Panonchov; Georgi Nikolov Hadzhi Teodoranov; Peter (barber) and his cousin Simo; Ivan Sakelarov Papazoolu (*chohadzhi*); Stamat Kosovali.

55. There are other examples of Arbanasi residents who were also sponsors of various books published from the 1850s onward. In his inventory of Greek books in Bulgaria, Manyo Stoyanov mentions six people from the eighteenth and nineteenth centuries. Stoyanov 1978: No. 301, 597, 1024, 1749.
56. Papazov 1937: 36.
57. There was only a Greek school and all Christians, not only Greeks and Albanians but also Bulgarians spoke Greek in the public and private space.
58. Slaveykov 1890: 382.
59. Cholov 1969.
60. Papazov 1937: 79.
61. Ibid., 61.
62. Ibid., 79.
63. Probably the author refers to his official position of *kaza vekili* and member of the *meclis* in Tarnovo, which gave an opportunity for personal enrichment.
64. Papazov 1937: 90.
65. Dimova 2011.
66. They both are registered as subscribers of Simeonov's book *Odigos tis evsevias*.
67. Papazov 1937: 10.
68. Ibid.

Chapter 9 Redrawing State Borders: Prosperity to Poverty in Ottoman and post-Ottoman Bitola (Monastir)

1. I used Bernard Lory's doctoral dissertation. Lory 2009: 4. He has recently published a book under the same title.
2. Lory, Popovic 1992: 79.
3. Dedijer 1913: 198.
4. Lory, Popovic 1992: 79.
5. Georgieva considers that until 1836, Bitola and Sofia were parallel centers of Rumelia. Georgieva 2007: 15.
6. Here we should mention the Russian occupation of Sofia during the Russo–Ottoman War (1828–9). In this way Sofia lost its significance from the previous period. Ibid., 17.
7. Ibid., 18. Cohen considers that Bitola became a seat of the Rumelian *eyalet* in 1831. Cohen 2004: 136.
8. Gounaris 2000: 79.
9. Sahara 2011: 27.
10. Dimeski 1982: 63.
11. In 1878, the Bitola *vilayet* was abolished for a short period, and the newly formed Bitola *sandzak* (district) was added to the Thessaloniki *vilayet*. In 1879, the Bitola *vilayet* was formed again and remained as such until 1912, i.e. until the end of Ottoman governance in Macedonia. Ibid., 67–8.
12. A number of Ottoman laws, adopted during the nineteenth century, positively influenced the development of Bitola. Some of these included: The Code of

Buildings (1848), the Law of Landownership (1858), the Regulation for trade (1862). Acun 2002: 274; Dimitrov 2004.

13. Cohen 2004: 136.
14. For migration to Bitola, see Gounaris 2001: 45; Dimitrov 2004: 11–14.
15. Robe 1937: 55.
16. For example, in 1856, there were 1875 workshops and shops. Anastasovski 2012: 197–8. The number of the crafts that existed varied: in 1828, there were 70 types of crafts and 30 guilds. The development of Bitola in the mid-nineteenth century contributed to the increase of crafts. Dimitrov 1998: 530; According to a British report from 1870, there were 69 guilds in Bitola. D. Ġorġiev 2003: 241.
17. D. Ġorġiev 2003: 56.
18. Birdal 2010.
19. Dimitrov 1998: 56–57.
20. Lory 2009: 605.
21. Lory, Popovic 1992: 81; Gerasimov 1979: 628.
22. Robe 1937: 56.
23. Palairet 2002: 346.
24. Lory, Popovic 1992: 81.
25. Cohen 2004: 136.
26. Lory, Popovic 1992: 82; Čipan 1978: 95.
27. Before the end of Ottoman rule, lectures in the schools were held in Turkish, Greek, Bulgarian, Rumanian, Ladino (Judeo-Spanish), and Serbian. In one Protestant and two Lazarist schools, the teaching was in English and French. Dimitrov 1998: 60.
28. During the second half of the nineteenth century, several banks were opened, such as the Ottoman Bank (1863), the Agricultural (1888), and the Thessaloniki Bank (1893).
29. Before the Balkan Wars Austro-Hungary, Russia, Italy, Great Britain, France, Germany, Greece, Serbia, Romania, and Bulgaria opened consular offices in Bitola.
30. Perry 1988.
31. For the organization and the beginning of the Ilinden Uprising, see V. Ġorġiev 2010: 267–346.
32. Lory 2009: 383.
33. For the preparations of the revolution, see D. Ġorġiev 2011.
34. *Britanskite konzuli* 2002: 422.
35. Ibid., 423.
36. Lory, Popovic 1992: 91.
37. *MH*, 1913, Vol. CIX, 124.
38. *Politika*, br. 3165, 7 November 1912.
39. Lory 2009: 502.
40. *ON*, br. 3, 20 January 1913, 5.
41. Ibid., 5.

42. *MH, 1913,* Vol. CIX, 223–4.
43. Svirčević 2013: 291–2.
44. *ON*, br. 4, 27 January 1913, 1.
45. Todorovski 1979: 102.
46. Ibid., 64.
47. Ibid., 223.
48. *ON*, br. 3, 20 January 1913, 3.
49. Ibid., 5.
50. *ON*, br. 5, 3 February 1913, 4.
51. Ibid., 4.
52. Ibid.,4.
53. *ON*, br. 3, 20 January 1913, 3.
54. *On*, br. 30, 6 December 1913, 11.
55. Gallon 2004: 516–7.
56. *ON*, br. 5, 3 February 1913, 3.
57. *ON*, br.4, 27 January 1913, 1.
58. Ibid., 1.
59. Todorovski 1979: 223.
60. Robe 1937: 58.
61. *ON*, br. 5, 3 February 1913, 5–6.
62. *Britanskite konzuli,* 432.
63. Todorovski 1979: 223.
64. *Britanski konzuli,* 432.
65. Ljubenova 2012: 15–47.
66. *ON*, br. 29, 20 November 1913, 11.
67. *Britanskite konzuli*, 436.
68. Ibid., 440.
69. Todorovski 1981: 84.
70. Ibid., 84.
71. *MH,* 1913, Vol. CIX, 124.
72. *ON*, br. 30, 6 December 1913, 11.
73. Svirčević 2013: 297–8.
74. Minoski 2006: 100–1.
75. *Report,* 1914: 176.
76. Ibid., 176.
77. Ibid., 166.
78. Ibid., 177.
79. Kukudis 2013: 456.
80. Ibid., 456.
81. Ibid., 456.
82. The refugees from Bitola were settled in Florina and a part of them moved to Thessaloniki. They organized their associations and showed a great political activity. During World War I and the Versailles Peace Conference, their representatives asked for Bitola's annexation to Greece. Chasiotis 2004: 213–29.

83. The Protestant Mission in Bitola was opened in 1873–4. Cacanoska 2001: 117; Richter 1910: 169.
84. *MH,* 1914, Vol. CX, 525.
85. After the Serbian forces entered Bitola, all schools in the city with the exception of the Protestant one, i.e., that one of the Lazarists, were closed. The more wealthy citizens wanted their children to continue their education there. *MH,* 1913, Vol. CIX, 224.
86. Tsanoff 1914: 77.
87. Ibid., 78.
88. *MH,* 1914, Vol. CX, 525.
89. *ON*, br. 28, 6 November 1913, 6–7.
90. Tsanoff 1914: 79.
91. According to Dimitrov, 4,116 wounded Serbian solders in the battles with the Austrian–Hungarian army arrived in Bitola. Dimitrov 1998: 62.
92. Tankovski-Lilin, Minovski 2009: 145.
93. *Annales*, tome 82, 1917: 687.
94. Ibid., 688.
95. Ibid., 690.
96. Petrov 1993:, 99–100.
97. Ibid., 266.
98. The editors of the newspaper were the military correspondents Nencho Iliev and Ivan Radoslavov. It was printed in the printing office by Hristo Kirijas. *Bŭlgarski periodičen pečat*, Vol. 3, 1969: 65.
99. Džonev 2008: 327.
100. Ibid., 340.
101. Todorovski 1981: 362.
102. Laffan 1918: 250.
103. Ibid., 253.
104. Lory 2009: 521.
105. Petrov 1993: 165.
106. *Annales*, tome 82, 706–7.
107. Tankovski-Lilin, Minovski 2009: 146.
108. Vojvodić, Živojinović 1970: 345.
109. *The New York Times*, 20 November 1916.
110. Todorovski 1981: 357.
111. Ibid., 357.
112. Several teachers born in Bitola, educated in the Exarchate's secondary school in Thessaloniki and graduates from the University of Sofia, thought in the Bulgarian schools during the Bulgarian rule. They did not leave the town along with the Bulgarian and the German armies. The Serbian authorities suspected that they remained with subversive intentions and wanted to expel them. Todorovski 1995: 57–8; 189–90.
113. Turan 2000: 124.
114. Reiss 1918: 128.

115. Tankovski-Lilin, Minovski 2009: 139.
116. Ibid., 139.
117. *MH,* 1917, Vol. CXIII, 329.
118. Tankovski-Lilin, Minovski 2009: 201.
119. Todorovski 1995: 105.
120. According to Esther Benbassa and Aron Rodrigue, the number of Jews in Bitola from 1907 to 1927 decreased to one half, or from 6,000 to 3,000. Benbassa, Rodrigue 2011: 401.
121. Devin Naar writes that Thessaloniki Jews were not impressed by the annexation of their city to the Greek side. Indeed, they felt marginalized there. Naar 2009: 55.
122. Dimovski-Colev 1996: 268.
123. Lory 2009: 531.
124. Meis 2011: 94.
125. Robe 1937: 57.
126. Garstang 1922: 348.
127. Vujović 1914: 4.
128. *Resultats definitifs* 1932: 88.
129. Kotek 2009: 27.
130. Lory 2009: 532.

Chapter 10 War, Dynasty, and Philanthropy: Kavala and the Khedivial Relief Campaign during the Balkan Wars (1912–13)

1. On Kavala during the First Balkan War, see Florentin 1929: 4–13. See also the following short reference in the *American Jewish Year Book*: "The occupation of Kavala (Nov. 15) was attended by the robbery of many Jews. Seven of the most prominent were carried off by Bulgarian bandits and released only after they had paid a ransom of $43,000. Assistance was rendered by the Khedive of Egypt to Jews as well as to the rest of the population." Friedenwald, Friedman 1913: 192.
2. For a survey of the main Balkan theatres of war, see Hall 2000.
3. On these new Ottoman practices of power and legitimacy, see Deringil 1998. For the shaping of dynastic symbolism in Egypt, see Toledano 1990: 50–67.
4. Winter 1985: 192.
5. On the definition of the poor and needy, perceived as entitled to society's charity among Muslim societies, see Singer 2008: 146–75.
6. Quataert 1999: 224–7.
7. This term is taken from Healy 2004: 262–72.
8. There is a growing body of literature on civilians during the age of modern warfare and the significance of philanthropy for the shaping of the home front and civil society. Wall, Winter 1988; Winter, Prost 2005: 152–72.

9. On the centralization and reinvention of imperial charity during the nineteenth century, see for the Ottoman Empire Özbek 1999: 1–33; idem 2005: 59–81; Singer 2014: 221–37. For Egypt, see Ener 2003a: 26–48; Singer 2008: 193–4; Pollard 2014: 239–57.
10. Ginio 2015, forthcoming.
11. A selection of his memories was published by Sonbol 2006.
12. On the use of charity by Ottoman sultans and their households to promote legitimacy and to serve social, cultural, and economic interests in the provinces, see Singer 2002. On Ottoman dynastic construction of iconic mosques to convey messages of power, continuity, and legitimacy, see Necipoğlu 1996: 23–36.
13. Halaçoğlu 1995: 54–5.
14. Pierre Nora coins the term *lieu de mémoire* to refer to symbolic sites of collective memory, which French society established as "memory aids" to preserve and to claim a shared past and illusion of eternity. Nora 1989: 7–25.
15. On the Ottoman reconstruction of Kavala during the sixteenth century, see Lowry 2008: 227–42; Kiel 1996: 149–55.
16. al-Sayyid Marsot 1984: 24.
17. Lowry and Erünsal 2011.
18. Mostras 1995: 143. This dictionary was published in St. Petersburg in 1873.
19. Toledano 1990: 16; idem, 1985: 141–59; Fahmy 1997: 26–9.
20. Ener 2003a: 10–11; idem, 2003b: 185–201.
21. Ener 2003a: 95.
22. Sultan Mahmud II (r. 1808–39) granted Mehmed Ali the tax revenues of the island of Thasos in perpetuity in return for the latter's role in retaking the holy cities of Hejaz from the Wahhābīs. Lowry, Erünsal 2011: 18–19; 39–48.
23. Hirszowicz 1972: 298–9; Kızıltoprak 2011.
24. al-Ayyūbī 1923: 5–9. On the positive perceptions of Alexander the Great's rule in Egypt and the return of Egypt to independence under the Ptolemaic dynasty, as presented in Egyptian historiography of the 1920s, see Gershoni, Jankowski 1986: 152–3.
25. Gorman 2003: 15–22; Gershoni, Jankowski 2004: 183–4.
26. Lowry, Erünsal 2011.
27. Ibid., 121–36.
28. Upon the deposal of the khedive ʻAbbas Hilmi in December 1914, his uncle, Husayn Kāmil ascended to the throne and declared himself sultan; his brother and successor, Fu'ād, adopted the title of "king" in 1922.
29. On the Egyptianization of the dynasty, see Toledano 1990: 22.
30. Lowry, Erünsal 2011: 130, 164; Uzer 1999: 280–1. Tahsin Bey, later Uzer, served as the governor of Drama during the khedive's visits to Kavala. As Kavala was under Drama's jurisdiction, he met with the khedive to learn about his plans regarding Kavala.
31. On the then so-called "Egyptian vakf", see Tsitselikis 2012: 356–9.
32. This was the newspaper's title as appeared in Latin alphabet on its first page.

33. On *al-Garidah*, see Ayalon 1995: 60. On the proliferation of the Egyptian press under ʿAbbas Hilmi and its increasing role in shaping public opinion, see Pollard 2005: 139–49.
34. *Al-Garidah*, No. 1696, 9 October 1912.
35. Interestingly enough, Egyptian authors used the European term "Balkan" rather than the prevailing Ottoman term of "Rumeli". On the term "Balkans" in Ottoman Turkish writing, see Boyar 2007: 30–41.
36. On the writing in Arabic on the Balkan Wars, see Ginio 2013: 594–617.
37. I chose to write his name in its Arabized form rather than in its Turkified version – Mehmed Ali – not to distinguish the prince from his famous ancestor, but rather to emphasize the Egyptianization of the ruling dynasty achieved by his time.
38. For the ceremonial opening meeting of the committee, and the different speeches, see *al-Garidah*, No. 1712, 28 October 1912.
39. On the Egyptian Red Crescent during the Balkan Wars, see *Osmanlı Hilâl-i Ahmer Cemiyeti*, 1329 [1913]: 178–85; al-Bustānī 1913: 206–14.
40. For detailed lists of contributions offered to the Egyptian Red Crescent, see *al-Muqattam*, 21 November 1912. Yūsuf al-Bustānī estimated that such public subscriptions gathered about 340,000 Egyptian pounds for the Association of Assistance and about 100,000 Egyptian pounds that were donated directly to the Egyptian Red Crescent. al-Bustānī 1913: 207.
41. *Al-Garidah*, No. 1743, 7 December 1912.
42. *Al-Garidah*, No. 1744, 8 December 1912. Egypt's neutrality enabled the Egyptian Red Crescent to establish field hospitals and to assist Ottoman victims of war on the different fronts. It was able to evacuate with its own vehicles 2,350 sick and wounded Ottoman soldiers from besieged Yanya to the port of Preveza that was already under Greek sway. The "Bahr al-Ahmer" boat, serving as a Red Crescent floating hospital, was able to transport 14,209 wounded soldiers and refugees from Salonica to Izmir; 700 from Preveza to Izmir and 6,081 from İşkodra to Izmir. Ömer 1330 [1914/5]: 55–6.
43. Özbek 2003: 203–20.
44. *Al-Garidah*, No. 1719, 5 November 1912. On the Ottoman "Extraordinary Commissioner to Egypt" and its changing status, see Peri 2005: 103–20.
45. *Al-Muqattam*, 25 November 1912.
46. *Al-Garidah*, No. 1739, 2 December 1912.
47. *Al-Garidah*, No. 1727, 13 November 1912. For other examples, see *al-Muqattam*, 28 November 1912; 16 December 1912.
48. Sonbol 2006: 11.
49. On the rise of pro-Ottoman feelings in Egypt following the British occupation of 1882, see Jankowski 1980: 229–35.
50. Hirszowicz 1972: 298–303.
51. The famous Ottoman historian Köprülzâde Mehmed Fuat published the short story "Süngü Altında" (Under the Bayonets) in the periodical *Halka Doğru* (1914). It recounted the massacres that took place in Doksad, a small village situated between Kavala and Drama. Duman 2005: 253–4. For the atrocities

that took place in the region of Kavala during the First Balkan War, see Boyar 2007: 144–5; Dinç 2008: 117–19.

52. Ginio 2015 (forthcoming).
53. For the atrocities that took place in Kavala against the local Muslim population, see, for one example based on German testimony, al-Bustānī 1913: 183.
54. İpek 1994: 39.
55. Halaçoğlu 1995: 55.
56. *Al-Garidah*, No. 1741, 4 December 1912.
57. *Al-Garidah*, No. 1746, 10 December 1912.
58. Halaçoğlu 1995: 54.
59. *Al-Garidah*, No. 1748, 12 December 1912.
60. *Al-Garidah*, No. 1749, 14 December 1912.
61. *Al-Garidah*, No. 1746, 10 December 1912.
62. Tannūs 1913: 140–1.

Chapter 11 National Interpretations of Misfortune and Welfare: the Paradigm of the Intellectuals of the Bulgarian Revival

1. For nationalism as a phenomenon of modernity, see Hobsbawm 1997; Anderson 1991; Gellner 1994; Smith 1991.
2. Eccleshall 2003: 98.
3. Ibid., 107.
4. Ibid., 108.
5. For classical liberalism, see van de Haar 2009; Conway 1995; Arblaster 1984.
6. Hobsbawm 1997: 23; Woolf 1996: 12.
7. Spencer, Wollman 2002: 6.
8. Tamir 1993: 58 ff.; Greenfeld 1992: 3–14. This is the civic or Western version of the nation, which was distinguished by an Eastern ethnic or cultural variant. Such a clear-cut distinction has been disputed, however. Brubaker 2004: 55–71.
9. For the political dimension of nationalism, see Anderson 1991: 6; Gellner 1994: 1; Hechter 2002: 7.
10. For liberal nationalism, see Heywood 2012: 168 ff.; Auer 2004.
11. Spencer, Wollman 2002: 7.
12. In Bulgarian historiography the term Bulgarian Revival (*Vŭzrazhdane*) refers to both the multifaceted process of the formation of the Bulgarian nation and the period during which this "nationalizing" activity was carried out, i.e. roughly the last 100 years of Ottoman rule. The beginning of the main phase of the Revival is usually placed in the 1830s. Daskalov 2004: 11 ff.
13. Boneva 2005: 123 ff.
14. Sampimon 2006: 159–215.

15. The aspiration for eccleciastical independence was put forward after the Crimean War (1853–6).
16. Nikov 2008; Boneva 2010.
17. Rakovski organized in Braila an unsuccessful attempt of a Greco–Bulgarian uprising as early as 1841, whereas during the Crimean War he armed a band (*cheta*) with the intention of joining the Russian troops, when they would enter the Bulgarian territory. Firkatian 1996: 27 ff.
18. Genchev 1991: 358 ff.; Boneva 2005: 359 ff.
19. Rakovski, Vol. III, 1984: 401.
20. Ibid., 461.
21. Ibid., 462.
22. Ibid., 470.
23. Quoted in English translation by Firkatian 1996: 159.
24. The first editor of *Narodnost* was Ivan Bogorov who was soon replaced by Ivan Grudev and in March 1868 by Ivan Kasabov. Borshukov 2003: 203–7.
25. *Narodnost,* No. 1, 21 October 1867.
26. *Narodnost,* No. 2, 27 October 1867.
27. *Narodnost,* No. 8, 1 December 1867.
28. Ibid.
29. *Narodnost,* No. 2, 27 October 1867.
30. *Narodnost,* No. 4, 11 November 1867.
31. *Narodnost,* No. 12, 1 January 1868.
32. Ibid.
33. Ibid.
34. *Narodnost,* No. 43, 30 October 1868.
35. Genchev 2011: 41.
36. Strashimirov, Vol. 1, 2014: 96–7.
37. Ibid., 230–1.
38. Ibid., 51.
39. Ibid., 220.
40. Ibid., 97.
41. Ibid., 231.
42. Ibid., 96.
43. Ibid., 220.
44. Karavelov, Vol. 12, 1992: 7–8.
45. *Svoboda,* No. 23, 10 April 1870.
46. *Svoboda,* No. 1, 2 July 1872.
47. The proposal was made by the conservative wing of the Committee through a *Report* compiled by Pantelei Kisimov and submitted to the Sultan. Jakimov 2003: 175–204.
48. Karavelov, Vol. 7, 1985: 54–5.
49. Ibid., 55; *Svoboda,* No. 1, 2 July 1872.
50. Karavelov, Vol. 12, 1992: 7–8.
51. Ibid., 7.

52. *Svoboda,* No. 15, 12 February 1870.
53. Karavelov, Vol. 12, 1992: 19.
54. Karavelov, Vol. 11, 1989: 20.
55. Ibid.
56. *Svoboda,* No. 41, 7 September 1870.
57. Karavelov, Vol. 12, 1992: 10.
58. Ibid.
59. *Svoboda,* No. 42, 16 September 1870.
60. Karavelov, Vol. 12, 1992: 11–13.
61. *Svoboda,* No. 11, 13 March 1871.
62. Karavelov, Vol. I, 1957: 459.
63. *Svoboda,* No. 42, 16 September 1870.
64. *Zname,* No. 4, 5 January 1875.
65. *Duma,* No. 1, 10 June 1871.
66. *Zname,* No. 19, 22 June 1875.
67. *Duma,* No. 2, 25 June 1871.
68. *Duma,* No. 3, 8 July 1871.
69. *Zname,* No. 3, 22 December 1874.
70. *Zname,* No. 1, 8 December 1874.
71. *Zname,* No. 4, 5 January 1875.
72. *Duma,* No. 2, 25 June 1871.
73. *Zname,* No. 2, 15 December 1874.
74. *Zname,* No. 7, 26 January 1875.
75. *Zname,* No. 9, 16 February 1875.
76. *Balgarska Dnevnica*, No. 16, 9 October 1857.
77. Ibid.
78. *Balgarska Dnevnica*, No. 10, 28 August 1857.
79. *Balgarska Dnevnica,* No. 9, 21 August 1857.
80. Strashimirov 2014: 50–1.
81. Ibid., 64.
82. *Phanariots* were the Orthodox state elite, named after their usual place of residence, the Fener/Phanarion in Constantinople. Faroqui 2006: 54.
83. *Svoboda,* No. 44, 15 April 1872.
84. Ibid.
85. Ibid.
86. *Svoboda,* No. 18, 5 March 1870.
87. Karavelov, Vol. 12, 1992: 24.
88. *Duma,* No. 2, 25 June 1871.
89. *Duma,* No. 1, 10 June 1871.
90. *Duma,* No. 4, 17 July 1871.
91. *Zname,* No. 16, 17 May 1875.
92. *Zname,* No. 7, 26 January 1875.
93. *Zname,* No. 16, 17 May 1875.
94. *Zname,* No. 20, 29 June 1875.

95. *Zname,* No. 23, 27 July 1875.
96. *Duma,* No. 1, 10 June 1871.
97. Although given the same nickname, they had a completely different profile than the "Young" of the diaspora.
98. Up until the 1830s, the Bulgarians together with the Greeks belonged to the unified Orthodox community, which was usually called the *Rum millet.* It included all Orthodox subjects in the Empire, irrespective of ethnic, linguistic, cultural or other differences, headed by the Patriarchate of Constantinople. Braude and Lewis 1982; The breakup was brought about by the prevalence of national ideology and the formation of national identities, which rendered the previous model unviable and led to differentiation on the basis of national rather than religious criteria. Stamatopoulos 2006: 253–73.
99. Naxidou 2012: 33–4.
100. Todev 2003: 374–6.
101. *Makedoniia*, No. 22, 29 April 1867.
102. Todev 2003: 382.
103. Ibid., 398.
104. Ibid., 406.
105. Ibid., 404–6.
106. Ibid., 406–8.
107. Ibid., 390.
108. Ibid., 376.
109. Undzhiev 1993: 95 ff.
110. Borshukov 2003: 122.
111. Arnaudov 1964: 443–80.
112. For example, Rakovski provided extensive information about the Italian struggle for unification, headed by Mazzini. *Balgarska Dnevnica,* No. 2, 3 July 1857; No. 3, 10 July 1857; No. 4, 17 July 1857; No. 5, 24 July 1857; No. 6, 30 July 1857; Karavelov made references to the uprising in Crete (1866). Danova 1972: 98–109; Mircheva 2006: 262–73.
113. In this sense his views are close to communist nationalism, which was adopted by the communist regimes in the twentieth century. Spencer, Wollman 1999: 80–1.

Chapter 12 "People's Welfare" as National Security: Serbian Liberals and Discourses on Economic Development in pre-Independence Serbia (1850s–1870s)

1. According to the first census of 1889, 32.65 percent of agricultural households owned a property that was less than 2 ha, or less than the required minimum for supporting a family; 39.96 percent owned a property the size of 2–5 ha, enough for supporting a family and a limited market production; and 20.31 percent

held properties of 5–10 ha. This small and autarchic property was further divided into lots and extensively cultivated. Đordević 1983: 414.

2. Gunst 1989: 53–83.
3. Lampe 1971: 11–19; Palairet 1997: 87–103.
4. Čalić 2004: 36, 417–29.
5. Smith 1991: 52–68.
6. Milosavljević 2002: 29–31.
7. Perović 1993: 19, 64.
8. Stokes 1989: 212.
9. Chirot 1986: 6.
10. Stokes 1989: 235–6.
11. Ibid., 244–5.
12. S. Jovanović 1990a: 33–63; Čubrilović 1982: 115–18, 148; Stoianovich 1959: 242–8.
13. Popović-Obradović 2013: 50–1.
14. S. Jovanović 1990a: 205–7.
15. Ibid., 76–79; Subotić 2001: 46–60; B. Mijatović 2001: 64–8.
16. Bešlin 2005: 151–64.
17. Samardžić 2010: 143–4.
18. Milićević 1970: 609–11.
19. V. Jovanović 2011: 59–85.
20. Mishkova 2004: 277.
21. Bešlin 2005: 278–286, 731–3; Samardžić 2009: 95–8.
22. S. Jovanović 1990a: 209–60; idem, 1990b: 295–307.
23. idem, 1990c: 21–72.
24. Mackenzie 2006: 70–85.
25. Stokes 1990: 11–14.
26. Popović-Obradović 2000: 30–3; Bešlin 2005: 851–67.
27. Popović-Obradović 2000: 27–9; Stokes 1990: 177–81; *Videlo*, 20 April 1880.
28. Mishkova 2006: 399.
29. idem, 2004: 277.
30. Bešlin 2005: 306.
31. Perović 2006: 31.
32. Nau 2002: 7–8.
33. Trgovčević 2003: 33–4.
34. Blagojević 1996: 98–9.
35. Stokes 1975: 35–7.
36. Blagojević 1996: 100–1.
37. Stokes 1975: 35–6.
38. Cukić, Vol. 1–3, 1851, 1862, 1853.
39. Č. Mijatović 1867; idem, 1869a; idem, 1869b.
40. Rošer, Vol. 1, 1863; Vol. 2, 1872.
41. Stokes 1975: 35–42.
42. Denes 2006: 5.

43. *Trgovačke novine*, No 5, 21 January 1861.
44. Blagojević 1996: 101.
45. Vučo 1981: 259–60; S. Jovanović 1990a: 93–5; Milić 1991: 370.
46. Samardžić 2012: 313–35.
47. C. Mijatović 2008: 39–58.
48. Cukić, Vol. 1, 1851.
49. *SN*, No. 80, 9 July 1859.
50. B. Mijatović 2008: 40.
51. *SN*, No 148, 31 December 1855.
52. During the period 1843–75, an average of 80.46 percent of the Serbian export was directed towards the Habsburg Monarchy, and its value increased by nearly four times (from 8,959,651 francs in 1843 to 35,014,874 in 1875). Milošević 1902: 6–24.
53. *SN*, January – February 1856.
54. *SN*, No 54, 19 March 1856.
55. S. Jovanović 1990b: 330–1.
56. B. Mijatović 2008: 52–4.
57. Čalić 2004: 35–74; Stojanović 2005: 121–5.
58. Blagojević 1996: 104–6.
59. S. Jovanović 1990b: 426–31.
60. idem, 1990c: 101–15; Vučo 1981: 152–69, 182–6.
61. Bešlin 2005: 731.
62. V. Jovanović, Vol. G, D, Đ, 1873: 602.
63. Blagojević 1996: 142–3.
64. *Srbija*, No 21, 13/25 March 1868.
65. Č. Mijatović 1871: 25–6, 49–51, 56–64.
66. Blagojević 1996: 99–101.
67. *Srbija*, January – April 1868; Bešlin 2005: 732–34.
68. Samardžić 2010: 27–44.
69. Popović-Obradović 2000: 30–4; Bešlin 2005: 852–9.
70. Petrović 1930: 87–99.
71. *Protokoli*, 1873: 493.
72. Ibid., 519.
73. Čalić 2004: 41; S. Jovanović 1990c: 181.
74. *Protokoli*, 1873: 479–80.
75. Petrović 1924: 30.
76. *Trgovačke novine*, No. 5, 21 January 1861.

Chapter 13 *Ricchi e Poveri*: Images of Wealth and Poverty in Nineteenth-Century Bulgarian Literature

1. Owning a car, earlier – a carriage – at some places and for some time marked wealth, but afterwards did not. In an ironic song of the singer Janis Joplin even

color TV could mark some kind of luxury and well-off life (something like Mercedes Benz and Porsche); only a few years later the same device will hardly mean wealth even in the third-world countries. "Oh lord won't you buy me a color TV. / Dialing for dollars is trying to find me. / I wait for delivery each day until 3. / So oh lord won't you buy me a color TV."

2. Aretov 2006.
3. Rural community, common among South Slavs, formed of one extended family or related families. It held its property and money in common, under the rule of the oldest (patriarch) member.
4. Todorov 1983: 118; Ianeva 1998: 3–36.
5. Danova 2011: 291–64.
6. Avramov 2007.
7. Along these lines, not without some exaggerations, the essayist Vladimir Svintila offers some interesting observations. Svintila 2007.
8. Palairet 1997.
9. Hadzhiyski 1966: 197.
10. Butler 1996: 127–9.
11. Popova 2004: 43. Quoted in Todorova 1987: 324.
12. There is an abundant literature on the travelers' stereotypes of Eastern Europe, see the pioneer study by Wolff 2004.
13. Mihaylova 2006.
14. Danova 1995; Detrez 2008: 75–95.
15. Slaveykov, Vol. 1, 1978: 172–174, 349. My translation is almost word-for-word and fails to render the poetic devices of the verses.
16. Hobsbawm 1969.
17. Penchev 1998.
18. Aretov 1983: 155–62; idem, 1990: 70–82.
19. Rusev 2003: 40–91.
20. Marinov 1994: 752–4.
21. Aretov 2004: 181–93.
22. Elin Pelin 1971: 5, 8.
23. Kolarov 1978: 204.

Conclusion

1. Among the few exceptions, see Kanner 2004; Mitev 2003; Zaimova, Aretov 2004; Bonner, Ener, Singer 2003; Korasidou 1995.
2. Mollat 1986: VII.

BIBLIOGRAPHY

About, Edmond. *I Ellada tou Othonos* (Athens, 1992).

Abrevaya Stein, Sarah. *Making Jews Modern: the Yiddish and Ladino Press in the Russian and Ottoman Empires* (Bloomington, 2004).

Abu-Manneh, Butrus. "The Islamic Roots of the Gülhane Rescript", *Die Welt des Islams* 34, 2 (1994): 173–203.

Acun, Fatma. "A portrait of the Ottoman cities", *The Muslim World* 92 (2002): 255–81.

Agoston, Gabor. *Guns for the Sultan: Military Power and the Weapons Industry in the Ottoman Empire* (New York, 2005).

Alexakis, Eleftherios. *Ta Geni kai I Oikogeneia stin Paradosiaki Koinonia tis Manis* (Athens, 1980).

——. *Ta Paidia tis Siopis: Oikogeneia, Syggeneia kai Gamos stous Arvanites tis N.A. Attikis-Lavreotikis, 1850–1940* (Athens, 1996).

Anastasovski, Nik. *Borbata za makedonskiot identitet 1870–1912* (Skopje, 2012).

Anastassiadou-Dumont, Méropi. ed. *Médecins et ingénieurs ottomans à l'age des nationalismes* (Paris/Istanbul, 2003).

Anderson, Benedict. *Imagined Communities* (London, 1991).

Angelomatis-Tsougarakis, Helen. "Women in the Greek War of Independence", in *Networks of Power in Modern Greece*, ed. Mark Mazower (London, 2008), 45–68.

Annales de la Congregation de la Mission (Lazaristes), t. 82 (Paris, 1917).

Anthimos Alexoudis of Amaseia. "Istoria ton Hreon tou Koinou kai ton legomenon Avlikon", *Ekklisiastiki Alitheia* 41 (1901): 406–7.

Apologismos pepragmenôn tēs en Chalkēdoni Philoptôchou Adelfotētos tôn Kyriôn kata ta etē 1901–02, 1902–03, 1903–04 (Istanbul, 1904).

Apostolidis, M., Al. Peev, eds. *Kondika na Plovdivskia abadzhiĭski esnaf*, Vol. 1–2 (Sofia, 1931).

Arblaster, Anthony. *The Rise and Decline of Western Liberalism* (Oxford, 1984).

Aretov, Nikolay. "Retseptsiyata na B. Franklin v Balgariya prez Vazrazhdaneto", *Literaturna misal* 4 (1983): 155–62.

——. *Prevodnata beletristika ot parvata polovina na 19 v. Razvitie, vrazki s originalnata knizhnina, problemi na retseptsiyata* (Sofia, 1990).

——. "Parite v literaturata. Povestta 'Beshe' na Vasil Popovich", in *Pari, dumi, pamet* (Sofia, 2004), 181–93.

——. *Natsionalna mitologiya i natsionalna literatura. Syuzheti, izgrazhdashti balgarskata natsionalna identichnost v slovesnostta ot 18 i 19 vek* (Sofia, 2006).

Argyriadis-Kervegan, Caroula. "Byzantine Law as practice and as History in the Nineteenth Century", in *Byzantium and the Modern Greek Identity*, eds David Ricks, Paul Magdalino (Brookfield, 1998), 35–47.

Armenopoulos, Konstantinos. *Procheiron Nomon I Exavivlos* (Athens, 1971).

Arnaudov, Mihail. *Liuben Karavelov. Zhivot, Delo, Epoha 1834–1879* (Sofia, 1964).

Asdrachas, Spyros, ed. *Elliniki Oikonomiki Istoria*, Vol. II (Athens, 2003).

Auer, Stefan. *Liberal Nationalism in Central Europe* (London, 2004).

Avramov, Rumen. Komunalniyat kapitalizam, Vols 1–3 (Sofia, 2007).

Ayalon, Ami. *The Press in the Arab Middle East – a History* (Oxford, 1995).

al-Ayyūbī, *Ilyās. Muhammad 'Alī: Siratuhu, wa-a'māluhu wa-athāruhu* (Cairo, 1923).

Badea-Păun, Gabriel. "Ascensiunea unui neam boieresc 'nou' – familia Bibescu", *AG* IV (IX), 3–4 (1997): 193–203.

Bakalaki, Alexandra. "Gender-Related Discourses and Representations of Cultural Specificity in Nineteenth-Century and Twentieth-Century Greece", *JMGS* 12, 1 (1994): 75–106.

Balaschev, Georgi, Diamandi Ihchiev. "Privilegiite na rayata v zemite, zaveshtani na chestitite gradove Meka i Medina", *Minalo*, 2 (1909): 156–75.

Barsoumian, Hagop. "The dual role of the Armenian *Amira* class within the Ottoman government and the Armenian Millet (1750–1850)", in *Christians and Jews in the Ottoman Empire,* eds Benjamin Braude and Bernard Lewis, Vol. 1 (New York, 1985), 171–84.

Bartholdy, Jakob Ludwig Salomo. *Taxidiotikes Entyposeis apo tin Ellada 1803–1804* (Athens, 1993).

Bastea, Eleni. *The Creation of Modern Athens* (Cambridge, 1999).

Benbassa, Esther. "L'École des Filles de l'Alliance Israélite Universelle à Galata", *Varia Turcica* XIII (1991): 201–36.

——. *Une diaspora sépharade en transition. Istanbul XIXe-XXe siècles* (Paris, 1993).

Benbassa, Esther, Aron Rodrigue. *Istorija na sefardskite Evrei* (Skopje, 2011).

Benveniste, Emile. *Le vocabulaire des institutions indo-européennes*, Vol. 1 (Paris, 1966).

Berindei, Dan. "Les descendants du prince Constantin Brâncoveanu et leur place dans l'histoire de la Roumanie. Généalogie et histoire", in *Nouveau recueil d'études généalogiques et héraldiques roumaines*, ed. Dan Berindei (Bucharest, 1988), 66–75.

——. "Urmaşii lui Constantin Brancovan şi locul lor în societatea românească. Genealogie şi istorie", in *Constantin Brancovan* (Bucharest, 1989), 275–85.

Bešlin, Branko. *Evropski uticaji na srpski liberalizam u XIX veku* (Novi Sad, 2005).

Bibesco, Georges. *Règne de Bibesco,* Vol. I, *Correspondance et documents* (1893); Vol. II, *Lois et décrets* (Paris, 1894).

Bikelas, Demetrius. "Statistics of the Kingdom of Greece", *Journal of the Statistical Society of London* 31, 3 (1868): 265–98.

Birdal, Murat. *The political economy of Ottoman public debt. Insolvency and European financial control in the late nineteenth century* (London, 2010).

Blagojević, Obren. *Ekonomska misao u Srbiji do Drugog svetskog rata* (Beograd, 1996).

Bojadžievski, Petar. *Zdravstveno-socijalnata politika na stranskite propagandi vo Bitola* (Štip, 2003).

Boneva, Vera. *Vazrazhdane: Balgariia i Balgarite v Prehod kam Novoto Vreme* (Shumen, 2005).

——. *Balgarskoto Carkovnonacionalno Dvizhenie 1856–1870* (Sofia, 2010).

Bonfield, Lloyd. "European Family Law", in *The History of the European Family*, eds David Kertzer, Marzio Barbagli, Vol. II (New Haven, 2002), 109–54.

Bonner, Michael, Mine Ener, Amy Singer, eds. *Poverty and Charity in Middle Eastern Contexts* (Albany, 2003).

Borshukov Georgi, *Istoriia na Balgarskata Zhurnalistika* 1844–1877 & 1878–1885 (Sofia, 2003).

Bourdieu, Pierre. *Le sens pratique* (Paris, 1980).

——. "The Forms of Capital", in *Handbook of Theory and Research for the Sociology of Education* (New York, 1986), 241–58.

Boyar, Ebru. *Ottomans, Turks and the Balkans: Empire Lost, Relations Altered* (London, 2007).

Bozkurt, Gülnihâl. *Alman-Ingiliz Belgerinin ve siyasî gelişmelerin isiği altında: Gayrimüslim Osmanlı vatandaşlarının hukukî durumu (1839–1914)* (Ankara, 1989).

Braude, Benjamin, Bernard Lewis, eds. *Christians and Jews in the Ottoman Empire*, Vols 1–2 (New York, 1982).

Braudel, Fernand. *The Wheels of Commerce. Civilization and Capitalism 15th – 18th Century*. Vol. 2 (London, 1982).

Brâncoveanu, Grigore. *Prince Gheorghe Bibescu Before the Public Opinion* (Bucharest, 1858).

Britanskite konzuli vo Makedonija 1797–1915, Dokumenti (Skopje, 2002).

Brubaker, Rogers. "The Manichean Myth: Rethinking the Distinction between 'Civic' and 'Ethnic' Nationalism", in *Nation and National Identity. The European Experience in Perspective*, eds Hanspeter Kriesi et al. (West Lafayette, 2004), 55–71.

al-Bustānī, Yūsuf. *Tarīkh Harb al-Balqān al-ūlā bayna al-Dawla al-'Āliya wa-al-Ittihād al-Balqānī al-Muallaf min al-Bulgār wa-al-Sirb wa-al-Yūnān wa-al-Jabal al-Aswad* [Cairo, 1913].

Butler, Thomas, comp. *Monumenta Bulgarica. A Bilingual Anthology of Bulgarian Texts from the 9th to the 19th centuries* (Ann Arbor, 1996).

Bŭlgarski periodičen pečat 1844–1944, Vol. 3 (Sofia, 1969).

Cacanoska, Ružica. "The emergence and development of Protestantism in Macedonia", *Religion, state & society* 29, 2 (2001): 115–19.

Carnarvon, Earl of. *Reminiscences of Athens and the Morea. Extracts from a Journal of Travels in Greece in 1839* (London, 1869).

Cassia, Paul Sant, Constantina Bada. *The Making of the Modern Greek Family* (Cambridge, 1992).

Cernovodeanu, Paul. "Coordonatele politicii externe a lui Constantin Brâncoveanu", in *Constantin Brâncoveanu,* eds Paul Cernovodeanu, Florin Constantiniu (Bucharest, 1989), 125–39.

——. "Clanuri, familii, autorităţi, puteri (Ţara Românească, secolele XV–XVII)", *AG* I (IV), 1–2 (1994): 77–86.

Cernovodeanu, Paul, Irina Gavrilă. *Arhondologiile Ţării Româneşti de la 1837* (Brăila, 2002).

Chasiotis, Loukianos. "Prosfygikes omades kai politikē. Ē periptōsē tōn Voreiomakedonōn (1913–1920, 1941–1950)", in *Prosfyges sta Balkania. Mnēmē kai ensōmatōsē*, eds Basil Gounaris, I. Michaēlidēs (Athens, 2004), 211–52.

Checkland, E.O.A., Checkland, S.G. *The Poor Law Report of 1834* (London, 1974).

Chekimoglou, Evangelos. "Eidēseis apo ton atitlo kôdika tēs ellēnikēs koinotētas Thessalonikēs peri tôn iatrôn kai tôn nosokomeiôn tēs poleôs (1792–1796)", in *I istoria tēs Iatrikēs stēn polē tēs Thessalonikēs* (Thessalonikē, 2005), 157–60.
Chilingirov, Stilian. *Dobrŭdzha i nasheto Vŭzrazhdane* (Sofia, 1917).
Chirot, Daniel. *Social Change in the Modern Era* (San Diego, 1986).
Cholakova, Margarita. *Bulgarsko zhensko dvizhenie prez Vazrazhdaneto 1857–1878* (Sofia, 1994).
Cholov, Petar. *Istoriya na grad Dryanovo* (Sofia, 1969).
Chouliarakis, Michail. *Geografiki, Dioikitiki kai Plythismiaki Exelixis tis Ellados 1821–1971*, Vol. A, Part I (Athens, 1973).
Chrēstidis, Michaēl. *Epistolarion koinôpheles* (Bucharest, 1837).
Churches, Christine. "Putting Women in their Place: Female Litigants at Whitehaven 1660–1760", in *Women Property and the Letters of the Law in Early Modern England*, eds Nancy Wright, Margaret Ferguson, A.R. Buck (Toronto, 2004), 50–65.
Cohen, Mark. "Disaster and change in an Ottoman Sephardic community: Moses Mantefiore and the Monastir fire of 1863", *Journal of Jewish Studies* 4, 1 (2004): 131–56.
Condurachi, Ioan. *Expunere rezumată a teoriei moştenitorilor în vechiul drept românesc* (Bucharest, 1919).
Conway, David. *Classical Liberalism. The Unvanquished Ideal* (New York, 1995).
Couroucli, Maria. "Dot et Société en Greèce Moderne", in *Femmes et Patrimoine dans les Sociétés Rurales de l'Europe Méditerranéenne*, ed. G. Ravis-Giordani (Paris, 1983), 327–48.
Cukić, Kosta. *Državne ekonomije*, 1–3 (Beograd 1851, 1862, 1853).
Çakır, Serpil. *Osmanlı Kadın Hareketi* (Istanbul, 1996).
Čalić, Mari-Žanin. *Socijalna istorija Srbije 1815–1941: usporeni napredak u industrijalizaciji* (Beograd, 2004).
Čipan, Boris. *Makedonskite gradovi vo XIX vek* (Skopje, 1978).
Čubrilović, Vasa. *Istorija političke misli u Srbiji 19. veka* (Beograd, 1982).
Danova, Nadia. "Le Retentissement de l'Insurrection Crétoise de 1866–1869 au sein de l'Opinion Publique Bulgare", *EB*, 2 (1972): 98–109.
——. ed. *Arkhiv na Konstantin Georgiev Fotinov*, Vol. 1 (Sofia, 2004).
——. *Ivan Dobrovski v perspektivata na bŭlgarskia XIX vek* (Sofia, 2008).
——. "Fragmenti ot istoriyata na izgrazhdaneto na pravnata kultura pri balgarite", *Kritika i humanizam* 7, 2 (2011): 201–264.
Danova, Nadia et al., eds. *Predstavata za "drugiya" na Balkanite* (Sofia, 1995).
Daskalov Roumen, *The Making of a Nation in the Balkans. Historiography of the Bulgarian Revival* (Budapest, 2004).
Daskalova, Krassimira. "Bulgarian Women's Movement (1850s–1940s)", in *Women's Movements. Networks and Debates in Post-Communist Countries in the 19th and 20th Centuries,* eds Edith Sauer, Margaret Lanzinger, Elizabeth Frysak (Köln, 2006), 413–38.
——. *Bulgarskiat uchitel prez Vazrazhdaneto* (Sofia, 1997).
Davidova, Evguenia. "Tŭrgovski kapital i otkupuvane na danŭtsi v Osmanskata imperia prez tretata chetvŭrt na XIX vek", *IP* 3–4, 2007: 64–75.
——. *Balkan Transitions to Modernity and Nation-States through the Eyes of Three Generations of Merchants (1780s–1890s)* (Leiden, 2013).
Davison, Roderic. *Reform in the Ottoman Empire, 1856–1876* (Princeton, 1963).

de Coulanges, Fustel. *La cité antique* (Paris, 1927), gallica.bnf.fr (Visited on 1 September 2014).

Dedijer, Jefto. *Nova Srbija* (Beograd, 1913).

Dénes, Ivan. "Liberalism and Nationalism: An Ambiguous Relationship", in *Liberty and the Search for Identity: Liberal Nationalisms and the Legacy of Empires*, ed. Ivan Dénes (Budapest, 2006), 1–17.

Deringil, Selim. *The Well-Protected Domains. Ideology and the Legitimation of Power in the Ottoman Empire, 1876–1909* (London, 1998); Greek edition (Athens, 2003).

Desan, Suzanne. *The Family on Trial in Revolutionary France* (Berkeley, 2004).

Detrez, Raymond. "'Lukavi gartsi' i 'nadmenni balgari.' Balgarski i gratski retsiprochni predstavi po vreme na tsarkovnata borba v Plovdiv prez 50-te godini na 19 vek", in *Vapreki razlichiyata. Interkulturni dialozi na Balkanite* (Sofia, 2008), 75–95.

Dimeski, Dimitar. *Makedonskoto nacionalnooslobodítelno dviženje vo Bitolskiot vilaet (1893–1903)* (Skopje, 1982).

Dimitrov, Nikola. "Migracii na doseluvanje i demografski promeni vo Bitola vo 19 vek", in *Bitola niz vekovite,* Vol. 7 (Bitola, 2004), 7–24.

——. *Bitola. Urban i geografski razoj* (Bitola, 1998).

Dimitrov, Strashimir. *Văstanieto ot 1850 godina v Bŭlgaria* (Sofia, 1972).

——. "Socialno-ikonomichesko razvitie na Vratsa ot vtorata polovina na XVIII vek do Krimskata voina", in *Istoria na Vratsa* (Sofia, 1976), 135–70.

——. "Buntovni dvizheniya v Tarnovsko i Iztochna Balgariya po vremena Chiprovskoto vastaniye", *IP* 10 (1988): 35–47.

Dimova, Marlena. "Belezhkite v edna ryadka gratska kniga ot Arbanasi", in *Fakti i mistifikatsii v starite tekstove* (Sofia, 2011), 449–75.

Dimovski-Colev, Gorgi."Bitola za vreme na Balkanskite vojni i na Prvata svetska vojna", in *Tvoreštvoto na braќata Manaki* (Skopje, 1996), 255–70.

Dincer, Aysu. "Wills, Marriage, and Business Contracts: Urban Women in Late Medieval Cyprus", *Gender and History* 24, 2 (2012): 310–32.

Dinç, Güney. *Mehmed Nail Bey'in Derlediği Kartpostallarla Balkan Savaşı (1912–1913)* (Istanbul, 2008).

"Dobruzha." *Entsiklopedicheskii Slovar'*. Vol. 10a (Brockhaus and Efron) (Saint Petersburg, 1893): 830–1.

Documente privind istoria României, B, XVI Century, Vol. III (Bucharest, 1952).

Doinov, Stefan. "Preselnicheski Dvizheniia ot Bŭlgarskite Zemi po Vreme na Rusko-Turskite Voini prez Pŭrvata Polovina na XIX v.", in *Bŭlgarskoto Vŭzrazhdane i Rusiia* (Sofia, 1981), 290–316.

Doxiadis, Evdoxios. *The Shackles of Modernity. Women, Property, and the Transition from the Ottoman Empire to the Greek State (1750–1850)* (Cambridge, Massachusetts, 2011).

——. "Standing in their Place: The Exclusion of Women from the Judicial System", *JMGS* 25, 1 (May 2007): 75–97.

Duman, Halûk Harun. *Balkanlara Veda: Basın ve Edebiyatta Balkan Savaşı (1912–1913)* (Istanbul, 2005).

Dumont, Paul. "Jewish communities in Turkey during the last decades of the nineteenth century in the light of the archives of the *Alliance Israélite Universelle*", in *Christians and Jews in the Ottoman Empire*, eds Benjamin Braude and Bernard Lewis, Vol. 1 (New York, 1985), 209–42.

Duprat, Catherine. *"Pour l'Amour de l'Humanité": Le temps des Philanthropes. La philanthropie parisienne des Lumières à la monarchie de Juillet*, Vol. 1 (Paris, 1993).

Džambazovski, Kliment. ed. *Grada za istoriju Makedonskog naroda iz arhiva Srbije*, Vol. 1, kn. I (Beograd, 1979).

Džonev, Angel. *Makedonija v železnpŭtnata politika na Bŭlgarija (1878–1918)* (Kjustendil, 2008).

Đordević, Dimitrije. "Srbija i srpsko društvo 1880-tih godina", *IČ* XXIX–XXX (1983): 413–26.

Eccleshall, Robert, et al. *Political Ideologies. An Introduction* (London, 2003).

Eisenstadt, S.N. "Multiple Modernities", *Daedalus* 129, 1 (2000): 1–29.

Ekmekçioğlu, Lerna, Melissa, Bilal, eds. *Bir Adalet Feryadı. Osmanlı'dan Türkiye'ye Beş Ermeni Feminist Yazar 1862–1933* (Istanbul, 2006).

Ekthesis Pepragmenôn tēs en Stavrodromiô Philoptôchou Adelfotētos tôn Kyriôn (Istanbul, 1876; 1885; 1896).

Elin Pelin. *Sachineniya*, Vol. 1 (Sofia, 1971).

Ener, Mine. "The Charity of the Khedive", in *Poverty and Charity in Middle Eastern Contexts*, eds Michael Bonner, Mine Ener, Amy Singer (Albany, 2003a), 185–201.

——. *Managing Egypt's Poor and the Politics of Benevolence, 1800–1952* (Princeton, 2003b).

L'Epoque Phanariote, International Symposium, October 1970 (Thessaloniki, 1970).

Erickson, Amy Louise. *Women and Property in Early Modern England* (New York, 1997).

Eroğlu, Münevver Güneş. *Armenians in the Ottoman Empire according to Ikdam 1914–1918*, MSc. Thesis (Middle East Technical University, Ankara, 2003).

Eryilmaz, Bilal. *Osmanlı Devletinde Gayrimüşlim tebaanin yonetimi* (Istanbul, 1996).

Exertzoglou, Harris. "To 'pronomiako' Zitima", *Ta Istorika* 16 (1992): 65–84.

Fahmy, Khaled. *All the Pasha's Men: Mehmed Ali, his Army and the Making of Modern Egypt* (Cambridge, 1997).

Fakiisko Predanie (Sofia, 1985).

Faroqui, Suraiya. *Koultoura kai kathemerinē zôē stēn Othomanikē autokratoria. Apo to Mesaiôna ôs tis arches tou 20ou aiôna* (Athens, 2000).

——, ed. *The Cambrigde History of Turkey.* Vol. 3 (Cambridge, 2006).

Filippides, Chrysanthos, Archbishop of Athens. "Oi Genikoi Kanonismoi tou Oikoumenikou Patriarheiou epi ti vasei tou kodikos TE' Patriarhikou Arheiofylakeiou (Praktika Ethnosynelefseos, 1858–1860)", *Praktika Akademias Athenon* (1946), 1–45.

Filitti, Ioan. *Arhiva Gh. Gr. Cantacuzino* (Bucharest, 1919).

——. *Proprietatea solului în Principatele Române până la 1864* (Bucharest).

Finlay, George. *History of the Greek Revolution and the Reign of King Otho* (London, 1971).

Firkatian, Mari. *The Forest Traveller. Georgi Stoikov Rakovski and Bulgarian Nationalism* (New York, 1996).

Florentin, Rephael Yosef. *Kózas Pasadas – Epizódyos de los Akontesimyentos ke se pasaron en Kavala del 1912 al 1918* (Kavala, 1929).

Fortna, Benjamin. "Islamic morality in Late Ottoman 'secular' schools", *IJMES* 32 (2000): 369–93.

Fotino, George. *Contribution à l'étude des origines de l'ancien droit coutumier roumain. Un chapitre de l'histoire de la propriété au Moyen Âge* (Paris, 1925).

Frieden, Nancy. *Russian Physicians in an Era of Reform and Revolution, 1856–1905* (Princeton, 1981).

Friedenwald, Herbert, H.G. Friedman, eds. *The American Jewish Year Book 5674: October 1913 to September 1914* (Philadelphia, 1913).

Friedl, Ernestine. *Vasilika, a Village in Modern Greece* (New York, 1962).

Gallon, Silvano. *Rapporti dei regi consoli d'Italia a Monastir (1895–1016)* (Bitola, 2004).

Garstang, A. "Welfare work in Macedonia", *The British journal of nursing* 69 (1922).

Gavrilova, Raïna. *Koleloto na zhivota* (Sofia, 1999).

Gedeôn, Manuel. *Istoria ton tou Christou peniton*, 1453–1913, Vols 3, 4 (Athens, 1939).

——. *Hē Zôodohos Pēgē kai ta idiaitera autēs prosartēmata* (Athens, 1886).

Geib, Gustav Karl. *Parousiasi tis Katastasis tou Dikaiou stin* (Athens, 1990).

Gellner, Ernest. *Nations and Nationalism* (Oxford, 1994).

Genchev, Nikolai. *Balgarsko Vazrazhdane* (Sofia, 1991).

——. *Vasil Levski* (Sofia, 2011).

Genç, Mehmet. "18. Yüzyılda Osmanlı Ekonomisi ve Savaş", *Toplumsal Araştırmalar Dergisi* 49 (April-May 1984): 52–61; 50 (1984): 86–93.

Georgescu, Vlad, *Ideile politice şi iluminismul in Principatele române 1750–1832* (Bucharest, 1972).

Georgieva, Gergana. "Administrative structure and government in the late eighteen and early nineteenth centuries: the functions and activities of the Vali of Rumelia", in *Ottoman rule and the Balkans 1760–1850,* eds Antonis Anastasopoulos, Elias Kolovos (Rethymno, 2007), 3–19.

——. *Arbanasi prez XV-XIX vek: sotsialno-ikonomicheski profil* (Varna, 2014).

Gerasimov, Ljubomir. "Knigata vo Makedonija vo prerodbata. Bibliotekata na semejstvotot Robevi", in *Školstvoto, prosvetata i kulturata vo Makedonija* (Skopje, 1979), 623–43.

Gerber, Haim. "Social and Economic Position of Women in an Ottoman City, Bursa 1600–1700", *IJMES* 12, 3 (1980): 231–44.

Gershoni, Israel, James Jankowski. *Egypt, Islam and the Arabs: The Search for Egyptian Nationhood, 1900–1930* (Oxford, 1986).

——. *Commemorating the Nation: Collective Memory, Public Commemoration, and National Identity in Twentieth-Century Egypt* (Chicago, 2004).

Ginio, Eyal. "Making Sense of the Defeat in the Balkan Wars: Voices from the Arab Provinces", in *War and Nationalism: The Balkan Wars, 1912–1913, and Their Sociopolitical Implications*, eds Hakan Yavuz, Isa Blumi (Salt Lake City, 2013), 594–617.

——. "Jewish Philanthropy and Mutual Assistance during the Balkan Wars: between Ottomanism and Communal Identities", in *The Balkan Wars 1912/13: Experience, Perception, Remembrance*, eds Katrina Boeckh, Mehmet Hacısalihoğlu, Sabine Rutar (forthcoming).

Giurova, Svetla, Nadia Danova. *Kniga za bŭlgarskite khadzhii* (Sofia, 1985).

Gobineau, Arthur de. *Sto Vasileio ton Ellinon* (Athens, 1999).

Godelier, Maurice. *Métamorphoses de la parenté* (Paris, 2010).

Gorman, Anthony. *Historians, State and Politics in Twentieth Century Egypt: Contesting the Nation* (New York, 2003).

Gorovei, Ştefan. "Clanuri, familii, autorităţi, puteri (Moldova, secolele XV–XVII)", *AG* I (VI), 1–2 (1994): 87–93.

Gorovei, Ştefan, Mihai Radulescu. "Constantin Basarab Brancovan. Strămoşii, înrudirile şi calea spre tron", *Anuarul Institutului de Istorie "A.D. Xenopol",* XXVII (1990): 220–37.

Gounaris, Basil. *Stis ochthe stou Ydragora. Oikougeneia, oikonomia kai astikē koinōnia stē Monastēri 1897–1912* (Athens, 2000).

——. "From peasant into urbanities, from village into nation: Ottoman Monastir in the early twentieth century", *European History Quarterly* 30, 1 (2001): 43–63.

Göçek, Fatma Müge. *Rise of the Bourgeoisie, Demise of Empire. Ottoman Westernization and Social Change* (New York, 1996).

Gradeva, Rossitsa. "Orthodox Christians in the Kadi Courts: The Practice of the Sofia Sheriat Court, Seventeenth Century", *Islamic Law and Society* 4, 1 (1997); 37–69.

——. "The Activities of a Kadi Court in Eighteenth-Century Rumeli: The Case of Hacıoğlu Pazarcık", *OM* 18, 1 (1999): 177–90.

——. "Villagers in International Trade: The Case of Chervena Voda, Seventeenth to the Beginning of the Eighteenth Centuries", *OM* 25, 1 (2006): 1–20.

Grecianu, Ştefan. "Contele N. Rosetti", *Revista pentru istorie, arhelologie şi filologie* V, 9 (1903): 213–45.

——. *Genealogiile documentate ale familiilor boiereşti,* Vols 1–2 (Bucharest, 1915).

Greenfeld, Liah. *Nationalism. Five Roads to Modernity* (Cambridge, 1992).

Gunst, Peter. "Agrarian Systems of Central and Eastern Europe", in *The Origins of Backwardness in Eastern Europe* (Berkeley, 1989), 53–91.

Gülsoy, Ufuk. "1828–1829 Osmanlı-Rus Savaşinda Rumeli'de Rus Işgaline Uğrayan Yerlerin Durumu", *Sultan II. Mahmud ve Reformları Semineri* (Istanbul, 1990).

——. *1828–1829 Osmanlı-Rus Savaşı'nda Rumeli'den Rusya'ya Göçürülen Reaya* (Istanbul, 1993).

Gyuzelev, Boyan. *Albantsi v Iztochnite Balkani* (Sofia, 2004).

Ġorġiev, Dragi. *Britanski dokumenti za istorijata na makedonskiot narod (1857–1885)*, Vol. 4 (Skopje, 2003).

——. *Spomenina Nijazi bej* (Skopje, 2011).

Ġorġiev, Vancho. *Podzemnata republika. Damjan Gruev i makedonskoto revolucionerno dviženje* (Skopje, 2010).

Hadzhiyski, Ivan. *Bit i dushevnost na balgarskiya narod* (Sofia, 1966).

Halaçoğlu, Ahmet. *Balkan Harbi sırasında Rumeli'den Türk Göçleri (1912–1913)* (Ankara, 1995).

Hall, Richard. *The Balkan Wars 1912–1913: Prelude to the First World War* (London, 2000).

Handman, Marie Elizabeth. "Astikos Kodikas kai Ethimiko Dikaio", in *Oikogeneia kai Periousia stin Ellada kai tin Kypro*, ed. Colette Piault (Athens, 1994), 239–49.

Hardwick, Julie. *The Practice of Patriarchy, Gender and the Politics of Household Authority in Early Modern France* (University Park, 1998).

Hasselquist, Fredrik. *Voyages and Travels in Levant* (London, 1766).

Healy, Maureen. *Vienna and the Fall of the Habsburg Empire: Total War and Everyday Life in World War I* (Cambridge, 2004).

Hechter, Michael. *Containing Nationalism* (Oxford, 2002).

Helladios, Alexandros. *Status Praesens Ecclesiae Graecae*, 1714.

Hering, Gunnar. *Das ökumenische Patriarchat und europäische Politik, 1620–1638* (Wiesbaden, 1968).

Heywood, Andrew. *Political Ideologies* (New York, 2012).

Hionidou, Violetta. "Domestic Service in three Greek Islands in the Later 19th and Early 20th Centuries", *History of the Family* 10 (2005): 473–89.

Hirszowicz, L. "The Sultan and the Khedive, 1892–1908", *MES* 8 (1972): 287–311.

Hobsbawm, Eric. *Bandits* (London, 1969).

——. *Nations and Nationalism since 1780* (Cambridge, 1997).

Houmanidis, Lazaros. *Oikonomiki Istoria tis Ellados*, Vol. B (Athens, 1990).

Howard, John. *An Account of the Principal Lazarettos in Europe; with various papers relative to the plague, together with further observations on some foreign prisons and hospitals, 2nd Edit with additions* (London, 1791).

Hughes, Diane. "From Brideprice to Dowry in Mediterranean Europe", *JFH* 3 (1978): 262–96.

Iancu, Andreea. "Adopter ou nourrir un enfant en Valachie, XVIIIe-XIXe siècles: norme et pratique. Etude de cas", *Méditerranées* 37 (2004): 237–77.

Ianeva, Svetla. "Regulatsiya na zanayatchiyskoto proizvodstvo v balgarskite zemi prez parvata polovina na 19 vek", *IP* 3–4 (1998): 3–36.

——. "Pŭtishta na industrializatsiata: protoindustriite v Evropa i v bŭlgarskite zemi (XVIII-XIX vek)", *IP* 5–6 (2000): 99–119.

——. "Otkupvacheskata deinost na bratia Khadzhitoshevi prez vtorata polovina na XIX vek", *IP* 3–4 (2007): 54–63.

——. "Nachaloto na inkorporatsiata na tsentralnobalkanskite provintsii na Osmanskata imperia v svetovnata ikonomicheska sistema (kraia na XVIII-XIX vek)", in *Balkanite, modernizatsia, identichnosti, idei* (Sofia, 2011a), 35–48.

——. *Bŭlgari – otkupvachi na danŭtsi vŭv fiskalnata sistema na Osmanskata imperia. Kŭm istoriata na bŭlgarskia delovi i sotsialen elit prez XIX vek* (Sofia, 2011b).

Ilchev, Ivan. *Reklamata prez Vŭzrazhdaneto* (Sofia, 1995).

Iorga, Nicolae. ed. *Genealogia Cantacuzinilor de Banul Mihai Cantacuzino* (Bucharest, 1902).

——. *Studii şi documente privitoare la istoria românilor*, Vol. VIII (Bucharest, 1904).

——. "Viaţa şi domnia lui Barbu D. Ştirbei, domn al Tării Româneşti (1849–1856)", *Analele Academiei. Memoriile Secţiunii Istorice* XXVII (1906): 347–52.

——. "Les diplômes impériaux de Constantin Brâncoveanu, prince de Valachie", *Revue des Etudes Sud-Est Européennes* XIV, 7–9 (1937a): 177–86.

——. *Histoire des Roumains et de la romanité orientale*, Vol. 2 (Bucharest, 1937b).

——. *Istoria literaturii române în secolul al XVIII lea (1688–1821)*, Vol. II (Bucarest, 1969).

İpek, Nedim. *Rumeli'den Anadolu'ya Türk Göçleri (1877–1890)* (Ankara, 1994).

Irechek, Konstantin. Patuvaniya po Balgaria (Sofia, 1974).

Islamoğlu-Inan, Huri, ed. *The Ottoman Empire and the World-Economy* (Cambridge, 1990).

Istoriya na Veliko Tarnovo, Vol. 2 (Tarnovo, 2000).

Ivanov, Yordan. *Balgarski starini iz Makedonia* (Sofia, 1931).

Jakimov, Georgi. *Pantelei Kisimov. Zhivot i Deinost* (Sofia, 2003).

Jankowski, James. "Ottomanism and Arabism in Egypt, 1860–1914", *The Muslim World* 70 (1980): 229–35.

Jelavich, Barbara. *Russia and the Romanian National Cause, 1858–1859* (Indiana, 1959).

Jovanović, Slobodan. *Vlada Milana Obrenovića* (Beograd, 1990a).

——. *Druga vlada Miloša i Mihaila* (Beograd, 1990b).

——, *Ustavobranitelji i njihova vlada* (Beograd, 1990c).

Jovanović, Vladimir. *Politički rečnik*, G, D, Đ (Beograd, 1873).

——. *Izabrani spisi* (Beograd, 2011).

Kaklamanaki, Roula. *I Thesi tis Gynaikas stin Oikogeneia, stin Koinonia, stin Politeia* (Athens, 1979).

Kalligas, Pavlos. *Systima Romaikou Dikaiou*, Vol. A (1878); Vol. B (1878); Vol. D (1930); Vol. E (Athens, 1876).

Kalpourtzi, Eva. *Syggenikes Scheseis kai Stratigikes Antallagon: To Paradeigma tis Naxou ton 17o Aiona* (Athens, 2001).

Kampouroglou, Dimitrios. *Istoria ton Athinaion* (Athens, 1969).

Kanner, Efi. *Ftôheia kai filanthrôpia stēn Orthodoxē koinotēta tēs Kônstantinoupolēs (1753–1912)* (Athens, 2004).

Kanonismos tēs En Phôtēra yper ton Aporôn Mathētôn Adelfotētos "O Sôtēr" (Istanbul, 1874).

Kanonismos tēs en Stavrodromiô Hellēnikēs Orthodoxou Koinotētos (Istanbul, 1876).

Kanonismos tēs En Therapeiois Agathoergou Adelfotētos (Istanbul, 1874).

Kanonismos tēs en Trapezounti Adelfotētos tôn Kyriôn Merimnēs (Trabzon, 1904).

Kanonismos tēs En Xyloportē Arôgou tôn Aporôn Mathētôn Adelfotētos "Ennea Mousai" (Istanbul, 1887).

Karachrēstos, Iôannēs. "Aïvali (Kydônies)" (2003). Politistikē Pylē tou Archipelagous tou Aigaio. http://www2.egeonet.gr/aigaio/Forms/fLemmaBodyExtended.aspx?lemmaID=3440 (Visited on 1 May 2014).

Karavelov Liuben. *Publicistikata na Liuben Karavelov*, Vol. I (Sofia, 1957).

——, *Sabrani Sachineniia*, Vol. 7, 11, 12 (Sofia, 1985, 1989, 1992).

Karlova, M. "Turetzkaya provintziya i eya sel'skaya i gorodskaya zhizn'. Puteshestvie po Makedonii i Albanii", *Vestnik Evropy* 5, 3 (1870): 721–53; 4 (1870): 150–90.

Karpat, Kemal. *Ottoman Population 1830–1914: Demographic and Social Characteristics* (Madison, 1985).

——. "Dobruca", *Türkiye Diyanet Vakfı – Islam Ansiklopedisi*, Vol. 9 (1994): 482–6.

Kasdagli, Aglaia. *Land and Marriage Settlements in the Aegean* (Venice, 1999).

Katsoulis Giorgis, Marios Nikolinakos, Vasilis Filias. *Oikonomiki Istoria tis Neoteris Elladas* (Athens, 1985).

Kelleher, Marie. "Hers by Right: Gendered Legal Assumptions and Women's Property in the Medieval Crown of Aragon", *Journal of Women's History* 22, 2 (2010): 34–55.

Kenderova, Stoyanka. "Construire une nation saine et vigoureuse: les médecins bulgares au XIXe siècle", in *Médecins et ingénieurs ottomans à l'âge des nationalismes* (Paris, 2003), 185–206.

Kévorkian, Raymond, Paul Paboudjian, *Les Arméniens dans l'Empire Ottoman à la veille du génocide* (Paris, 1992).

Kharizanov, Vasil. ed. *Istoria na grad* Vratsa, Vol. 1 (Sofia, 1976).

——. "Proizvodstvo i tŭrgovia sŭs svila v Severozapadna Bŭlgaria prez poslednata chetvŭrt na XVIII i pŭrvata chetvŭrt na XIX vek", *Izvestia na Bŭlgarskoto istorichesko druzhestvo* 30 (1977): 57–70.

Kiel, Machiel. *Art and Society in Bulgaria in the Turkish Period* (Assen-Maastricht, 1985).

——. "Ottoman Building Activity Along the Via Egnatia: The Cases of Pazargah, Kavala and Firecik", in *The Via Egnatia under Ottoman Rule, 1380–1699,* ed. Elizabeth Zachariadou (Rethymnon, 1996), 145–58.

Kitromilides, Paschalis. *Neohellēnikos Diafôtismos. Oi politikes kai koinônikes idees* (Athens, 1996).

Kızıltoprak, Süleyman. *II. Abdülhamid Han'ın Dış Politikası ve Taşöz Operasyonu* (Izmir, 2011).
Klapisch-Zuber, Christiane. *Les généalogies florentines du XIVe et du XVe siècle*, in *Le modèle familial européen. Normes, déviances, contrôle du pouvoir* (Rome, 1986).
——. *La maison et le nom. Stratégies et rituels dans l'Italie de la Renaissance* (Paris, 1990).
——. *L'ombre des ancêtres. Essai sur l'imaginaire médieval de la parenté* (Paris, 2000).
Kolarov, Stefan. *Georgi Karaslavov. Literaturna anketa* (Sofia, 1978).
Konortas, Paraskevas. *Othômanikes theôrēseis gia to Oikoumeniko Patriarcheio (17os- arhes 20ou aiôna)* (Athens, 1998).
Konstantinov, Hristo. Opisanie na grada Veliko Tarnovo i okolnostta mu (Tarnovo, 1893).
Korasidou, Maria. *Oi athlioi tôn Athēnôn kai oi therapeutes tous: ftôheia kai filanthrôpia stēn ellēnikē prôteuousa ton 19o aiôna* (Athens, 1995).
Kostov, Dimitar. *Arbanasi* (Sofia, 1959).
Kotek, Joël. "Les villes – frontières au XX siecle: 'Etre et ne presque plus etre'", in *L'Europe et ses villes–frontières*, ed. Joël Kotek (Paris, 2009), 15–32.
Koukou, Eleni. *Oi Koinotikoi Thesmoi stis Kyklades kata tin Tourkokratia – Anekdota Eggrafa* (Athens, 1989).
Kryzhanovskaia, K.P., E.M. Ruseev. *Ustroistvo Zadunaiskikh Pereselentsev v Bessarabii i Deiatel'nost A.P. Iushnevskogo: Sbornik Dokumentov* (Kishinev, 1957).
Kuehn, Thomas. "Women, Marriage, and Patria Potestas in late Medieval Florence", in *Law, Family, and Women: Toward a Legal Anthropology of Renaissance Italy*, ed. Thomas Kuehn (Chicago, 1991), 197–211.
Kukudis, Asterios. *Vlasite. Metropoli i dijaspora* (Skopje, 2013).
Kurnaz, Şefika. *II. Meşrutiyet Döneminde Türk Kadını* (Istanbul, 1996).
Kyriazis, Nota. "Feminism and the State of Women in Greece", in *Greece Prepares for the Twenty First Century*, eds Dimitris Constas, Theofanis Stavrou (Washington, DC, 1995), 267–301.
Laffan, R. *The guardians of the gate. Historical lectures on the Serbs* (Oxford, 1918).
Laiou, Angeliki. *Gender, Society, and Economic Life in Byzantium* (Brookfield, 1992).
Laiou, Sophia. "Christian Women in an Ottoman World: Interpersonal and Family Cases Brought Before the Shari'a Courts During the Seventeenth and Eighteenth Centuries", in *Women in the Ottoman Balkans*, eds Amila Buturovic, Irvin Cemil Schick (New York, 2007), 243–71.
Lambiri-Dimaki, Jane. "Dowry in Modern Greece: An Institution at the Crossroads between Persistence and Decline", in *The Marriage Bargain*, ed. Marion Kaplan (New York, 1985), 165–78.
Lampe, John. *Financial Structure and the Economic Development of Serbia 1878–1912*, PhD thesis (Madison, 1971).
Land, Joy. *Corresponding Lives: Women Educators of the Alliance Israélite Universelle School for Girls in the City of Tunis, 1882–1914*, PhD Dissertation (Los Angeles, UCLA, 2006).
Lanza, Janine. *From Wives to Widows in Early Modern Paris* (Burlington, 2007).
Lazaretou, Sophia. "The Drachma, Foreign creditors, and the International Monetary System: Tales of a Currency during the 19th and early 20th Centuries", *Explorations in Economic History* 42 (2005): 202–36.
Leake, William. *Travels in Northern Greece*. Vol. 1 (Amsterdam, 1967).
Lecca, Octav-George. *Familiile boereşti române. Istorie şi genealogie* (Bucureşti, 1899).
Lefebvre, Henry. *The Production of Social Space* (Oxford, 1991).

Leontidou, Lila. "Gynaikeia Ergasia stis Poleis: Mia Antifatiki Kataktisi", in *I Ellada ton Gynaikon,* eds Evtychia Leontidou, Sagrid Ammer (Athens, 1992), 104–16.

Lévi-Strauss, Claude. "Nobles sauvages", in *Culture, science et developpement: contribution à une histoire de l'homme: mélange en l'honneur de Charles Morazé* (Toulouse, 1979).

Lewis, Bernard. *The Emergence of Modern Turkey* (London, 1961).

Liata, Eftychia. *Times kai agatha stin Athina (1839–1846)* (Athens, 1984).

Libaridian, Gerard. "What Was Revolutionary about Armenian Revolutionary Parties in the Ottoman Empire?" in *A Question of Genocide: Armenians and Turks at the End of the Ottoman Empire,* eds Ronald Grigor Suny, Fatma Müge Göçek, Norman M. Naimark (Oxford, 2011), 82–112.

Lindemann, Mary. *Medicine and Society in Early Modern Europe* (Cambridge, 2010).

Ljubenova, Lizbet. *Poslednite bŭlgarski vladici v Makedonija* (Sofia, 2012).

Logodosia tes epi tēs anegerseôs tou en Ypsomatheiois Kentrikou Parthenagogeiou Eidikēs Epitropēs (Istanbul, 1875).

Logoi kai euthynai tēs en Megalô Reumati tou Vosporou Eforias tôn Dēmotikôn ekpaideutēriôn gia to sholiko etos 1888–1889 (Samos, 1889).

Lory, Bernard. *La ville Balkanissime, Bitola 1800–1918*, Thèse (Paris, 2009).

Lory, Bernard, Aleksandar Popovic. "Au Carefour des Balkans, Bitola 1816–1918", in *Villes ottomans a la fin de l'empire* (Paris, 1992), 75–93.

Lowry, Heath. *The Shaping of the Ottoman Balkans, 1350–1500: The Conquest, Settlement and Infrastructural Development of Northern Greece* (Istanbul, 2008).

Lowry, Heath, İsmail Erünsel. *Remembering One's Roots – Mehmed Ali Paşa of Egypt's Links to the Macedonian Town of Kavala: Architectural Monuments, Inscriptions and Documents* (Istanbul, 2011).

Lyberatos, Andreas. "Men of the Sultan: the Beğlik Sheep Tax Collection System and the Rise of a Bulgarian National Bourgeoisie in Nineteenth-century Plovdiv", *Turkish Historical Review* 1 (2010): 55–85.

Mackenzie, David. *Jovan Ristic: Outstanding Serbian Statesman* (Boulder, 2006).

Maksudyan, Nazân. "Orphans, cities, and the state: vocational orphanages (Islahhanes) and 'Reform' in Late Ottoman urban space", *IJMES* 43 (2011): 493–511.

——. "'Missions 2': les 'missions' occidentales dans l'Empire ottoman, de 1800 à 1918", in *Dictionnaire de l'Empire Ottoman*, eds Nicolas Vatin, Gilles Veinstein, François Georgeon (Paris, forthcoming).

Mamoukas, Andreas. *To Kata tin Anagennisin tis Ellados itoi Syllogi ton peri tin Anagenomenin Ellada Syntachthenton Politevmaton, Nomon, kai Allon Episimon Praxeon apo tou 1821 Mechri tou Telous tou 1832*, Vol. 9 (Athens, 1941).

Manolova-Nikolova, Nadia. *Chumavite Vremena (1700–1850)* (Sofia, 2004).

Maridakis, Georgios. *To Astikon Dikaion eis tais Nearais ton Byzantinon Aytokratoron* (Athens, 1922).

Marinov, Dimitŭr. "Dimitraki Khadzhi Toshov. Gradivo za novata ni istoria", *Bŭlgarska sbirka* 1, 6 (1894): 432–47.

——. *Narodna vyara i religiozni narodni obichai* (Sofia, 1994).

Marinska, Khristina. "Ezikova kharakteristika na korespondentsiata prez Vŭzrazhdaneto v grad Vratsa (spored 'Semeen archiv na Khadzhitoshevi')", in *Problemi na sotsiolingvistikata* (Sofia, 2011), 222–6.

Markova, Zina. *Bŭlgarskoto tsŭrkovno-natsionalno dvizhenie do Krimskata voîna* (Sofia, 1976).

——. *Bŭlgarskata Ekzarhija, 1870–1879* (Sofia, 1989).

Maropoulou, Marina. "I Politiki ton Ekklisiastikon kai Koinotikon Archon sto Zitima tis Avxisis tou Posou tis Proikas", in *Oikogeneia kai Periousia stin Ellada kai tin Kypro,* ed. Colette Piault (Athens, 1994), 111–20.

Maslev, Stoyan. *Targoviyata mezhdu balgarskite zemi i Transilvaniya prez XVI-XVII vek* (Sofia, 1991).

Masters, Bruce. "The Sultan's Entrepreneurs: The Avrupa Tüccaris and the Hayriye Tuccaris in Syria", *IJMES* 24 6 (1992): 579–97.

Matmazel Talya, "Çocukların libasi ve muhâfaza-i Sıhhatı", *HMG*, Nisan 1312/1896.

Maurer, Georg Ludwig von. *O Ellinikos Laos* (Athens, 1976).

Mazhdrakova-Chavdarova, Ogniana. *Vŭzrozhdenetsŭt Stefan Penev Akhtar* (Sofia, 1985).

McGowan, Bruce. *Economic Life in Ottoman Europe: Taxation, Trade and the Struggle for Land, 1600–1800* (Cambridge, 1981).

McMillan, James. *France and Women 1785–1914* (New York, 2000).

Meijer, Gerrit, Sjoerd Meijer. "Influence of the Code Civil in the Netherlands", *European Journal of Law and Economics* 14 (2002): 227–36.

Meis, Itzhak. *Makedonska hronika: prikazna za sefardskite Evrei na Balkanot* (Skopje, 2011).

Meshcheriuk, Ivan. *Pereselenie Bolgar v Iuzhnuiu Besarabiiu 1828–1834 gg.* (Kishinev, 1965).

Michailidis-Nouaros, Georgios. "Paratiriseis sto Klironomiko Ethimo tis Karpathou", *Etaireia Karpathiakon Meleton* 3 (1984): 7–27.

Mihaylova, Katya. *Stranstvashtiyat slyap pevets prosyak vav folklornata kultura na slavyanite* (Sofia, 2006).

Mijatović, Boško. "Iskušenja liberalizma Koste Cukića", in *Liberalna misao u Srbiji: prilozi istoriji liberalizma od kraja XVIII do sredine XX veka*, eds Jovica Trkulja, Dušan Popović (Beograd, 2001), 63–107.

——, ed. *Srpski ekonomisti do 1914: zbornik tekstova* (Beograd, 2008).

Mijatović, Čedomilj. *Izvod iz politične ekonomike* (Beograd, 1867).

——. *Nauka o državnom gazdinstvu ili nauka o financiji, po Lorencu Stajnu i drugima* (Beograd, 1869a).

——. *Kratka nauka o državnom gazdinstvu ili nauka o financiji* (Beograd, 1869b).

——. *Treba li nam železnica* (Beograd, 1871)

Milić, Danica. "Ilija Garašanin i privreda Srbije", in *Ilija Garašanin*, ed. Vladimir Stojančević (Beograd, 1991), 369–75.

Milićević, Jovan. "Prilog poznavanju porekla srbijanskog parlamentarizma", *Zbornik Filozofskog fakulteta* XI, 1 (1970): 609–26.

Milosavljević, Olivera, *U tradiciji nacionalizma ili stereotipi srpskih intelektualaca XX veka o "nama" i "drugima"* (Beograd, 2002).

Milošević, S. *Spoljna trgovina Srbije od 1843–1875 godine* (Beograd, 1902).

Miller, William. *Greek Life in Town and Country* (London, 1905).

Minoski, Mihajlo. *Makedonija vo meǵunarodnite dogovori,* Vol. 1 (Skopje, 2006).

Mircheva, Keti. "Balgarskiiat 'prochit' na Macini v kraia na 60-te i 70-te godini na XIX vek)", in *Balgari i Italianci prez Vekobete v Borbi za Nezavisimost i Darzhavnost* (Sofia, 2006), 262–73.

Mirow, M.C. "The Code Napoleon: Buried but Ruling in Latin America", *Denver Journal of International Law and Policy* 179 (2004–2005): 179–94.

Mishkova, Diana. "The Uses of National Identity in the Balkans", in *Balkan Identities: Nation and Memory*, ed. Maria Todorova (New York, 2004), 269–93.

——. "The Interesting Anomaly of Balkan Liberalism", in *Liberty and the Search for Identity: Liberal Nationalisms and the Legacy of Empires*, ed. Ivan Dénes (Budapest, 2006), 399–456.

Mitev, Plamen., ed. *Daritelstvo i vzaimopomosht v Bŭlgarskoto obshtestvo* (XVI – *nachaloto na XIX vek*) (Sofia, 2003).

Molho, Rena. *Oi Evraioi tēs Thessalonikes, 1856–1919. Mia idiaiterē koinotēta* (Athens, 2001)

——. *Salonica and Istanbul, Social, Political and Cultural Aspects of Jewish Life* (Istanbul, 2005).

Mollat, Michel. *The Poor in the Middle Ages. An Essay in Social History* (New Haven, 1986).

Morris, R. J. *Men, Women, and Property in England 1780–1870* (Cambridge, 2005).

Mostras, C. *Dictionnaire géographique de l'Empire Ottoman* (Istanbul, 1995).

Mutafov, Vasil."Za etnicheskiya, sotsialniya i stopanski oblik na selo Arbanasi prez XVII vek", *Godishnik na muzeite of Severna Balgaria* V (1979): 83–95.

Mutafova, Krassimira. *Staroprestolniyat Tarnov* (Tarnovo, 2002).

Naar, Devin. "Between 'New Greece' and 'the new World': Thessaloniki Jewish Emmigration to America", *Journal of the Hellenic diaspora* 35 (2009): 45–89.

Nahum, Henri. "Charisme et pouvoir d'un médecin jiuf. Moise Allatini (1809–1882), 'le père de Salonique'", in *Médecins et ingénieurs ottomans à l'age des nationalisms*, ed. Méropi Anastassiadou-Dumont (Paris, 2003), 49–62.

Nau, Heino Heinrich. "History Matters: From Historical Economics to Modern Institutionalism", in *The Historicity of Economics: Continuities and Discontinuities of Historical Thought in 19th and 20th Century Economics*, eds Heino Nau, Bertram Schefold (Berlin, 2002), 1–22.

Naxidou, Eleonora. "The Routes to the Bulgarian National Movement. Simultaneously Homogenous and Polymorphous", *ADAM Akademi Sosyal Bilimler Dergisi,* 21 (2012): 25–42.

Nazarska, Georgeta. "The Vienna School of Medicine and Bulgarian Medicine and Health Care (1840s–1910s)" in *Medicine Within and Between the Habsburg and Ottoman Empires. 18th–19th Centuries*, ed. Teodora Sechel (Bochum, 2011), 39–51.

Necipoğlu, Gürlü. "Dynastic Imprints on the Cityscape: The Collective Message of Imperial Funerary Mosque Complexes in Istanbul", in *Cimetières et traditions funéraires dans le Monde Islamique*, eds Jean-Louis Bacqué-Grammont, Aksel Tibet (Ankara, 1996), 23–36.

Nikolopoulos, B., A. Kakoulidis. *Syllogi Apanton ton Nomon, Diatagmaton Egkyklion, Odigion kai Eidopoiiseon ton Ypourgeion Synthikon tis Ellados meta Allon Ethnon*, Vol. A (1859); Vol. B (Athens, 1860).

Nikov, Petar. *Vazrazhdane na Balgarskiia Narod. Carkovno-Nacionalni Borbi i Postizheniia* (Sofia, 2008).

Nora, Pierre. "Between Memory and History: Les Lieux de Mémoire", *Representations* 26 (1989): 7–25.

Norton, Caroline. *English Laws for Women in the Nineteenth Century* (Westport, 1981).

Opis na osmanoturski dokumenti za zanayati i targoviya (XVI-XIX vek) (Sofia, 1993).

Ortayli, Iber. *İmparatorluğun En Uzun Yüzyılı* (İstanbul, 1983); Greek edition (Athens, 2004).

——. *Studies on Ottoman Transformation* (Istanbul, 1994).

Osmanlı Hilâl-i Ahmer Cemiyeti 1329–1331 Salnamesi (Istanbul, 1329 [1913]).

Osmanlı Kadınları Çalıştırma Cemiyeti Islamiyyesi Nizamnamesi (Istanbul, 1913).

Osmanlı- Türk Hanımları Esirgeme Derneği Nizamnamesi (Istanbul, 1913).

Ovcharov, Nikolai. "Migration des ouvriers du chantier naval et des marins du littoral bulgare de la Mer Noire au cours de la première moitié du XIXe Siècle", in *Shipbuilding and Ships in the Eastern Mediterranean during the 18th and 19th Centuries*, ed. Kostas Damianidis (Chios, 1999), 93–5.

Ömer, Besim. *Hanım Efendilere Hilâl-i Ahmere dair Konferans* (Istanbul, 1330 [1914/5]).

Özbek, Nadir. "The politics of poor relief in the late Ottoman Empire 1876–1914", *NPT* 21 (1999): 1–33.

——. "Imperial Gifts and Sultanic Legitimation during the Late Ottoman Empire, 1876–1909", in *Poverty and Charity in Middle Eastern Contexts*, eds Michael Bonner, Mine Ener, Amy Singer (Albany, 2003), 203–20.

——. "Philanthropic activity, Ottoman patriotism and the Hamidian regime, 1876–1909", *IJMES* 37 (2005): 59–81.

——. "'Beggars' and 'vagrants' in Ottoman state policy and public discourse, 1876–1914", *MES* 45/5 (2009): 783–801.

Özcan, Ufuk. "Two perceptions of economy in the last century of Ottoman Empire: The Liberal and Nationalist-Statist Movements", *International Journal of Turcologia* VIII/15 (2013): 17–42.

Palairet, Michael. *The Balkan economies c.1800–1912. Evolution without development* (Cambridge, 1997, 2002).

Pantazopoulos, Nikolaos. *I Entaxi tis Elladas stin Evropaiki Koinotita. I Symvoli tis Antivasileias kai tou Othona 1833–1843* (Athens, 1988).

——. "Georg Ludwig von Maurer, I Pros Evropaika Protypa Oloklirotiki Strofi tis Neoellinikis Nomothesias", in *Epistimoniki Epetiris Scholis Nomikon kai Oikonomikon* 13 (1968): 1346–506.

——. *Apo tis "Logias" Paradoseos eis ton Astikon Kodika* (Thessaloniki, 1965).

Papadopoullos, Theodoros. *The History of the Greek Church and people under Turkish domination* (Brussels, 1952).

Papagianni, Eleftheria. *I Nomologia ton Ekklisiastikon Dikastirion tis Byzantinis kai Metabyzantynis Periodou, se Themata Perousiakou* (Athens, 1997).

Papamichos-Chronakis, Paris. *Hellēnes, Evraioi, Dönme emboroi tēs Thessalonikēs 1882–1919. Taxikoi kai ethnotikoi metashēmatismoi se trohia exellēnismou*, PhD dissertation (Rethymno, University of Crete, 2011).

Paparrigopoulos, Petros. *To En Elladi Ischyon Astikon Dikaion*, Vol. 8 (Athens, 1875).

Papazov, Dimitar. "Selo Arbanasi. Lichni spomeni i sabrani Danni", *SBAN* 31 (1937): 1–94.

Paskaleva, Virzhinia. "Sŭdba i bitie na ungarsko-polskata emigratsia v Osmanskata imperia (1849–1850)", *IP* 5–6 (2000): 226–51.

Paspatis, Alexandros. *Ypomnēma peri tou Graekikou Nosokomeiou tôn Epta Pyrgôn* (Athens, 1862).

Pateman, Carol. *The Sexual Contract* (Stanford, 1988).

Penchev, Bojko. *Tagite na kraevekovieto* (Sofia, 1998).

Peri, Oded. "Ottoman Symbolism in British-Occupied Egypt, 1882–1909", *MES* 41, 1 (2005): 103–20.

Periodiko tou En Kônstantinoupolei Hellēnikou Philologikou Syllogou. "Dēmosiai dialexeis genomenai en tô Philologikô Syllogô apo tou 1870–1920", *Istanbul Hellenic Literary Association's Review* (Istanbul, 1913–21).

Perović, Latinka. *Srpsko-ruske revolucionarne veze: prilozi za istoriju narodnjaštva u Srbiji* (Beograd, 1993).

——. *Između anarhije i autokratije: srpsko društvo na prelazima vekova (XIX–XXI)* (Beograd, 2006).

Perry, Duncan. *The politics of terror. The Macedonian revolutionary movements 1893–1903* (Durham, 1988).

Petriceicu-Haşdeu, Bogdan. *Etymologicum Magnum Romaniae. Dicţionarul limbei istorice şi poporane a românilor*, Vol. III (Bucarest, 1893).

Petrov, Petŭr. *Naučna ekspedicija v Makedonija i Pomoravieto 1916* (Sofia, 1993)

Petrović, Jovan. *Prelaz seljaka u varoši i radnike* (Beograd, 1924).

——. *Okućje ili zaštita zemljoradničkog minimuma* (Beograd, 1930).

Pharmakopoulos, Nikolaos. *Peri Progamiaias Doreas* (Athens, 1886).

Philergos Etaireia. *Ekthesis tôn kata to etos 1872–73 ergasiôn, hypovlētheisa tē Z' etēsia genikē syneleusei tēn 6/18 Maiou 1873* (Istanbul, 1873).

——. *Ekthesis tôn kata to etos 1873–74 ergasiôn, hypovlētheisa tē H' etēsia genikē syneleusei tēn 19/31 Maiou 1874* (Istanbul, 1874).

Philliou, Christine. *Biography of an Empire. Governing Ottomans in an Age of Revolution* (Berkeley, 2011).

Phillips, Roderick. *Putting Asunder* (Cambridge, 1988).

Philoptôchos Adelfotēs tôn Kyriôn Megalou Revmatos "Hē philanthrôpia." Ekthesis tôn pepragmenôn. Etos A' (Istanbul, 1907).

Pinson, Mark. "Ottoman Bulgaria in the First Tansimat Period – The Revolts in Nish (1841) and Vidin (1850)", *MES* 11, 2 (1975): 103–46.

Pippidi, Andrei. *Hommes et idées du Sud-Est européen à l'aube de l'âge moderne* (Bucarest, 1980).

Podbrani osmanski dokumenti za Tarnovo i Tarnovska kaza (Tarnovo, 2012).

Pollard, Lisa. *Nurturing the Nation: The Family Politics of Modernizing, Colonizing, and Liberating Egypt, 1805–1923* (Berkeley, 2005).

——. "Egyptian by Association: Charitable States and Service Societies, circa 1850–1945", *IJMES* 46 (2014): 239–57.

Popgeorgiev, Iordan. "Grad Vratsa. Prinos kŭm istoriata mu", *SBNU* 20 (1904): 1–75.

Popova, Elena. "Zlatoto v narodnata kultura na balgarite prez osmanskiya period", in *Pari, dumi, pamet* (Sofia, 2004), 42–9.

Popović, D.J. *O Cincarima. Prilozi pitanju postanka našeg građanskog društva* (Beograd, 2000).

Popović-Obradović, Olga. "Idea and Practice of Constitutionality in Serbia in 1869-1914 Period", in *Helsinki Files, 3: Russia, Serbia, Montenegro*, eds Jelica Kurjak, Olga Popović-Obradović, Mijat Šuković (Beograd, 2000), 25–69.

——. *The Parliamentary System in Serbia 1903–1914* (Beograd, 2013).

Porter, Roy. *Disease, Medicine and Society in England 1550–1860* (Houndmills, 1987).

Promitzer, Christian. "Stimulating the Hidden Dispositions of South-Eastern Europe. The Plague in the Russo-Turkish War of 1828–29 and the Introduction of Quarantine on the Lower Danube", in *Medicine Within and Between the Habsburg and Ottoman Empires. 18th–19th Centuries*, ed. Teodora Sechel (Bochum, 2011), 78–107.

Protokoli Narodne skupštine koja je držana u Kragujevcu 1873 god (Beograd, 1873).

Prpa, Branka, ed. *Živeti u Beogradu 1837–1841. Dokumenta uprave grada Beograda*, Vols 1–2 (Beograd, 2003–4).

Psychogios, Dimitris. *Proika, Foroi, Stafida kai Psomi, Oikonomia kai Oikogeneia stin Agrotiki Ellada tou 19ou Aiona* (Athens, 1995).

Quataert, Jean. "Mobilizing Philanthropy in the Service of War: The Female Rituals of Care in the New Germany, 1871–1914", in *Anticipating Total War: The German and American Experiences, 1871–1914*, eds Manfred Boemeke, Roger Chickering, Stig Förster (Washington, DC, 1999), 217–38.

Racheva, Vania. "Za edin agent na kniaz Miloš Obrenović. Ili shtrikh ot politicheskata kariera na Dimitŭr Mustakov", in *Balkanskite izmerenia na familiata Mustakovi*, eds Plamen Mitev, Vania Racheva (Sofia, 2008), 200–38.

Radulescu, Andrei. ed. *Legiuirea Caragea* (Bucharest, 1955).

——. ed. *Indreptarea legii 1962* (Bucharest, 1962).

Rakovski, Georgi. *Sachineniia*, Vol. III (Sofia, 1984).

Refik, Ahmet. *Balgariya pod tursko upravlenie* (Sofia, 1938).

Reiss, A. R. *The Kingdom of Serbia. Infringements of the rules and laws of war committed by the Austro–Bulgaro–Germans* (London, 1918).

Report of the International commission to inquire into the causes and conduct of the Balkan wars, Carnegie Endowment (Washington, DC, 1914).

Resultats definitifs de la recensement de la population du 31 janvier 1921 (Sarajevo, 1932).

Richter, J. *A History of Protestant missions in the Near East* (Edinburgh, 1910).

Robarts, Andrew. "The Danube *Vilayet* and the Bulgar-Turkish compromise proposal of 1867 in Bulgarian Historiography", *International Journal of Turkish Studies* 14, 1&2 (2008): 61–74.

Robe, Teodosi A."Bitolj, njegov postanak, razvitak do početka XX veka", *Luč* 1 (1937): 49–59.

Rodrigue, Aron. *French Jews, Turkish Jews: The Alliance Israélite Universelle and the Politics of Jewish Schooling in Turkey* (Bloomington, 1990).

Rose, Nicholas. "Identity, genealogy, history", in *Questions of Cultural Identity*, eds Stuart Hall, Paul du Gay (London, 1996), 128–50.

Rosetti, Radu. *Familia Rosetti*, Vol. I (Bucharest, 1938).

Rošer, Vilhelm. *Sistema narodne privrede*, 1, *Osnovi narodne privrede* (1863); *2, Narodna ekonomika poljske privrede: ručna i poučna knjiga za državne i poljske privrednike* (Beograd, 1872).

Rowe, Victoria. "Armenian Writers and Women's Rights Discourse in Turn-of-the-Twentieth-Century Constantinople", *Aspasia* 2 (2008): 44–69.

Rusev, Ivan. "Balgarskite uchebnitsi po targoviya prez Vazrazhdaneto (1830s-1870s)", *IP* 5–6 (2003): 40–91.

Sachelarie, Ovid, Nicolae Stoicescu, eds. *Instituţii feudale din ţările române. Dicţionar* (Bucharest, 1988).

Sahara, Tetsuya. "The Ottoman City Council and the beginning of modernization of urban space in the Balkans", in *The City in the Ottoman Empire. Migration and the Making of Urban Modernity*, eds Ulrike Freitag et al. (London, 2011), 26–50.

Sakkis, Dimitris. *Neosystato Elliniko Kratos 1833–1848*, Vol. A (Athens, 2001).

Salzmann, Ariel. "Citizens in Search of a State: The Limits of Political Participation in the Late Ottoman Empire", in *Extending Citizenship, Reconfiguring States,* eds Michael Hanagan, Charles Tilly (New York, 1999), 39–45.

Samardžić, Momir. "Serbian liberals and the struggle for the National Assembly in the mid-19th century", in *Institutional change and stability: conflicts, transition and social values*, eds Andreas Gemes, Florentia Peyrou, Ioannis Xydopoulos (Pisa, 2009), 89–109.

——. *Roads to Europe: Serbian politics and the railway issue, 1878–1881* (Pisa, 2010).
——. "Projekat transbalkanske železnice i politika Srbije u vreme ustavobranitelja 1851–1858", *Srpske studije* 3 (2012): 313–35.
Samiou, Dimitra. "To Feministiko Kinima stin Ellada (1860–1960)", in *I Ellada ton Gynaikon*, eds Eytychia Leontidou, Sigrid Ammer (Athens, 1992), 57–63.
Sampimon, Janette. *Becoming Bulgarian* (Amsterdam, 2006).
Saraceno, Chiara. "Women, Family, and the Law, 1750–1942", *JFH* 15 (1990): 427–42.
al-Sayyid Marsot, Afaf Lutfi. *Egypt in the Reign of Muhammad Ali* (Cambridge, 1984).
Scurtu, Vasile. *Termenii de înrudire în limba română* (Bucharest, 1966).
Sechel, Teodora Daniela. "Contagion Theories in the Habsburg Monarchy (1770–1830)", in *Medicine Within and Between the Habsburg and Ottoman Empires. 18th-19th Centuries*, ed. Teodora Sechel (Bochum, 2011), 55–77.
Senders Pedersen, Joyce. "Victorian Liberal Feminism and the 'Idea' of Work", in *Women and Work Culture Britain c.1850–1950,* eds Krista Cowmand, Louise Jackson (Burlington, 2005), 27–47.
Sfyroeras, Vasilios. *Istoria tis Neoteras Ellados, I Periodos tis Vasileias tou Othonos (1832–1862)* (Athens, 1970).
Shanley, Mary Lyndon. *Feminism, Marriage, and the Law in Victorian England 1850–1895* (Princeton, 1989).
Shatzmiller, Maya. "Aspects of Women's Participation in the Economic Life of Later Medieval Islam: Occupations and Mentalities", *Arabica* 35, 1 (1988): 36–58.
Simeonidis, Ioannis. *Odigos tis evsevias* (Constantinoupolis, 1850).
Singer, Amy. *Constructing Ottoman Beneficence: An Imperial Soup Kitchen in Jerusalem* (Albany, 2002).
——. *Charity in Islamic Societies* (Cambridge, 2008).
——."The Last Imaret? An Imperial Ottoman Firman from 1308/1890", in *The Ottoman Middle East: Studies in Honor of Amnon Cohen*, eds Eyal Ginio, Elie Podeh (Leiden, 2014), 221–37.
Slaveykov, Petko R. "Izvlecheniya iz Letopisa na pop Yovcho ot Tryavna", *SBNU* 3 (1890): 381–8.
——. *Sachineniya*, Vol. 1 (Sofia, 1978).
Smith, Anthony. *National Identity* (London, 1991).
Smochowska-Petrowa, Wanda. *Michal Czajkowski – Sadik Pasha i Bŭlgarskoto Vŭzrazhdane* (Sofia, 1973).
Snegarov, Ivan. "Drug tarnovski tsarkoven kodeks za ushilishta, enoriyski tsarkvi i manastiri", *Godishnik na Sofiyiskiya Universitet, BF* 18, 2 (1940/1): 49–53.
——. "Grŭtski kodeks na Plovdivskata mitropolia", *SBAN* XLI, 2 (1946): 179–396.
Sofronii Vračanski. *Žitie i stradaniya gresnago Sofroniya* (Sofia, 1989).
Sokolov, Ivan. *Konstantinopolskaja cerkov v 19 veka. Oput istoriceskovo izsledovanija*, Vol.1 (Petersburg, 1904).
Somel, Selçuk Akşin. *The Modernization of Public Education in the Ottoman Empire, 1839–1908: Islamization, Autocracy and Discipline* (Leiden, 2001).
Sonbol, Amira, ed. *The Last Khedive of Egypt: Memoirs of Abbas Hilmi II* (Cairo, 2006).
Spencer, Philip, Wollman Howard. "Nationalism, Politics and Democracy in the Development of Post-Communist Societies", in *Ethnicity and Nationalism in East Central Europe and the Balkans*, eds Thanasis Sfikas, Christopher Williams (Aldershot, 1999), 73–121.

——. *Nationalism. A Critical Introduction* (London, 2002).

Stahl, Henri. H. *Satele devălmaşe româneşti*, Vols I–III (Bucharest, 1998).

Stahl, Paul. "La consanguinité fictive. Quelques exemples balkaniques", *Revue des études roumaines* XVI (1981): 47–62.

——. *Household, village and village confederation in Southeastern Europe* (New York, 1986).

Stamatopoulos, Dimitrios. *Metarrythmisi kai Ekkosmikefsi: pros mia anasynthesi tis Istorias tou Oikoumenikou Patriarheiou ton 19o aiona* (Athens, 2003).

——. "From Millets to Minorities in the 19th Century Ottoman Empire: an Ambiguous Modernization", in *Citizenship in Historical Perspective*, eds S. Ellis, G. Hálfadanarson, A. Isaacs (Pisa, 2006), 253–73.

——. "The Splitting of the Orthodox *Millet* as a Secularizing Process: The Clerical–Lay Assembly of the Bulgarian Exarchate (Istanbul 1871)", in *Griechische Kultur in Südosteuropa in der Neuzeit. Beiträge zum Symposium in memoriam Gunnar Hering*, eds Herausgegeben von Maria Stassinopoulou, Ioannis Zelepos, *Byzantina et Neograeca Vindobonensia XXVI* (2008): 243–70.

——. "The Bulgarian Schism Revisited", *Modern Greek Studies Yearbook* 24/25 (2008–9): 105–25.

——. "The Christian Orthodox Family in Crisis: The Ecumenical Patriarchate's Courts and the reconstruction of the private sphere in Southeast Europe (19th–20th c.)", in *Problems of Crime and Violence in Europe, 1780–2000: Essays in criminal justice,* eds Efi Avdela, Shani D'Cruze, Judith Rowbotham (Lewiston, 2010), 91–118.

——. "Bulgarian Patriarchs during the Age of the Greek Revolution: Modern Greek Enlightenment and the Rise of the Neophanariotism", in *(Mis)Understanding the Balkans. Essays in Honour of Raymond Detrez*, eds Michel De Dobbeleer, Stijn Vervaet (Ghent, 2013), 45–57.

Stambolski, Khristo. *Avtobiografia, dnevnitsi i spomeni*, Vol. 1 (1852–1868) (Sofia, 1927).

Staves, Susan. *Married Women's Separate Property in England 1660–1833* (Cambridge, 1990).

Stefanov, Vasil. *Bŭlgarskata meditsina prez Vŭzrazhdaneto* (Sofia, 1980).

Stoianovich, Traian. "The Pattern of Serbian Intellectual Evolution, 1830–1880", *Comparative Studies in Society and History* 1, 3 (1959): 242–72.

——. "The Conquering Balkan Orthodox Merchant", in *Between East and West: The Balkan and Mediterranean Worlds*, Vol. 2 (New Rochelle, 1992), 1–77; *JEH* 20, 2 (June 1960): 234–313.

Stoicescu, Nicolae. *Dicţionar al marilor dregători din Ţara Românească şi Moldova, sec. XIV–XVII* (Bucharest, 1971).

Stojanović, Dubravka. "Ulje na vodi: politika i društvo u modernoj istoriji Srbije", in *Srbija 1804–2004: tri videnja ili poziv na dijalog* (Beograd, 2005), 115–48.

Stojanovski, Nikola. *Zdravstvena kultura vo Veles i Veleshko od minaloto do krajot na 20 vek* (Veles, 1999).

Stokes, Gale. *Legitimacy through liberalism: Vladimir Jovanović and the transformation of Serbian politics* (Seattle, 1975).

——. "The Social Origins of East European Politics", in *The Origins of Backwardness in Eastern Europe*, ed. Daniel Chirot (Berkeley, 1989), 210–51.

——. *Politics as Development: the Emergence of Political Parties in Nineteenth Century Serbia* (Durham, 1990).

Stone, Lawrence. *Road to Divorce, England 1530–1987* (Oxford, 1990).
Stoyanov, Manyo. *Stari gratski knigi v Balgaria* (Sofia, 1978).
Strashimirov, Dimitar. ed. *Vasil Levski. Zhivot, Dela, Izvori,* Vol. I (Sofia, 2014).
Subotić, Milan. "Liberalna misao Dimitrija Matića", in *Liberalna misao u Srbiji: prilozi istoriji liberalizma od kraja XVIII do sredine XX veka*, eds Jovica Trkulja, Dušan Popović (Beograd, 2001), 45–61.
Svintila, Vladimir. *Etyudi po narodopsihologiya na balgarina* (Sofia, 2007).
Svirčević, Miroslav. "The New territories of Serbia after the Balkan wars of 1912–1913. The establishment of the first local authorities", *Balcanica* 44 (2013): 285–306.
Svolopoulos, Constantinos. "L'initiation de Mourad V à la Franc-Maçonnerie par Cléanthi Scalieri: aux origines du mouvement libéral en Turquie", *BS* 21 (1980): 441–57.
Svoronos, Alexandros. *Ta Ellinika Syntagmata 1822–1952* (Athens, 1972).
Symeonidou-Alatopoulou, Charis. "I Exelixis tou Thesmou tis Proikas stin Ellada 1956–1974", *Epitheorisi Koinonikon Erevnon* 36/37 (1979): 322–40.
Ta egainia tôn en Vathyrryaki sholeiôn (Istanbul, 1871).
Tamir, Yael. *Liberal Nationalism* (Princeton, 1993).
Tankovski-Lilin, Ġorgi, Nikola Minovski. *Bitola i Bitolsko vo Balkanskite i vo Prvata svetska vojna (1912–1918)* (Bitola, 2009).
Tannūs, Tawfīq. *Tarīkh al-Harb al-Balqānīya* (Alexandria, 1913).
Tarashoeva, Valeria et al., eds. *Semeen arhiv na Khadzhitoshevi (1827–1878)*, Vol. 2 (Vratsa, 2002).
Tarchila, Petru. "The History of Romanian Civil Codes Evolution", *Journal of Humanistic and Social Studies* III, 2 (2012): 153–8
Teal-i Vatan Osmanlı Hanımlar Cemiyeti Nizamnamesi (Istanbul, 1909).
Thiersch, Frederic. *I Ellada tou Kapodistria*, Vol. B (Athens, 1972).
Thompson, Francis. *The Rise of Respectable Society: A Social History of Victorian Britain, 1820–1900* (Cambridge, 1988).
Titorov, Iov. *Bŭlgarite v Bessarabia* (Sofia, 1903).
Todev, Ilia. *Stoian Chomakov (1819–1893). Zhivot, delo, potomtsi*, Vol. 1, 2 (Sofia, 2003).
Todorov, Nikolai. *The Balkan City 1400–1900* (Seattle, 1983).
Todorova, Mariya, ed., *Patepisi za Balkanite*, Vol. 7 (Sofia, 1987).
Todorovski, Gligor. *Srpski izvori za istorijata na makedonskiot narod 1913–1917* (1981); *1912–1914* (Skopje, 1979).
——. *Srpski izvori za istorijata na makedonskiot narod. Srpskata reokupacija na Bitola i bitolsko 1916–1917* (Skopje, 1995).
Toledano, Ehud. "Mehmet Ali Paşa or Muhammad Ali Basha? An Historiographical Appraisal in the Wake of a Recent Book", *MES* 21, 4 (1985): 141–59.
——. State and Society in Mid-Nineteenth-Century Egypt (Cambridge, 1990).
Tomara-Sideri, Matoula, Nikos Sideris. *Sygkrotisi kai Diadochi ton Geneon stin Ellada tou 19ou Aiona* (Athens, 1986).
Tonev, Velko. "Natsionalnoobrazuvashti Protsesi v Severoiztochna Bŭlgariia i Dobrudzha", in *Bŭlgarskata Natsiia prez Vŭzrazhdaneto* (Sofia, 1980), 264–99.
Traikov, Veselin. "Bŭlgarskata Emigratsia vŭv Vlashko sled Rusko-Tŭrskata Voina ot 1828–1829", in *Odrinskiat Mir i Balkanskite Narodi* (Sofia, 1981), 156–62.
Trgovčević, Ljubinka. *Planirana elita: o studentima iz Srbije na evropskim univerzitetima u 19. veku* (Beograd, 2003).

Triantafyllopoulos, Konstantinos. *Ekthesis kai Proschedion Nomou Peri ton Logon tou Diazygiou kai Synepeion Tinon Aytou* (Athens, 1918).
Trompoukēs, Kônstantinos. *Ē Ellēnikē iatrikē stēn Kônstantinouplolē 1856–1923* (Athens, 2000).
Tsanoff, Vladimir. *Reports and letters of American missionaries referring to the distribution of the nationalities in the former provinces of European Turkey* (Sofia, 1914).
Tsitselikis, Konstantinos. *Old and New Islam in Greece: From Historical Minorities to Immigrant Newcomers* (Leiden, 2012).
Tsonchev, Petŭr. *Iz stopanskoto minalo na Gabrovo* (Sofia, 1996).
Tsvetkova, Bistra. "Turski dokumenti za statusa na nyakoi selishta vav Velikotarnovski okrag prez XVII vek", *Izvestiya na oblastniya istoricheski Muzey Tarnovo* 3 (1966): 61–8.
Turan, Ömer. "American Protestant missionaries in Monastir, 1912–1917: Secondary Actors in the Construction of Balkan Nationalisms", *MES* 36, 4 (2000): 119–36.
Undzhiev, Ivan. *Vasil Levski. Biografiia* (Sofia, 1993).
Urechia, Vasile. *Istoria românilor*, Vol. VIII (Bucharest, 1897).
Uzer, Tahsin. *Makedonya Eşkiyalık Tarihi ve Son Osmanlı Yönetimi* (Ankara, 1999).
Vachev, Hitko. *Tsarkovniyat ansambal v Arbanasi* (Varna, 2006).
——. *Nekropolite pri tsarkvite "Rozhdestvo Hristovo" i "Sv. Archangeli Michail i Gavrail"* (Tarnovo, 2008).
Valassis, Georgios Men. "Tina peri Patrikis Exousias kata to Dikaion tou Meta tin Alosin Ellinismou", in *Themata Genikis Theorias kai Philosophias Dikaiou*, ed. Stavrou Stavropoulou (Athens, 1970), 530–49.
Van de Haar, Edwin. *Classical Liberalism and International Relations Theory. Hume, Smith, Mises, and Hayek* (New York, 2009).
Varika, Eleni. *I Exegersi ton Kyrion* (Athens, 2004a).
——. "National and Gender Identities in Turn of the Century Greece", in *Women's Emancipation Movements in the 19th Century*, eds Sylvia Paletschek, Bianka Pietrow-Ennker (Stanford, 2004b), 263–79.
Veliki, Konstantin. "Za targoviyata na balgarskite gradove s Avstriya v kraya na XVIII I nachaloto na XIX vek", *IP* 6 (1959): 61–74.
Vîrtosu, Emil and Ion. *Aşezămintele Brâncoveneşti. O sută de ani de la înfiinţare, 1838–1938* (Bucharest, 1938).
Vneshniaia Politika Rossii XIX i Nachala XX Veka: Dokumenty Rossiiskogo Ministerstva Inostrannykh Del (Moscow, 1960).
Vojvodić, Mihajlo, Dragoljub Živojinović. *Veliki rat Srbije 1914–1918* (Beograd, 1970).
"Vospominaniia Doktora Zeidlitsa o Turetskom Pokhod 1829 Goda", *Russkii Arkhiv* 1–4 (1878): 412–35.
Vranousis, Leandros. ed. *Rigas* (Athens, 1953).
Vučo, Nikola. *Razvoj industrije u Srbiji u XIX veku* (Beograd, 1981).
Vujović, M. *Rečnik mesta u oslobođenoj oblasti Stare Srbije po službenim podatcima* (Beograd, 1914).
Vŭzvŭzova-Karateodorova, Kirila et al., eds. *Semeen arhiv na Khadzhitoshevi (1751–1827)*, Vol. 1 (Sofia, 1984).
Walker, Mary. *Through Macedonia to the Albanian Lakes* (London, 1864).
Wall, Richard, Jay Winter, eds. *The Upheaval of War: Family, Work and Welfare in Europe 1914–1918* (Cambridge, 1988).

Wallerstein, Immanuel, Reşat Kasaba. "Incorporation into the World Economy: Change in the Structure of the Ottoman Empire, 1750–1839", in *Economie et sociétés dans l'Empire ottoman (fin du XVIIIe – début du XXe siècle)* (Paris, 1983), 336–54.

Watson, Alan. ed. *The Digest of Justinian*, Vol. 2 (Philadelphia, 1998).

Weisner, Merry. *Women and Gender in Early Modern Europe* (Cambridge, 1993).

Werner, Michael, Bénédicte Zimmermann. "Beyond Comparison: *Histoire croisée* and the Challenge of Reflexivity", *History and Theory* 45, 1 (2006): 30–50.

Whittle, Jane. "Servants in Rural England *c.*1450–1650: Hired Work as a Means of Accumulating Wealth and Skills Before Marriage", in *The Marital Economy in Scandinavia and Britain 1400–1900*, eds Maria Agren, Amy Louise Erickson (Burlington, 2005), 89–110.

Wilkinson, William. *An Account of the Principalities with Various Political Observations Relating to them* (London, 1820); 2nd ed. (New York, 1971).

Winter, Jay. *The Great War and the British People* (London, 1985).

Winter, Jay, Antoine Prost. *The Great War in History: Debates and Controversies, 1914 to the Present* (Cambridge, 2005).

Wolff, Larry. *Inventing Eastern Europe* (Stanford, 2004).

Woolf, Stuart. "Introduction", in *Nationalism in Europe, 1815 to the Present. A Reader*, ed. Stuart Woolf (London, 1996), 1–39.

Wright, Nancy, Margaret Ferguson, "Introduction", in *Women, Property, and the Letters of the Law in Early Modern England*, eds Nancy Wright, Margaret Ferguson, A.R. Buck (Toronto, 2004), 3–22.

Yildirim, Nuran. "Le role des médecins turcs dans la transmission du savoir", in *Médecins et ingénieurs ottomans à l'age des nationalisms* (Paris, 2003), 127–70.

Zaimova, Raja, Nikolay Aretov, eds. *Pari, dumi, pamet* (Sofia, 2004).

Zepos Panagiotis. *I Neotera Elliniki Epistimi tou Astikou Dikaiou* (Athens, 1954).

——. *Ta Nomika Ethima tis Peloponnisou*, ed. Méropi Anastassiadou-Dumont (Athens, 1976).

Zervos, Spyros. *Recherches sur les Phanariots et leur idéologie politique (1666–1821)*, Thése de doctorat, 2 Vol. (Paris, 1990).

INDEX